Psychology and the Law

Psychology and the Law

Research Frontiers

NATIONAL UNIVERSITY LIBRARY

Edited by
Gordon Bermant
Battelle Memorial Institute

Charlan Nemeth
University of British Columbia

Neil Vidmar
University of Western Ontario

Lexington Books
D.C. Heath and Company
Lexington, Massachusetts
Toronto

Library of Congress Cataloging in Publication Data

Main entry under title:
  Psychology and the law.

  Proceedings of a conference held June 12-14, 1975 at the Battelle
Seattle Research Center and sponsored by Battelle Memorial Institute.
  Includes index.
  1. Psychology, Forensic—Congresses. 2. Sociological jurisprudence—
Congresses. I. Bermant, Gordon. II. Nemeth, Charlan. III. Vidmar, Neil.
IV. Battelle Memorial Institute, Columbus, Ohio.
Law   347.06'6   75-40628
ISBN 0-669-00452-9

In accord with that part of the charge of its founder, Gordon Battelle, to
assist in the education of men, it is the commitment of Battelle to
encourage the distribution of information. This is done in part by
supporting conferences and meetings and by encouraging the publication
of reports and proceedings. Toward that objective, Battelle retains a
royalty-free right to unrestricted use of all material within the Work for
use in the performance of its scientific research, for scholarship, and to
promote the progress of science and the useful arts.

Contents

List of Figures

List of Tables

Preface

On June 12-14, 1975, a conference called Psychological and Social Factors in Legal Processes was held at the Battelle Seattle Research Center. The conference was the culmination of a period of study and research by Battelle Center Fellow Gordon Bermant and Visiting Fellows Gerald Dworkin, Charlan Nemeth, Neil Vidmar, and Lauren Wispé. Also involved in the planning of the meeting was Duncan Chappell, Director of Battelle's Law and Justice Study Center. The current volume grew from the papers presented at the Battelle conference.

This conference was the last to be sponsored by the Battelle Institute program in Behavioral and Social Sciences as it had been conceived in 1969. During these years, the program sponsored the research and publications of more than a dozen scholars, for periods of time ranging from two months to six years. Those of us who have been fortunate enough to benefit from Battelle's generosity are grateful to the officers of the Battelle Memorial Institute who, in various ways, contributed greatly to the success of the program: Tommy Ambrose, Russ Dayton, Ev Irish, Bill Kern, and Ron Paul. In addition, the staff of the Battelle Seattle Research Center has always been extraordinary in its commitment to the efforts of scholars whose usefulness they must sometimes, at least, have wondered about.

For every book there is at least one person who has taken on the burden of making sure things get done right. Sometimes, perhaps inevitably, assuming this responsibility leads to bearing the brunt of pique expressed by authors concerned lest their prose be sullied or their footnotes altered. For this book, at the last minute when we needed her most, Faith Fogarty took on the heavy load of bringing all the manuscripts into final form. As the editors who get the credit, we thank her very much indeed.

Gordon Bermant
Charlan Nemeth
Neil Vidmar

List of Participants, Social and Psychological Factors in Legal Processes Conference

Richard A. Berk
Department of Sociology
Northwestern University

Gordon Bermant
Battelle Seattle Research Center

Robert Buckhout
Center for Responsive Psychology
Brooklyn College

Robert A. Burt
School of Law
University of Michigan

Duncan Chappell
Battelle-Law & Justice Study Center

Richard Christie
Department of Psychology
Columbia University

Anthony N. Doob
Department of Psychology
University of Toronto

Gerald Dworkin
Department of Philosophy
University of Illinois-Chicago Circle

Joseph Ebersole
Federal Judicial Center

Phoebe Ellsworth
Department of Psychology
Yale University

Lawrence C. Farmer
School of Law
Brigham Young University

Bernard Grofman
Department of Political Science
SUNY at Stonybrook

V. Lee Hamilton
Department of Sociology
University of Michigan

Robert Hogan
Department of Psychology
Johns Hopkins University

Robert E. Jones
Multnomah County Circuit Court

Beth Loftus
Department of Psychology
University of Washington

Wallace Loh
School of Law
University of Washington

Lester Mazor
Center for the Study of Law & Society
University of California

Mary McGuire
Department of Psychology
University of Washington

Gerald R. Miller
School of Communication
Michigan State University

Herman Mitchell
Department of Psychology
University of Washington

Charlan Nemeth
Department of Psychology
University of British Columbia

Thomas Ostrom
Department of Psychology
Ohio State University

Alice Padawer-Singer
Bureau of Applied Social Research
Columbia University

Albert Pepitone
Department of Psychology
University of Pennsylvania

Anthony Platt
School of Criminology
University of California

Raymond Roberts
Superior Court, California

Milton Rokeach
Department of Sociology
Washington State University

Paul Rush
Educational Television
University of California

Ezra Stotland
Program in Society & Justice
University of Washington

Neil Vidmar
Department of Psychology
University of Western Ontario

Gerald R. Williams
School of Law
Brigham Young University

Part I:
Overview

1

Psychology and the Law: Status and Challenge

Gordon Bermant
Charlan Nemeth
Neil Vidmar

In the first section of this chapter, we present a brief overview of the current status of various aspects of psycholegal research. To do this we rely on a simple trichotomy of the justice system and a number of recently published works that, in our opinion, accurately portray recent developments in the field. For each branch of the system we attempt to specify the major challenges facing psychological researchers and practitioners.

This review is the backdrop against which we go on to our second task, which is to provide a preview of the chapters by the other contributors to this volume. The reader will note that the compass of the other chapters is narrower than the scope of the entire field. This selection was intentional, for advances in research and application relating psychology to the law do not occur uniformly at all places along the border. It is our belief that the chapters in the book represent some of the most important and fruitful current research and applied work.

Hermann Ebbinghaus said of psychology, in 1908, that it had a long past but only a short history. We may say of legal psychology at this time that it has a short past and an even briefer history. Although Hugo Münsterberg applied the psychology of his day to courtroom practices early in the century (see Münsterberg, 1907), the idea did not catch on, and Münsterberg's efforts brought him only disfavor from the rest of the psychological establishment (Boring, 1950). As Kolasa (1972) has noted, the work of Hutchins and Slesinger (for example, 1928, 1938), Burtt (1931), and Louisell (1955) serve as important markers on the path of psycholegal studies that Münsterberg pioneered. This work has to do with psychological factors influencing eyewitness identification and courtroom testimony. The relevance of basic psychological principles regarding perception, memory, and suggestibility to these important legal activities has continued to challenge experimental psychologists and psychologically oriented legal analysts (Buckhout, 1976; Levine & Tapp, 1973; Loftus, 1974; Trankell, 1972). These studies represent just one facet of psychology's role in the courtroom. We will discuss some of them more fully below, under that heading.

The activities of the court represent one function of the legal system: the adjudication of disputes. Two other functions may be listed as having obvious psychological relevance: enforcement and corrections. In both cases our attention is usually directed to the criminal justice system, to the police, and prison officials, respectively.

3

Although the American conception of the penitentiary began with an ideal of rehabilitation (Rothman, 1971), the actual involvement of psychologists in correctional programs could not begin until much later. As we describe more fully below, initial enthusiasms for extensive therapeutic programs in prisons have been dampened by several factors. Correctional psychology now faces major challenges. The involvement of psychologists with police forces is even more recent than correctional psychology. The most effective roles for psychologists in the police setting remain to be developed.

It is important to emphasize that each branch of legal psychology presents only one of several possible social science perspectives on the legal system. Anthropologists, sociologists, and psychiatrists have all made major contributions to systematizing our understanding of how the system works (or does not) and how social science may be applied in the interests of securing a more uniform distribution of justice (Friedman, 1975; Katz, Goldstein, & Dershowitz, 1967; Pospisil, 1974; Slovenko, 1973).

Now we will turn to a closer look at the status of legal psychology as it applies to the police, the courts, and prisons.

Psychology and Law Enforcement

Psychologists joined other behavioral and social scientists during the 1960s, in response to the stimulus of increased federal concern and funding, to bring their talents to bear on the improvement of police services and police-community relations.

In retrospect, we must recall the emergencies that engulfed many major cities at that time. Police forces had the primary responsibility to deal with demonstrations and riots of unprecedented scale. It is unsurprising that many mistakes were made, that the police took a beating in the press and in the eyes of the communities they were obliged to protect, and that political pressure would be great to bring whatever behavioral and social science had to offer to play on the problems. However, given the size and complexity of the problems and the state of development of relevant psychological and social theory and skills, it would have been very surprising had psychologists' activities been particularly successful. And, in fact, they were not.

Psychologically based policy recommendations about police functions would be based, ideally, on fundamental research into the causes of crime and the behavior of persons who commit crimes. However, there is some reason to believe that this ideal is practically unattainable. Certainly, currently accepted social psychological and sociological conceptions of criminal behavior, and the police and community response to it, have not led to generally successful program recommendations or applications for police departments (Brodsky, 1973; Stotland, 1975a). Causal theories of criminal behavior have emphasized behavioral determinants that are beyond the reach of alteration by means of available public policy processes. This, at least, is the view of one visible critic of social science research in the criminal justice system (Wilson, 1975), who has suggested that the most influential criminological theories (Sutherland & Cressey, 1966) have pointed to causal factors so deeply embedded in the fabric of the society that they are practically immutable:

If we regard any crime-prevention or crime-reduction program as defective because it does not address the "root causes" of crime, then we shall commit ourselves to futile acts that frustrate the citizen while they ignore the criminal. . . . [T]he most profound understanding may impede or even distort, rather than facilitate, choice, because much of this knowledge is of what is immutable and necessary, not what is variable or contingent [Wilson, 1975, pp. 51, 58].

Wilson suggests that policy analysis will be more effective than causal analysis in providing sound recommendations for police practice. In this case, the psychologist's role would emphasize careful design and implementation of evaluations of different forms of police activity organization, including, for example, changes in the density of foot patrolmen per beat, random versus proactive preventive patrol, team policing practice, "crime-specific" strategies to pinpoint particular classes of crime, and police-community relations programs. There need be no fundamental psychological theory behind the reasoning that leads to the initiation of the project, but the psychologist can have a valuable role in insuring that the standards of measurement and interpretation used in the project and its evaluation are kept as high as possible.

A recent overview of research and evaluation in police-community relations programs (Stotland, 1975a) suggests that the disappointing and even counterproductive results of a number of these efforts have resulted in increased understanding of how to approach their implementation in the future. It is now clear that interracial attitudes (whether within police ranks or police attitudes toward the public) can be worsened during the conduct of in-service training programs designed to improve them (Singer, 1975; Teahan, 1975a, 1975b). More generally, in-service programs designed and implemented by outside "experts" are generally mistrusted by police (for example, Reddy & Lansky, 1975); periods of trust building and careful diplomacy between police and psychologists appear to be essential requirements for a successful outcome (Stotland & Guppy, 1975). Second, while the single most common activity of police community relations units has been the establishment of Speaker's Bureaus (Reasons & Wirth, 1975), accumulated experience indicates that increased one-way communication from police to community has little chance of improving cooperation between members of the two groups. Kelly (1975a) is adamant that the key to improved police-community relations does not reside in communication per se but in properly redistributed power relations between the police and the community: ". . . the perpetual polishing of the police side of the police-community coin is not enough" (Kelly, 1975a, p. 75). Basing her views on an evaluation of an experimental police-community relations project in Washington, D.C., in which the community eventually elected a Citizen's Board with substantial authority over the project, Kelly concludes that:

Those in the police establishment have to change, to move over, to let those knocking at the door come in. At the same time, the inpatient door-knockers must change; they must learn to navigate the system, to perform the required functions, to understand why the police function has existed since time immemorial, and, as importantly, how it functions positively as well as how it performs poorly [Kelly, 1975a, p. 85].

The question is, of course, how the desirable power realignments, if in fact they are desirable, are to be brought about. One is reminded of Wilson's skepticism about the possibilities for fundamental change. Stotland (1975b) expresses the view that one way to reduce natural community resentment of police power is to increase the extent to which police exercise their usefulness in performing nonthreatening public service functions. Police who are perceived as generally helpful and nonthreatening will be more likely to receive cooperation under circumstances when they must resort to force or threat of violence. This certainly appears to be a plausible position, but it is not universally accepted.

Kelly's evaluation experience suggested that neither the police nor the community in a high crime-rate area considered the social work role of police to be important when contrasted to the need for control of the predatory crimes of burglary, robbery, assault, and rape. While the community might react against police abuse of their power, the primary complaint was against police ineffectiveness in the control of crime. The same point has been made by Wilson (1975, p. 103) who cites Campbell and Schuman (1968, pp. 41-45) to the effect that more than half the blacks surveyed for the report expressed the opinion that the police were slow to respond to calls for help.

Hence, there appears to be a policy dilemma: Should severely limited financial resources be placed in support of direct crime-control police maneuvers, which may fail for lack of community support and understanding, or in support of attempts to improve attitudes between police and community, which may fail for lack of substantive effect on criminal activity? It is not obvious that psychological theory has a great deal to offer in the resolution of this problem. But psychologists can surely be useful as formative evaluators, critics of research design and interpretation, and facilitators of open communication within police forces and between police and the community they serve.

Psychology and the Courts

The activities of courts provide a natural and important focus for psychological interest. The bulk of research has been aimed at understanding the jury process.

While experiments using mock jurors in law school moot courts were being conducted in the 1930s (Weld & Danzig, 1940; Weld & Roff, 1938), the major thrust began in the mid-1950s with the formation of the University of Chicago Jury Project. During its lifetime, members of the project contributed scores of books and articles to the literature of jury functioning, the most influential being *The American Jury*, by Kalven and Zeisel (1966).

This study was based on reports of more than 3,500 criminal jury trials filed by the 555 judges who presided at them. To begin with, the study reported on the degree of disparity between what the jury decided and what the judge would have decided had the decision been his to make. Judges and juries agreed in approximately 75 percent of the cases. Disagreements were produced predominantly by the jury's greater likelihood of acquitting the defendant; it was very rare for the jury to convict when the judge would have acquitted. Having established this measure of disparity, the study provided detailed analyses of legal and social-psychological factors within the trials that might have accounted for it. The authors concluded with a strong positive note in favor of the jury system as it is constituted.

Since the publication of *The American Jury*, Zeisel has spoken out on several occasions against what he takes to be erosions of the jury's significance in American trial practice (Zeisel, 1971; Zeisel & Diamond, 1974). His concern is that the apparent evolution to juries with fewer than twelve persons, and to decision criteria of less than unanimity, will markedly decrease the quality of justice that juries will be able to provide. Further analysis of the issue has been provided by Lempert (1975) and by Grofman and Nemeth in the current volume.

Experimental work on jury functioning done in academic contexts has sometimes lacked the practical policy focus that would make it relevant to actual trial practice. The desirability of maximizing verisimilitude in the experimental setting, of exercising caution about generalizing to group responses from data based only on individuals, and of forming research hypotheses based on policy-relevant legal issues is becoming more appreciated as academic psychologists and jurists continue to interact.

The jury trial occurs in the larger context of the adversarial legal process. The dramatic quality inherent in our trials is due to the explicitly competitive relationship established between the attorneys representing both sides. The judge's role is relatively passive, similar to that of an umpire in an athletic contest; the judge's bench is elevated above the floor of the court, a symbol of the status of the role and its distance from the competition between lawyers. The jury also remains passive, constrained from asking questions throughout the trial. The witnesses are active only insofar as the attorneys allow them to be. They answer the questions asked of them and then depart. The idea of "a day in court" is thus the idea of a stylized event, with ritual aspects, in which two sides to an issue battle to convince a third party about different versions of the truth.

Our legal tradition holds that this procedure for adjudicating legal disputes provides for more justice, on balance, than would other procedures. In particular, the tradition holds that the adversarial system is preferable to the so-called inquisitorial system prevalent in the courts of continental Europe. The fundamental principle of the inquisitorial system is that the court, not the attorneys, is responsible for details of trial conduct, with the goal of uncovering all the relevant evidence and achieving an objective view of the truth of the matter. The inquisitorial judge is therefore much more active than a judge acting in an adversarial trial. The tradition holds that an unbiased judge, or panel of judges, seeking and organizing information with the cooperation of attorneys for both parties and additional consultants retained by the court, will get closer to the truth, and hence to a just legal decision, than will the finder of fact acting within the adversarial system.

Under the title of *Procedural Justice*, Thibaut and Walker (1975) have summarized their experimental investigations of individual responses to adversarial and inquisitorial procedures. In addition to contrasting the national legal traditions as described above, the authors emphasize that there are several approximations to the inquisitorial process within different branches of the American legal system. For example, presidential commissions (Kerner Commission, Warren Commission, and so forth) and congressional committees operate on an inquisitorial basis. Legal decisions of federal administrative agencies are often made on the basis of some form of inquisitorial investigation rather than adversarial trial. And military courts-martial represent a mixture of systems in which separate advocates are assigned by central authority to represent the interests of the accused and the service.

Finally, there is much in the way of inquisitorial procedure practiced in our juvenile courts, though the recent trend is to bring more of the "due process" found in adult courts into juvenile proceedings.

On the whole, then, while we are committed to adversarial process in the conduct of our adult civil and criminal trials, we do not uniformly practice it in our other fact-finding and legal decision-making institutions. But perhaps we should. Alternatively, perhaps we should increase the extent of inquisitorial process in our trial courts. Obviously, more than psychology is required to consider these conjectures intelligently. Psychological information is relevant, however, and the intent of Thibaut and Walker's work was to supply it and to argue from research findings to policy conclusions.

The results of their experiments have convinced Thibaut and Walker that more, not less, adversarial procedure should be brought into administrative and other legal decision-making. They also believe that there is a potentially dangerous erosion of adversarial process in civil trials in federal court settings. While their data do not allow the conclusions that the adversarial process always brings out more facts, they do suggest that the process discourages premature closure on available information and brings out more facts on behalf of a criminal defendant. They also conclude, on the basis of very complex data, that the adversarial process allows participants a greater sense of satisfaction with trial outcome.

Thibaut and Walker summarize by saying "It is perhaps the main finding of the body of our research, therefore, that for litigation the class of procedures commonly called 'adversary' is clearly superior" (p. 118). They then make recommendations about specific legal decision-making settings in which use of adversarial process would be most just: disputed claims over federal disability benefits, teacher dismissal and student suspension cases, and disputes over appropriate punishments within prisons. Their confidence in the superiority of adversarial process increases with the seriousness of the conflict and the lack of an accepted standard for determining the validity of the conflicting claims.

The experiments and conclusions of Thibaut and Walker represent an extensive and serious attempt to bring the procedures of experimental social psychology to bear on questions of immediate policy relevance. It must not be overlooked that these experiments were conducted with college and law school students under conditions of low similarity to actual litigation. All of their results are of the paper-and-pencil variety. Therefore we may wonder how general the findings are. Do they in fact apply to conditions of actual litigation, as Thibaut and Walker assert that they do? Here, then, is one of the challenges facing the psychologist interested in the legal system: to move from the generalizations and policy recommendations generated by this set of experiments to tests and evaluations of them in real settings.

As a third and final topic in this brief sampler of issues relating psychology and the courts, we will discuss one aspect of the psychology of evidence: factors influencing criminal identification by victims and other witnesses. The topic is obviously important to both the police and the courts. To begin with, there is a widespread belief among laypersons that eyewitness accounts of crimes are accurate. The belief has a number of consequences for criminal prosecutions and trial proceedings. First, the police often depend on eyewitness identification of a suspect in order to generate a case strong enough for prosecution. Even with the best of intentions, the police have a vested interest in achieving a "definite" identification. Second, criminal suspects with prior records of conviction may be more tempted to plea bargain if they have been identified by an eyewitness, even if the identification is incorrect. And third, juries may give greater credence to eyewitness testimony than it deserves.

Levine and Tapp (1973) have reviewed the psychology of criminal identification in the context of recent Supreme Court decisions and federal legislation. In three cases decided in 1967 the court recognized that the accuracy of eyewitness identification of a suspect in a police lineup could be subject to many distorting influences. To guard against these influences the court specified, in general terms, that suspects had a right to counsel during exposure in a lineup. The language of the decision was open to different interpretations by lower courts. Of particular importance was the timing of the right to counsel in regard to indictment of the suspect by a grand jury: Did the right to counsel exist in both pre-indictment and post-indictment lineups, or only in post-indictment lineups? The issue is important because of its potential influence on police tactics and possible defenses against false identifications. In a 1972 decision the court rules that the right to counsel held only for post-indictment lineups. Levine and Tapp believe that this decision marked a "withdrawal by the courts from an area essential to the improvement of the criminal justice system" (p. 1081). Hence they were concerned to review what we know about the factors influencing criminal identifications and to recommend procedures to reduce the likelihood of false identifications.

There have been a number of convincing demonstrations that perceptions and memories of unexpected dramatic events are typically distorted (for example, Trankell, 1972, pp. 33-55). It is also quite clear that the details of witness reports can be influenced by the form in which the reports are elicited (Loftus, 1974; Marshall, Marquis, & Oskamp, 1971). These effects are easily demonstrated in persons who have neither deep emotional involvement in the outcome of their reports, as does a victim, nor institutional involvement in achieving a "positive" identification, as do the police. Several lines of psychological evidence show that the presence of these additional factors further decreases the accuracy of perception and memory. Hence there are good psychological reasons for being concerned about the exaggerated importance of eyewitness identifications for indictments and trial testimony.

Levine and Tapp cite several recommendations for improving the lineup procedure. Witnesses should be screened for auditory and visual deficiencies. Police questioning should proceed in a nonleading, structured fashion. Witnesses to the same event should be segregated before, during, and after the lineup. The officers conducting the lineup should not be part of the investigating team. Contact between police and witnesses should be minimal during the conduct of the lineup. Witnesses should be exposed to multiple lineups and to the possibility that the suspect is not present in any of them. The suspect should not be singled out for any special treatment during the lineup. Other participants in the lineup should not all differ from the suspect in obvious ways. Finally, "live" lineups might be replaced by filmed or videotaped segments in which the suspect and others in the lineup appear in a number of standard postures and movements.

Levine and Tapp note that this final suggestion highlights the need for further basic research in the factors influencing individual identification. The challenges to experimental and social psychologists are clear. In this psycholegal area, perhaps more than in any other, we already possess the theory and method to make important practical contributions.

Psychology in Corrections

Correctional psychology is in trouble. Americans are uncertain about what they want their prisons to accomplish. During the 1950s and 1960s there was a great growth in the "rehabilitative ideology," the view that prison life could be designed to cure or reform antisocial tendencies. Along with this view grew the variety of possible therapies, from sensitivity training and encounter groups to aversive conditioning with Anectine. A distinguished psychoanalyst wrote *The Crime of Punishment* (Menninger, 1966), in which he argued for complete adoption of a theraupeutic model for the penal system. Subsequently, when it appeared that therapeutic goals could not be accomplished within the confines of large penal institutions, there was a change in thematic emphasis from rehabilitation outside the community to reintegration with it; the goal was to create decentralized or community-based correctional facilities. But this move occurred at a time of unprecedented growth in the rate of violent crime, and with this growth has come a disenchantment with rehabilitation as a goal of incarceration. One very experienced observer has described the current mood in these terms:

Our political leadership senses that public opinion is prepared to mass along a hard line on crime. From every point on the political spectrum our performance is described as an abysmal failure. From the President himself on down, high officials call for mandatory sentences as a cure for the leniency of the courts. The hard line becomes ever more firm, reinforced by the fear in the streets and the Uniform Crime Statistics [Conrad, 1975, p. 3].

Intellectual justification for the change in emphasis away from rehabilitation has been provided by some of the most influential legal and social scholars in the nation. Thus Norval Morris has argued that:

... penal purposes are properly retributive, deterrent, and incapacitative. Attempts to add reformative purposes to that mixture—as an objective of the sanction as distinguished from collateral aspirations—yield neither clemency, justice, nor, as presently administered, social utility [Morris, 1974, p. 1161].

James Q. Wilson, after reviewing the largely negative evidence about the effectiveness of rehabilitative efforts in prisons, has concluded that:

In retrospect, little of this should have been surprising. It requires not merely optimistic but heroic assumptions about the nature of man to lead one to suppose that a person, finally sentenced after (in most cases) many brushes with the law, and having devoted a good part of his youth and young adulthood to misbehavior of every sort, should, by either the solemnity of prison or the skillfulness of a counselor, come to see the error of his ways and to experience a transformation of his character . . . . [In an alternative system] we would view the correctional system as having a very different function—namely, to isolate and punish [Wilson, 1975, pp. 170, 172].

Neither Morris nor Wilson wants to discontinue rehabilitative efforts in the prison system; rather, they believe it is fruitless to found or justify the prison system on the rehabilitative principle.

Similarly, Judge David Bazelon, whose landmark *Durham* decision in 1954 (214 F. 2d 862 D.C. Circuit) effectively opened courtroom doors to more extensive and technical participation by psychiatrists in the determination of insanity, has become disenchanted with the application of psychological principles to corrections. He speculates that the fundamental postulates of correctional psychology, roughly the "medical model," may make it impossible for psychology to reach the central correctional problem: conditions arising from gross social inequities. And he suggests that the potential role of psychology in corrections has been "greatly overstated" (Bazelon, 1973, p. 153).

Alongside these technical and fiscal concerns with correctional psychology have arisen serious doubts about the ethics of intervention through behavioral and social technologies. Ethical arguments have focused on the use of behavior modification in prison settings, the informed consent of prisoners serving as participants in research programs, and indeterminate or unpredictable prison sentences (Burt, 1974; Dershowitz, 1974; Gaylin, 1975, Katz, 1972; Klerman, 1975; London, 1969; Orland & Tyler, 1974; Sarason & Sarason, in press; Stolz, in press). One consequence of these ethical concerns has been a substantial restriction on the experimental work that can be done within institutional settings. During 1974, for example, the Federal Bureau of Prisons and the Law Enforcement Assistance Administration made major reductions in the funding of behavior science-based research programs. The biggest cutbacks were in behavior modification programs. There have also been litigation and legislative action taken against "therapeutic prisons" and therapy programs within prisons (Gaylin & Blatte, 1975; Goldberger, 1975; Trotter, 1975; U.S. Senate, 1974). It appears that whatever success these large-scale programs and smaller projects may claim (Brodsky, 1973, chapters 7 and 8), it is insufficient to overcome the negative evaluations that have been made on the grounds of effectiveness, cost, morality, and legality.

What is to be done? Gottfredson (1973) believes psychologists are uniquely qualified to work on five major challenges facing correctional institutions. First, current confusion about fundamentals should be eliminated by the adoption of an internally consistent theory. The second, related challenge is to develop a taxonomy of offenders or offender behavior that can be applied to meeting institutional goals. Designing and testing the theory and taxonomy in programs of treatment and control constitutes the third challenge. The fourth challenge is to provide accurate monitoring and evaluation of programs in place, in order to aid agencies to meet their specified goals. And finally, psychologists must be challenged to develop the most effective means of disseminating their findings to the appropriate interest groups. Taken as guides to action, these are surely worthwhile challenges for the correctional psychologist. One hopes they do not represent too little too late in the face of current antagonisms.

There is of course more to the relation between psychology and corrections than psychologically-based programs within prisons. Consider the role psychologists may play in the current debate over capital punishment. For example, when the Supreme Court handed down *Furman v. Georgia* (408 U.S. 238, 1972), the majority of five who found capital punishment "cruel and unusual" cited diverse reasons for their opinions. Justice Marshall, in particular, offered reasons that were susceptible to empirical test. Put most simply, Justice Marshall argued that the majority of Americans who favor the death penalty do so because they are ignorant or misinformed about its ability to deter capital crime. However, he also recognized that popular approval of capital punishment might be based in part on a desire for retribution, in which case information about the ineffectiveness of executions as a general deterrent would not decrease the extent of popular support.

Sarat and Vidmar (1976) have tested the "Marshall hypothesis" by an experimental opinion poll in which some respondents were informed about either the utilitarian or humanitarian arguments against capital punishment, while a control group was given information about an irrelevant legal matter. Attitudes toward capital punishment, including assessment of the strength of desire for retribution, were assessed before and after receiving the information. The results of the study were in substantial agreement with Justice Marshall's position. To begin with, most respondents were generally uninformed about the data relating to the ineffectiveness of capital punishment as a general deterrent. Secondly, providing factual information produced a significant reduction in the percentage of support for capital punishment. However, individuals whose initial support was based on desire for retribution were relatively unaffected by the factual information. The effect of humanitarian information on attitude change was nonsignificant.

This study represents one of a number of possible applications of psychological method to important policy issues in the area of criminal punishment. Surely the largest challenge facing legal psychologists is to maximize our legitimate contribution to the decisions that will be made on these issues.

Preview of the Volume

The remaining thirteen chapters of this volume are divisible into three sections: psychological jurisprudence (Chapter 2), external and internal legal socialization (Chapters 3-6), and psychological analyses of courtroom procedures (Chapters 7-14). Here we will present an overview of each section.

The Dangers of Legal Benevolence

In Chapter 2 Robert Burt makes a scholarly analysis of the legal reform movement in the field of mental illness. His criticisms and conclusions are germane to enforcement practices, sentencing guidelines, and the nature of the prison-like mental hospitals that detain persons who have been committed involuntarily.

Burt presents two themes that concern the current reform movement. First, the current concept of mental illness has been redefined to the extent that a person officially classified as "mentally ill" bears a stigma that makes eventual reassimilation into the social mainstream unnecessarily difficult. Major elements of proposed reform include the development of community-based mental health care facilities to replace the current out-of-the-way, prison-like state mental hospitals as well as major revision of current mental illness civil commitment statutes. The second theme is that additional public financial resources should be provided for the treatment of those labelled as mentally ill; in current legal parlance, the mentally ill have "the right to treatment."

Burt points out that these two themes bear a contrapuntal, if not competitive, relation to each other. On the one hand reformers claim that the "mentally ill" have been unfairly stigmatized and separated from the rest of society and that both they and the majority would benefit from their reintegration into the community. On the other hand they claim that the "mentally ill" are not being given a sufficiently large share of public resources; as a result of their special status, they deserve more. The major purpose of Burt's essay is to illuminate, through social psychological analysis, how these themes work together and how they exemplify, for one category of deviance, a deep feature of public response to all categories of deviance.

Three concepts are keys to Burt's analysis; stigma (a mark of disgrace or reproach), segregation (both conceptual and spatial; for example "the mentally ill are different from the rest of us, hence they should be kept apart from us"), and benevolence (an inclination to do good).

In barest outline, his argument takes the following form: persons who force themselves into public attention by appearing to be either threatening or incapable of coping for themselves arouse feelings of fear or revulsion in others. Historically, for diverse reasons, numerous personal features have become stigmata producing these feelings; skin color is probably the most obvious.

Benevolence occurs when the deviant person appears to be threatening not our safety but rather our time and effort (for example a drunk lying sprawled asleep on the sidewalk, or an old lady wandering without apparent aim along a city street), then the revulsion and anger at having our personal space invaded must be masked; the mask takes the form of benevolence. In the guise of "helping" we achieve the goal of removing the deviant person from public view: the drunk and the wandering old lady can be "institutionalized" with surprising ease.

Burt illustrates the extent to which benevolence can unwittingly mask control by referring to the now well-known case of *Lake v. Cameron*, which was decided in the Court of Appeals for the District of Columbia Circuit in 1966. At the time of the decision, Mrs. Lake had been detained involuntarily in St. Elizabeth's Hospital in the District of Columbia for four years for no reason other than that she had a tendency to "wander" in what police and psychiatrists believed to be a disoriented way. During the years of her confinement she was offered no therapy to remedy her wandering; indeed the official justification for her continued involuntary confinement was the prevention of her wandering. The official psychiatric label for Mrs. Lake was "chronic brain syndrome associated with arteriosclerosis, with psychotic reaction." Burt points out that while "the vocabulary is medical/psychiatric, the treatment provided is custody for its own sake." Once Mrs. Lake entered the boundaries of the "mental health establishment," the medico-legal label of incompetence branded her in a way that allowed detention to be confused with treatment, neither of which Mrs. Lake had requested. The Court of Appeals attempted to remedy the situation by insisting that, in cases like Mrs. Lake's, the state must provide "the least restrictive alternative" in its attempt to protect those who, apparently, neither protect themselves nor desire the protection of the state. In order to prevent legitimate attempts at benevolence to mask, albeit unwittingly, the enforced segregation of those who make the majority merely uncomfortable by virtue of their behavior, the court rules that no more may legally be done than is necessary to restrict the committed person's freedom of action. One way to accomplish this end is to decentralize the facilities in which those whom we purport to help are constrained to live. Community-based mental health centers, by this argument, serve two important functions: first, they prevent the isolation of "them" from "us," thereby, in Burt's terms, "permitting a fuller appreciation and tolerance ... of human variability." Second, they have the potential to provide therapy by permitting the gradual reintroduction of those who have been removed from society's mainstream.

Burt emphasizes that his argument is not the cynical one that whenever we act to help we end by doing the opposite:

The burden of my argument is not that we must never act to help one another. It is rather that we must be rigorously suspicious of that motive when it is linked, however tangentially, to fear of those we mean to help.

Finally, in a series of nicely drawn parallels, Burt points out that the majority continues to treat minorities, blacks in particular, with much of the same stigmatizing, segregating benevolence that characterizes its approach to the mentally disabled. The same psychological and social mechanisms are at work in the two cases, and there are equivalent dangers to both groups. A partial solution to the worst abuses of benevolence, in addition to minimizing spatial segregation, is to specify definite time limitations on any program that creates different classes of social participation, whether these be special college admissions programs based on race or involuntary commitment programs based on mental disability. As different as these programs may seem on the surface, they share the tendency to perpetuate the problems they were intended to solve.

Three Aspects of Legal Socialization

The term legal socialization refers to the development of attitudes and behavior with respect to laws and the operation of the legal system. Following Friedman's (1975) distinction between external and internal legal cultures, we may distinguish between external and internal legal socialization. By external legal socialization we mean the development of legal attitudes and behavior within the general populations that begins in childhood but is not limited to it. By internal legal socialization we mean the formation and change of legal attitudes and behavior within legal practitioners, for example, police, lawyers, judges, and so on. The first of our three chapters presents a theory of external legal socialization, while the second two deal, in quite different ways, with two aspects of internal legal socialization.

In Chapter 3 Robert Hogan presents an overview of his approach to the theory of legal socialization in children and relates the theory to guidelines for the drafting of effective legislation. Hogan argues that individuals pass through two stages before reaching the final forms of their law-related reasoning and behavioral tendencies. The first stage, labelled attunement to rules, is successfully completed when the child makes an accommodation to adult authority that stems from the proper combination of warmth and discipline administered by its parents. Affection and discipline are independent dimensions of parental response to children; affection coupled with strong, consistent discipline appears to produce the highest degree of attunement to rules—that is, the child has internalized the limits of conduct that his parents have imposed.

The second stage of legal socialization, labelled sensitivity to social expectations, corresponds in time approximately with the development of the child's peer-group relations. Whereas in the earlier stage of development the child was learning rules, he now must learn norms and values, primarily through peer-group experience. A key element in this process is developing a sense of reciprocity, which leads to what the philosopher John Rawls has called the ethics of association. Rewarding peer-group experiences will lead to the secure internalization of the norms and values of the group; to the extent that the children at this stage are properly supervised by adults, the norms and values of the peer group will reflect the principles and ideologies of the adult society and thus are an introduction to adult life.

During the final stage of socialization, labelled ideological maturity, the individual organizes previous experiences with rules and social expectations into a coherent system of beliefs from which the correctness of obedience or disobedience to external rules or laws may be assessed. The autonomous or principled person organizes the rules and principles under an ideology that becomes an important part of his sense of self. Actions in violation of the internalized rules produce guilt; usually, therefore, such actions are avoided.

How may this characterization of the process of legal socialization be applied to the practical business of legislation? Based on the stages of socialization, Hogan conjectures that an effective law will reflect the attributes of all three stages. To begin with, the law will be perceived as emanating from legitimate, respectable authority, thus being analogous to earlier relations to parents. Secondly, the law will be perceived as fair or just, which means that it will appear to treat like cases alike and different cases differently. In this way the law will have the characteristic of the rules of reciprocity or fair play that developed during the period of initial peer-group affiliations. And finally, the law will be consistent with the highest or sacred beliefs of the society. It can be obeyed without demanding behavior inconsistent with the abstractions of personal ideology.

To the extent that legislators appear to be (and, one might hope, indeed are) personally representative of the high standards they set for others by virtue of the laws they enact, then to that extent we may expect greater obedience to law. When corruption and cynicism are discovered in high places, however, citizens tend to view legislation as coming from incompletely legitimate authority; disobedience is facilitated. Under such circumstances, using the law as an instrument of progressive social reform becomes seriously problematic.

Anthony Platt (with Randi Pollock) deals with a highly interesting and important aspect of adult legal socialization, namely, changes in the attitudes of young lawyers as a result of working in the Office of the Public Defender. While other studies have focused primarily on how public defenders do their jobs and their effectiveness in defending clients (see, for example, Alschuler, 1975; Skolnick, 1967), Platt examines the political and bureaucratic pressures within the organization itself, how these pressures affect recruitment into the job, and their impact on the attitudes, motivation, and subsequent legal careers of the people exposed to them.

The main subjects of Platt's study are present and former members of the Public Defender's Office in Alameda County, California, acknowledged to be one of the best offices in the nation. For the most part, lawyers who choose to work in the office are motivated by the desire to gain extensive legal experience: the nature and quality of the cases coming to the office insure that its lawyers will gain trial experience and have more individual responsibility for the conduct of cases, than in any other first job out of law school. In addition, many of the young people are motivated by a sense of high public purpose, for they see themselves as defending the underdog who cannot afford private counsel. Platt notes, however, that public defenders in Cook County (Chicago) were less likely to express job preference in terms of moral and political beliefs; rather they were more likely to regard their job as "second best to a job in the District Attorney's

Office and as an instrumentality for advancing their careers." Platt's data also indicate differences in the background and career aspirations of persons who become public defenders and those who become prosecuting attorneys.

Whatever their reasons for joining the Public Defender's Office, however, the data show that very few of them remain for long: between 1960 and 1968 the median duration in the job was 2.5 years. Platt ascribes these brief periods of tenure to the pernicious effects of the weak political and fiscal situation in which public defenders find themselves. In Platt's view the Public Defender's Office is under the political thumb of an oppressive criminal justice system. Political realities force the Office into a low profile position in which ideological and bureaucratic conservatism are virtually mandatory for survival. The adversary system is compromised. Lack of funds, heavy case load, general lack of public interest, and even a lack of adequate appreciation of their work by their own clients create cynicism and, in the jargon of the trade, these young lawyers become "burned out." They leave their typically "poor, powerless, and disproportionately Third World" clients for the greater financial rewards of working with the middle class.

Attrition in the office, Platt asserts, would be decreased if legal education provided a more realistic picture of life as a public defender. What constitutes realism in this portrayal is inevitably a matter of political ideology as well as of practical sociology. Platt draws his political theory from the literature of the radical left and argues that the socialization process in the Public Defender's Office, which emphasizes technical virtuosity and professionalism, segregates the lawyers from their natural affiliation with their clients. While there is a degree of autonomy unusual in other beginning legal jobs, the young defenders are hemmed about with bureaucratic restrictions and divisions of labor that prevent them from attempting to change the organizational goals of the office while meeting its daily demands.

In Platt's opinion the solution to the waste of time and effort accompanying the rapid turnover of lawyers in the Public Defender's Office cannot be remedied by reform movements. The key issue is that the office, as part of the larger criminal justice system, operates as an instrument of class and racial exploitation. The role of the public defender has the sort of benevolence attached to it that Burt complains about in his chapter. While in principle this role is service to the poor, it is effectively prevented from doing the best possible job by fiscal and bureaucratic hamstringing, and hence it operates to insure a maximum of social control over those who seek help from it. The disillusionment of the young defenders stems from their comprehension, at whatever level of articulation, of the contradiction inherent in their position. Until the contradiction is resolved at the level of the entire system, the development from idealism to cynicism is inevitable.

There are, of course, less revolutionary perspectives regarding both the problems of public defenders and their effectiveness. Platt's chapter must be viewed in the context of work by other authors who have reached conclusions at least partially at variance with his. For example, Platt argues that by its very bureaucratic nature the Public Defender's Office must compromise its adversarial role—a role that is essential in the Anglo-American system of justice. Skolnick (1967) studied public defenders in another California county and concluded that in some respects the Public Defender has greater flexibility to maintain an adversarial posture than the private defense attorney. Alschuler (1975) has reached a similar conclusion: while the Public Defender is susceptible to bureaucratic pressures and other disadvantages, in comparison to the private defense attorney, he often has greater influence with the prosecutor's office, better channels for pre-trial discovery, better access to knowledge about and resources in the criminal justice system, and is more likely to have the sympathy of the judge. Indeed, there is evidence suggesting that public defenders are more likely to go to trial than to plea bargain. They are also likely to obtain better outcomes for their clients when they do make a plea agreement, especially when such factors as type of client, the offense, defendant's bail status, and prior criminal record are controlled.

Yet, all serious students of the subject acknowledge that the defendant is, more often than not, a secondary figure in the process. Both public and private legal counsel have broader interests—maintaining a high volume of clients for financial reasons, fostering a "good" relationship with the prosecutor, bending to bureaucratic pressures—that conflict with the client's interests. Then, in Blumberg's (1967) apt phrasing, law is practiced as a confidence game and the client is "conned" by his counsel into compromising or surrendering the rights to which he is due. Thus, even if one does not agree with Platt's political perspective, it must be acknowledged that he raises some provocative questions about legal justice and the process of internal legal socialization.

The chapter by Williams, England, Farmer, and Blumenthal is addressed to another aspect of the lawyer's job. These authors make a preliminary report on a project directed toward investigating the effectiveness of legal negotiation. While litigation may be the most visible form of legal dispute resolution, it is only the tip of an iceberg. In an overwhelming majority of criminal cases, pleas are negotiated or charges are dropped before the case comes to trial. As many as 90 percent of civil case filings are settled before coming to trial. However, even these statistics ignore the disputes that could potentially become legal disputes, but are resolved without recourse to the first stages of litigation. Instead parties solve their conflicts through informal negotiation or third-party interventions such as mediation and arbitration. Further, recent research on the role of the courts (for example, Friedman & Percival, 1976) indicates that, at least in the civil law, formal adjudication is likely to become even less frequent as society continues to urbanize and grow in complexity.

Traditionally, lawyers have been identified as dealing primarily with the technicalities of litigation, but in fact they play a crucial role in the informal conflict resolution process (see Ross, 1970; Sarat, 1976). While social scientists have recently begun to turn their attention to these nonadjudicatory mechanisms (for example, Abel, 1973; Felsteiner, 1974; Sarat & Grossman, 1976), only anecdotal information exists on the precise functions of the lawyer in these proceedings and the social psychological dynamics involved in occupying these roles.

Williams et al. have, therefore, chosen a project that is ripe with opportunities to contribute important knowledge. They have drawn upon several sources of literature and information to develop some specific, empirically testable hypotheses about effective legal negotiating. Underlying their research are the explicit theoretical assumptions that legal negotiations take place in the context of informal but well-defined and commonly held professional norms and that a legal negotiator's effectiveness depends in large measure upon the degree to which he learns and adheres to these norms. Their work thus illuminates another facet of legal culture and socialization.

Psychological Analysis of Courtroom Procedures

This third and largest section of the book considers four aspects of courtroom practice: psychological factors in the presentation of evidence (Chapter 7), consequences of changes in jury size and decision rule on deliberation outcomes (Chapters 8 and 9), potential advantages and disadvantages of substituting videotape trial presentations for traditional, "live" performances (Chapters 10 and 11), and the use of sociological and psychological methods in the selection of jurors during the *voir dire* phase of a trial (Chapters 12, 13, and 14).

In Chapter 7 Anthony Doob discusses experimental results and policy conclusions in regard to jurors' abilities to weigh properly certain forms of evidence. For example, what ought to be the significance, in a criminal trial, of the defendant's past criminal record? On the one hand our intuition tells us that past convictions for related crimes are indicative of a character that could commit such a crime again—that is, we believe the evidence of past convictions to be germane to our estimates of guilt in the current case. On the other hand we know very well that the defendant is not being tried for what he may have done in the past, nor for what kind of person he is, but only on the current charge; hence the information about his past ought not to be relevant. In Canada, where Doob has done his research, the law takes a compromise course. If the defendant's past criminal record is mentioned during testimony, the judge instructs the jury that it may use the information only to determine the credibility of the defendant's testimony, not to determine his guilt on the current charge. The question is, of course, whether the jury can avoid the inference that the accused's past record increases the likelihood of his current guilt.

Doob presents experimental evidence suggesting that jurors may not be able to avoid the inference. Judge's instructions may not be sufficient to alleviate the jury's tendency to reconvict a previously convicted offender. And in a related study, Doob demonstrates, for both actual and experimental situations, that if jurors know that a defendant has been incarcerated prior to trial (as opposed to being released on bail), then they are more likely to convict or otherwise deal severely with him. Although arguments from these results to policy conclusions regarding the availability of bail must be made in the context of many other factors, the experimental findings are useful in suggesting what kinds of biases may be operating as a result of particular administrative procedures.

Chapters 8 and 9 exemplify two distinct approaches to understanding the significance of recent Supreme Court decisions allowing juries composed of less than twelve members (*Williams v. Florida*, 399 U.S. 78, 1970; *Colgove v. Battin*, 413 U.S. 149, 1973) and decision criteria of less than unanimity (*Johnson v. Louisiana*, 406 U.S. 356, 1972; *Apodaca et al. v. Oregon* 406 U.S. 404, 1972). In Chapter 8 Bernard Grofman uses mathematical probabilities to ascertain the impacts of six versus twelve person juries and of unanimity versus nonunanimity decision criteria, given different first-ballot vote distributions. The model demonstrates quite clearly the advantage of an initial majority. Most verdicts are in the direction initially held by a majority. This conclusion, offered from a theoretical perspective, is in agreement with the empirical evidence provided by Kalven and Zeisel (1966) in their analysis of 225 trials. Grofman, however, provides refinements in his assessment of the impact of these changes in jury procedures. Through his analyses, we see the relative proportions of verdicts going "guilty," "not guilty," or hanging, as a function of size of the group and the requirements of the decision—that is, two-thirds majority, five-sixths majority, and unanimity.

Grofman's assumptions are clear and his model provides a rationale for possible subsequent changes in the law. However clear the model, it is also clear that the modelling method has some limitations. For example, the models offered by Grofman require some restrictive assumptions. They do not take into account the fact that some people are more persuasive than others; and they do not address the dynamics of group interaction. Further, they deal solely with outcome distribution, or the probability of a given verdict.

Chapter 9, by Charlan Nemeth, focuses on these interactive dynamics as a function of the allowance of nonunanimity. In addition to concerns over verdict distribution as a function of unanimity versus nonunanimity, this chapter also addresses itself to the concept of due process and to the *perception* that justice has been administered. While replicating previous results showing that non-unanimity does not lead to statistically different outcomes than does unanimity, Nemeth points out that the nature of the jury's interactions is substantially affected by the change in decision rule. Juries operating with a less-than-unanimity decision criterion spend less time in deliberation; the deliberation is characterized by less robust discussion. It is characterized by fewer task-oriented comments. And the jurors are less likely to agree with the verdict or be convinced that justice has been administered. Thus, while verdict outcome may not be significantly affected, Nemeth's analysis suggests that due process and the symbolic function of the jury may be compromised by the allowance of nonunanimity. To the extent that the Supreme Court decisions on nonunanimity were based upon the various justices' opinions concerning the likely social influence processes that would occur, Nemeth's empirical findings suggest that the dissenting justices' theory was closer to the empirical facts than those offering the majority Court opinion.

Chapters 10 and 11 provide experimental analyses of the use of videotape as a means of jury trial presentation. The substitution of videotape for "live" trial testimony began in the early 1970s, primarily in the Erie County, Ohio, court of Judge James L. McCrystal. Judge McCrystal has written at length on the advantages of videotaped trials (for example, McCrystal, 1973), and some commentators have joined in his optimistic appraisals (Morril, 1970; Kornblum, 1972). More cautious notes have been sounded by other analysts (Bermant & Jacoubovitch, 1975; Doret, 1974), particularly in regard to the complete substitution of video for live presentation in single cases. However, almost all critics have agreed on the desirability of increased partial uses of the medium, for example in recording the depositions of experts or witnesses who might be unavailable at the date of trial.

Chapter 10, by Gerald Miller, and Chapter 11, by Larry Farmer and associates, approached the experimental analysis of complete prerecorded trials in very similar fashion. Both investigators take pains to achieve reality within the experimental setting; indeed Miller's group went to the extent of telling the experimental jury that the case was actual. And both groups made direct comparisons of individual juror responses to videotaped and live presentations of the same trial. The dependent variables selected for analysis were similar but not identical. While the results of the two studies are similar, the authors are not in consensus in regard to interpretation. Miller is generally more sanguine than Farmer et al. about the neutrality of the video medium in the creation of juror attitudes or biases. The differences between the outcomes of the two studies do not warrant large differences of interpretation. While more laboratory research will probably clarify our understanding of the impact of videotape presentations of legal material, we would also urge the evaluation of the medium's use in actual trial settings. There has been some post-trial polling of jurors who have participated in actual videotaped trials (Bermant, Chappell, Crockett, Jacoubovitch, & McGuire, 1975), and the Federal Judicial Center has begun a project to track the use of videotape in several district courts. Continuation of this work, combined with experiments in simulation, should provide the empirical support necessary for a sound policy decision regarding extensive use of videotape as a substitute for live trial presentation.

The final three chapters present experience and experiment in regard to the most publicized and controversial recent application of behavioral science to courtroom practice: the use of sociological and psychological data and insight during the selection of the jury, the *voir dire*. There has been a good deal of speculation about the usefulness and propriety of these techniques (for example, Bermant, McKinley, Jacoubovitch, & Sanstad, 1974; Etzioni, 1974; Shapley, 1974; Spector, 1974), but relatively few solid reports or analyses (Schulman, Shaver, Colman, Emrich, & Christie, 1973). Systematic presentations for lawyers have appeared only in the last year or so (Ginger, 1975; Kairys et al., 1975).

In Chapter 12 Lee Hamilton provides an experimental analysis of some limiting conditions on the relationship between authoritarianism and behavior on a jury. The "authoritarian personality," one who is highly submissive to authority and punitive to subordinates, has been a major target for psychologists aiding defense counsel in political conspiracy trials. The operative theory is that highly authoritarian individuals will be prone to accept the government's version of the case and vote for conviction on the conspiracy charges.

Earlier experimental research has tended to support this generalization. Hence, when possible, defense attorneys will exercise a peremptory challenge to an apparently highly authoritarian venireperson. In her chapter Hamilton demonstrates that under certain circumstances highly authoritarian individuals are *less* likely to convict a defendant than are low authoritarians. Nevertheless, Hamilton reports, when highly authoritarian individuals do convict a defendant, they are more punitive (as measured by duration of recommended sentence) than less authoritarian individuals.

In Chapter 13 Richard Christie shares a number of his experiences as a psychologist for the defense in several of the well-known conspiracy trials. Christie points out that the social scientist brings with him a methodological expertise but, perhaps even more importantly, he brings with him insights into interactive processes. Thus, the social scientist not only offers a profile of the "good" juror from the point of view of a particular advocate, but he also brings insight into who is likely to be persuaded, who will be the most persuasive, what cliques are likely to be formed, and so forth. This input, rather than being definitive, is creatively interwoven with the insights of the attorneys and the defendant. Together, there is an artful collaboration among people who bring different kinds of expertise toward the same end. The search is for agreement between these different sources.

The final chapter, by Richard Berk, begins with the raiding of the Illinois Black Panther Party headquarters by the Chicago Police Department on December 4, 1969. During the raid two Panthers, Mark Clark and Fred Hampton, were killed. Berk is presently involved as a social scientist for the plaintiffs in a civil suit that is now pending[1] on behalf of the dead and surviving Black Panthers. Berk brings to us the daily workings of a social science team

---

[1] As of the summer of 1976, the case (*Iberia, Hampton, administratrix, etc. et al. v. Edward Hanrahan et al.*, no. 70 C 1384, consolidated) was being heard in the U.S. District Court of the Northern District of Illinois, Eastern Division.

plagued by too little time, too little money, and occasional lapses in morale. Specifically, he shows us the trials and tribulations, the mechanics and the processes by which a team attempts to determine predictor variables that will be of aid to the plaintiff's attorneys in their usage of peremptory challenges.

In these two chapters we find a sensitive portrayal of the social scientist in collaboration with attorneys. We are instructed in the art as well as the science of this collaboration. And in the process, we get a glimpse of the problems associated with the *usefulness* of social science research for trials.

How effective has scientific jury selection been in the special trials in which it has been used? To what extent do these methods have applicability to general criminal trials? Answers to these two questions are crucial for assessing whether such endeavors justify the considerable money-time-effort costs involved. They are also important in attempts to examine the broader social and ethical issues involved.

It should be noted from the outset that at present the data are far too incomplete to yield more than the most tentative conclusions. Nevertheless, even in the absence of hard data we can pose the questions that must ultimately be entertained when better data are collected. We may also draw upon existing bodies of related social science data to speculate about what the outcome of such evaluation studies will be.

On the surface at least, scientific jury selection has been a generally successful enterprise. According to his own account, hypnoanalyst Bryan (1971) has never been on the losing side in the dozens of cases in which he has participated as part of the jury selection team. With the exception of a conviction on a minor charge in the Harrisburg trial and a conviction in the first of the Attica trials, all of the other cases that have involved social scientists and have gone to the jury resulted in favorable defense verdicts. Moreover, legal counsel in all of these trials have been favorably impressed by the techniques and have attributed successful trial outcomes as being at least partially due to successful jury selection. Finally, the Schulman-Christie team has conducted post-trial interviews with jurors in an attempt to determine how they voted initially, the dynamics of juror interaction, their perceptions of the trial process and so on, in an attempt to gauge the predictive ability of their techniques. They claim a success rate exceeding 70 percent accuracy. However, we wish to argue that in the absence of an appropriate study design, none of these indices constitutes an adequate criterion of success.

Consider, first, the criterion of jury acquittals. It is important to note that scientific jury selection techniques have always been confounded with other factors that could have caused the verdict outcome. The trial is a complex process involving interaction of the litigants, their counsel, the judge, the nature of the evidence, and other variables. The interplay of any of these factors or combination of these factors, rather than the jury selection endeavors, might have been responsible for the favorable verdicts. For example, any legal counsel who recruits social scientists for jury selection is also likely to initiate other innovative techniques and devote extraordinary energies in presenting his client's position. As another example it should be noted that in most of the political trials in which these techniques have been used, the government's case was generally weak (especially after much evidence was ruled inadmissible), and this factor alone may have resulted in pressures for acquittal that even adversely prejudiced jurors could not have resisted. Finally, because the *voir dire* may serve an educative function as well as an information gathering function, a secondary effect of social science techniques may have been to sensitize the jurors about prejudice or racism; this secondary effect, rather than selection per se, may have contributed to the acquittals. While this last example suggests some utility of social science for the jury process, it does not prove jury selection effective. In short, any number of factors may have affected jury decisions in complex ways; the conditions for a "time" experiment (Campbell & Stanley, 1961), in which the effects of jury selection procedures alone could be systematically assessed, have never been met.

A second factor to consider is what we can call the *marginal effectiveness* of the selection techniques—that is, to what extent do the social science techniques result in the elimination of biased jurors who would not ordinarily be eliminated from the jury panel using the conventional jury selection techniques? Note again that in all of the cases surveyed, the social scientists' input was always used in conjunction with traditional techniques; scientific input was only one element in the final decisions about acceptability of jurors. Despite some claims to the contrary (Broeder, 1965; Levit, Nelson, Bell, & Chernick, 1971), there is evidence that standard *voir dire* techniques are successful in eliminating biased jurors (Gutman, 1973; Padawer-Singer, Singer & Singer, 1974). Especially in the trials to which we are referring, with the high calibre defense counsel teams skilled at all phases of the trial process including *voir dire*, the question arises as to whether the final jury composition would have been similar even if social scientists had not participated. (We assume that extensive *voir dire* would have been allowed anyway.)

Although it should be obvious that neither legal counsel's faith in the efficacy of the new techniques nor the participating social scientists' beliefs about them, is a reliable criterion. Yet these statements of faith are largely responsible for the publicity and popularity the techniques have achieved. It need only be noted that the perceived effectiveness may be a result of investment in time, money, and energy into the process. The psychological literature is replete with studies showing that heavy investment in an activity results in rationalizing processes to justify the effort.

A major evaluational difficulty is that, since the privacy of actual jury deliberations has been completely protected by Congress (Katz, 1972, chapter 2), we must rely on post-trial interviews with jurors to determine what went on in the jury room. Although there is some unreliability inherent in such measures of recall, it would not appear to be an unduly serious problem. The Schulman-Christie research team has used this approach and they claim a 70 percent or better accuracy rate in predicting juror behavior. Unfortunately, the number of cases which went to trial after their techniques had been utilized is very small, and therefore the reliability of their figures is open to some question. Moreover, even if acceptable reliability can be demonstrated, such data do not come to grips with the issue of the marginal effectiveness over conventional selection techniques.

In short, despite widespread publicity and increased demand for its utilization, the present state of data collection does not allow us to draw any conclusions about the predictive efficacy of scientific jury selection. This does not mean that it is nonexistent, only that there is no reliable evidence either way.

References

Abel, R.L. A comparative theory of dispute institutions in society. *Law and Society Review*, 1973, *8*, 217-347.

Alschuler, A.W. The defense attorney's role in plea bargaining. *Yale Law Journal*, 1975, *84*, 1179-1315.

Bazelon, D.L. Psychologists in corrections—Are they doing good for the offender or well for themselves? In S.L. Brodsky (Ed.), *Psychologists in the criminal justice system*. Urbana: University of Illinois Press, 1973.

Bermant, G., Chappell, D., Crockett, G.T., Jacoubovitch, M.-D., & McGuire, M. Juror responses to prerecorded videotape trial presentations in California and Ohio. *Hastings Law Journal*, 1975, *26*, 975-998.

Bermant, G., & Jacoubovitch, M.-D. Fish out of water: A brief overview of some social and psychological concerns about videotaped trials. *Hastings Law Journal*, 1975, *26*, 999-1011.

Bermant, G., McKinley, W., & Jacoubovitch, M.-D., & Sanstad, A. Psycholegal collaboration. *Harvard Law Record*, April 26, 1974, 11.

Blumberg, A.F. Practice of law as a confidence game: Organizational cooptation of a profession. *Law and Society Review*, 1967, *1*, 15-39.

Boring, E.G. *A story of experimental psychology*. New York: Appleton-Century-Crofts, 1950.

Brodsky, S.L. *Psychologists in the criminal justice system*. Urbana: University of Illinois Press, 1973.

Broeder, D. Voir dire examination: An empirical study. *Southern California Law Review*, 1965, *38*, 503-528.

Bryan, W.J., Jr. *The chosen ones*. New York: Vantage Press, 1971.

Buckhout, R. Guilt by fabrication: Psychology and the eyewitness. In M.H. Siegel & H.P. Zeigler (Eds.), *Psychological research—The inside story*. New York: Harper & Row, 1976.

Burt, R.A. Of mad dogs and scientists: The perils of the "criminal-insane." *University of Pennsylvania Law Review*, 1974, *123*, 258-296.

Burtt, H. *Legal psychology*. New York: Prentice-Hall, 1931.

Campbell, A., & Schuman, H. Racial attitudes in fifteen American cities. In *Supplemental studies for the National Advisory Commission on Civil Disorders*. Washington, D.C.: U.S. Government Printing Office, 1968.

Campbell, D.T. & Stanley, J.C. Experimental and quasi-experimental designs for research on teaching. In N.L. Gage (Ed.), *Handbook of research on teaching*. Chicago: Rand McNally, 1963.

Conrad, J.P. We should never have promised a hospital. *Federal Probation*, 1975, *39*, 3-9.

Dershowitz, A.M. Indeterminate confinement: Letting the therapy fit the harm. *University of Pennsylvania Law Review*, 1974, *123*, 297-339.

Doret, D. Trial by videotape—Can justice be seen to be done? *Temple Law Quarterly*, 1974, *47*, 228-268.

Ebbinghaus, H. *Abriss der Psychologie*, 1908.

Etzioni, A. Creating an imbalance. *Trial*, 1974, *10*, 28-30.

Felstiner, W.L.F. Influences of social organization on dispute processing. *Law and Society Review*, 1974, *9*, 63-94.

Friedman, L.M. *The legal system—A social science perspective*. New York: Russell Sage Foundation, 1975.

Friedman, L.M. & Percival, R.V. A tale of two courts: Litigation in Alameda and San Benito counties. *Law and Society Review*, 1976, *10*, 267-302.

Gaylin, W. *Partial justice*. New York: Knopf, 1974.

Gaylin, W., & Blatte, H. Behavior modification in prisons. *American Criminal Law Review*, 1975, *13*, 11-36.

Ginger, A.F. *Jury selection in criminal trials*. Tiburon, Calif.: Lawpress, 1975.

Goldberg, D. Court challenges to prison behavior modification programs: A case study. *American Criminal Law Review*, 1975, *13*, 37-68.

Gottfredson, D.M. Five challenges. In S.L. Brodsky (Ed.), *Psychologists in the criminal justice system*. Urbana: University of Illiois Press, 1973.

Gutman, F.M. The attorney-conducted voir dire of jurors: A constitutional right. *Brooklyn Law Review*, 1973, *39*, 291-303.

Hutchins, R.M., & Slesinger, D. Some observations on the law of evidence—spontaneous exclamations. *Columbia Law Review*, 1928, 28, 432-440.

Hutchins, R.M., & Slesinger, D. Some obesrvations on the law of evidence—memory. *Harvard Law Review*, 1938, *41*, 860-873.

Kairys, D., Schulman, J., & Harring, S. (Eds.), *The jury system: New methods for reducing prejudice.* Prepared by the National Jury Project and the National Lawyers Guild. Philadelphia: Philadelphia Resistance Print Shop, 1975.

Kalven, H., & Zeisel, H. *The American jury.* Chicago: University of Chicago Press, 1966.

Katz, J. *Experimentation with human beings.* New York: Russell Sage Foundation, 1972.

Katz, J., Goldstein, J., & Dershowitz, A.M. *Psychoanalysis, psychiatry, and law.* New York: The Free Press, 1967.

Kelly, R.M. Generalizations from an OEO experiment in Washington, D.C. *Journal of Social Issues*, 1975, *31*, 57-86. (a)

Kelly, R.M. Comments on a view from management. *Journal of Social Issues*, 1975, *31*, 95-98. (b)

Klerman, G. Behavior control and the limits of reform. *Hastings Center Report*, 1975, 5, 40-45.

Kolasa, B.J. Psychology and law. *American Psychologist*, 1972, *27*, 499-503.

Kornblum, G.O. Videotape in civil cases. *Hastings Law Journal*, 1972, *24*, 9-36.

Lempert, R.O. Uncovering "nondiscernible" differences: Empirical research and the jury-size cases. *Michigan Law Review*, 1975, *73*, 643-708.

Levine, F.J., & Tapp, J.L. The psychology of criminal identification: The gap from *Wade* to *Kirby. University of Pennsylvania Law Review*, 1973, *121*, 1079-1131.

Levit, W., Nelson, D., Bell, V., & Chernick, R. Expediting voir dire: An empirical study. *Southern California Law Review*, 1971, *44*, 916-995.

Loftus, E. Reconstructing memory: The incredible eyewitness. *Psychology Today*, December 1974, pp. 116-119.

London, P. *Behavior control.* New York: Harper & Row, 1969.

Louisell, D.W. The psychologist in today's legal world. *Minnesota Law Review*, 1955, *39*, 235-272.

Marshall, J., Marquis, K., & Oskamp, S. Effects of kind of question and atmosphere of interrogation on accuracy and completeness of testimony. *Harvard Law Review*, 1971, *84*, 1620-1643.

McCrystal, J.L. Videotape trials: Relief for our congested courts. *Denver Law Journal*, 1973, *44*, 463-488.

Menninger, K. *The crime of punishment.* New York: The Viking Press, 1966.

Morrill, A.E. Enter—The video tape trial. *The John Marshall Journal of Practice and Procedure*, 1970, *3*, 237-258.

Morris, N. The future of imprisonment: Toward a punitive philosophy. *Michigan Law Review*, 1974, *72*, 1161-1180.

Münsterburg, H. *Psychology on the witness stand.* New York: S.S. McClure, 1907.

Orland, L., & Tyler, H.R. *Justice in sentencing.* Mineola, New York: The Foundation Press, 1974.

Padawer-Singer, A., & Barton, A. Free press-fair trial. In R. Simon (Ed.), *The jury system: A critical analysis,* Beverly Hills, Calif.: Sage Publications, in press, 1976.

Padawer-Singer, A.M., Singer, A., & Singer R. Voir dire by two lawyers: An essential safeguard. *Judicature,* 1974, *57,* 386-391.

Pospisil, L. *Anthropology of law: A comparative theory.* New Haven: Human Relations Area File Press, 1974.

Radzinowitz, L., & Wolfgang, M.E. *Crime and justice.* 3 vols. New York: Basic Books, 1971.

Reasons, C.E., & Wirth, B.A. Police-community relations units: A national survey. *Journal of Social Issues,* 1975, *31,* 27-34.

Reddy, W.B., & Lansky, L.M. Nothing but the facts—and some observations on norms and values: The history of a consultation with a metropolitan police division. *Journal of Social Issues,* 1975, *31,* 123-138.

Ross, H.L. *Settled out of court.* Chicago: Aldine, 1970.

Rothman, D. *The discovery of the asylum: Social order and disorder in the new republic.* Boston: Little, Brown, 1971.

Sarason, I.G., & Sarason, B.R. Comments on ethical issues in behavior modification. In G. Bermant, H. Kelman, & D. Warwick (Eds.), *Ethics of social intervention.* Washington, D.C.: Hemisphere Publishing Co., in press, 1976.

Sarat, A. Choice of legal procedure: Litigation in a small-claims court. *Law and Society Review,* in press.

Sarat, A., & Grossman, J. Courts and conflict resolution: Problems in the mobilization of adjudication. *American Political Science Review,* 1975, *69,* 1200-1217.

Sarat, A., & Vidmar, N. Public opinion, the death penalty, and the eighth amendment: Testing the Marshall hypothesis. In H. Bedau & C. Pierce (Eds.), *Capital punishment in the United States.* New York: AMF Press, 1976.

Schulman, J., Shaver, P., Colman, R., Emrich, B., & Christie, R. Recipe for a jury. *Psychology Today,* May 1973, pp. 37-44, 77, 79-84.

Shapley, D. Jury selection: Social scientists gamble in an already loaded game. *Science,* 1974, *185,* 1033-1034.

Slovenko, R. *Psychiatry and law.* Boston: Little, Brown, 1973.

Singer, H.A. Police action—Community action. *Journal of Social Issues,* 1975, *31,* 99-106.

Skolnick, J. Social control in the adversary system. *Journal of Conflict Resolution*, 1967, *11*, 54-60.

Spector, P. Scientific jury selection warps justice. *Harvard Law Record*, February 8, 1974, p. 14.

Stotland, E. (Ed.). Police and community. *Journal of Social Issues*, 1975, *31*, 1. (a)

Stotland, E. Police power and community power: A final editorial comment. *Journal of Social Issues*, 1975, *31*, 217-218. (b)

Stotland, E., & Guppy, W. Community relations training in the Seattle police academy. *Journal of Social Issues*, 1975, *31*, 139-144.

Stolz, S.B. Ethical issues in behavior modification. In G. Bermant, H. Kelman, & D. Warwick (Eds.), *Ethics of social intervention*. Washington, D.C.: Hemisphere Publishing Co., in press, 1976.

Sutherland, E.H., & Cressey, D.R. *Principles of criminology*, 7th Ed., Rev. Philadelphia: J.B. Lippincott, 1966.

Teahan, J.E. Role playing and group experience to facilitate attitude and value changes among black and white police officers. *Journal of Social Issues*, 1975, *31*, 35-46. (a)

Teahan, J.E. A longitudinal study of attitude shifts among black and white police officers. *Journal of Social Issues*, 1975, 31, 47-56. (b)

Thibaut, J., & Walker, L. *Procedural justice*. Hillsdale, N.J.: Laurence Erlbaum Associates, 1975.

Trankell, A. *Reliability of evidence*. Stockholm: Beckmans, 1972.

Trotter, S. Patuxent: "Therapeutic" prison faces test. *APA Monitor*, May 1975, *6*, 1, 4, 12.

U.S. Senate. Committee on the Judiciary. Subcommittee on Constitutional Rights. *Individual rights and the federal role in behavior modification*. Washington, D.C.: U.S. Government Printing Office, 1974.

Weld, H.P., & Danzig, E.R. A study of the way in which a verdict is reached by a jury. *American Journal of Psychology*, 1940, *52*, 518-536.

Weld, H.P., & Roff, M.F. A study in the formation of opinion based upon legal evidence. *American Journal of Psychology*, 1938, *51*, 609-628.

Wilson, J.Q. *Thinking about crime*. New York: Basic Books, 1975.

Zeisel, H. . . . And then there were none: The diminution of the federal jury. *University of Chicago Law Review*, 1976, *38*, 710-724.

Zeisel, H., & Diamond, S.S. "Convincing empirical evidence" on the six person jury. *University of Chicago Law Review*, 1974, *41*, 281-295.

Part II:
Psychological Jurisprudence

2 Helping Suspect Groups to Disappear

Robert A. Burt

During recent years intense legal reform efforts have been directed toward social care of the mentally ill and mentally retarded. Two different themes have characterized these efforts. First, claims have been made that these depictions should be given virtually no social significance—that "mental illness" is a fictitious social construct and that "mental retardation," while not wholly fictive, has been given grossly exaggerated social importance. From this stance reform proposals have come for the abolition of mental illness civil commitment, for example (Szasz, 1963, 1970), and for community "normalization" as the keystone in social response to the mentally retarded (Hobbs, 1975a). But there is a competing, or at least contrapuntal, theme raised with equal intensity in reform efforts: more resources should be provided for the mentally ill and retarded as such. Continued social differentiation of these statuses is at least implicit in claims for implementation of financially costly "rights to treatment" in institutions for the mentally ill and retarded[1] and for special educational facilities for the retarded to implement a "right to education."[2]

These two themes are not necessarily mutually exclusive. For many mentally retarded persons, for example, the prospects of independent living in the general community are dim without intensive and expensive training directed toward that goal. Our traditional policies toward the retarded—excluding them as such from general public educational facilities and providing special programs only in large-scale geographically isolated nightmarish institutions—have dramatically worked against the ultimate possibility of "normal" (essentially undifferentiated) community life for the retarded (Hobbs, 1975b).

Thus there can be clear logic in joining together these two reformist themes—no stigmatizing separation but commitment of separate resources to work against stigmatizing separation—but there is still tension between them. In practical terms the tension can be seen in the recent litigative efforts to implement the "right to treatment." Some courts that have been persuaded to embrace this rhetoric have focussed their attention on improving conditions within the large-scale institutions for the mentally ill and retarded and have given

---

[1] See, for example, *Wyatt v. Stickney*, 344 F. Supp. 387 (M.D. Ala. 1972), *aff'd sub nom. Wyatt v. Aderhold*, 503 F.2d 1305 (5th Cir. 1974); *Rouse v. Cameron*, 373 F.2d 451 (D.C. Cir. 1966).

[2] See, for example, *Pennsylvania Association for Retarded Children v. Commonwealth of Pennsylvania*, 343 F. Supp. 279 (E.D. Pa. 1972); *Mills v. Board of Education*, 348 F. Supp. 866 (D.D.C. 1972).

33

little more than lip-service to the goal of ending the stigmatizing segregation inherent in the very existence of these institutions (Burt, 1975).[3]

In this presentation, I want to explore some aspects of the tension between these two reformist goals. There is at heart here a fundamental question of social psychology: Why should consciously intended benevolence toward a stigmatized group work to emphasize, rather than diminish, stigma? The question can, I think, be brought into clear focus by considering current legal reform efforts directed toward the mentally ill and retarded.

The first step in this inquiry is to identify the psychological link between benevolent offers of assistance and impositions of social stigma. The link is this: "benevolence" necessarily implies inequality between a donor and a potential actual recipient. The donor, that is, believes that the recipient "needs help." At the moment when this need is perceived, the donor also perceives that he has power—both the needed help and the capacity to bestow or withold it—that the recipient lacks.

This inequality of power is not inevitably permanent or perjorative. To the contrary, such inequality is an important aspect of the most mutually satisfying and intimate human relationships. But viewing benevolence from this perspective (as an expression of power inequality) begins to illuminate the reasons for tension between the reformist goals noted above regarding stigmatized groups.

A central hallmark of stigma is inequality of power.[4] Accordingly, benevolence toward stigmatized people can be as much an expression and exacerbation of stigma as a well-meaning, effective instrument toward its elimination. The critical question for evaluating reform strategy for stigmatized groups is thus to differentiate useful from harmful benevolence. To do this we must look carefully for the reasons that stigma has been imposed on these groups—to see why equality of power has been withheld from them so that we might identify and guard against parallel motivations for benevolent attitudes and actions that, as noted, necessarily imply inequality.

Stigma and Benevolence toward the Mentally Disabled

There are many reasons and a few ways that stigma has been imposed on the mentally disabled in this society. The most striking initial fact is that at least

[3] But compare the settlement recently reached in the litigation directed at the New York state mental retardation institution, which points toward a different direction. See "State agrees to transfer 2,650 out of Willowbrook," *The New York Times*, April 22, 1975, p. 1.

[4] Chief Justice Stone's famous footnote in the *Carolene Products* case reflects this proposition. He called for "more searching judicial inquiry" regarding legislation affecting "discrete and insular minorit[ies]"—that is, stigmatized groups—because "prejudice . . . tends seriously to curtail the operation of those political processes ordinarily to be relied upon to protect minorities" (*United States v. Carolene Products Co.*, 304 U.S. 144, 153, n.4 [1938]).

since the end of the nineteenth century, the keystone of our social response to mental illness and retardation has been discrete conceptual categorization linked to spatial separation of these persons from the "normal" population (Rothman, 1971). Even among "abnormal" populations such as criminals, the "mentally disabled" have been conceptually and spatially segregated (Burt, 1974a). A rhetoric of benevolence has been invoked to justify this separate treatment—that the mentally disabled "need help" (and that "mentally ill criminals" deserve "help" rather than "punishment"). Benevolent rhetoric here has taken the special cast of medical nomenclature invoked by medical personnel. Two separate questions must be explored. First, what social function has been served by the conceptual-spatial segregation of the mentally disabled as such? Second, how has the rhetoric of benevolence, and its specific medical incarnation, related to this social separatist function?

I want to explore these two questions primarily through an important contemporary law reform case. In *Lake v. Cameron*, decided in 1966, the United States Court of Appeals for the District of Columbia Circuit—the most prominent court in the country addressing legal issues of mental disabilities—announced the principle that when the state takes power to protect a person because of mental disability, the state must provide the "least restrictive alternative" to accomplish its protective purpose.[5] This principle was particularly intended to disfavor the traditional pattern of confinement in geographically isolated institutions and thus to stand against the spatially segregating aspects of our past policies toward the mentally disabled. This principle has since obtained great currency in court decisions and legislative reforms regarding both mental illness and mental retardation statuses (Chambers, 1972). Nonetheless, the *Lake* Court held fast to the old tradition in two ways—special conceptual categorization of mental disability and the rhetoric of benevolence—and these traditions catalyzed the old dynamic of degradation masked by kindly smiles at least for Mrs. Catherine Lake, the first putative beneficiary of this important legal reform.

Mrs. Lake, in 1966, was a sixty-four-year-old woman who by then had been confined for four years in St. Elizabeth's Hospital, the large-scale isolated mental institution for Washington, D.C.[6] She had come to official attention one afternoon in 1962 when a police officer noticed her, as he put it, "wandering around" on a downtown Washington street directly across from the Department of Justice. According to the transcript of her civil commitment proceeding, Mrs. Lake that day had been at the Department of Justice seeking restoration of a pension that she had received until several years earlier because of her dead son's naval service. The policeman, that afternoon, asked Mrs. Lake to account for her

---

[5] 364 F.2d 657 (D.C. Cir. 1966).

[6] All of the quoted depictions of Mrs. Lake's case, except as specifically indicated, are drawn from her initial commitment and subsequent habeas corpus proceeding prior to the Court of Appeals remand. Various portions of that transcript appear in the Court of Appeals decision (364 F.2d 657 [D.C. Cir. 1966]), the District Court decision on remand (267 F. Supp. 155 [D.D.C. 1967]), and Katz, Goldstein & Dershowitz (1967, pp. 552-553).

presence on the street and, it appears, she explained her mission to the Justice Department. The officer then asked where Mrs. Lake was heading and, according to him, she could not "remember her last address." Mrs. Lake was then taken into state custody from which she was never released until her death some ten years later (and, it should be noted, six years after her landmark victory of principle in the United States Court of Appeals).

Thus far in the narrative, one might wonder why a citizen walking in daylight on a public street should have been approached at all by a police officer and asked to account for herself. But though Mrs. Lake clearly knew where she was (since she had found her way to the Department of Justice for what seemed a plausible purpose) the officer not only demanded an accounting but concluded that Mrs. Lake did not know where she was going next. The officer was not irrational to reach this latter conclusion, since Mrs. Lake could not give her street address. But still, it did not occur to the officer to conclude that since Mrs. Lake had clearly found her way that day to a place she intended to be, she might find her way to another intended place that day though she could not remember the address.

Something about Mrs. Lake's street presence made the officer see her as "wandering," which provoked his initial question, and her nonresponse confirmed that diagnosis. Throughout all of the subsequent court proceedings about her, this depiction (that Mrs. Lake was a "wanderer") stuck and was the sole justification offered by the state for its decision to confine her in a state mental institution.

For example, a psychiatrist testifying to her need for confinement stated that after her initial commitment to St. Elizabeth's, she once "wandered away" from the hospital and thirty-two hours later was found "wandering in the streets not too far from the hospital." Following the Court of Appeals directive that the state provide the "least restrictive alternative" possible to protect Mrs. Lake, the trial court on remand affirmed continued confinement at St. Elizabeth's on this ground:

The purpose of her confinement in a closed ward is to prevent her from wandering. Her medical background indicates that she has a strong propensity, when in a confused and disoriented state, to wander aimlessly through the streets until eventually picked up. . . . This Court finds . . . that constant supervision is not only proper but required for the safety of this patient.[7]

Again, as in her initial contact with the police officer, no one evaluating her "wandering" from St. Elizabeth's gave much credit to the clear fact that Mrs. Lake didn't want to stay there and might have intentionally escaped but got lost because she was unfamiliar with the environs of the hospital. Mrs. Lake herself had testified quite clearly about her desires in the court proceedings: "I feel I am

[7] *Lake v. Cameron*, 267 F. Supp. 155, 158 (D.D.C. 1967).

thoroughly competent," she said. "I always took care of myself. . . . I never would want to be in an insane asylum. . . . I don't think any person would want to be in an insane asylum."

What, then, led Mrs. Lake into state custody? If the episodes charged of "street wandering" were in fact plausibly explicable (she meant to be across from the Justice Department and to escape from St. Elizabeth's Hospital), what did the policeman, psychiatrist, and judge mean when they said she "wander[ed] aimlessly" and dangerously? This much, I think, was meant. Mrs. Lake looked strange on the streets, like a "senile old lady." One can read in the interstices of the court proceedings that she most likely dressed oddly, rather like the rag-tag old ladies seen on many public streets fishing in trash barrels for newspaper and other treasures to fill their paper shopping sacks. Further, Mrs. Lake most likely strolled rather than strode purposively on a downtown business street and, more significantly, she evidently had a disoriented look to her facial expressions.

The St. Elizabeth's psychiatrist testified that she "has shown memory defect for remote and recent events"; that when she returned from her thirty-two hour elopement from the hospital "she thought she had been away just a few hours"; and that she "cannot give dates" of significant events in her life. In short, Mrs. Lake's mind "wandered"—and, it seems, quite patently so even to a casual street observer—and in this sense, she "wandered" the streets. Ironically, this information might also have been used to support Mrs. Lake's claim for freedom. Her inability to remember dates and time might equally extend to numbers, such as her street address, and this memory lapse thus need not demonstrate that she could not have found her way home in 1962 as readily as she had found her way to the Department of Justice. But no such significance was given to this diagnostic detail. This "disorientation" was instead further evidence of her need to be kept off public streets.

Mrs. Lake did not believe she needed this. To the contrary, Mrs. Lake clearly testified that she wanted and felt competent to be free. It follows, then, that we—that is, society—needed to believe she needed this, or else we would acquiesce in her depiction of her needs. From this perspective (our need, not hers), we can approach the first question I posed earlier: In Mrs. Lake's case, what social function was served by our conceptual-spatial segregation of her? Why was it important for us that she be removed from "wandering" on the public streets?

Erving Goffman has brilliantly, I think, sketched our reasons. The heart of the matter, as Goffman sees it, is that Mrs. Lake's public presentation failed to give an "adequately normal account" of herself indicating to others that she could safely be disattended. Her failure to participate in the minute decorum of public places forced us in turn more rigorously to extrude her since her apparent public disorientation suggested that she would not keep herself from intruding on us. In this sense Mrs. Lake "wandered" unacceptably from the "normal" and "safely disattendable" presence demanded in public places.

Goffman (1971) has explored the vast social significance of minute infractions practiced by a person like Mrs. Lake. For him, Mrs. Lake's "wandering" is no small matter:

The most disruptive thing [he states] a well organism can do is to acquire a deadly contagious disease. The most disruptive thing a person can do is fail to keep a place that others feel can't be changed for him. Whatever the cause of the offender's psychological state—and clearly this may sometimes be organic—the social significance of the disease is that its carrier somehow hits upon the way that things can be made hot for us [p. 389].

"The social significance," Goffman concludes, "of the confusion he creates may be as profound and basic as social existence can get" (p. 389).

The urgent need provoked by Mrs. Lake's street presentation is suggested by this observation of Goffman's:

Individuals in modern society must jointly use fixed service equipment in public places and the fixed passageways leading to and from these places. A society such as ours could not afford the facilities found in public places unless this equipment were used there by streams of people. It is inevitable, then, that citizens must expose themselves both to physical settings over which they have little control and to the very close presence of others over whose selection they have little to say. The settings can bring disease and injury to those in them. And others present can introduce all the basic dangers inherent in co-presence: physical attack, sexual molestation, robbery, passage blocking, importunity, and insult [p. 329].

In his various writings, Goffman has explicated the incredibly rich and varied techniques of social etiquette that most people habitually deploy to provide the reassurance needed to keep calm in public places. Consider, for example, his depiction of the etiquette for eye-contact between strangers passing on a public street. Goffman (1963a) calls this "civil inattention":

[O]ne gives to another enough visual notice to demonstrate that one appreciates that the other is present (and that one admits openly to having seen him), while at the next moment withdrawing one's attention from him so as to express that he does not constitute a target of special curiosity or design.

In performing this courtesy the eyes of the looker may pass over the eyes of the other, but no "recognition" is typically allowed. Where the courtesy is performed between two persons passing on the street, civil inattention may take the special form of eyeing the other up to approximately eight feet, during which time sides of the street are apportioned by gesture, and then casting the eyes down as the other passes—a kind of dimming of lights. In any case, we have here what is perhaps the slightest of interpersonal rituals, yet one that constantly regulates the social intercourse of persons in our society.

By according civil inattention, the individual implies that he has no reason to suspect the intentions of the others present and no reason to fear the others, be hostile to them, or wish to avoid them. . . . This demonstrates that he has nothing to fear or avoid in being seen and being seen seeing, and that he is not ashamed of himself or of the place and company in which he finds himself. It will therefore be necessary for him to have a certain "directness" of eye expression. . . . [T]he individual's gaze ought not to be guarded or averted or absent or defensively dramatic, as if "something were going on." Indeed, the exhibition of such deflected eye expressions may be taken as a symptom of some kind of mental disturbance [pp. 84-85].

The individual's participation in these extraordinarily complex and commonplace public rituals finally, for Goffman, amounts to this: "situational improprieties . . . constitute evidence that the individual is not prepared to keep his place," and this "behavior . . . must create organizational havoc and havoc in the minds of [others]" (1971, pp. 355-356). This does not mean that everyone's public behavior must be rigidly identical, never surprising, never alarming. It does mean, however, that every person who behaves "oddly" in public places must be prepared to

provide an account . . . suggesting that although things look strange, they are really explicable, and, furthermore, are explicable in a way that will remove cause for concern. In thus accounting for their act, the alarming individuals need not show that they are acting properly or from ordinary concerns—only that they have a reason for their action and that once this reason is understood by the [alarmed] subject, he will see the act as one that need not disturb him further [Goffman, 1971, p. 262].

Social response to Mrs. Lake's "wandering," as Goffman sees it, parallels fears of—and our reasons for spatially and conceptually confining—others who more obviously threaten our communal peace. But still, a puzzle remains about Catherine Lake's banishment from the public streets. Our obvious and justified fear leads us to take power from convicted murderers and rapists and to depict their lessened power with various stigmas, such as "criminal." For Mrs. Lake, however, this matter seems vastly overblown. What clear relation does this odd old lady have to our collective needs to defend against the primitive terror that Goffman sees as underlying the minute rituals of public life? Mrs. Lake, at most, obviously threatened only her own well-being, and even that threat may have been greatly overstated.

Goffman's concept of "civil inattention" provides the missing piece of this puzzle. Mrs. Lake's public behavior did not so much inspire fear as intimate the possibility that something might be fearful. But fear itself is a painful emotion. We mean to avoid it wherever possible. Because our public streets are filled with fearful potential, our street behavior signalling "civil inattention" of one another permits each of us to ignore fearful possibilities. Any stranger's failure to observe these niceties might ultimately provoke us all into massive fear. But before we are pressed to this painful, psychologically costly feeling, we typically deploy other defensive maneuvers to restore the *status quo ante*. The basic defensive goal is to avoid fear, not to experience and act on it. The essential strategy toward that goal is to disattend fearful people (or the fearful potential in all people). This strategy was deployed in the skirmish with Mrs. Lake in this way: if she won't actively participate in our social decorum, and thus give us good reason to disattend her, we will take affirmative action to ignore her. We accomplish this by benevolence, by offering help to her regardless of whether she wants that help.

This defensive use of benevolence can be seen in the initial moments of the transaction between Mrs. Lake and the police officer. First, the officer was briefly alarmed at seeing something out of the ordinary within his official realm of responsibility. Second, probably even before he spoke to Mrs. Lake, the officer was much relieved to see that this was only a "harmless, senile old lady." Third, he felt kindly toward her, willing to help and protect her, in substantial part to consolidate his belief that she was no threat to him because she needed him to protect her. The officer has thus banished fear and his own impulses for aggressive response from his conscious reaction to Mrs. Lake. The strength of this wish, and the corresponding intensity of the officer's psychological commitment to his own beneficence, led him to ignore the possibility that Mrs. Lake neither wanted nor needed his help.

This, however, is just one possible explanation of the officer's motives for taking Mrs. Lake into custody. He may, for example, have been responding more to bureaucratic imperatives (to add an item of activity to his daily work sheet, for example) than to any interactional psychological imperative regarding Mrs. Lake. But beginning with his initial report of the encounter, the officer invoked the rhetoric of benevolence, and all of the formal participants who followed his action—psychiatrists, attorneys, and judges—justified Mrs. Lake's continued confinement in this same rhetoric. These other participants may also have been moved by varying bureaucratic imperatives. But their uniform invocation of this rhetoric and their assumption that it most acceptably explained and justified their actions indicates that they, and the public they addresss, are most comfortable "feeling benevolent" toward Mrs. Lake. Thus, my depiction of this officer's motives sees him as a social actor, the public's dramatic surrogate, expressing the predominant social view of the transaction irrespective of his individual commitment to that view.

There is another aspect to this transaction—another reason for the officer to fear Mrs. Lake and to fear that fear—which Goffman's perspective somewhat obscures. Mrs. Lake's disorientation suggests not only that she might directly threaten our communal security; it suggests also that she is helpless, lost, and utterly dependent on the caretaking of others. She is, in this sense, the paradigmatic infant and reminds us all that we too were once so dependent. Her invocation of that memory, to passersby and the officer on the street, is only fleeting, just as her invocation of assaultive potential would only be instantaneously perceived. But in both guises she reminds us of the possibility that we may be powerless to defend ourselves, and thus her presence drives us to proclaim the contrary: we have power and she does not. To ward off our own feelings of helplessness and dependency, we insist that she is the needy one, regardless of her view, or the actuality, of her own needs. The officer's stance in this transaction thus reflects that aspect of our collective benevolence that leads us to disattend the object's real need for our help and to assume that the object is not our equal but is more a needy child than a responsible adult.

There is, of course, another aspect to social benevolence: the recipient needs and can truly benefit from our help. It would be wrong and socially harmful to ignore this. Overlooking the possible reality of social benevolence would deny that we can ever provide for one another in need (Katz, 1969). To ignore Mrs. Lake, that is, when she appears disoriented and in trouble is to stifle social altruism and to deny that, in any measure, we are our brothers' keepers.

But once again the critical ambiguity presents itself: As Mrs. Lake's "keeper," are we more her helper or her jailer? This contradictory tension is necessarily posed by our benevolent stance toward her. By "helping" her, we have asserted that we are more powerful than she. The strength of our commitment to maintaining this power inequality comes from fear and, more precisely, from fear of fear. This commitment led us ultimately to confine Mrs. Lake though any pretense of thereby "helping" her had become a brutal parody. We subjected her to life imprisonment, tore her from the company of her husband and sister (however odd and inadequate they also appeared in testimony at her commitment proceedings), and confined her in conditions of extreme indignity—all in order to "protect" her.

Here another puzzling question appears. How could we keep the pretense of benevolence through this decade and allow Mrs. Lake to remain imprisoned under protest? The answer is, I think, deeply unsettling in its implications. We kept faith in our own good will, and kept Mrs. Lake confined, by insistently disattending her and by so firmly denying her equal status with us that she became a "nonperson." We refused to acknowledge that our benevolent feelings toward her contained dramatically contradictory elements, and as we inflicted more suffering on her while professing our good intentions, it became increasingly painful for us to acknowledge how shamefully we had behaved. We thus looked away from her in part to avoid our guilt at what we had done to her. But more than this, if we looked with any objectivity at the true import of her lengthy confinement, one uncomfortable thought must emerge: though we professed to help her, we were in fact imprisoning her as if she were a criminal. We locked her away initially, however, in order to avoid fearing her. It would defeat that purpose to acknowledge fear at the end.

From the perspective of Mrs. Lake's case, several possibilities for differentiating useful from harmful benevolence regarding the mentally disabled can now be explored. Some reformers have suggested that the basic problem lies in the very existence of civil commitment statutes that permit us to take "beneficent custody" of Mrs. Lake, notwithstanding her protestation (see, for example, Szasz, 1963, 1970). This position correctly sees the dark aspects of benevolence, and the difficulties of demarking those aspects from truer altruism. But this attitude denies both the possibility of such altruism and the psychological reality that Mrs. Lake might need—and might ultimately welcome—our assistance, and yet be so disoriented that she cannot clearly hear our offer of help.

As Katz (1969) points out:

Most persons whom society involuntarily commits are consciously and unconsciously so convinced that no one cares, indeed they look at offers of help with such suspicion, that a sustained period of exposure to an unaccustomed world of trust, respect, and care is required in order to attempt to modify these beliefs. . . . Behind the conscious refusal of treatment, other unconscious wishes also operate—to be protected, to be cared for, to be sustained, to be helped. What weight should be given to these wishes when they are almost drowned out by words which damn their own self and the world [p. 771]?

To deny the possibility of altruism and to turn away from her would cruelly ignore her needs, and our needs to believe we are members of a caretaking community.

If the possibility of civil commitment should not be ruled out, can our manner of providing benevolence, the conditions of commitment, be usefully reformed? Two distinct aspects of our techniques for responding to the mentally disabled should be separately considered here: spatial segregation and conceptual segregation. The premise of those reformers who urge abolition of the large-scale, geographically remote institutions is that eroding spatial segregation of the mentally disabled will in itself tame the excesses of our benevolent pretensions. But I am skeptical of this.

I have noted that the underlying intention of the Court of Appeals, in its heralded decision in Mrs. Lake's case, was to press toward "deinstitutionalization" and community placement by requiring the state to provide the "least restrictive alternative available" for civilly committed persons. But we ignored the possibility, for Mrs. Lake, that community placement would be "restrictive enough" to help her just as insistently as we ignored the possibility that she didn't need our help. Judge Wright, in a concurring opinion to the Court of Appeals decision, stated that "while the [state] may be able to make some provision for Mrs. Lake's safety . . . , the permissible alternatives, on the record before us, do not include full-time involuntary commitment."[8] The majority opinion, by Judge Bazelon, suggested that Mrs. Lake might be "sufficiently protected if she were required to carry an identification card on her person so that the police or others could take her home if she should wander. . . .[9] The

[8] 364 F.2d 662 (D.C. Cir. 1966).
[9] Id., at 661.

trial court, on remand, nevertheless found that full-time institutional confinement was the "least restrictive alternative" possible to stop Mrs. Lake's "wandering."[10]

Mrs. Lake's experience suggests the aptness of David Rothman's prediction for the future course of the "deinstitutionalization" movement for the mentally disabled: the old large-scale institutions are closed; small group homes are used instead for the mentally disabled and are scattered throughout the community; soon arguments "for economies of scale and more efficient service provision" lead these community group homes to be clustered together under one roof—and we are back where we started (Rothman, 1973).

The likelihood that these efforts will walk us round in circles comes from the continued relevance of the functions and seductions of the conceptual segregation implicit in our old patterns of dealing with the mentally disabled and the underlying functions of that segregation—that is, disguise and denial of our intense fear of "non-normality" through "benevolently motivated" actions toward the feared group. Our conceptualization regarding the mentally disabled as a group (that "they" are less competent than "us," less than fully human) first of all permits us to disattend them, as noted. But this conceptualization gathers force on its own and, with disturbing ease, removes psychological restraints to authorize infliction of terrifying cruelty on these "nonpersons," these dehumanized beings. This has been the psychology that has led to infliction of nightmarish brutality on the inmates of our institutions for the mentally ill and retarded.[11] The seductive dangers of this conceptual segregation as such can be more fully illuminated by exploring in some detail a further aspect of the benevolent face we turn toward the mentally disabled: the invocation of medical science.

Traditionally the vocabulary and personnel of the medical sciences has been employed for taking custody of the mentally disabled. On its face, this scientific ethos appears to offer the curative prospects that might keep faith with our promise of benevolence. But in fact this medical/psychiatric model has frequently been invoked where there is patently no hope of cure or, indeed, any plausible application of general medical or psychiatric methodology toward cure.

Mrs. Lake, for example, immediately attracted a medical/psychiatric label: "chronic brain syndrome associated with arteriosclerosis, with psychotic reaction." But the treatment regime prescribed by the doctors had no medical or psychiatric content. The psychiatrist at St. Elizabeth's assigned to treat Mrs.

---

[10] 267 F. Supp. 155, 158 (D.D.C. 1967).

[11] Reviewing conditions at the Alabama state institution for the retarded, the District Court found as follows: "Primitive conditions . . . atmosphere of futility and despair which envelops both staff and residents . . . legislative neglect has been catastrophic; atrocities occur daily. . . . The gravity and immediacy of the situation cannot be overemphasized" (*Wyatt v. Stickney*, 344 F. Supp. 387, 393 [M.D. Ala. 1972]). The New York state institution was similarly "depicted as a place of horror" in extensive litigative testimony (see *The New York Times, supra* n. 3).

Lake testified that "[t] he only danger is her exposure in wandering away" and that, accordingly, "if she has . . . supervision, she would be no problem" (Katz, Goldstein, & Dershowitz, 1967, p. 553). This is a stark depiction of the reality underlying typical invocations of civil commitment statutes: the vocabulary is medical/psychiatric; the treatment provided is custody for its own sake (see, generally, Livermore, Malmquist, & Meehl, 1968). The doctors thus in one sense were simply restating the dual aspects of the policeman's initial encounter with Mrs. Lake: benevolent protestations that permit her comfortably to be removed from the public streets. But the doctors do more than restate this purpose; they reinforce it, thereby giving the benevolent protestations an added patina of plausibility.

There might seem to be a further puzzle here: Why have the doctors been so willing to collaborate in this double-faced dealing? One legal reformist answer has been, in effect, that the doctors involved in civil commitment proceedings were poorly trained and that the state institutions were poorly funded. The premise of this position (better personnel and more money would give reality to the benevolent promises) has been apparently accepted by many advocates of a court-enforced "right to treatment" for residents of state institutions for the mentally ill and retarded (see, for example, Bazelon, 1969). The obstacles toward that happy goal are typically portrayed as essentially practical and political: Where will the competent doctors be found? How can the legislatures be forced and cajoled toward an adequate funding level? But I think the problems in matching the promise and performance of benevolence are more fundamentally insoluble than these premises admit.

The reformers overlook the ease with which the scientific ethos legitimates precisely the double-dealing that is the target for reform. The reasons for this legitimation indicate the general harmfulness of conceptual segregation of the mentally disabled as special objects of benevolence. The ethos of medical science expresses, in this society, the paradigm of our collective commitment to caretaking benevolence. There are instructive tensions in that ethos, not only for the mentally disabled but for all objects of medical care. Medical science can offer true help to suffering patients. But the medical ethos can equally express our impulses to banish disturbing people from our ken by "eliminating" them.

The psychological linkage can be illustrated in simplest form by considering the mental processes of a surgeon with his knife poised over the supine body restrained before him on the operating table. To some degree, however fleetingly and denied, the surgeon must "dehumanize" that person—that is, see him as a laboratory organism, a mechanical assemblage of working parts—in order comfortably to plunge the knife. Surgery is not the only branch of medicine, or the human sciences in general, that requires some degree of conceptual dehumanization of its beneficiaries. This is an underlying characteristic of the scientific ethos generally (see, for example, Callahan, 1973).

There is nothing inherently wrong with this thought modality. To the contrary, great social benefits have come from scientists' capacity to think systematically about human beings as organisms functioning on physical principles similar to other animals. Further, it is essential that the surgeon poised with his knife be able momentarily to "dehumanize" his patient—to see him as a laboratory animal or a machine—so that he can overlook the patient's abject fear and the intense pain caused by the process of surgery itself. The surgeon is further assisted by his educated belief that the procedure will benefit the patient in the long run and that the patient wants his momentary fears and pain to be disregarded. But if benevolence may be practiced only when the practitioner suppresses his own instinctual sympathy with the immediate suffering of a fellow human being before him, the psychological preconditions for great and destructive confusions are created. The destructive implications of these confusions are chillingly demonstrated by some recent data from the social sciences that I want to consider here at length.

Stanley Milgram (1974), a psychologist at Yale University, designed an ingenious set of experiments to test obedience to authority that commands infliction of considerable pain on others. Milgram's subjects were drawn from a cross-section of the New Haven and Bridgeport, Connecticut, populations by newspaper advertisements and telephone solicitation. They were asked to participate in experiments to test the effect of punishment on learning. Upon arriving at the laboratory, the subjects were met by a gray-coated technician and another apparent subject (who was in fact a trained actor). By rigged drawing of lots, the subjects were chosen as "teachers" and the actor chosen as "learner." The "learner" was then strapped in a chair, and the "teacher" was instructed by the experimenter to give memory tests to the learner and to administer electric shocks of increasing severity for each wrong answer. The teacher-subject administered the shocks by depressing different levers on an instrument panel before him; the levers had thirty gradations designated from 15 to 450 volts, and these voltage designations were grouped together under labels ranging from "slight shock" at 15 volts, "extreme intensity shock" at 255 volts, "danger: severe shock" at 375 volts, and only an artful "XXX" at 435 volts.

During the entire sequence, the "learner" was in fact not shocked at all, though the teacher-subject's belief that he was actually administering very painful shocks was reinforced in a number of ways, including the administration to the subject himself of a jarring 75 volt shock from this apparatus at the beginning of the experiment. The learner-victim responded to the subject's acts in depressing the shock levers in this way:

[T]he victim indicated no discomfort until the 75-volt shock was administered, at which time there was a little grunt. . . . [A]t 120 volts the victim shouted to the experimenter that the shocks were becoming painful. Painful groans were heard on administration of the 135-volt shock, and at the 150 volts the victim cried out, "Experimenter, get me out of here! I won't be in the experiment any more! I refuse to go on!" Cries of this type continue with generally rising intensity, so that at 180 volts the victim cried out, "I can't stand the pain," and by 270 volts his response to the shock was definitely an agonized scream. Throughout, from 150 volts on, he insisted that he be let out of the experiment. At 300 volts the victim shouted in desperation that he would no longer provide answers to the memory test [Milgram, 1974, p. 23].

Whenever the teacher-subject turned questioningly to the laboratory technician during this sequence, the experimenter-technician would direct him to continue the memory test and the escalating electric shocks. The experimenter's direction followed this regular sequence, as described by Milgram:

Prod 1: "Please continue," or, "Please go on."
Prod 2: "The experiment requires that you continue."
Prod 3: "It is absolutely essential that you continue."
Prod 4: "You have no other choice, you *must* go on" [p. 21].

If the teacher-subject asked whether the learner-victim was being harmed by the shocks, the experimenter-technician would respond, "Although the shocks may be painful, there is no permanent tissue damage, so please go on."

The purpose of the experiment was to see whether and when the teacher-subject would refuse to continue administering the shocks. The results were profoundly disturbing. In one variation, with the victim in an adjoining room but clearly audible, twenty-five of forty teacher-subjects (62.5%) administered the highest shock levels possible, at the XXX designations, in obedience to the experimenter's direction. With the victim in the same room, sixteen of forty (40%) escalated the shocks to the highest limits. With the subject and victim side by side, and the subject required to press the victim's hand onto a metal plate to administer the shock, twelve of forty (30%) continued through the XXX level (see Milgram, 1974, Table 2, pp. 34-35). In another set of variations, the victim mentioned as he was being strapped into the chair that he had "a slight heart condition." When the shock level reached 150 volts, the victim stated that his heart was "starting to bother" him, and he repeated this complaint several times with, finally, an "intense and prolonged agonized scream" at 330 volts. This variation did not change the experimental results at all (pp. 55-57). Milgram concluded, "Probably there is nothing the victim can say that will uniformly generate disobedience; for the teacher's actions are not controlled by him" (p. 57).

It is hard to understand fully what did control the teacher-subjects' actions. In an obvious sense, of course, the experimenter was in control. But the crucial question is why the teacher-subjects were willing to yield control of their actions to the experimenter and to engage in recklessly cruel conduct toward another human being. The mystique of science, which cloaked the experimenter, was likely an important determinant here. In other variations of this experiment, the subject was left alone in the laboratory though the experimenter first told him "he was free to select any shock level on any of the trials." In this variation, twenty-eight of forty "went no higher than the [learner-victim's] first indication of discomfort, and thirty-eight did not go beyond the point where the learner vehemently protested [150 volts]" (p. 72). In yet another variation, the gray-coated technician was called away from the laboratory (on a ruse) and authorized the experiment to be conducted by an "ordinary man" (another actor who appeared to arrive at the laboratory at the same time as the teacher-subject). In this variation, only four subjects of twenty (20%) obeyed the "ordinary man's" directives to administer the maximum possible shocks (Milgram, 1974, Table 4, p. 94).

These experiments also offer some suggestive data about the relative importance of spatial and conceptual segregation. It is notable that increasing the physical distance between teacher and victim increased the teacher's willingness to ignore the victim's expressed pain. Thus sixty-two percent of the teachers administered the XXX shock levels with the victim clearly audible but in an adjoining room, while thirty percent of the teachers went to this limit when required to take the victim's hand and press it onto a metal plate to administer the shock. Although eroding spatial segregation did diminish the infliction of cruelty, it is nonetheless significant that so many people were willing to pursue the goals of science single-mindedly and oblivious to the expressed pain of a human being touching them.

The Milgram experiments suggest a central role to the self-justifying norms of science in another, ironic way. The conduct of the experiments themselves has been sharply attacked on the ground that Milgram deceived his subjects in multiple ways and led them unwittingly into an experience that for the obedient subjects brought them "to live with the realization that they were willing to yield to destructive authority to the point of inflicting extreme pain on a fellow human being" (Kelman, 1967, p. 5). Milgram himself discounted this criticism by describing postexperimental measures to avoid adverse impact on the subjects and by stating that follow-up studies of his subjects revealed no psychological harm. He suggested, at least by implication, that the absence of adverse impact on the subjects is itself an intriguing finding of the experiment (Milgram, 1974, pp. 193-202). Milgram may be correct in these observations, but it is nonetheless clear that he took extraordinary risks with the future emotional well-being of his subjects in these experiments. His vivid depictions of their stress in administering the shocks is itself testimony to this (pp. 44-54, 73-88). It is further clear that if Milgram had simply lured people into these practices for his own personal amusement, we would not hesitate to condemn his action as grotesque sadism. The question is complex, but Milgram finds professional and personal refuge through the ethos of science. The lesson is tautly drawn: ethos can make victimizers and victims of any of us.

How then, for the mentally disabled, can we accomplish the goal I initially posited—to differentiate between useful and harmful beneficence? We must first of all acknowledge that our benevolence always implies inequality of power between donor and recipient. We must then admit that we fear the mentally disabled, even an apparently "harmless old lady" such as Catherine Lake. Because we need to comfort ourselves that we are more powerful than those we fear, our "benevolent feelings" toward the mentally disabled are particularly suspect. But we must take care not to turn away from our "benevolent" feelings any more than we disregard our fear. The central, ultimate goal is to keep firmly in sight that these people (who inspire both fear and benevolence) are people like "us"; they have equal claim to full human status and are fully as "competent," notwithstanding their different characteristics. In this sense, our goal is to end permanent conceptual segregation of the mentally disabled, because that segregation necessarily implies permanent inequality of power and competence and that implication can too readily gather destructive momentum.

We can implement this prescription for Mrs. Lake, even if we offer her help by ignoring her protestations that she does not want our help. That initial transaction does conceptually segregate her as less competent than her caretakers. But, as noted earlier, she and we may well benefit from this benevolence. Nonetheless we must then act on our suspicion of our motives. We must guard against the likelihood that our solicitous coercion will move toward brutal parody by rigorously demarcating our contradictory roles of "helper" and "jailer" as Mrs. Lake's keepers. For this purpose the simple passage of time seems the most apt measure. We are converted from Mrs. Lake's helper to her jailer when we have offered our help most graphically to her—that is, by placing her for some brief time where we mean to help her—and, for whatever reasons, Mrs. Lake continues to refuse our help. When that time has come, we should permit her to return to the streets. We may feel she will suffer grievously there, and we may see some ambivalence on her part about this as well. But she says she wants to go. The only clear, concretely demonstrable harm from that decision will fall on Mrs. Lake herself. Our insistence that Mrs. Lake can define "harm" and "help" for herself is a measure of our tolerance of her autonomy and of helpless and aggressive feelings within ourselves (see Katz, 1969, pp. 772-775).[12]

Stigma and Benevolence toward Blacks

The preceding discussion has application beyond those who are considered mentally disabled. There are important parallels between our social response to

---

[12]We are properly reluctant to permit those who have concretely harmed others—that is, convicted criminal offenders—to define dispositions for themselves. But when we have joined beneficient protestations to our forthright wishes to protect ourselves from the harm inflicted by these persons, destructive confusions have proliferated. I have addressed this subject at some length in "Of Mad Dogs and Scientists: The Perils of the 'Criminal-Insane'" (Burt, 1974a), where I suggested that the only way to demark our decent from our darker motives is to abolish special rigid categorizations for the "mentally disabled" among those who are "criminals." The underlying theme is the same there as here: we must learn to see a wide range of variability among all "criminals" to disenthrall ourselves from the supposed special fearfulness of the "criminal-insane."

such persons and to blacks, both in our slave past and in current reformist efforts. Both groups inspire intense fear among the majority (the "normal"/the "oppressor") population. For slaves, the incipient question was always revolt. As Genovese (1974) points out:

The panic of the slaveholders at the slightest hint of slave insurrection revealed what lay beneath their endless self-congratulations over the supposed docility, contentment, and loyalty of their slave [p. 595].

In regard to the mentally ill and retarded, the analogous fear has been of unpredictable and senseless assault. This fear was reflected in the empirically unsupportable proposition asserted by the Nebraska Supreme Court in upholding the state compulsory sterilization law: "It is an established fact that mental deficiency accelerates sexual impulses and any tendencies toward crime to a harmful degree."[13]

And yet, notwithstanding this fear—or because of its very intensity—our institutionalized social response to slaves and the mentally abnormal has been colored over by self-conscious beneficence. Though fear has lurked just off stage, the social script has demanded that on stage we smile benignly and offer care and sustenance toward these poor unfortunates who, after all, know no better. Consider, for example, the proudly proclaimed paternalism of the slave plantations (see Genovese, 1974, pp. 3-112) or the self-righteous justification of the insanity defense in the criminal law that it would be wrong to "blame" the offender no matter how terrifying the offense.[14]

But this beneficent face toward slaves and the mentally ill and retarded has always masked barely acknowledged hypocrisy. Terrible degradations have been practiced on both groups, and there is reason to think that these degradations have been less restrained, been made more terrible, precisely because we have hidden our fear with benign smiles. For slaves, the ferocious white response to open revolt (or to minute breaches of decorum toward whites) has been intensified by accusations of betrayal, of "ingratitude," as if deference were specially owed because of white paternalism (see Genovese, 1974, pp. 97-112). For the mentally ill and retarded, the fate of those found not guilty for insanity of a criminal offense exemplifies the same thing—that worse indignities, longer confinements, more lasting stigmatization, are inflicted on those "excused from blame" on the grounds of insanity than for those who are straightforwardly convicted for the criminal offense (Burt, 1974a, pp. 261-262, 280-289).

This same intertwining of degradation and protestations of benevolence can be seen in our current response to blacks and the mentally disabled. Particularly during this century, and outside the South, residential segregation for blacks and remote institutionalization for the mentally ill and retarded have effectively kept

---

[13] *In re Cavitt*, 182 Neb. 712, 716, 157 N.W. 2d 171, 177 (1968), *appeal dismissed*, 396 U.S. 996 (1970).

[14] See *Durham v. United States*, 214 F.2d 862, 876 (D.C. Cir. 1954), Royal Commission on Capital Punishment, 1949-53 Report, CMD. No. 8932 at 98 (1953).

both groups from general social visibility (for example, see Harrington, 1962, pp. 1-18). But first the blacks and then the mentally disabled have come dramatically into view again especially during the past generation. Since World War II, blacks have been "rediscovered" as a victimized, brutalized group in this society (see Myrdal, 1944), and the post-Civil War abolitionist amendments to the Constitution have been given refurbished meaning. In legal parlance, segregation by race came to be characterized a constitutionally "suspect" classification (see Developments in the law, 1969). During the past decade, we have seen a similar discovery of the mentally disabled as a victimized group, and a similar constitutional theory has been advanced, by some at least, on their behalf (see Mental illness . . . , 1974; Burt, 1975).

The contemporary parallels do not end here. More recently, legal reform strategies pursued for both groups have taken the same twist. Compensatory programs, giving special benefits to blacks as such, have direct analogies in the constitutionally based claims of the mentally ill for a "right to treatment" and of the mentally retarded for a "right to education." Implementation of these claimed constitutional rights for the mentally disabled requires allocation of substantial financial resources for programs clearly limited to this group as such. For black compensatory programs, the tension between the legal stance that race is a "suspect categorization" and claims for race-limited programs is resolved, purportedly, by demonstrating that the latter programs are "beneficent" uses of racial criteria (see, generally, Gunther & Dowling, 1970). For the mentally disabled, this theoretical tension has not been so sharply etched; the tradition of "benevolence" toward the mentally disabled has roots so deep in public rhetoric that court invocation of that theme has seemed self-evidently natural.[15]

As with the mentally disabled, I would not argue that there can be no social reality to the good intentions or the good effects of black compensatory programs. But as with the mentally disabled, I believe it necessary—and quite difficult—to differentiate useful from harmful benevolence motivating implementation of these programs. The ultimate goal for blacks is clear: race as such should no longer connote differences in power or competence. But when the means toward realizing this goal depend on the "benevolence" of whites, implications of inequality stubbornly remain.

Judicial and legislative vindications, during the past generation, of black claims for equality did not initially seem caught in this contradictory web. The principles of justice, the ethic of entitlement, that could be invoked to support black claims muted, if not altogether contradicted, any sense that whites were now charitably bestowing gifts on blacks whom they had previously wronged. But today, as objectively measured and subjectively felt inequalities persist and reformers press for strategies that seem increasingly costly, the self-evident

---

[15] Compare *Rouse v. Cameron*, 373 F.2d 451, 452-53 (D.C. Cir. 1967): "The purpose of involuntary hospitalization is treatment, not punishment. . . . Commitment . . . is permissible because of its humane therapeutic goals."

entitlement of blacks for many claims to compensatory programs appears more attenuated. I am not suggesting that these claims are unjust, but rather that they appear more obviously to rest on appeals to white benevolence than to self-evidently clear claims of black entitlement to "equal justice."

Discussing recent Supreme Court decisions' reliance on past racial discrimination as the premise for ordering far-reaching compensatory programs, Owen Fiss (1974) has noted that attenuated force of the ethical tenet now invoked. He states:

[F]our considerations prompt me to question whether the Court is giving too big a task to the concept of past discrimination. First, the ethical void still exists when the cost of the remedy is placed on those who were neither perpetrators nor beneficiaries of the past wrongful conduct. It may, for example, be unfair to hold an employer accountable for past discrimination in a realm totally divorced from his control, such as a public school system. Second, under the past discrimination analysis, the identity between the victim of the discrimination and the beneficiary of judicial action tends to disintegrate; to the extent that it does, the ethical basis of the beneficiary's claim loses force. Third, the causal connection between past discrimination and present results may be significantly more tenuous than what the courts declare it to be. There is a heavy reliance on presumptions—presumptions that formally, but not practically, permit a rebuttal. For example, the dual school system might have played a role in causing the segregated residential pattern of a community or the poor performance of Blacks on voter qualification or employment tests; but the evidence compels none of these connections. Difficult as it is for the alleged victims to prove any of these connections, it is equally difficult for the alleged discriminators to prove the opposite. The concept of past discrimination has led us to rely on an odd species of empirical propositions—ones that cannot be proved or disproved. Fourth, courts do not limit the remedy in these cases to eliminating the portion of the undesired result that they can in all fairness attribute to past discrimination. A judicial conclusion that there is some causal connection between the past discrimination and a portion of the undesired result is used as a triggering mechanism—the predicate for an order elminating the entire undesired result.

Although these problems with the past discrimination concept should not preclude its use altogether, they do indicate that reliance on the concept should be limited and hesitant [p. 770].

One contemporary example particularly illustrates this conceptual shift. Special admission programs for blacks to universities and professional schools, with avowedly lower entrance criteria than for whites, have been implemented by many institutions, though no claim has been proven that these institutions practiced past racial discrimination[16] or that current entrance criteria were clearly unjust on any basis.[17] These programs are not wholly devoid of appeals

---

[16] See *DeFunis v. Odegaard*, 94 S.Ct. 1704 (1974).

[17] There is a dearth of validated data on whether standard law school admissions criteria disfavor blacks, but the meager evidence available suggests that currently used predictors of law school performance are at least as accurate for blacks as for whites, and perhaps more so. See the Educational Testing Service report by Schrader & Pitcher, *Predicting law school grades for Black American law students*, published in 1973.

to principles of entitlement: racial discriminations in education, employment, and other aspects of broader social organization have all markedly contributed to the underrepresentation of blacks in universities and in the professions. But these are claims of relatively global injustice. The particular institutions that choose to implement these special programs can plausibley assert that they are acting more from social altruism than from any clear sense of personal or institutional wrongdoing.

As with the discussion of benevolence toward the mentally disabled, to identify black special admissions programs as resting on social altruism does not condemn them or reveal them as necessarily fraudulent. Many powerful arguments can be advanced to support the social wisdom, and to predict the ultimately beneficial results, of these programs (see, for example, Bittker, 1962; Graglia, 1970; Karst & Horowitz, 1974; O'Neil, 1971; Sandalow, 1975). If more than a generation after the decision in *Brown v. Board of Education,*[18] for example, all law schools of national stature remained white preserves, that self-evidently appears socially baneful if not necessarily "unjust."

But nonetheless there are ominous implications in these programs. If their initial impetus comes from white benevolence, this in itself implies that the donor is more powerful, more competent, than the recipient. The specific format of the gift dramatically reinforces that implication. These programs proclaim on their face that blacks are less than the equal of whites in the same educational institution. Elaborate arguments have been offered to assert that these credentials differences are wholly illusory.[19] But if they are illusory, their continued application to white admissions raises nagging questions. This avowed double standard necessarily imposes a stigmatizing conceptual separation between blacks and whites, even though that standard is followed in the service of ending spatial segregation.

The central problem posed by black special admissions programs for higher education is that these institutions proudly purport to be based on the principle of rewarding meritorious performance. Although there may be disagreements about the accuracy of various performance measures, it is clear particularly for postgraduate and professional education that a wide range of variability in performance is not and should not be tolerated. The nub of the resentment stimulated for both blacks and whites by the special admissions programs is the suspicion that the schools and professions have embarked implicitly and deceptively toward creating a two-track system. In this inconsistency, and in the breach of the performance merit principle graphically avowed by the special admissions program itself, are the seeds of the degrading underside of benevolence for stigmatized groups. "We" (those who are judged by performance merit)

[18] 347 U.S. 483 (1954).
[19] Compare Justice Douglas' speculations in his dissent in *DeFunis v. Odegaard* (94 Sup. Ct. at 1715): "Insofar as LSAT tests reflect the dimensions and orientation of the Organization Man they do a disservice to minorities. I personally know that admissions tests were once used to eliminate Jews. How many other minorities they aim at I do not know."

will resent "them" (who are judged by race) for their threat to our definition of social worth and "normality." "They" in turn will resent "us" for purporting to offer equality but persistently and proudly invoking the meritocratic principle while visibly judging blacks by a different and implicitly degrading criteria.

Thus, although the two groups may no longer be spatially segregated, both groups are likely to be driven toward infliction of increasingly angry stigmata of conceptual segregation. Ultimately we may find ourselves close to our starting point. Black slavery, after all, was not characterized by spatial segregation. The two races mixed together every day. But they remained in separate worlds, each resenting, fearing, and smiling benignly toward the other. The premise of the existing black compensatory programs is that spatial integration is itself good, but the contemporary invocation of that premise excessively discounts the stigmatizing risks of accomplishing integration by perpetuating conceptual segregation of the races.

The initial hope for the black special admissions programs was that they were temporary expedients intended to erode spatial segregation of the races while many social forces worked toward equality judged by traditional merit standards. But if this hope is not realized, and these programs seek acceptance as permanent social fixtures, we must face the question identified earlier regarding reform strategies for mental disabilities: whether spatial or conceptual segregation is ultimately more unequal, more stigmatizing, and more destructively dehumanizing. That earlier discussion does not yield a simple answer to the problem here. It does offer a warning, however, that ending spatial segregation alone does not reliably diminish stigma, but that the continuation of conceptual segregation, even for the most apparently benevolent motives, feeds the psychological dynamic that initially led to imposition of stigmatizing inequalities.

I am not suggesting that black special admissions programs were initially unwise, or that the altruistic arguments advanced for them were fraudulent. I am suggesting that the lessons drawn from the discussion of reform efforts for mental disabilities point toward great caution and rigorous insistence that the impulses to degrade and dehumanize the objects of our bounty be acknowledged and restricted so that we might be appropriately and decently helpful to those we mean to help. Thus I would ask the same question, ultimately, for a black special admissions program that I asked for Mrs. Lake's benevolent confinement: For whose clear, concretely demonstrable benefit is it continued, and when precisely will it end?

The particular relevance of this question to these programs is suggested by another parallel with the earlier discussion of the many contradictory motivations underlying benevolence toward the mentally disabled. Adoption of black special admission programs in universities has taken place against a backdrop of overt racial violence and fear, from urban ghetto riots to seizures of university campuses. Few university administrators or faculties would be willing to admit that fear led them to adopt these programs. The arguments on the substantive merits of such programs were sufficiently weighty that, from a rational perspective, fear need not have played any role. But it is an inescapable fact that there was good reason for fear of racial violence at the time most of the current programs were intensely debated and adopted. Our fervent belief that fear had no influence in our actions, that our motives were wholly rational and altruistic, should be viewed with the same skepticism that our motives and actions in confining Catherine Lake deserved. We did not feel fear toward her, but that was because we insisted that she was less competent and less powerful than we precisely in order to avoid feeling fear of her. For Mrs. Lake, the underlying truth about our benevolence toward her emerged only slowly—until, at last, few could mistake the true import of her life imprisonment at our hands. Must we wait an equivalent time before acknowledging the destructive contradictions inherent in these special programs for blacks?[20]

The importance of ultimately ending these racially restrictive programs is not diminished by the fact that many blacks (or most, or all) ask the continuance of these programs. The social and psychological dynamic that brings hurtful benevolence to those we fear can be deceptively seductive for all who are fearful—the "them" as well as the "us." For all stigmatized groups, it is painful to yield the protective definitions of "group differences" and to venture into ordinary intercourse without recurrent (and often implicitly belittling) reference to those differences. The bed "we" have made for "them," after all, has its comforts as well as its chafing restrictions.

It is not inconsistent to act on Mrs. Lake's expressed desire to be free and yet to refuse to act on blacks' expressed desires for racially limited compensatory programs. The premise for confining Mrs. Lake and granting special benefits to blacks as such is ultimately the same: "we" treat "them" as less competent than "we." Avoiding such treatment is helpful, I think, for "them." This argument is, of course, a plea for benevolence and that should raise suspicions. Beyond that, however, avoiding such treatment is important for "us." In these actions we are defining ourselves as well as others. Our collective decisions regarding which individual and group desires we choose to honor necessarily reflect our views of what kinds of relationships we mean to have among ourselves, what kinds of human beings we see one another to be.[21]

[20] One final ironic parallel should be noted. Consideration of the constitutional claims for black and for mentally disabled compensatory programs has reached the Supreme Court in virtually a dead heat. During the 1973 term, the Court considered, and then backed away from resolving, the constitutionality of special black admissions programs to public universities (*DeFunis v. Odegaard*, 94 Sup. Ct. 1704 [1974]). During the 1974 term, the Court had on its docket its first case addressing the constitutional right to treatment for the mentally ill (*O'Conner v. Donaldson, cert: granted*, 95 *Sup. Ct.* 171 [1974]).

[21] Erik Erikson (1969) has invoked the term "pseudo-speciation" to connote social divisions of "us" and "them," as I have used the notion in this discussion. Erikson concludes that "where an emphasis on the pseudo-species prevails—as in much of colonial history—the

No matter how fervently "compensatory benefits" are sought by their putative beneficiaries, the time must come in the foreseeable future, I believe, when we refuse to accept such racially limited "benefits" as a permanent social arrangement. My argument for this position is based on the same principles that would support the social policy of refusing to honor a person's expressed desire to sell his blood for commercial profit (see Titmuss, 1971, pp. 237-246) or a prisoner's desire to be the subject of experimental psychosurgery (see Burt, 1974b, pp. 31-34). In all of these instances, the request can plausibly be based on the requester's rational view of his best interests. But in these instances, all of us are implicated in a diminution of that person's intrinsic worth, from our perspective if not self-evidently and immediately from his. We are commonly our brothers' keepers in this sense: we define one another for another. In this, therefore, we should take special care to practice the Golden Rule.

Stigma in Benevolence as a Social Reform Idiom

The parallels drawn in this discussion between the themes of contemporary legal reforms regarding blacks and the mentally disabled can be extended to other groups as well. Many newly self-conscious groups have recently been pressing forward to claim the same victimized status and commitment for social redress: women, children, and homosexuals are prominent, current examples. Perceptions of group victimization (with the victims feeling stigmatized, oppressed, and claiming compensation and with the victimizers feeling guilty, fearful, and benevolently accommodating) seem to have become the stereotypic social reform idiom of our day.

Current claims for women's liberation point most directly to an underlying theme of this discussion: social "benevolence" can express both helpful caretaking and galling stigmatization. Opponents of the Equal Rights Amendment,[22] for example, have claimed that it would invalidate statutory exemptions for women from the military draft or from onerous labor conditions as if that were a self-evident argument against the amendment. Proponents have claimed that the purported benevolence underlying these exemptions is merely symptomatic of a general denigration of women and that these arguments demonstrate constricted "male chauvinist" vision (see, generally, Brown, Emerson, Falk, & Freedman, 1971; Equal rights for women, 1971).

development of every participant individual is endangered by various combinations of guilt and rage which prevent true development, even where knowledge and expertise abound" (p. 433). In another work, Erikson (1975) states, "All the members of a given communality—whether differentiated by age, sex, race, or class—are inseparable in their influence on one another: each, by the way he sees himself, will influence the way all others see themselves; and such a simple statement, when multiplied, becomes a whole network of potentially fateful interdependencies . . . " (p. 187).

[22] Proposed Amdt. XXVII, submitted to the states on March 22, 1972.

The proponents of women's liberation have clearly struck a resonant chord in the society. The widespread sense of discovery that the stigmata imposed on blacks were analogous to the contemporary status of women points to a larger commonality: today, quite strikingly, something has gone awry in our past almost somatic beliefs that traditional caretakers mean well toward those in their care.[23] But unless we can clearly identify what has gone wrong and identify the basic components of the complaint. it seems likely that we will see only increasingly angry and uncomprehending confrontation between the old donors and the old recipients.

We may anticipate the same psychological dynamic for response to the new militancy of women that was sketched earlier regarding the response to other stigmatized groups. For whatever reasons that eroded for the recipients the old assumptions about benevolence and gave stark appearance to the power implications of that social attitude, those reasons work similarly to unsettle the donors. The reciprocally upsetting character of this reexamination of social benevolence can be starkly seen in the response of professional educators to new assertions of "students' rights"—the most currently visible claim to establish childhood as an inherently stigmatizing status (see, generally, Tribe, in press, 1975). Consider the question posed in 1968 by the President of Columbia University as he stood in the shambles of his private office after the student demonstrators had returned it to him. President Kirk asked, "My God, how could human beings do a thing like this?" Erving Goffman translated that question into its more pervasive significance; he rejoined: "The great sociological question, of course, is not [Kirk's] , . . . but rather how is it that human beings do this sort of thing so rarely. How come persons in authority have been so overwhelmingly successful in conning those beneath them into keeping the hell out of their offices?" (1971, p. 288).

Seeing this question in the context of social attitudes toward women and children points to the psychological value most directly at stake in all of this discussion of stigmatized status. The basic question, I believe, for all of the expressions of benevolence between donor and recipient is whether that attitude, and the actions based on it, lead toward mutual respect for individual integrity. Whatever the psychological wellsprings of this attitude, or its precise definitional content, it was evident that the students who seized President Kirk's office did not believe that he or the educational profession generally were adequately respectful of them. In this transaction, the absence of a belief in "the good parent" is most starkly revealed—that is, the good parent who necessarily is

---

[23] Even judicial decisions reveal this attitude, in newly heightened skepticism toward educators (for example, *Tinker v. Des Moines School Dist.*, 393 U.S. 503 [1969]; *Goss v. Lopez*, 95 *Sup. Ct.* 729 [1975]); toward social welfare bureaucracies (for example, *In re Gault*, 387 U.S. 1 [1967]; *Goldberg v. Kelly*, 397 U.S. 254 [1970]); and toward the medical profession, as reflected in new rules requiring more extensive disclosure to patients of information traditionally withheld by "professional discretion" (for example, *Canterbury v. Spence*, 464 F.2d 722 D.C. Cir., *cert. denied*, 409 U.S. 1064 [1972]; Capron, 1974).

stronger than, and knows more than, his child, but who uses that superior strength and knowledge only in the service of leading his child toward mature strength and knowledge.

Invocation of the parenting imagery highlights the central conceptual issue that divides the donors and recipients—caretakers and cared-for, stigmatizers and stigmatized—as this discussion has proceeded. That issue is the definition of "equality." Put in simplest terms, the "good parent" is prepared for his child to differ significantly from him—that is, to grow into "his own person." That difference may mean that the child becomes stronger than the parent in the parent's own terms, or different from the parent in seeking values that the parent finds deeply unsettling (Erikson, 1968, pp. 91-141).

The "bad parent" fears such differences, or even the potential for them. This parent has great opportunity and temptation for abuse of his power. For the child confronted with this threatened parent, a critical psychological barrier is presented. In fighting for his right to be himself, the child is robbed of the experience of mutual trust and respect. He cannot pursue a sense of personal integrity in the context of a mutually reciprocal relationship in which differences can be tokens of pride. For this threatened and threatening child, differences are stark hallmarks of power and of fear. For this child, any difference connotes inequality, and any inequality will be ruthlessly, fearfully, and unfairly exploited. Peace—restored calm—thus appears possible only at the end of warfare in which power has become precisely equal and differences have been levelled.

This increasing intolerance for differences of any sort among people is the psychological underpinning of the increasing use of "stigma" as the idiom depicting contemporary social relations. Goffman's thinking is again instructive. He has shown that stigmatized status implies a "stigma theory" that the stigmatized person is "not quite human," and this theory carries an ideology "to explain his inferiority and account for the danger he represents" (Goffman, 1963b, p. 5). Further, the stigma theory provides a construct for social reality for both stigmatizer and stigmatized. It carries more than an explanation of inferiority; it implies a complementary status of superiority, which is the status of a "normal human being." Goffman (1963b) observes:

[I]t seems possible for an individual to fail to live up to what we effectively demand of him, and yet be relatively untouched by this failure; insulated by his alienation, protected by identity beliefs of his own, he feels that he is a full-fledged normal human being, and that we are the ones who are not quite human. He bears a stigma but does not seem to be impressed or repentant about doing so. . . . In America at present, however, separate systems of honor seem to be on the decline. The stigmatized individual tends to hold the same beliefs about identity that we do; this is a pivotal fact. His deepest feelings about what he is may be his sense of being a "normal person," a human being like anyone else, a person, therefore, who deserves a fair chance and a fair break. The notion of "normal human being" . . . seems to provide the basic imagery through which laymen currently conceive of themselves [p. 7].

The contemporary prominence of stigma as a social construct threatens to distort the perceptions of both those who seem themselves as stigmatizers and as stigmatized. The proposition that a person—child, woman, aged, black—is visibly "different" expresses no necessary value stance. But the stigmatizer says, "You are not normal, you are not full-fledged, you must be confined." Then the stigmatized is increasingly tempted to rejoin, "I am normal, I am full-fledged, I can be free—because I am really no different." Thus the goal of mutual respect for autonomy, for individual integrity, is lost; not because pursuit of that goal has been defeated, but because the goal does not appear anywhere on the standards for battle.

The grip that this levelled version of equality has on our contemporary imagination is suggested, I think, by current popular concern with the potential for genetic cloning. The technological capacity for human cloning—that is, assexual reproduction of exact genetic carbon copy humans—is by all accounts remotely futuristic, if at all attainable (see Eisenberg, in preparation, 1976). But the popular attention lavished on this possibility, with its mixtures of awe and terror, suggests that it offers an ultimate embodiment of "normality" as we are discussing it here. If, that is, everyone were exactly alike, all would share everyone's deepest assumptions and no one need fear anyone.

Concern with social normality has been notably heightened by recent experiences of racial and student riots. As Goffman (1971) observes, "The vulnerability of public life is what we are coming more and more to see, if only because we are becoming more aware of the areas and intricacies of mutual trust presupposed in public order" (p. 331).

Reflecting on the "new garrison architecture" of urban buildings generally, Goffman (1971) notes:

building maintenance managers of urban public housing have acquired an experience of our times that is deep, dumb, and terrifying. And citizens at large have learned the sociological lesson that their easefulness had been dependent all along on the self-restraint sustained by potential offenders who have never had many reasons for being respectful [pp. 289-290].

The pervasive mistrust of difference, of human variability, fundamentally underlies the idiom of stigmatization. This mistrust characterizes all of the stigmatizing attitudes and conduct discussed in this presentation, whether the differences are between the mentally "normal" and "abnormal," between black and white, or between men and women. It has further expression in the commitment to group solidarity among both the stigmatizers and stigmatized, the "balkanization" of our social lives and roles into various groups of "us" and "them" (see Footnote 21). This attitude is in fundamental conflict with possibilities for social realization of mutually satisfying relationships based on respect for individual diversity and autonomy.

But no easy prescription for social action follows from this analysis. The fact is that, for whatever complex constellations of reasons, we no longer can comfortably, somatically trust in the good will of traditional caretakers. Although in some ways we may regret our lost innocence, the corrosion worked by this skeptic acid will not vanish by an act of will. Even jeremiads from the pulpit of the Supreme Court will not restore this faith.[24] And in many ways this naive faith should not be regained. When we look objectively at what has been done, in the name of benevolence, to blacks, to the mentally disabled (such as Mrs. Lake), or to children (such as those processed by the juvenile courts), it is clear that our trust in traditional caretakers was quite excessive. Regaining lost innocence would be no bargain for anyone. Jettisoning any possibility of faith in social benevolence toward "different people" would, however, be an equally costly transaction.

No specific agenda for action follows from this analysis. A specific attitude does follow, however, for evaluating reforms proposed purportedly to benefit persons viewed as previously stigmatized. When claims are advanced to eliminate all possible differences between the previous victims and their oppressors, we should search skeptically for the fantasy of levelled equality in this claim. That fantasy is the impulse, for example, behind claims for proportional representation of blacks and women in every aspect of social life no matter how tangentially related to clearly inappropriate and socially harmful inequalities.[25] That fantasy impels claims that the law should treat the judgmental capacities of latency or even early adolescent children as equal to adults. Behind such claims is the conviction that any visible difference connotes inequality of power and that any such inequality will be ruthlessly exploited.[26]

It is wrong and harmful to act on this conviction, but not necessarily because the conviction is wholly unrealistic. Rather, reforms premised on this basis will be illusory. These reforms will inevitably become part of the problem

[24] Justice Blackmun, for example, asserted that "the [welfare] caseworker is not a sleuth but rather, we trust, is a friend in need" to justify the Court's ruling that caseworkers need not obtain warrants for compelled visits to welfare recipients' homes (*Wyman v. James*, 400 U.S. 309, 323 [1971]. Similarly, Justice Powell dissented from the Court's ruling that some procedural formality must precede school suspensions, stating, "We have relied for generations upon the experience, good faith and dedication of those who staff our public schools . . . " and that "one role of the teacher in our society historically has been an honored and respected one, rooted in the experience of decades that has left for most of us warm memories of our teachers . . . " (*Goss v. Lopez*, 95 *Sup. Ct.* 729, 746 & n. 12 [1975]). For a consideration of the competing premises toward institutionalized benevolence revealed in recent Supreme Court decisions regarding state programs for children, see R. Burt, 1971.

[25] Consider, for example, the claims put forward in initial HEW guidelines (though ultimately rejected) to mandate equal expenditures on all athletic programs for males and females in all educational facilities receiving Federal funds.

[26] Consider, for example, the draft regulation promulgated by HEW to mandate the consent of children as young as seven for certain kinds of mental experimentation on them (National Academy of Sciences, 1975, pp. 112-13). Regarding the complexity of obtaining or relying on the consent of adolescents and younger children, see R. Burt, in press, 1976.

rather than its solution because this premise expresses the same destructive psychological dynamic that impelled the initial stigmatizing uses of inequality. Levelled equality may bring an apparent peace, but it is the calm of an exhausted battlefield, a momentary respite between an endless series of destructive engagements. The necessary precondition for interrupting this vicious psychology is to see it for what it is. From that clear vision, a more precise analysis can follow to assess the relative importance of differences among people.

The premise of this assessment would be that some, but not all, socially perceived differences between people are inappropriate and should be reformed. The hallmark of this impropriety is the connotation that the difference permanently diminishes the competence and thus the respect-worthiness of the affected individual in his or others' eyes. Unfortunately, this hallmark is not a self-applying litmus test. It can be read properly only if we can comfortably accept, deep in the wellsprings of our individual and collective identities, that all differences between people may imply inequality but that all inequalities need not connote exploitation. Without this fully felt belief, there is no real possibility for social trust or for mutual respect of one another's individual autonomies. Without this trust and respect, truly harmonious peace will always elude our grasp.

References

Bazelon, D. Implementing the right to treatment. *University of Chicago Law Review*, 1969, *36*, 742-754.

Bittker, B. The race relations. *Yale Law Journal*, 1962, *71*, 1387-1423.

Brown, B.A., Emerson, T.I., Falk, G., & Freedman, A.E. The Equal Rights Amendment: A constitutional basis for equal rights for women. *Yale Law Journal*, 1971, *80*, 871-985.

Burt, R. Forcing protection on children and their parents: The impact of *Wyman v. James. Michigan Law Review*, 1971, *69*, 1259-1310.

Burt, R. Of mad dogs and scientists: The perils of the criminal insane. *University of Pennsylvania Law Review*, 1974, *123*, 258-296. (a)

Burt, R. Why we should keep prisoners from the doctors: Reflections on the Detroit psychosurgery trial. *Hastings Center Report*, 1974, *5*, 25-34. (b)

Burt, R. Judicial action to aid the retarded. In N. Hobbs (Ed.), *Issues in the classification of children* (Vol. II). San Francisco: Jossey-Bass, 1975.

Burt, R. Developing constitutional rights in, of and for children. *Law and Contemporary Problems*, in press, 1976.

Callahan, D.J. *The tyranny of survival.* New York: Macmillan, 1973.

Capron, A.M. Informed consent in catastrophic disease research and treatment. *University of Pennsylvania Law Review*, 1974, *123*, 340-438.

Chambers, D.L. Alternatives to civil commitment of the mentally ill: Practical guides and constitutional imperatives. *Michigan Law Review*, 1972, *70*, 1108-1200.

Developments in the law—Equal protection. *Harvard Law Review*, 1969, *82*, 1065-1192.

Eisenberg, L. The psychopathology of clonal man. In A. Milunsky (Ed.), *Genetics and the law.* Book in preparation, 1976.

Equal rights for women: A symposium on the proposed constitutional amendment. *Harvard Civil Rights and Civil Liberties Law Review*, 1971, *6*, 215-287.

Erikson, E.H. The life cycle: Epigenesis of identity. In his *Identity, youth, and crisis.* New York: W.W. Norton, 1968.

Erikson, E.H. *Gandhi's truth on the origins of militant violence.* New York: W.W. Norton, 1969.

Erikson, E.H. *Life history and the historical moment.* New York: W.W. Norton, 1975.

Fiss, O.M. The fate of an idea whose time has come: Antidiscrimination law in the second decade after *Brown v. Board of Education. University of Chicago Law Review*, 1974, *41*, 742-773.

Genovese, E. *Roll, Jordon, roll: The world the slaves made.* New York: Pantheon Books, 1974.

Goffman, E. *Behavior in public places.* New York: Free Press, 1963. (a)

Goffman, E. *Stigma: Notes on the management of spoiled identity.* Englewood Cliffs, N.J.: Prentice-Hall, 1963. (b)

Goffman, E. *Relations in public: Microstudies of the public order.* New York: Basic Books, 1971.

Graglia, L. Special admission of the "culturally deprived" to law school. *University of Pennsylvania Law Review*, 1970, *119*, 351-363.

Gunther, G., & Dowling, N.T. *Cases and materials on constitutional law* (8th ed.). Mineola, N.Y.: Foundation Press, 1970.

Harrington, M. *The other America: Poverty in the United States.* New York: Macmillan, 1962.

Hobbs, N. *The futures of children: Categories, labels and their consequences.* San Francisco: Jossey-Bass, 1975. (a)

Hobbs, N. (Ed.). *Issues in the classification of children* (2 vols.). San Francisco: Jossey-Bass, 1975. (b)

Karst, K.L., & Horowitz, H.W. Affirmative action and equal protection. *Virginia Law Review*, 1974, *60*, 955-974.

Katz, J. The right to treatment—An enchanting legal fiction? *University of Chicago Law Review*, 1969, *36*, 755-783.

Katz, J., Goldstein, J., & Dershowitz, A. *Psychoanalysis, psychiatry and law.* New York: Free Press, 1967.

Kelman, H.C. Human use of human subjects: The problem of deception in social psychological experiments. *Psychological Bulletin*, 1967, *67*, 1-11.

Livermore, J.M., Malmquist, C.P., & Meehl, P.E. On the justifications for civil commitment. *University of Pennsylvania Law Review*, 1968, *117*, 75-96.

Mental illness: A suspect classification? *Yale Law Journal*, 1974, *83*, 1237-1270.

Milgram, S. *Obedience to authority: An experimental view.* New York: Harper & Row, 1974.

Myrdal, G. *An American dilemma: The Negro problem and modern democracy.* New York: Harper & Bros., 1944.

National Academy of Sciences. *Experiments and research with humans: Values in conflict.* Washington, D.C.: National Academy of Sciences, 1975.

O'Neil, R.M. Preferential admissions: Equalizing the access of minority groups to higher education. *Yale Law Journal*, 1971, *80*, 699-767.

Rothman, D.J. *The discovery of the asylum.* Boston: Little, Brown, 1971.

Rothman, D.J. Decarcerating prisoners and patients. *Civil Liberties Review*, 1973, *1*, 8-30.

Sandalow, T. Racial preferences in higher education: Political responsibility and the judicial role. *University of Chicago Law Review*, 1975, *42*, 653-703.

Szasz, T. *Law, liberty and psychiatry.* New York: Macmillan, 1963.

Szasz, T. *The manufacture of madness: A comparative study of the Inquisition and the mental health movement.* New York: Harper & Row, 1970.

Titmuss, R.M. *The gift relationship: From human blood to social policy.* New York: Pantheon Books, 1971.

Tribe, L. Childhood, suspect classifications, and conclusive presumptions: Three linked riddles. *Law and Contemporary Problems*, in press, 1975.

Part III:
Three Forms of Legal
Socialization

3

Legal Socialization

Robert Hogan

By human goodness is meant not fineness of physique, but a right condition of the psyche. That being so, it is evident that the statesman ought to have some inkling of psychology.

Aristotle, *The Nichomachean Ethics*

An Overview of Legal Socialization

As the foregoing quotation suggests, Aristotle thought there was a natural relationship between law and psychology. The two disciplines are most clearly joined in what psychologists call the socialization process. The Oxford English Dictionary defines *to socialize* as "to render social, to make fit for living in society." As used by social psychologists, socialization refers to those events that cause people to develop their particular (and usually favorable) orientations to the rules, values, and customs of their society. Legal socialization, then, is concerned with the development of people's attitudes and behaviors with regard to a particular set of social rules, the manifest law.

The subject is particularly important for attorneys, criminologists, and criminal justice workers because ultimately it should clarify those conditions under which law will have maximum effect in regulating social conduct. This information, in turn, will shed light on the possibility that the law can be used by planners and policymakers as an instrument of social reform.

Since the mid-1950s social psychologists have become increasingly interested in legal socialization. Their writing on this topic can be divided into two broad classes depending on whether it is concerned with content or process.

The content literature describes children's attitudes toward the law at various age levels. Adelson, Green, and O'Neil (1969), Gallatin and Adelson (1971), and Hess and Torney (1968) have made important contributions to this topic. The content literature is rather extensive and is difficult to summarize briefly, but Adelson et al.'s findings convey the flavor—that is, over time children are increasingly able to think in terms of legal principles and to see law in a relativistic, pragmatic, utilitarian way as an instrument for achieving social ends.

The process literature is based on one of two principal theories of the process of legal socialization. The first, also outlined by Hess and Torney (originally in the context of political socialization) assumes that four distinct sets of influences determine the manner in which children orient themselves to the legal system:

The *accumulation model* describes legal socialization as a process wherein, over time, children steadily acquire units of knowledge about the law; this model explains the contribution of the school system to legal socialization.

The *interpersonal transfer model* holds that a child transfers to authority figures (policemen, judges, and so forth) those attitudes and behavior developed *vis-à-vis* his parents; this model is used to explain the emotional loading of a child's relationship to authority.

The *ideintification model* describes legal socialization in terms of direct imitation by a child of adult attitudes toward some aspect of the law; this model would explain such phenomena as a child's attitude toward capital punishment.

The *cognitive-developmental model* maintains that a child's conception of the law is modified by his stage of intellectual development; this model is primarily useful for explaining how a child develops complex and abstract legal ideas such as distributive justice and natural rights.

The second process theory of legal socialization, described in detail by Tapp and Levine (1974) and Tapp and Kohlberg (1971), is probably the best known view of this subject. Here legal socialization is equated with the development of legal reasoning (defined in terms of how laws are justified); this reasoning is seen as evolving through three levels. At the preconventional level, legal reasoning is grounded in physical fear of authority and deference to power. At the second or law maintenance level, laws are justified in terms of their ability to regulate society. Level three is called post-conventional; it is a "law-creating, legislative perspective" wherein laws are justified in terms of certain abstract and personally defined conceptions of justice. This second process theory is primarily concerned with the development of conscious, publically stated attitudes toward the law; as such, it is a very "rational" model: " . . . the ultimate appeal of a cognitive-developmental explanation of legal thought is its emphasis on rationality and its refusal to accept the preeminence of irrationality" (Tapp & Levine, 1974, p. 11).

These two process theories of legal socialization were imported from other (related) fields: Hess and Torney, for example, are students of political socialization; and the Tapp and Kohlberg model comes from moral development. This importation is no accident. Process theories necessarily belong to the study of socialization broadly defined, and they take *legal* socialization as a special case. Only content studies of legal socialization contain subject matter specific to the field.

The process models discussed above are important contributions to the study of legal socialization, and they have stimulated some very useful research.

At the same time, however, they tend to foster a serious misconception—that is, a child's consciousness of rules is important in itself and the child's actual behavior with regard to these rules is irrelevant or at least not very important. Process research consists almost exclusively of inquiring about children's conscious attitudes toward the law, or of asking them to comment on hypothetical legal dilemmas and situations. But this research repeatedly demonstrates that even fairly young children distinguish between what they think they should do or say in a situation, and what they actually would do or say (cf. Zillman & Sears, 1971, p. 119). That children can do this points up the importance of Ichheiser's (1970) distinction between "views in principle" and "views in fact." As Ichheiser notes, views in principle are those we have about social and legal issues in general, and they have no serious implications for our actions; they reveal only how we think we would or should act in certain hypothetical situations. In contrast with our views in principle, our views in fact actually determine our actions. The problem is that most people don't know what their views in fact actually are, and when asked, they typically state their views in principle. The point to be made here is that to the degree that legal socialization research studies only children's theoretical legal judgments, it is sampling their views in principle and is studying the social psychological equivalent of phlogiston. Since one of the primary issues in legal socialization research concerns the psychological conditions that affect the usefulness of law as a regulator of social conduct, it would seem reasonable for investigators to focus on those attitudinal variables that are known (or are at least likely) to have behavioral consequences.

There is a second misconception fostered by process research. The rationalist view that motivates it (the view that people's conscious opinions and judgments are the cause (or at least a major determinant) of their actions) represents what Freud, Jung, and William James called the intellectualist fallacy (cf. McDougall, 1908, p. 323; Rawls, 1971, p. 470). The problem is that, just because we know a person can state a rule or legal principle, why should we assume that person will follow it? Similarly, this rationalism accounts for the fact that these models contain no reference to the moral passions; no mention of guilt, remorse, and painful moral introspection; no description of man's irrational sense of honor. They seem unconcerned with the kinds of conflicts between private belief and respect for public authority that can cause one to resign from high public office, or push one to the edge of madness and despair. We have instead tepid accounts of how children's theoretical legal attitudes change over time.

An Alternative Model of Legal Socialization

In a very influential analysis, Kelman (1961) identified three sets of reasons for following a socially defined rule—that is, three levels of legal socialization. The first set of reasons, labelled *compliance*, results in relatively superficial rule observance. Compliance occurs when one follows a rule with the hope of gaining a favorable reaction from certain others. Here rule observance is a function of the degree to which one is observed by the relevant others. In the second case, which Kelman calls *identification*, one follows a rule in order to preserve a social relationship that is personally rewarding, a relationship that enhances one's feelings of self-esteem. If a person finds a particular relationship satisfying, he will tend to act in accordance with the expectations of the others with whom he is involved, and these expectations coincidentally will reflect the norms and rules of the group. Identification is similar to compliance in that the rules aren't seen as intrinsically worthwhile; it differs from compliance in that the person actually believes in the norms and rules that he adopts. Moreover, the person will follow these rules in private as long as the role relationship remains satisfying.

Kelman's third type of rule following is called *internalization*. It occurs when a law appears to be compatible with a person's existing value system. In such cases the law is assimilated effortlessly to a person's character structure, and it is thereafter followed and defended in an unambivalent, almost unconscious manner. Kelman emphasizes that internalization is not necessarily or even primarily a rational process. Laws are internalized essentially without regard for their logical consistency with one's existing values, and they are subsequently observed whether or not one is being watched, and regardless of the wishes of one's friends and associates. Only when laws have been internalized in Kelman's sense can legal socialization be considered complete.

The next question is, what social experiences and development processes produce an internalized orientation to the law? In the remainder of this paper I will describe a model of legal socialization that focuses on the processes underlying internalization of the law. Like the Tapp and Kohlberg theory described earlier, this model was initially derived from the study of moral development.

Before moving into the details of the model itself, I should describe the assumptions on which it is based. The model assumes that beyond survival requirements, man needs social interaction, predictability, and order and that his cultural and legal systems reflect these needs. Three separate lines of research support these assumptions.

The first line of research is exemplified by recent work in anthropology (cf. Mayr, 1963), which suggests that for the major portion of his time on earth, man lived in small hunting groups. During this period of his development, man seemed largely concerned with killing game and members of competing groups as efficiently as possible. Individual survival depended on the quality of the group rather than the talent of particular members; efficient social organization (defined in terms of laws, language, leadership structure, and so forth) rather than brain size promoted man's survival and ultimately his evolutionary success. This line of reasoning suggests, then, that man has a deep organic need for his culture and that legal systems are not arbitrary accretions of history continually threatened with obsolescence. Rather, part of what it means to be human is to have a system of law.

A second line of research, ably summarized by Bowlby (1969), suggests that children (and people in general) require social interaction with preferred others on a predictable basis. Conversely, they fear unpredictability and isolation. (In man's evolutionary past he was most vulnerable when alone and in a strange environment.) People seem happiest in the company of familiar companions in a predictable environment; infants in particular become severely disturbed—in some cases even die—when these requirements aren't met.

A third line of research, conducted by my colleagues at Johns Hopkins (cf. Garvey, 1974; Garvey & Hogan, 1973), points to the conclusion that children need social interaction, probably from birth, and that by age three and one-half, they have developed a considerable range of conventional, rule-governed means for carrying out this interaction. Moreover, the rules that structure their interaction often become so important that many small children stop playing rather than allow the rules to be broken—that is, for example, when playing with girls, many little boys will quit rather than be "Mommy."

Restating the main point, three lines of research suggest that man needs social interaction on a predictable and orderly basis and that his cultural and legal systems reflect these needs. In brief, we have the image of man as a rule-formulating and rule-following animal, with research suggesting that these rule-oriented tendencies reflect human biology and promote human survival. With this image in mind we can now turn to a discussion of how internalized attitudes toward the law develop.

Starting from an initial unsocialized state, internalized compliance with legal and social rules seems to pass through three forms or levels; the attainment of each level is precipitated by changes in a child's life circumstances. The first is characterized by *attunement to rules*; the second is marked by *sensitivity to social expectations and concern for the well-being of others*; the third is defined by *ideological maturity*. Several earlier writers proposed similar stages, although arriving at them from very different perspectives. Emile Durkheim (1961), for example, described a person's integration into his social groups as passing through three levels. The first is defined by a sense of loyalty and duty to the rules of the group; the second is achieved by adopting impersonal, group-defined goals for one's actions; the third is reached by a conscious and rational understanding of the group's purposes. William McDougall (1908) described moral development in terms of three stages. In the first, one's conduct is regulated by fear of punishment; in the second, conduct is governed by social praise and blame; and in the third, one's conduct and sense of self-worth depend on the maintenance of certain abstract moral principles.

Rawls (1971) elaborates his discussion of a theory of justice by describing moral development in terms of three stages that he calls the ethics of authority, the ethics of association, and the ethics of principle. The parallels between Rawls' views and those presented below are obvious and extensive.

Attunement to Rules

Among the many problems confronting a very young child, two stand out: procuring care and attention from adult caretakers and making sense out of the social world that surrounds him. For the social scientist, a key problem is to explain why the initially amoral infant would allow himself to be guided by adult rules. This is a puzzle because, as Rawls (1971) notes, "The child's having a morality of authority [being attuned to rules] consists in his being disposed without the prospect of reward and punishment to follow certain precepts that not only may appear to him largely arbitrary but which in no way appeal to his original inclinations" (p.466). This distinguishing feature of the first level of internalization has nothing to do with the rules per se—that is, the child doesn't incorporate a set of rules in the same way as he would eat a box of cookies. Rather, the critical transformation concerns the accommodation that a child makes to adult authority. If a child sees his parents as benevolent and trustworthy sources of support and guidance, he will be disposed to accept their rules and commands regardless of their content. If the parents are not so viewed, a child will tend to regard authority with suspicion and even resentment—he will be resistant to rules regardless of their content.

The specific chemistry of the parent-child interaction that engenders attunement to rules is not well understood. Nonetheless, two points about this early transformation are apparent. First, Waddington (1967) points out that the survival of culture necessarily requires the role of authority acceptor; children would be unable to learn language (or the safe foods to eat, or danger signs) unless they were willing to accept the arbitrary pairing of certain random sounds with various meanings. And there is in principle no difference between language learning and the acquisition of any other rule system or aspect of culture. Second, there is evidence to suggest that within the first twelve months of life, maternal warmth and sensitivity to an infant's needs are sufficient to produce internalization of maternal commands; given the "proper" parent-child atmosphere, infants seem innately disposed toward obedience (cf. Stayton, Hogan, & Ainsworth, 1971). As an infant begins to creep around, however, its caretakers must increasingly restrict its behavior. Generally speaking, a child will be most attuned to rules if it is treated in a warm but restrictive fashion—that is, if it receives love and nurturance combined with prompt and consistent disapproval for disobedience. Warm but permissive parents, on the other hand, produce self-confident children who are not attuned to rules. Parents who are cold and restrictive tend to have children who are hostile toward authority, but who publicly conform to rules. Parents who are cold and permissive tend to produce delinquent children.

To restate the point, the first level of legal socialization (the first stage in developing internalized compliance with the law) involves attunement to rules; this entails recognizing that social situations are governed by rules, learning what these rules are, and adjusting to them in an effortless, unambivalent way. Moreover, by adopting parental rules (for example, language and so forth), a child is able simultaneously to secure parental care and to begin making sense of its environment. As Rawls (1971) notes, a child will become attuned to the rules under the following conditions: "First, the parents must love the child and be worthy objects of his admiration. In this way they arouse in him a sense of his own value and the desire to become the sort of person that they are. Secondly, they must enunciate clear and intelligible (and of course justifiable) rules adapted to the child's level of comprehension. In addition they should set out the reasons for these injunctions so far as these can be understood; they must also follow these precepts insofar as they apply to them as well. The parents should exemplify the morality that they enjoin and make explicit its underlying principles as time goes on" (pp. 465-466). The point, however, is that a child doesn't incorporate rules per se, rather, he becomes attuned to the existence and operation of rules, so that when he enters any given situation, he expects rules to apply; his job is to determine what they are.

Understanding this permits us to make sense of some otherwise rather curious findings in the legal socialization literature. For example, Torney (1971) notes that relative to lower-class and upper-middle-class children, lower-middle class children have more favorable attitudes toward the police. She explains these findings in terms of different social-class-related experiences with policemen—that is, lower-middle-class children have generally positive experiences with the police, while the experiences of lower-class and upper-middle-class children are generally negative. But how many normal seven-year-olds have had significant contact with the police? A more parsimonious answer is that social class differences in child rearing lead to differences in attunement to rules and different orientations to adult authority generally. These social class differences in orientation to adult authority are then reflected in children's attitudes toward the police.

Finally, I might note that if a child is attuned to rules and loves and trusts his parents, he will tend to feel guilty when he breaks these rules. The guilt associated with this stage is a composite of fear of parental punishment and fear of parental rejection. Rejection, in particular, is a blow to a child's self-esteem and symbolizes parental abandonment. Rawls (1971) disagrees; he observes that ". . . love and trust will give rise to feelings of guilt once the parental injunctions are disobeyed. Admittedly in the case of the child it is sometimes difficult to distinguish feelings of guilt from the fear of punishment, and especially from the dread of the loss of parental love and affection . . . I have supposed, however, that even in the child's case we can separate (authority) guilt feelings from fear and anxiety" (p. 465).

Sensitivity to Social Expectations

The second level of legal socialization entails developing internalized compliance with the norms, values, and principles of one's society. How does this come about? Throughout the history of mankind very young children have been faced with the problem of making an accommodation to adult authority. Typically, however, by the time a child is five, he has been replaced at the center of family attention by a younger sibling. Changes within the family, in conjunction with a child's naturally expanding sociability, cause him to spend increasing time away from his parents, usually with his peers. Making one's way in the peer group is a major problem at this point in life and to the degree that a child remains scrupulously loyal to parental rules and adult authority, his way will be hindered. At this point, a child must accommodate himself to a greatly altered—that is, more general and abstract—set of rules or risk becoming a social isolate. To the degree that the children of a culture are sensibly supervised, the norms of the peer group will approximate the norms of adult society.

As Mead (1934) and Piaget (1964) pointed out so well, the major vehicle for the socialization of children at this age is games and the experience of cooperation. Through games, children are exposed to a range of adult values, including, most importantly, the norms of reciprocity and the concept of fairness. In the first period of legal socialization children become attuned to *rules.* In the second period, however, they develop an internalized orientation to adult *norms* and *values*—through peer group experience. And as Rawls (1971) points out, the notions of reciprocity and fairness in childhood turn into the concept of justice in adulthood.

Although the preadolescent child is able to articulate many adult values and principles (cf. Adelson et al., 1969), the question remains as to how they become internalized. In very general terms, internalization is a function of the development of empathy (Hogan, 1973), which can be broken down into two psychological processes. The first is sensitivity to social expectations. I remember a boy in my seventh-grade class who was vastly unpopular; he routinely alienated his classmates and was sublimely indifferent to their attempts to socialize him. He was one of the most obtuse and insensitive people I have ever met—and remained so into adulthood. I watched him one day in the company of his parents at a supermarket. The parents obviously worshipped the ground the boy walked on; apparently their solicitude and unqualified affection made it unnecessary for him to develop the introspection and attentiveness to social cues that lead to sensitivity to social expectations—a sensitivity which, in turn, provides cues for regulating one's behavior.

The second process that seems to engender an internalized orientation to norms and values is concern for the welfare of those people with whom one interacts (in a child's case, the extended family and the peer group). How do people come to care about the welfare of their social groups? Freud (1960) suggested that when people work together toward a common goal, ties of affection "naturally" spring up. Rawls (1971) is more specific. Sensitivity to social expectations develops as children experience reciprocity in the family, school, neighborhood, and peer group. "Thus if those engaged in a system of social cooperation regularly act with evident intention to uphold its just (or fair) rules, bonds of friendship and mutual trust tend to develop among them, thereby holding them even more securely to the scheme" (Rawls, 1971, p. 470). Thus, ". . . the evident intention to honor one's obligations and duties is seen as a form of good will, and this recognition arouses feelings of friendship and trust in return" (p. 471). These bonds of friendship and trust lead to a concern for the welfare of others and to an internalized orientation to the norms and values appropriate to this second level of legal socialization.

Once a set of norms and values has been incorporated, a person will tend to feel guilty if they are violated. These feelings of guilt, perhaps rooted in fear of social disapproval, are manifested in a willingness to make reparations, to admit blame, and to be less indignant when others violate the same norms. If this capacity for guilt is missing, then there are no genuine ties of friendship and mutual trust among the members of the group, and one's orientation to these norms and values is not internalized.

To summarize this discussion, the second level of legal socialization consists in developing an internalized orientation to the norms, values, and principles implicit in the laws of one's society. This process starts when a child leaves the exclusive care of his parents and begins to accommodate himself to the demands of his peer group, neighborhood, and school. Being required to cooperate with others, experiencing reciprocity in peer play, perceiving that certain ideals are upheld by attractive members of the group are all factors that sensitize a child to social expectations and engender a concern for the welfare of the group. This leads to what Rawls (1971) calls the ethics of association; here the ideals and norms of one's social group are seen as one's own and one feels guilty when these norms are violated.

Ideological Maturity

According to Jung (1934) the critical problem facing an adolescent is choosing a mate and a career. According to Erikson (1950), however, neither choice is possible unless a person has a sense of personal identity—that is, some knowledge of who he is and what he stands for. Another way of putting this is to say that a major problem for an adolescent is to make sense of the competing and often contradictory lessons learned in the family, neighborhood, and peer group. From the viewpoint of legal socialization, the problem is to explain a person's internalized orientation to the rules and principles of law when such an orientation runs counter to the wishes and expectations of his parents and peer group. From the viewpoint of social theorists, the problem is that a person who is attuned to rules, sensitive to social expectations, and concerned about the welfare of his social groups will be necessarily committed to the status quo. Consequently, a proper model of legal socialization must make provisions for constructive nonconformity, for prosocial deviation from established patterns of conduct.

At the first level of legal socialization one must learn to live with authority; at the second level, one must learn to live with other people; but at the third level, one must learn to live with oneself. Rawls (1971) calls this final level of internalization the ethics of principle. As he remarks, although a person at the second level "... understands the principles of justice, his motive for complying with them ... springs largely from his ties of friendship and fellow feeling for others, and his concern for the approbation of wider society .... Once a morality of principle is accepted, however, moral attitudes are no longer connected solely with the well-being and approval of particular individuals and groups, but are shaped by a conception of right chosen irrespective of these contingencies" (p. 475).

We are concerned here with what, in another context (Hogan, 1973, 1975a), I called autonomy, or autonomous observance of legal and social rules. The problem of autonomy has vexed social psychology for years. Part of the difficulty is methodological—that is, it is hard to distinguish autonomous behavior from simple, immature anticonformity (cf. Hollander & Willis, 1967). Perhaps the biggest problem, however, is conceptual and definitional. The tradition of ethical individualism exemplified by Friedriche Nietzsche, for example, defines autonomous moral behavior as conformity to internal rather than external laws; truly moral (and autonomous) conduct is guided by one's personally derived standards of right and wrong. Although this individualistic view is widely popular (for example, Kohlberg, 1963), it is untenable for practical and psychological reasons. On the one hand, society would be impossible if citizens refused to comply with any laws but their own. On the other hand, the unpredictable and anomic society that would follow from the Nietzschean ethic violates man's need for a predictable and orderly social environment. Nietzschean autonomy, like the existentialist's notion of authentic existence, presupposes a stable social order.

It is also worth noting that this individualistic view of autonomy is relatively parochial, and reflects the negative side of American intellectuals' ambivalent attitude toward culture (cf. Hogan, 1975b). According to this view, man is seen as fundamentally humane and reasonable, his wickedness caused by corrupt, social institutions; it is culture, not human nature, that sets the limits of human perfectability. Individuality, autonomy, and personal freedom are seen as highly desirable states of being, possible only by transcending the constraints of culture. But there are at least two equally defensible alternatives to this liberal view of man's relation to society. On the one hand, there is the traditional conservative view that man is fundamentally anarchistic and antisocial, that culture is the flimsy last line of defense protecting us from the depredations of our fellows. On the other hand, there is the traditional biological view that man evolved as a culture-bearing, norm-respecting animal, that he achieves his essential humanity only through becoming a well-integrated member of a human community. Here culture is seen as supporting and enhancing, rather than stultifying, individual development. The individualistic view of autonomy, then, represents an arbitrary, parochial position, and there are no historical, logical, or empirical grounds for preferring it over the conservative or the biological view.

It seems to me that autonomous conduct doesn't refer to autonomy with regard to the rules, values, and principles of a society, but with regard to the current opinions of other people—peers and figures of authority. The autonomous or principled person upholds the highest moral and legal ideals of his society without concern for their contemporary popularity. (This means, for example, allowing the American Nazi Party and the Ku Klux Klan the same rights of assembly and free speech that more socially acceptable political groups enjoy.)

How does autonomous or principled rule compliance come about? The best empirical work on the subject has been conducted by Baumrind (1971). She has identified a set of child-rearing practices that characterize "authoritative" parents. Such parents provide clear guidelines for their children's behavior, explain their rules, allow for rational discussion of specific prescriptions, but adhere to the principle that there will be some rules in any event. Perhaps the truly critical feature of such parents is that they are themselves autonomous in that they provide models of autonomous adult behavior. This feature may be more important than any discrete pattern of child-rearing practices.

William James and William McDougall proposed definitions of autonomy similar to that presented above—that is, one is autonomous with regard to other people rather than with regard to social rules and principles. They explained the development of autonomous rule observance in terms of what is today known as reference group theory: over time, some people come to be concerned about the approval and censure of a group of judges more distinguished or elevated than their own family and friends. These judges may be historical personages, even—in the case of Socrates, for example—semifictional characters. Although they no longer have a temporal existence, they embody the best traditions of one's culture or society. By being concerned with their approval rather than that of one's peers, one achieves a measure of autonomy while remaining generally in tune with the rules and precepts of one's society. McDougall (1923) was particularly clear about this; as he remarked: "The man who stands up against the prevailing public opinion . . . has found some higher court of appeal, the verdict of which he esteems more highly . . . and whose approval he desires more strongly, than that of the mass of mankind . . . in short, he has learned to judge his conduct as it would appear to a purely ideal spectator . . . . In this way . . . a man may become, as it is said, 'a law unto himself' " (pp. 441-442).

Autonomy can also be understood through an analysis of the role of ideology in personality development. As mentioned above, one of the major problems facing an adolescent is to integrate the conflicting requirements of parents, peers, school, and neighborhood. This integration is made possible through ideological maturity. Ideological maturity is a function of having organized one's experiences and aspirations in terms of a coherent philosophy, political perspective, religion, or set of family ideals. To achieve ideological maturity, the adolescent needs two supporting features in the environment—adult models of autonomy on the one hand, and a history, a tradition, a political philosophy, or a culturally based ideology on the other—on which he can draw. Problems will develop, of course, when the relevant adult models and cultural traditions are absent.

Erikson (1950) also emphasizes the role of ideology in adolescent identity formation, and Gallatin and Adelson (1971) provide evidence that eighteen-year-olds are in fact inclined to formulate ideologies. As they remark: "To lend coherence to his anticipated adult life, some order to his decisions, the adolescent needs to develop what Erikson (1959) has loosely termed an 'ideology of religion' or what Inhelder and Piaget (1958) call 'a feeling for ideals' " (p. 105).

In addition to providing a structure for organizing the adolescent's life, an ideology also gives him a sacred rationalization for the rules adopted from his parents, and for the norms and principles learned in his peer group. The sacred or numinous quality of ideologies in part accounts for the extraordinary tenacity and independence of the views of persons at this level of legal socialization. When the rules and principles of one's culture have been organized under an ideology, they become a part of one's identity, and their violation produces the most profound psychological distress.

Conclusion

The complete argument can now be stated very quickly. For the rules, values, and principles of one's society to be fully internalized in Kelman's (1961) sense, legal socialization must pass through three levels. In the first, one internalizes *rules* by accommodating oneself to loving but controlling parents. At the second level, one internalizes *principles* by accommodating oneself to a peer community in which certain standards (for example, fairness and cooperation) are maintained by virtue of judicious adult supervision. At the third level, one organizes these rules and principles under an ideology, usually by accommodating oneself to one's cultural and ethnic history; this organization gives the rules and principles acquired earlier a sacred quality that makes their violation almost unimaginable.

With this model in mind we now have a tool for answering a broad, policy-related question that arises repeatedly in the legal socialization literature. Phrased most generally, the question concerns what can be achieved in terms of social reform by legislative means. Is it not the case, as observed by Andeneas (1971), for example, that the effectiveness of a law will depend in large measure on people's motivation to do that which is regulated? Alternatively, to what degree is law constrained by the moral sentiments of a population, and to what degree can law be used as an independent agent of social reform? As Zimring and Hawkins (1971) point out, little is known about the factors that militate for or against the success of law in changing customary behavior. The model of legal socialization presented above suggests that there are circumstances under which laws will be highly effective regardless of people's motivation to do that which is regulated. What might these circumstances be?

There are three conditions that a piece of legislation must meet in order to be maximally effective; these conditions are prefigured in the three stages of legal socialization discussed above. The first condition is that it must be seen as emanating from legitimate authority—that is, the law-making body must be regarded as credible, as worthy of respect and veneration, as authentically concerned with the welfare of its constituency, as exemplars of probity and integrity. In most normal societies the larger proportion of the population will be attuned to rules; however, the behavioral dispositions that this attunement entails are most readily elicited by authority that is legitimate.

The second condition promoting the efficacy of law can be stated in several different ways. One statement is that the law must be perceived as relevant to the ongoing activities and concerns of the group. Another way of phrasing this is to say that the law must be seen as promoting the interests of the group in an even-handed way; it must not confer special favor on any particular subgroup. Alternatively, the law must be perceived as causing equal hardship for everyone subject to it; no particular subgroup should be singled out for special abuse. All of these conditions amount to saying that the law must be fair or just, according to Hart's (1961) definition of justice as treating like cases alike and different ones differently. The principle underlying this second condition is that the behavioral dispositions entailed by sensitivity to social expectations and concern for the welfare of the group are most readily elicited by laws that are just.

The third enabling condition of law is that it must be seen as consonant with the values, traditions, and history of the persons subject to it. To be most effective, law must be perceived as an organic part of the heritage and principles of that culture. When laws seem part of what the members of a culture regard as sacred, they will most strongly elicit the behavioral dispositions entailed by ideological maturity.

Summarizing the above, laws have their greatest potential as agents of social reform when they are perceived as legitimate, fair, and consistent with what people hold to be sacred.

This raises a final question, one that concerns the possibility of using the law as an instrument of social reform in the United States. The model of legal socialization presented above, in conjunction with the current climate of opinion in America, suggests a rather bleak view of this possibility. With regard to the perceived legitimacy of American government, Richardson (1975) refers to a 1974 University of Michigan poll and remarks that confidence in government at all levels has been falling steadily at least since the late 1950s; he fears that people may have become so cynical about government that they are no longer willing to believe any public message, no matter how honestly or candidly given. The finding that politicians rank lower than TV news broadcasters in public trust and esteem further underscores the notion that the moral authority and legitimacy of legislators has been seriously eroded (Newscasters . . . , 1974, p. 28).

With regard to the perceived fairness of our political institutions, it is widely believed that government at all levels routinely confers favors on preferred special interest groups. In addition, a study by Abravanel and Busch (1975) suggests that participatory democracy and experience with the political system, while increasing people's political competency, may actually produce negative feelings toward the political system itself—that is, political distrust is a consequence of participation in politics. Between 1966 and 1975 disaffection from government doubled (from 29% to 59%; see Public disaffection . . . , 1974, p. 87). A majority of every segment of our population distrusts government and regards the economic system as unfair. As suggested above, authority must be seen as even-handed if it is to compel admiration and respect. The perceived unfairness of our public institutions in part accounts for the widespread mood of alienation and distrust that pervades the land.

The third requirement for effective law is that it be regarded as consistent with the tradition and history of the culture. Here we have a particularly intransigent problem because, other than the crass marketplace mentality of laissez faire economics, there seems to be no distinctive American political philosophy. Freedman (1975) suggests that the doctrine of the separation of powers might represent the distinctive American political ideology. But, as he further notes, the American public has historically been ambivalent with regard to the notion of federal regulation of local affairs, so this particular ideological foundation supports nothing. Nagai (1972) points out that the traditional American themes of pragmatism, technological efficiency, anti-intellectualism, and avoidance of ideological analysis have cost America its capacity for self-restoration at a time when all the forces at work in society seem to alienate, isolate, and divide the individual members of the body politic. The widespread distrust of politicians and legislators, the perceived injustice of many of our institutions, and the apparent fact that little is sacred beyond the profit motive seem to raise serious obstacles to the possibility of using the law as an instrument of social reform in America.

References

Abravanel, M.D., & Busch, R.J. Political competence, political trust, and the action orientations of university students. *The Journal of Politics*, 1975, *37*, 57-82.

Adelson, J., Green, B., & O'Neil, R. Growth of the idea of law in adolescence. *Developmental Psychology*, 1969, *4*, 327-332.

Andeneas, J. The moral or educative influence of criminal law. *Journal of Social Issues*, 1971, *27*, 17-32.

Baumrind, D. Current patterns of parental authority. *Developmental Psychology*, 1971, *4* (Pt.2).

Bowlby, J. *Attachment and loss* (Vol. 1). *Attachment*. New York: Basic Books, 1969.

Durkheim, E. *Moral education*. New York: Free Press, 1961.

Erikson, E. *Childhood and society*. New York: Norton, 1950.

Erikson, E. Identity and the life cycle. *Psychological Issues*, 1959, *1*(1, Whole Monograph 1).

Freedman, J.O. Crisis and legitimacy in the administrative process. *Stanford Law Review*, 1975, *27*, 1041-1076.

Freud, S. *Group psychology and the analysis of the ego*. New York: Bantam, 1960.

Gallatin, J., & Adelson, J. Legal guarantees of individual freedom: A cross-national study of the development of political thought. *Journal of Social Issues*, 1971, *27*, 93-108.

Garvey, C. Some properties of social play. *Merrill-Palmer Quarterly*, 1974, *20*, 163-180.

Garvey, C., & Hogan, R. Social speech and social interaction: Egocentrism revisited. *Child Development*, 1973, *44*, 562-568.

Hess, R.D., & Torney, J.V. *The development of political attitudes in children*. New York: Anchor Books, 1968.

Hogan, R. The structure of moral character and the explanation of moral action. *Journal of Youth and Adolescence*, 1975, *4*, 1-15. (a)

Hogan, R. Theoretical egocentrism and the problem of compliance. *American Psychologist*, 1975, *30*, 533-540. (b)

Hogan, R. Moral conduct and moral character. *Psychological Bulletin*, 1973, *79*, 217-232.

Hollander, E.P., & Willis, R.H. Some current issues in the psychology of conformity and nonconformity. *Psychological Bulletin*, 1967, *68*, 62-76.

Ichheiser, G. *Appearances and reality*. San Francisco: Jossey-Bass, 1970.

Inhelder, B., & Piaget, J. *The growth of logical thinking from childhood to adolescence.* New York: Basic Books, 1958.

Jung, C.G. *Modern man in search of a soul.* New York: Harcourt Brace, 1933.

Kelman, H.C. Processes of opinion change. *Public Opinion Quarterly*, 1961, *25*, 57-78.

Kohlberg, L. The development of children's orientation towards a moral order. *Vita Humana*, 1963, *6*, 11-331.

Mayr, E. *Populations, species, and evolution.* Cambridge: Harvard University Press, 1963.

McDougall, W. *Social psychology.* London: Methuen, 1908.

McDougall, W. *Outline of psychology.* New York: Scribner, 1923.

Mead, G.H. *Mind, self, and society.* Chicago: University of Chicago Press, 1934.

Nagai, Y. The United States is disintegrating. *Psychology Today*, May 1972, pp. 24, 26-27, 93-94.

Newscasters inspire more public trust than politicians. *Current Opinion*, 1974, *2* 28.

Piaget, J. *The moral judgment of the child.* New York: Free Press, 1964.

Public disaffection at record high. *Current Opinion*, 1974, *2*, 87.

Rawls, J. *A theory of justice.* Cambridge, Mass.: Harvard University Press, 1971.

Richardson, E. Dynamics of citizenship: Confidence, capacity, consensus. *National Civic Review*, 1975, *5*, 234-237.

Stayton, D., Hogan, R., & Ainsworth, M.D.S. Infant obedience and maternal behavior: The origins of socialization reconsidered. *Child Development*, 1971, *42*, 1057-1069.

Tapp, J.L., & Kohlberg, L. Developing senses of law and legal justice. *Journal of Social Issues*, 1971, *27*, 65-92.

Tapp, J.L., & Levine, F.J. Legal socialization: Strategies for an ethical legality. *Stanford Law Review*, 1974, *27*, 1-72.

Torney, J.V. Socialization of attitudes toward the legal system. *Journal of Social Issues*, 1971, *27*, 137-154.

Waddington, C.H. *The ethical animal.* Chicago: University of Chicago Press, 1967.

Zellman, G.L., & Sears, D.O. Childhood origins of tolerance for dissent. *Journal of Social Issues*, 1971, *27*, 109-136.

Zimring, F., & Hawkins, G. The legal threat as an instrument of social change. *Journal of Social Issues*, 1971, *27*, 33-48.

<table>
<tr><td>**4**</td><td>

Channeling Lawyers: The Careers of Public Defenders

Anthony Platt
Randi Pollock
</td></tr>
</table>

Introduction

Overview

This paper concerns the careers and ideology of lawyers who have worked in a public defender's office in Alameda County—a highly populated and industrial community on the West Coast. While partly building on a variety of studies on occupational careers inside and outside the criminal justice system (Hughes, 1959; Carr-Saunders & Wilson, 1933; Janowitz, 1964; Slocum, 1966), this study also attempts to place the concept of "career" in a larger social and political context by borrowing from recent contributions to theories of the state and the "new" working class (Miliband, 1969; Mallet, 1963; Gorz, 1972; Il Manifesto, 1972).

In general, there are very few appreciative studies of the working conditions and attitudes of persons who staff the criminal justice bureaucracies. They are popularly characterized as "faceless bureaucrats," "public servants," or "insidious technocrats"—depending on the author's political perspective. Public defenders, like other sectors of the law enforcement labor force, have been victimized by this kind of stereotyping. They are either uncritically celebrated by government and professional authorities as indispensable public servants[1] or they are depicted by critics and muck-rakers as lackeys of prosecutors or, at best, dangerous do-gooders (Sudnow, 1965; Platt, Schechter & Tiffany, 1968; Casper, 1971).

The research for this paper is based on a pilot study in Chicago, sponsored by the Center for Studies in Criminal Justice, University of Chicago, and a research project supported by the Center for the Study of Law and Society, University of California at Berkeley. Sharon Dunkle Marks in Chicago and Suzi Tanguay and Jay Adams in Berkeley provided essential help in collecting and interpreting data. Herman Schwendinger gave supportive criticism of a first draft. We are especially grateful to the many present and past members of the Public Defender's Office who gave us their time and confidence.

This chapter is reprinted with permission from "Channeling Lawyers: The Careers of Public Defenders," by Anthony Platt and Randi Pollock, published in *Issues in Criminology*, Volume 9, Number 1 (spring 1974), pp. 1-31 by the graduate students of the School of Criminology at the University of California, Berkeley.

[1] According to the American Bar Foundation (1955, p. 90) for example, "the public defender's office is one of the most valuable contributions in modern times to the administration of criminal justice." Similarly uncritical comments can be found in the President's Commission on Law Enforcement and Administration of Justice (1967, especially chapter 5).

This case-study is designed to present a more accurate and sympathetic portrait of people who work as public defenders—why they enter Public Defender Offices, how they are recruited, who remain to make a career as public defenders, who leave and why, and how their subsequent careers develop. It is also about what the job of public defender does to people's aspirations, identities, values and human potentialities. Hopefully, this analysis has larger implications for understanding some of the problems and dilemmas faced by a growing and important sector of the labor force who work as "servants of the state" (Miliband, 1969, pp. 119-145).

Methodology

A list of all sixty-four attorneys who worked in the Alameda County Public Defender Office (PDO) between 1927 and 1969 was compiled and chronologically ordered. Minimal background and career information was collected through public and official records. Extensive interviews—partly structured and partly open-ended—were conducted with 75 percent (48) of the former PDO attorneys, and a small number of important or helpful informants were re-interviewed. Two of the interviewees, as friends of the authors, helped to evaluate the reliability and accuracy of data collected through interviews.

In addition, minimal background and career information was collected on the 58 attorneys who were employed in the PDO as of May, 1971. Through interviews and questionnaires, more extensive data were gathered on 64 percent (37) of these attorneys. Additional data were derived from annual budget reports, local newspapers, published articles and office memoranda. In summary, this study is based primarily on data concerning 122 attorneys in the PDO, 85 (70%) of whom were researched in considerable depth. Comparative references in this paper are derived from a larger project on the legal careers of public defenders in Cook County, Illinois, and prosecutors in Alameda County, California.[2]

Development of the Public Defender System

The public defender system, as distinguished from other kinds of legal aid, was first implemented in Los Angeles in 1914, though it had been discussed since the early 1890s (Silverstein, 1965). Typically, it involves salaried lawyers who devote all or most of their time to the specialized practice of representing poor defendants charged with criminal offenses. Defender systems vary considerably in the kinds of cases they handle, in the quality of legal service, and in their

---

[2] The results of the Cook County study have not been published. The other study is partially reported by Suzi Tanguay (1967).

territorial jurisdiction (Silverstein, 1965, chapter 3). According to the National Legal Aid and Defender Association, there are approximately over 1,000 public defenders in the United States, of whom about half are full time (President's Commission on Law Enforcement and Administration of Justice, 1967). While the assigned counsel system is used in most counties (approximately 2,750 of the 3,100 counties in the country), the public defender system is presently in operation in about 270 counties (including many large cities) and handles approximately one-third of all felony defendants in the country (President's . . . , 1967; see also Silverstein, 1965, pp. 40-45; James, 1972, p. 129).

Public defender systems were adopted in most large urban jurisdictions because they offer a more efficient and centralized method of processing a high volume of cases (President's Commission on Law Enforcement and Administration of Justice, 1967, p. 59). Since the majority of criminal defendants are poor and incapable of retaining a private attorney,[3] there is an ever-increasing need for free legal services. The public defender system has grown considerably in recent years, partly as a general reflection of the expansion of state bureaucracies and more specifically as a result of efforts to centralize and rationalize the criminal justice system.

Alameda County Public Defender Office

Alameda County, located on the coast of northern California, includes a large industrial city (Oakland) and a college town (Berkeley). The Public Defender's Office has its central office in Oakland, a sprawling and ugly metropolis which suffers, like many American cities, from chronic unemployment, deteriorating public services, and an economy reminiscent of the depression. Its unemployment rate is about twice the national average and its welfare caseload is the second largest in California. One-quarter of all families in Oakland live in extreme poverty (at less than $4,000 per annum) and almost half of all families in the city live in deprivation or worse. In the flatlands area of the city, where blacks, chicanos and poor whites live, almost half of the eligible work force is either unemployed or subemployed (Hayes, 1972, pp. 45-46). Although Oakland's total population has been declining slightly in the last ten years, its proportion of black residents has been gradually increasing. Over 90,000 blacks, approximately one-quarter of the city's population, live in Oakland (Lunch, 1970).

Though Oakland is typical of many moderate-sized American cities confronted by profound economic and political problems, it has a national reputation among professionals and policy-makers for an above-average system

---

[3] The President's Commission conservatively estimated that approximately 60 percent of all felony defendants and close to 50 percent of all misdemeanor defendants are unable to retain a private attorney.

of criminal justice. The Police Department is reputed to have high professional standards and is governed by a reform-minded Chief; the District Attorney's Office has trained several well-known professionals and politicians, and has a reputation for honesty and high standards; and the Public Defender's Office is locally and nationally recognized for its technical competence, high ethical standards, excellent training program and freedom from political interference. This study, therefore, is about a public defender system which, comparatively speaking, ranks very high and sets standards which other offices try to emulate.

Alameda County's PDO was created by a county charter passed in 1926, in accord with provisions of a statute passed by the California legislature in 1921, permitting the extension of the public defender system in Los Angeles to other more populous counties of the state (Ivens, 1939). Alameda's PDO was supported by many notables and leaders in the community, including the local District Attorney and Grand Jury (Ivens, 1939, p. 66). On January 18, 1927, Alameda County's Board of Supervisors unanimously ratified the state law and appointed a prominent Oakland attorney as Public Defender for the county. A few years later, the Alameda County Grand Jury reported that the PDO not only provides "experienced counsel for accused persons unable to pay fees, but it brings the public interest into a closer bearing on the problems of dealing with the offenders. Trials under this system are more expeditious, sufficient court time being saved to pay the cost of the public defender and possibly even result in economy. The cost per case handled is only about $18." In short, the PDO was suggested and supported by elite members of the judiciary and political system. In this respect, it was no different from many welfare reforms which accompanied the rise of corporate capitalism at the turn of the century (Kolko, 1967; Weinstein, 1969).

When the first Public Defender took office in 1927, his total budget was less than $7,500 and he supplemented his income by maintaining a civil practice. During his twenty-four-year office as Chief Public Defender, from 1927 to 1951, his staff increased to four lawyers and his budget to $27,000. The PDO continued to slowly grow during the 1950s, adding more lawyers and becoming a full-time operation. During the late 1960s it suddenly expanded into a complex organization requiring a division of labor and specialization of skills. When the fourth Chief Public Defender entered office in 1963, there were five lawyers handling 1,964 cases; by 1968, there were thirty-eight lawyers handling 16,500 cases. As of May 1971, the PDO consisted of fifty-eight lawyers (of whom six were in supervisory positions) and ten investigators processing almost 20,000 cases annually.

Entering the Public Defender Office

Recruitment: The Employer's Perspective

While Alameda County's District Attorney Office is elective, the Public Defender is appointed by the Board of Supervisors to whom he is legally and politically responsible. Assistant Public Defenders, however, are governed by the Civil Service Commission which is designed, in theory at least, to protect them from political interference. Since the Public Defender plays a key role in the recruitment and selection of Assistants, it is important to understand some basic political features of his Office.

Between 1927 and 1971, there have been five Chief Public Defenders. Public Defender One, who held office from 1927 to 1951, was previously a deputy clerk in the District Court of Appeal. He was appointed as first Public Defender with the support of a federal judge, who "put in a good word for me," and the local District Attorney, whom he later supported in his successful bid for Attorney General. In the early days of the PDO, the staff was very small and the Public Defender had difficulty recruiting young attorneys because salaries were inadequate and Assistants were required to supplement their income through private practice.

Public Defender Two, who held office from 1951 to 1959, was a senior trial attorney in Alameda's District Attorney Office before his appointment as Public Defender. His political connections on the Board of Supervisors and the power of the local District Attorney combined to defeat his competitors in the PDO. Public Defender Three, 1959-1963, came from the ranks and was groomed for the job by his predecessor. After his appointment as judge in 1963, he was succeeded by Public Defender Four who also had been a life-long civil servant working as a Probation Officer and Assistant Public Defender for many years. The present Public Defender, appointed in 1970, was the personal choice of his predecessor and had worked in the Office for about fifteen years, except for a brief and unsuccessful episode in private practice. His selection as Chief Public Defender was helped by his long friendship with the present District Attorney, whom he has known since college.

Thus, in forty-four years there have been only five Public Defenders, indicating the remarkable stability and continuity of Alameda's PDO. The leadership selection process has been exclusive and ingrown, dominated by a powerful District Attorney's Office and conservative Board of Supervisors. Since the Public Defender and his budget are almost totally dependent on the support of these two organizations, it is not surprising that all five Public Defenders are men of diplomatic restraint and caution, ideologically and bureaucratically conservative, avoiding publicity and controversy.

In the earlier days of the Office, the civil service exam was a formality incidental to the main problem of finding lawyers willing to work as Assistants. Public Defender One personally recruited a couple of acquaintances and other recruits were referred to him by judges and local law schools. As the Office became larger and more formalized in the 1950s, more systematic efforts were made to recruit young law school graduates. The Public Defender gave talks at local law schools and the Office developed a summer internship program to attract law students.

The Public Defender has always had a great deal of control over the civil service exam. Civil service regulations require that a prospective Assistant pass a written and oral exam[4] and place in the top three on the overall test. The written exam is superficial and counts much less than the oral exam which is typically administered by Alameda County's Public Defender together with a public defender from another county and a local private attorney.[5] The oral exam is open-ended and covers a range of formal and informal topics. The whole process is sufficiently flexible for the Public Defender to select any candidate, with the exception of outrageous failures:

When I took the test, they had a written and an oral test, which supposedly gave some objectivity to it because you had to get a certain grade on the written and a certain grade on the oral. But as a practical matter it was a joke because one of the guys who took the test with me failed the written but the boss wanted him. . . . They wanted him because they liked him. He was a kind of healthy jock-like fellow who they figured wouldn't make any worries. So they wired it up so that he would do very well on the orals so he would just barely get over the line on the civil service exam. They just arranged it. You see, they control the civil service panel [Interview #25].

While minimum standards of educational and technical competence are required, the Public Defender still has many opportunities to select candidates whom he personally or ideologically approves. For example, he hires Assistants provisionally before taking the exam, thus giving them priority even over other applicants who score better on the tests:

I didn't take the tests (originally) . . . They had a system where they could hire you provisionally subject to review and when the test came up you took it and of course by that time you couldn't help but pass it [Interview #53].

The Public Defender can also control the selection process by waiting until his choice becomes eligible through encouraging the top three candidates to take other jobs.

Until the mid-1960s, the PDO always had a problem in finding young lawyers who met their formal and informal standards of eligibility. The post-war boom in the legal profession made it difficult for the PDO to compete with private firms and businesses which offered more money and better career opportunities. For those with political and governmental ambitions, the District Attorney's Office was a much more effective vehicle of upward mobility (Tanguay, 1967, chapter 4). Throughout the 1950s and into the early 1960s, a determined law school graduate could get into the PDO if he or she exhibited proper demeanor and had character references from reputable professionals:

---

[4] The written exam is no longer required.

[5] The local private attorney is often an ex-Assistant from Alameda's PDO, this ensuring a cooperative relationship between the PDO and the private bar.

For hiring at that time (1964), you could pretty much, if you were really interested in it, . . . get a job there because there weren't that many people interested. If you were kind of interested and aggressive, you could probably work there. . . . That's not true any more because it's highly competitive now. It wasn't very competitive at the time I went in [Interview #9].

When the PDO was smaller and not characterized by a division of labor and responsibilities, there was a "tremendous esprit de corps and feeling of loyalty to the office," according to an ex-Public Defender. New Assistants were personally recruited and smooth functioning of the Office was maintained on an ad hoc and informal basis. In the last ten years, the character of the PDO and legal marketplace have significantly changed. Prior to 1968, the PDO had at most seventeen attorneys on the staff; four years later, over 60 were employed in the same office. Whereas previously the PDO had difficulty recruiting Assistants, it now has too many applicants and law school graduates vigorously compete for every opening. The expansion of the PDO is consistent with the increasing centralization of power and management of social life by the state,[6] as well as with the disproportionate growth of professional and technical workers within the labor force (Gintis, 1970, pp. 13-43). In addition, the PDO is one of the few places where young attorneys can get paid while gaining extensive trial experience and working with poor clients.

The increased size and popularity of the PDO was accompanied by the development of more regulated methods of recruitment and an internal system of hierarchical controls. This is characterized by organizational distinctions between administrators and staff attorneys, the development of technical specializations (juvenile law, appellate work, felony trials, etc.), and a division of labor based on experience and seniority. The era of "esprit de corps" was formally concluded when the majority of Assistants recently joined the union which represents state and county employees and demanded better working conditions.

Antagonisms within the Office between Assistants and administrators are not solely "bread and butter" disputes over pay and fringe benefits. They also involve different concepts of the appropriate role of public defenders. This was dramatically illustrated in 1967 when a small group of Assistants signed a "Lawyers Against the War in Vietnam" petition which appeared in local newspapers. The Public Defender criticized the signers for "unprofessional conduct" and accused them of disloyalty to the Office. He argued that public demonstrations of militancy or involvement in controversial political issues weakened the Office by attracting bad publicity, annoying an already conservative Board of Supervisors, hurting clients by prejudicing judges and juries, and

[6] This analysis is developed in the work of Ralph Miliband (1969), Gabriel Kolko (1967, 1969) and James Weinstein (1969, 1972).

complicating their working relationship with the District Attorney's Office.[7] The controversy was quickly ended when several Assistants either resigned or were "encouraged to leave." "Up to that point," says an ex-Assistant, "everybody thought that the Public Defender (and his Chief Assistant) were just the greatest people in the world. Everybody loved his job. It was just really rosy and this thing blew the lid off everything. And ever since then this Office has been really shaky" (Interview #9). According to another ex-Assistant, "that one incident was the turning point in a lot of people's attitudes in the Office and in fact it began the great departure of the group that I was part of, which was about ten lawyers" (Interview #55).

So long as there was no apparent conflict within the Office, its regulating principles remained hidden behind the rhetoric of professionalism and political neutrality:

Another thing I had as a policy as Public Defender—no individual self-aggrandizement and hunting for headlines and courting the newspapers and grandstand stunts. . . . I told everybody who came to work for me: 'If you're riding some hobby-horse and some kick, then you're not going to work for me.' I wanted no zealots, no person who had a philosophy of this, that and the other thing. I was not on the side of crime, I was not on the side of criminal and anti-social behavior. Nobody who worked for me was going to be either (Interview #29).

We feel that the more obscurely we live the more likely it is that we will be permitted to do what we think we ought to do. Basically, I think the public and the Board of Supervisors do not look on us with favor because, to be oversimplified about it, I think they have a kind of gut reaction that we are employed to raise impediments in the way of the conviction of bad people. . . . So we have always felt that we will stay out of the press. We have never called, to my knowledge, in all my years in the office, a press conference. . . . We have tried to avoid letting causes swamp cases. . . . I think in terms of representing a person in court on a criminal charge if you, as a lawyer, permit yourself to be swept up in causes, you're likely to blow your case [Interview #26].

When political contradictions in the society directly affected the PDO, as exemplified in the "Vietnam incident," the mask of legitimation was suddenly ripped off and the administrative staff temporarily lost control. This was caused not by any change in policy but through the realization by several Assistants that the neutrality and independence of the PDO is a fiction, that it in fact depends for its existence on continued good relationships with and loyalty to local political elites and the District Attorney's Office.

While this incident revealed a certain naiveté on the part of some Assistants, it also served as a warning to PDO administrators to pay closer attention to the ideology and moral character of new applicants. Public Defender Five rejects applicants who "have been involved in political activities to the extent where I

[7]The Chief District Attorney at that time was a strong anti-communist and had organized a division within his Office to prosecute radical political activists.

think they can no longer view the situation or our situation rationally" (Interview #19). Persons who are too "idealistic" or "scholastic" are also discouraged. "I think a good deal of idealism is helpful if it's channeled properly," commented another administrator. "You have to temper your idealism with a practical sense of reality" (Interview #53).

Background of Public Defenders

The PDO, like the criminal bar and other unglamorous forms of legal practice, is a route of upward mobility for the children of the skilled and semi-skilled working class, of minor entrepreneurs, salaried professionals and middle-management personnel (Cf. Ladinsky, 1963; Wood, 1967; Carlin, 1962). About 90 percent of the grandparents of PDO lawyers were born in Europe; their parents, as children of immigrants, were modestly successful in economic terms, though less than one-third of their fathers completed college education. With one or two exceptions, their parents did not accumulate any significant wealth and the PDO lawyers were required to either work their way through college or support themselves with the help of the GI bill and other kinds of loans.

In terms of religious, educational and political background, PDO lawyers are comparable to lawyers in other public defender offices but differ in many important respects from their adversaries in the District Attorney's Office. A minority of public defenders was brought up as Protestants or related religions (41%), while the remainder came from Catholic (20%), Jewish (20%) and agnostic (19%) families. About 37 percent of the PDO attorneys were educated in high-ranking state university law schools and the rest were distributed through a variety of modest and low-ranking state and city law schools. Close to 50 percent finished in the top third of their law school classes, while over 10 percent finished in the lower third.

In terms of political affiliation, PDO lawyers are for the most part liberals. Until 1969, only 20 percent of the PDO lawyers were registered as Republicans; between 1969 and 1971, this declined to approximately 11 percent. Democrats presently account for about 68 percent (an increase of about 12 percent since 1969) and 16 percent identify themselves as Independents and to the political left of the Democratic party. The left-liberal ideology of PDO lawyers is further reflected in their membership in organizations like the ACLU, the Lawyers Guild, and various anti-war groups. A small group of Assistants also worked in the Peace and Freedom Party, supporting Robert Scheer's Senate campaign.

Between 1927 and 1971, there were one black and seven women lawyers in the PDO. This is a reflection of institutionalized racism and sexism in the legal profession (1 percent of the national bar is black and 3 percent women), as well as in the specific programs of government and industry in Alameda county.[8] As

---

[8] As of 1966, there were 4,164 judges and lawyers in Oakland, of which only 1.3 percent were blacks. See Hayes (1972, p. 51).

of 1971, there was no affirmative action policy in the PDO, and the legal problems of the white and Third World poor continued to be handled for the most part by white men who received their training in an educational system based on class and caste privileges.[9] The present Chief Public Defender intends to continue these policies:

My own personal prejudices are opposed to the selection of anyone on the basis of race. I neither favor it or am against it. . . . I would like to have about 3 or 4 women on the staff. . . . There are cases where it is better balanced and better theory and actually more realistic practice to use a woman. They have defects too—they can't get into jails, they can't be locked up in interview rooms with some of the people. . . . So if we had too great a percentage of them, we would lose flexibility in some of these areas [Interview #19].

The Alameda county PDO recruits its lawyers from persons with varied working and middle-class white backgrounds, more typically from non-Protestant families, with liberal political affiliations and an education in state or city law schools. A comparable study of forty-five lawyers who worked in Cook County's PDO between 1930 and 1967 revealed a similar profile: forty-one whites, five blacks; twenty-five Catholics, twelve Jews; twenty-six attended local law schools; and the overwhelming majority were registered Democrats and came from working-class backgrounds (Platt, 1968).

Lawyers in Alameda County District Attorney's Office, however, differ from attorneys in the PDO in several important ways. A study of over 150 attorneys who worked in the District Attorney's Office between 1926 and 1969 indicated that they are predominantly Republicans (at least 64%), more likely to have Catholic backgrounds (36%), 71 percent came from middle and upper-middle class families, and many were active in athletics or social clubs while in college. During this forty-three-year period, there were only four Jews, five women and three blacks in the District Attorney's Office (Tanguay, 1967, chapter 1).

These differences in social-economic background confirm the well-established fact that organizations regularly use informal criteria, such as class background and political affiliation, in addition to technical competence when assessing the reliability of potential recruits (Becker & Strauss, 1956). The distinctions between the two offices also indicate that the PDO does not try to compete with corporate law firms or the District Attorney's Office in trying to recruit more conservative lawyers trained in elite law schools who are potential partners in business law firms or career politicians. Rather the PDO seeks lawyers interested in civil service careers or preparing for extensive trial work. In this respect, it plays an important role in channeling lawyers into careers consistent with their class background and with the demands of the legal marketplace.

---

[9] As a major study of legal careers concluded, "in its attraction and appeal to young people the law seems to do its fishing in restricted waters stocked largely with the product of professional families, private schools, and the upper social strata" (Warkov & Zelan, 1965).

Although there are significant differences in the social upbringing of public defenders and prosecutors, there are also several similarities which suggest that recruitment is based on more complex factors than simply economic or religious background. Ralph Miliband has pointed out that the recruitment of civil servants in advanced capitalist countries is "no longer in the main determined on the basis of social provenance or religious affiliation" (Miliband, 1969, p. 123). And Gabriel Kolko similarly concluded in a study of federal executives that "there is no evidence whatsoever to prove that social and educational origins determine policies of state" (Kolko, 1969, pp. 14-15). Social background is an important indicator of potential performance but it is certainly not an assurance of reliability and ideological soundness, as the "Vietnam incident" clearly demonstrated. For this reason, PDO administrators make every effort to recruit Assistants who are ideologically prepared to follow their leadership, to accept existing regulations in the Office, and to subordinate any personal idiosyncracies to the prevailing administrative consensus. During their interviews for jobs in the PDO, applicants are clearly told what is expected of them:

When I came into the Office, (the Public Defender) indicated that this was not an ACLU office. . . . He said we were here to make the system work in the best way possible. . . . We were not necessarily engaged in the process of advocating major social change through the processes of the Office itself [Interview #45].

It was the only interview I ever had in my life where it took 20 minutes to tell me what was *wrong* with the job. (The Public Defender) had the view that he didn't want people coming in naively and he made it a point to tell me what was wrong with the Office . . . [Interview #57].

The people in the Office who interviewed me were very explicit in telling me that, 'We represent cases not causes.' . . . They sort of hold their breath and hire you and try to caution you and hope that you turn out not to be a troublemaker [Interview #52].

Motivation and Aspiration

Recruitment is a process of interaction. While the employer holds the power of evaluating various formal and informal criteria of assessment, the potential employee is also a participant in the recruitment process and his demeanor, intentions and credentials influence the chances of employment. For the overwhelming majority of recruits, the PDO serves as the initial step in a consciously selected career. For most it is the first job involving criminal trial work, a specialized form of practice which prepares lawyers not only for general practice but for most specialities involving extensive *trial* work. Lawyers entering the PDO typically understand that this choice is the beginning of a specialized legal career.

This is a fairly recent phenomenon, dating back to the expansion of the legal profession in the 1950s. Previously, lawyers entering the PDO were glad to get a job, any job, because it was a matter of "making a living in those days"

(Interview #38). Career lines and long-range planning were not entertained because the legal marketplace was unstable and unpredictable. As one lawyer who left the PDO in 1946 commented, "I am a child of the great depression and it's only in the last few years that I've really been able to feel that when one loses one's job this is not necessarily the end of the world . . . " (Interview #15).

During the last fifteen to twenty years, ideological preference has played an important role in the selection of legal careers. Before 1960, a considerable number of lawyers applied for jobs in both District Attorney and Public Defender Offices, regarding them as equally capable of providing technical training. The two offices were not regarded as morally or politically antagonistic. This attitude started to change in the late 1950s, and by the early 1960s young attorneys expressed an ideological preference for the PDO:

I don't have a DA personality. I am, for example, diametrically opposed to the death penalty, and if you're going to be a DA that's a built-in limitation [Interview #39].

I wanted to do trial work and I wanted to help people whom I considered to be deprived and underprivileged, and it seemed to me that the P.D.'s Office was the avenue to go into [Interview #29].

I did not wish to work for a D.A.'s Office particularly because at that time I identified very strongly with the oppressed and downtrodden [Interview #15].

I think my whole inclination at that point was connected to my theological background and I was just upset, I think, with the law and I didn't think that people should pay for legal services . . . [Interview #44].

These attitudes are typically held by most potential Assistants in the PDO on the grounds that they are "not inclined to prosecution," "not prosecution-minded," or are "opposed to the death penalty."

But ideology is *not* the essential issue in job preference. The majority of applicants seek out a job in the PDO in order to get trial experience in preparation for a future career in private practice. This aspiration can be expressed crudely—"I was there just to sort of rape the Office of experience and to go out and become a criminal law attorney" (Interview #24)—or in more professional terms:

I think this (PDO) is a good training ground for a reservoir of skilled criminal lawyers who can go out and practice and participate as members of the private bar in the practice of criminal law [Interview #36].

Most applicants want a technical and professional apprenticeship in an Office which does not violate their moral and political beliefs:

I don't like prosecuting. I'd much rather defend . . . I don't think you get very good training as a prosecutor. You don't really learn how to try a case as a prosecutor because you never learn how to cross-examine. Prosecutors don't have as much opportunity to cross-examine [Interview #25].

Prosecution is regarded as a comparatively simple job, given the high number of guilty pleas, the investigative and political support of the police, and the anti-defendant perspective of most judges and juries. Aspiring trial lawyers argue that the PDO is a better place to sharpen one's wits and master informal strategies as well as develop technical competence. This view is reflected in the comments of two Assistants who worked in both a PD and DA Office:

It's easy to be a DA—and I was one for a few short months—because you've got all the facts on your side and generally all you have to do is ask a few simple questions and let the witnesses answer and you've got the case won. The only way you ever won a case on the defense side is through some generally very imaginative work because all the cards are stacked against you. The type of odds you have as PD breeds more imaginative thinking and more confidence as a trial lawyer . . . [Interview #28].

I don't enjoy (prosecution) work as much; it's not as challenging. It's more cut and dried. You don't have to use your imagination. You're served your case on a silver platter literally and all you have to do is serve it up. What the PD has to do is take an extraordinarily weak case and fabricate out a whole cloth, as it were, to give himself a reasonable defense. Not 'fabricating,' mind you, but using imagination to take weak points and trying to deal with them [Interview #36].

Prior to 1960, some lawyers entering the PDO were not certain about their career plans and regarded the Office as a place to evaluate different possibilities, including a civil service career in a PDO. "I didn't enter the Office," said one ex-Assistant, "with the specific expectation of staying there two years and then leaving. That was not clear in my mind as I think it was clear in other people's minds. I came in with the idea if I liked the work I would have no reason to leave and might stay a considerable period of time" (Interview #52). Those who are uncertain about their careers quickly learn from their colleagues that opportunities for promotion and success within the PDO are limited and that most intend to leave after they have accumulated sufficient experience, contacts and technical expertise. The official policy of the PDO recognizes and legitimizes the temporary commitment of its recruits. According to the present Chief PD:

If they want to learn all there is to learn about the practical application of trial work or the rules of evidence and then they want to go out and progress into the other fields of trial work, I have no objection to it. . . . I would ask that they (Assistants) give me at least two years of their time. But apart from that I assume we're lucky to keep them and I assume that they're free to go. . . . Once you become a trial lawyer in this Office, you're probably as good after two years as about 85-90% of the trial attorneys in the area. You will have had as many trials as the average practitioner has in his lifetime [Interview #19].

The majority of lawyers entering the PDO view their experience as a form of technical and professional apprenticeship, a means for developing informal contacts in the private bar and exploring various job possibilities. In this sense, the PDO is not unlike other public organizations (hospitals and welfare agencies, for example) which perform training services for the private sector and are faced with a constant turnover of personnel.[10] PDO lawyers are, to use Alvin Gouldner's distinction, typically "cosmopolitans" rather than "locals" because their commitment to a professional career transcends their loyalty to the organization (Gouldner, 1957, pp. 446-467). While the PDO is *formally* concerned about recruiting lawyers interested in and committed to a life-time of public service, it is informally and openly recognized that the Office cannot expect to keep most of its Assistants beyond two or three years. There are obvious organizational disadvantages with this policy: the need for an ongoing training program, the loss of specially skilled personnel, and the inability to develop esprit de corps. But there are also considerable advantages: the rapid turnover prevents Assistants from developing an effective organization vis-à-vis Administrators; recruits are more dependent and more easily managed; and the PDO achieves some legitimacy with the Board of Supervisors and Bar Associations as a service and training center for the private bar.

While most Assistants regard their commitment to the PDO as temporary and instrumental, we do not intend to imply that these lawyers are merely opportunists who use the Office as a vehicle to advance their own careers and narrow self-interest. Many Assistants are motivated by a genuine concern for the lives and problems of poor defendants; many attempt to reconcile their professional aspirations with their moral and political beliefs; and others are unclear about their career plans and regard the PDO as an opportunity to explore different job possibilities. This is strikingly different from public defenders in Cook County, many of whom regard a job in the PDO as second-best to a job in the District Attorney's Office and as an instrumentality for advancing their careers.[11]

Lawyers who begin their legal careers in Alameda County District Attorney's Office do it for comparable reasons to their counterparts in the PDO. For the majority, it is regarded as an opportunity to learn technical skills, to gain extensive trial practice, to become visible and accessible to the job market, and to develop contacts which might be useful to their careers. Their choice of the District Attorney's Office as opposed to the PDO is motivated partly by ideological reasons but more importantly by aspirations for a political career or a job in an elite law firm (Tanguay, 1967, chapter 2). But lawyers in both offices are in basic agreement on one point: despite variations in motivations and aspirations, very few plan to pursue careers as civil servants.

---

[10] For an overview of related studies, see Becker and Strauss (1956).

[11] Between 1930 and 1967, 16 out of a total of 45 public defenders left Cook County's PDO to join the District Attorney's Office.

Staying and Leaving

Career Public Defenders

Very few lawyers in the PDO become career public servants. Of the sixty-four attorneys in the Office between 1927 and 1969, only eight made a career out of the job—four as Chief Public Defenders in Alameda County and four in public defender offices in other counties. Of the fifty-eight attorneys employed in the PDO as of May 1971, only five claimed that they seriously intended to remain in the Office as a career. Similar findings were reported in studies of the District Attorney's Office and Cook County's PDO (Tanguay, 1967; Platt, 1968).

To develop a successful career in the PDO requires a great deal of patience, persistence and luck. The pyramid structure of the PDO bureaucracy makes it almost impossible for a recruit to reasonably anticipate promotion to Chief Public Defender. In the last forty-four years, there have only been five Chief Public Defenders in Alameda and one of these was recruited from the District Attorney's Office. Appointment as Chief Public Defender requires the support of the Board of Supervisors and the District Attorney's Office, as well as several years of trial and administrative experience. Some Assistants hope to achieve the position of Chief PD in other counties, but this also requires informal sponsorship from judges or District Attorneys and the competition for these positions is intense and often unpredictable. Many Assistants who enter the Office with the intention of making it their career quickly change their minds when they assess their chances of promotion. "I didn't think," said one ex-Assistant, "that I wanted to spend the rest of my life as 'the number three man in the Public Defender Office'" (Interview #23).

Those who stay in the PDO do so for a variety of reasons. Some claim that the job is more secure and exciting than private practice. "What I think keeps me here," says an Assistant, "is the sense of great challenge and the sense of ingenuity that's able to be used" (Interview #53). Some prefer a salaried job to the unpredictable income and demeaning aspects of fee collecting in private practice; others enjoy constant trial work and argue that "private lawyers do not have as much of a need to be in court . . . " (Interview #47).

Becoming a career public defender is not so much a positive choice as it is a process of attrition and inevitability. For the Assistant who neither wants nor is capable of successful private practice in criminal or general practice, there are very few options. The cautious civil servant is not likely to be attracted to the economically precarious existence of solo practice[12] and established law firms are not usually interested in recruiting older Assistants who have forsaken trial work for administrative duties. Upward mobility in the PDO, therefore, may be a consequence of failing to leave the office "at the right time" or to be recruited into a law firm.[13]

---

[12] On the organization and conditions of solo practice, see Carlin (1962).

[13] For similar observations about the mobility of teachers and lawyers, see Howard S. Becker (1952, pp. 470-477) and Erwin O. Smigel (1964, pp. 74-85).

Failure to leave the Office, however, does not guarantee successful promotion. Organizational success, as C. Wright Mills observed, is a "series of small calculations, stretched over the working lifetime of the individual: a bureaucracy is no testing field for heroes." Promotion depends on "agility rather than ability, on 'getting along' in a context of associates, superiors, and rules," and "on loyalty to, or even identity with, one's own firm, rather than entrepreneurial virtuosity" (Mills, 1956, p. 263). It is not surprising, then, that Chief Public Defenders are not charismatic leaders but rather cautious bureaucrats who "don't make waves" and will "do anything to keep people from being mad, which means doing nothing" (Interview #25). The career Public Defender rejects the entrepreneurial ethos of private practice and pursues the gradual accumulation of power and responsibility through hard work, patience and diplomacy. Most Assistants, however, regard the "occupational climb" as psychologically draining and economically limited, preferring instead to take their chances in the "open market" of private practice.

Burning Out

Most Assistants only stay in the PDO long enough to complete their apprenticeship and become qualified for private practice. Prior to 1960, the median length of stay in the Office was 4.75 years; from 1960 to 1968, the median dropped to 2.5 years. Similarly, lawyers in Cook County's PDO (1930-67) stayed for a median of 3.0 years and in the District Attorney's Office (1926-70) for about 4.0 years. Fluctuations in the length of stay are primarily determined by the availability of jobs in the legal marketplace.[14]

There are several reasons for leaving the PDO: some are fired or "cooled out" for inefficiency or unprofessional conduct; some are recruited into better paying jobs in private law firms; some seek the independence and challenge of solo practice; and some become disillusioned and jaded. Most Assistants leave for more than one reason, typically a combination of an opportunity in private practice and disenchantment with the PDO. Assistants refer to the latter process as "burning out."

Many young lawyers enter the PDO with confused liberal commitments, rather broad notions about how they can contribute to changing the world, and enormous amounts of energy and optimism. By the time they leave the Office, their idealism has developed into cynical pragmatism, resulting from the realities of professional practice.[15] The following comments typify the attitudes of the majority of Assistants:

---

[14] For example, the present economic crisis has increased the length of stay in Alameda County's PDO, though most Assistants are ready to move on after two years.

[15] For a comparable study of medical students, see Howard S. Becker and Blanche Geer (1958, pp. 50-56).

The public defenders are steeped in a tradition where you don't win things, where you lose everything, where you're constantly demoralized and where the DA's always on top [Interview #9].

I was becoming callous. . . . I tried I don't know how many death penalty cases in the last two years. Well, a fellow just can't keep trying that kind of case without either losing his mind or becoming somewhat callous. . . . When I found that happening I became dissatisfied with the business and decided to get out of it [Interview #13].

In about two and a half years I felt a certain routine setting in. . . . There's just so many ways you can commit a burglary and just so many ways you can commit a robbery. And these things boil down to the same cross-examination for the purpose of shaking an identification witness. . . . I felt that I was getting too hardened and I wasn't going to be able to do the kind of job that I should be able to do. . . . You're burned out, you know, you've done it. You give an awful lot and you get damn little, except pretty good pay and at some point you just poop out [Interview #44].

The realities of the PDO differ dramatically from formal descriptions of criminal courts portrayed in law school. Law students do not expect to be "bucking a stacked deck all the time" (Interview #12); nor do they view themselves as potential "salesmen" required to "get along with people you don't like" (Interview #56). After a short time in the PDO, however, Assistants learn to "never become personally involved in cases," to "build a shield around yourself," and to develop "professional detachment" (Interviews #7, 12, and 56).

The duties of lawyers in the PDO are time-consuming, technical and specialized. They include determining the economic eligibility of clients, conducting pre-trial investigations, interviewing witnesses, negotiating pleas and sentences with prosecutors, defending persons charged with everything from traffic offenses to murder, preparing sentencing reports, writing appeal briefs, and doing public relations and community speaking. These tasks have become bureaucratically organized and specialized according to function so that Assistants rarely handle a client's case from beginning to end. In addition, the cooperative ethic of the criminal courts requires an attitude of accommodation and willingness to work harmoniously with different actors in the system (Skolnick, 1967, pp. 52-70). According to a former Chief District Attorney, the ideal temperament required of persons working in the criminal courts is stability:

I didn't want any oddballs or queers or eccentrics, you see. I wanted somebody that's well-rounded. That's why I didn't pay too much attention whether they were phi betas or Coif or law review because sometimes these brilliant guys can be awfully odd. They can be oddballs and give you trouble. . . . Stability was very important—yes, stability, working with others, and getting along with other people.

This view is reciprocated by an ex-Chief Public Defender who characterized his Assistants by their "ability to be practical and to compromise."

The realities of the job—mechanical processing of cases, lack of adequate resources and time for proper research and pretrial investigation, the availability of extensive resources (for example, the police) to the District Attorney's Office, and the prosecutorial bias of judges—not only cultivate an attitude of cynicism to the job but also to clients. Occasionally, this cynicism develops into explicit animosity and prejudice:

What makes the job difficult for public defenders is the clients. . . . The fact of the matter is that you're dealing with the scum of the earth and they'll stab you in the back at the first opportunity. They'll walk over you and anybody else to get what they want. They're one cut above the animal—in fact, they're by and large worse. . . . They're just the lowest of the low. . . . Oddly enough, I wasn't bothered by the clients any more than a scientist in a lab dealing with extremely dangerous virus is bothered by virulents. He's careful because he recognizes that if you're dealing with bubonic plague, you're very careful how you handle it . . . [Interview #21].

An ex-Public Defender similarly described his experience in the Office as a "voyage through a sewer in a glass-bottomed boat," while an ex-Assistant classified some of his clients as the "great unwashed" and observed that "most colored people just scream and yell" (Interviews #27 and 42).

This kind of explicit prejudice is rare among ex-Assistants; typically, their hostility is implicit and ambivalent, reflecting feelings of guilt about the betrayal of their original liberal idealism:

About the time I was getting ready to leave, I'd almost figured I was as eager to prosecute my client as I was to defend him. I think that's psychologically the time when you've got to get out of that sort of situation. . . . I got disillusioned [Interview #15].

I started out with some kind of avenging zeal to protect these people who'd been ensnared in the clutches of the law. And I grew progressively sourer and had progressively less patience with them as I stayed there, and it finally got so that my animosities for them were very thinly disguised. I just didn't like them by and large. Nobody else liked them either really, but some of them were a little more patient finally than I became . . . [Interview #20].

Various Assistants claim that their clients lie, are sullen and distrustful, and are ungrateful. As one Assistant reflected, "in all the cases I handled in the Public Defender's Office, even if I won a fantastic victory, the defendant never said 'thank you' " (Interview #40). Given their inaccurate expectations of the job, it is not surprising that Assistants become "less sympathetic the longer they've been on the job. They've seen more; they've been burned more times" (Interview #52).

Most Assistants report that they develop an immunity to the job and become somewhat callous. "The job is like a doctor's job. After a while a doctor gets tired of seeing forty people a day with colds. He tells them to take aspirins, drink juice and go to bed. What else can you do?" (Interview #52). An ex-Assistant, now working in another PDO, also found the medical analogy appropriate:

Public Defender work is an ordinary mundane thing. It's patching up people in the first-aid sense.... It's something like being in an emergency ward all the time. There's nothing but emergencies. You try to help a lot of people who come in that front door and patch up the big gaping holes that they all have in them, but you don't really ... make a great medical finding ... [Interview #48].

By the time Assistants are ready to leave the PDO, many are embittered, cynical and burned out. This process partly derives from the failure of law schools to properly prepare students for professional realities; and this is reinforced on the job when Assistants learn that "success" is characterized by an ability to be accommodating, manipulative and pragmatic. The emphasis on mass processing of cases, technical virtuosity and salesmanship, which characterizes the PDO, is interpreted by most Assistants as an indication of the hopelessness and inevitability of the situation. The experience in the PDO is generally an embittering rather than radicalizing process, for Assistants leave the Office with an attitude of futility and defeatism about the possibility of making major changes in society.[16]

Leaving

While most Assistants voluntarily leave the PDO because they are burned out and have better opportunities in private practice, a small minority is "forced to resign" or "cooled out." This group ranges from persons accused of immoral behavior (drug use, alcoholism, etc.) to those considered inefficient or technically incompetent. The former is considered a liability to the PDO because they are likely to generate public scandals or incur charges of professional misconduct. Given the vulnerability of the PDO to criticism from the local Board of Supervisors and the media, the "heavy drinker" and "known drug user" are encouraged to leave the Office rather than risk exposure or prosecution.

"Inefficiency" is broadly defined to include inappropriate etiquette (too long hair, an untrimmed moustache, flashy clothes, etc.), poor judgment and demeanor (overly aggressive behavior in court, abrasive relationships with judges and prosecutors, etc.), and even "sentimentality" defined according to sexist

[16] By contrast, ex-prosecutors in Alameda County generally report that their experiences in the District Attorney's Office conform to their expectations and ideology.

standards (one lawyer was encouraged to leave because she "handled every case like it was Leopold and Loeb"). Assistants who are unable to remain personable and cooperative while processing large numbers of cases are liable to the charge of "inefficiency":

She wasn't a good PD in the sense that she couldn't handle volume. She just wasn't willing to handle cases on a volume basis. She wanted to act like a private lawyer and the Office couldn't afford to give her that much time. . . . [Assistant C.] didn't make a very good appearance in court. He was a nice-looking guy but he looked slow and talked rather hesitantly, and he wasn't aggressive enough to make him sound good. He got a couple of bad reviews from judges and they just very summarily got rid of him [Interview #25].

There are several options open to an organization that wants to remove or neutralize an employee who is considered inefficient or "unsuitable." He can be fired, or moved laterally within the organization, or demoted, or even promoted to an honorific but essentially powerless position (Levenson, 1961, pp. 362-375). In the PDO, as in most formal organizations, employees are rarely fired but rather "encouraged to leave":

I can never remember a person being outwardly fired. A couple of people were told they wouldn't be suitable for PD's. Saying 'Your're fired'—they don't do that. It's too dangerous, there may be a hearing later or something . . . [Interview #52].

The Office said, 'You're never going to be happy here because you believe in justice for everyone and we can't do that.' . . . He (Public Defender) told me five months before I left that he thought I wasn't going to be happy there, that it wasn't suited for my personality and that I should think about looking elsewhere for a job [Interview #16].

He wasn't told to leave the day after tomorrow or anything like that. He was given to understand that it would be in everybody's interests if he looked elsewhere for a job [Interview #39].

This pressure to leave is invariably successful because Assistants cannot risk getting bad references for future jobs. Moreover, if they refuse to resign, Office administrators can informally punish them by, for example, holding up pay increases or assigning them to less interesting duties in municipal or juvenile court. The reluctance of the Office to explicitly fire wayward employees stems from a desire to maintain organizational integrity and avoid bad publicity. As Edwin Lemert has observed in more general terms:

Even when the person is almost totally excluded and informally isolated within an organization, he may have power outside. This weighs heavily when the external power can be invoked in some way, or when it automatically leads to raising questions as to the internal workings of the organization. This touches upon the more salient reason for reluctance to eject an uncooperative and retaliatory person, even when he is relatively unimportant to the organization.

We refer to a kind of negative power derived from the vulnerability of organizations to unfavorable publicity and exposure of their private lives that are likely if the crisis proceeds to formal hearings, case review, or litigation (Lemert, 1967, p. 204).

The majority of Assistants, however, leave voluntarily and with the reluctant approval of administrators who have become used to seeing trained personnel leave for more lucrative jobs in private practice.

The Careers of Ex-Assistants

With the exception of a small group of tired and disillusioned "drop-outs" who turned to art, poetry, teaching, missionary work, yoga and travel, the majority of Assistants was recruited into small to medium-size general practice firms in the local area. After two or three years, most Assistants are ready to leave the PDO in search of greater professional autonomy and more money. "The thing is," said an ex-Assistant now specializing in criminal practice, "that it gets to a point where you get so competent that you really want to be your own man" (Interview #9). Another typical ex-Assistant said that he left the PDO because "I felt I'd had enough of it. I wanted to try private practice. My wife was going to have a baby and I was afraid that if I got locked in on a civil service salary after having a child, it would be harder to get out" (Interview #34).

The "criminal bar" in Alameda, as in most counties, is small and its participants know each other and maintain informal ties through contact in the courts, client referrals, and occasional social activities (Skolnick, 1967). General practice lawyers do a considerable amount of criminal work and they are able to do first-hand evaluations of Assistants when they are defending a "crime partner" of a client of the PDO. They also have many opportunities to observe Assistants while waiting for their own cases to be called. It is within this informal context that assistants become familiar with the legal marketplace and are eventually recruited into private practice.

About one-third of the ex-Assistants entered specialized practices—usually criminal or personal injury work. The remainder, with a few exceptions, entered general practices involving criminal, family, personal injury, probate and other routine kinds of law. The kind of law practice in which ex-Assistants work ranges from solo practice (about 28%) to medium-sized partnerships or associateships (about 45%). Ex-Assistants are not to be found in large firms practicing business or corporate law. Their annual incomes, which are typical of general practitioners involved in volume business and "small fee" cases, range from under $20,000 (about 35%) to over $30,000 (about 8%). In this respect, ex-Assistants in Alameda county are very similar to criminal lawyers and general practitioners in Detroit and New York who went directly into private practice from law school (Ladinsky, 1963; Carlin, 1962).

By contrast, ex-prosecutors from Alameda county are less likely to go into criminal law practice (13%) and more likely to go into personal injury (26%) and corporate law practice (26%). Forty percent of ex-prosecutors (compared with 13 percent of all attorneys nationally) became partners in law firms, while only 14 percent (compared with 80 percent of all attorneys nationally) are in solo practice or salaried associates. Differences between ex-public defenders and ex-prosecutors are most clearly demonstrated in income levels: 39 percent of ex-prosecutors earn between $20,000 and $40,000 annually, while another 15 percent earn between $40,000 and $60,000.

Very few ex-Assistants from the PDO participated in local politics. One became a member of the Oakland city council and four were eventually rewarded with judgeships (three in municipal and one in superior court). The PDO, unlike the District Attorney's Office, is not a route into local or state politics. It even may count against lawyers with political aspirations because of its negative associations with "charity" law and "defense of criminals." On the other hand, most Assistants are not interested in political careers and prefer, as Jack Ladinsky (1963) has observed of solo lawyers in Detroit, to test their entrepreneurial and technical skills in the highly competitive marketplace of general practice.

Ex-prosecutors, who are generally more interested in pursuing political careers, discover that the District Attorney's Office is not only a good place to make contacts but also serves as a certifier of their technical competence and ideological reliability. Twenty-two percent of ex-prosecutors moved on to jobs in state and federal prosecuting agencies, federal legislation, and state legislative and executive bodies. In addition, another 10 percent became judges in courts ranging from local municipal court to the United States Supreme Court (Tanguay, 1967, chapter 4).

While ex-prosecutors leave the District Attorney's Office to become the functionaries of economic and political elites, ex-Assistants usually remain in general practice and discover that they have exchanged old problems—excessive caseloads, limited resources, bureaucratic inflexibility, ungrateful clients, etc.—for new burdens and crises—competing for clients with lay organizations (accountants, insurance agencies, real estate companies, savings and loan associations, etc.), collecting fees, rising overhead costs, and long hours of work. The only way out of this channel is to try to cross over into another profession like teaching, or to drop out of professional work completely. The former requires enormous discipline and conviction, while the latter demands the total reversal of some thirty years of socialization.

Summary and Conclusions

In this essay, we have followed the careers of lawyers who spent some time in a Public Defender's Office in the years between 1927 and 1971. The Office has considerably changed and grown during this period, beginning as a very small and part-time operation in the 1920s, gradually becoming more stable and respectable during the 1950s, and emerging in the late 1960s as a medium-sized bureaucracy characterized by a hierarchial division of labor and a formal apparatus of recruitment, training and promotion.

During the 1950s, the background, motivation and careers of ex-Assistants began to follow a general pattern. Most recruits were male, white, from working and lower-middle class origins, and with non-Protestant and liberal political backgrounds. Typical new Assistants regarded the PDO as a place to develop technical skills and professional values in an atmosphere which would not violate their liberal political principles. Very few Assistants planned to make a career in the PDO and only a small minority remained as career civil servants. Their decision to remain was typically motivated by either an unwillingness or inability to successfully compete in the marketplace of private practice rather than by a positive commitment to a public service career. Most lawyers, however, left the PDO after an average of two and a half years, feeling "burned out" and often embittered by the realities of professional practice in a public office. While a few Assistants were cooled out and encouraged to leave, the majority left voluntarily to continue their legal careers locally in solo to medium-sized private firms.

While this study provides a clearer understanding of specific legal careers, it also raised more general questions about the relationship between the State, the legal profession and public service. The PDO is an example of how the State subsidizes the apprenticeship and training of professionals who in the final analysis devote themselves to the practice of law for profit. It is through the PDO that young lawyers are professionally socialized and introduced to the legal marketplace. As in other public institutions—notably county hospitals, welfare departments and ghetto high schools—the clients of the PDO are poor, powerless and disproportionately Third World. After lawyers in the PDO have completed their apprenticeship and refined their technical skills, they generally leave the PDO to enter private practice and defend predominantly middle-class clients.

This analysis, however, does not imply that lawyers join the PDO with the intention of instrumentally exploiting poor clients in order to develop profitable skills. On the contrary, most recruits are ideologically liberal, conceive of their work in humanitarian terms, and initially undertake their work with enthusiasm and optimism. Pragmatism and cynicism are not motivating factors for joining the PDO but instead gradually develop as a consequence of working there. The PDO is generally a disillusioning experience for young lawyers who at one time considered devoting themselves to public service careers.

Rather than becoming radicalized by their experience in the PDO, most Assistants became embittered and alienated from political action. Malaise rather than rebellion characterized their frustrations.[17] This occurs for several reasons. First, the lack of a proper education about the nature and role of legal

[17] For more general comments on this process, see Il Manifesto (1972, pp. 78-81).

institutions in society lays the grounds for the development of cynicism. With the exception of the National Lawyers Guild, law students are not exposed to an analysis of the political economy of law or to other models of professional practice which might allow them to combine a reasonable salary with public service. Secondly, by the time they leave the PDO, they are usually married, have children and have become accustomed to a comfortable life style. Their life style and financial responsibilities make it difficult to take risks in a different kind of occupation or even to make radical changes within the legal profession. And finally, the emphasis on technical virtuosity and professionalism, which characterizes the socialization process in the PDO, serves to reduce political consciousness and increase social distance from oppressed groups (Miliband, 1969, pp. 119-145). This last point needs further elaboration.

Lawyers in the PDO occupy an ambiguous position in the labor force and society comparable to scientists, technicians, engineers and other professionals. While they are an occupationally privileged group by virtue of their education, training and income, at the same time they have no independent access to productive property and minimum control over the conditions of their work. Though their life-styles are "middle-class," they are also part of a "new working class of educated labor necessitated by the increasingly technological and scientific character of the process of production" (Marcuse, 1971, 1972, p. 3). As State workers performing unglamorous and professionally unrewarding work, public defenders are subject to additional exploitation and indignity.

Compared with most workers, Assistants possess a relative degree of control over their work. But their autonomy is tolerated only so long as it does not violate the operating conditions of the PDO. The illusion of autonomy is maintained through constant reference to "professional discretion" (Il Manifesto, 1972, p. 71). Control of Assistants, however, is maintained by the hierarchy of bureaucratic power and by the division of labor into technically disconnected roles. The former provides a mechanism for maintaining compliance with organizational goals, while the latter assures that Assistants are "inserted into a microcosm that allows them no overall view" (Il Manifesto, 1972, p. 73).

According to this case study of a relatively enlightened county, public defenders do not as a rule examine the source and conditions of their own exploitation as workers. Rather they see themselves as enlightened and privileged professionals who, as James Weinstein has similarly observed of the student movement, tend to neglect their own grievances and "relate to the under-classes only through feelings of guilt and liberal missionary politics" (Weinstein, 1972, p. 49). The relationship of public defenders to their clients is, at its best, one of benevolent service, sustained by an ideology which emphasizes political neutrality, efficiency, and technocratic rationality (Gorz, 1964, pp. 120-125). Many Assistants become aware that their work primarily consists of ameliorism and band-aid reform. They even acknowledge that the solution to "crime" lies in the economic and political transformation of society. But these are seen as "problems" to be solved in another context and by other persons, while Assistants adapt to their role as inevitable and "realistic." They come to justify their role as mediators between the poor and the courts, resigned to seeking occasional loopholes in the system, softening its more explicitly repressive features, and attempting to rescue the victims of blatant injustices. But even this makeshift effort to link everyday work with liberal humanitarianism proves inadequate, since most Assistants are regarded with resentment, ingratitude or indifference by their clients. When they leave the PDO, they have become cynical and embittered, alienated from politics, and preoccupied with problems of survival and success in the legal marketplace.

The process we have described is not, of course, unique to public defenders. Neal Shover (1972) has reported on the routine development of cynicism in correctional workers, Arthur Niederhoffer (1967) on comparable traits in police officers, and Abraham Blumberg's study (1967, p. 158) of probation officers concluded that "frustrated as professionals, stripped of real decision-making power, lacking a genuine career motif, and assigned relatively low status by the community, it is not surprising that (they) often develop a high degree of cynicism."

The basic solution to these problems does not lie in more training, better facilities, more money,[18] or even recruitment of more women and Third World professionals. As recent studies have indicated, the recruitment of black probation officers and police officers makes little difference to the treatment received by oppressed groups and even tends to increase the marginality, isolation and cynicism of Third World professionals (Blumberg, 1967, chapter 7; Alex, 1969). So long as the criminal justice system is used as an instrument of class and racial exploitation, its employees cannot expect to resolve the contradictions inherent in their role as servants of the state. The solution to the cynicism and disillusionment of public defenders lies not only in devising new ways of offering their service to the victims of oppression, but also in contesting the fragmentation, meaninglessness and exploitation of their own work.

References

Alex, N. *Black in blue: A study of the negro policeman.* New York: Appleton, 1969.

American Bar Foundation. *The administration of criminal justice in the United States.* Chicago: American Bar Foundation, 1955.

Becker, H.S. "The career of the Chicago public school teacher." *American Journal of Sociology*, 1952, *57*, 470-477.

[18] As suggested, for example, by the President's Commission (1967) and Howard James (1972).

Becker, H.S., & Geer, B. "The fate of idealism in medical school." *American Sociological Review*, 1958, *23*, 50-56.

Becker, H.S., & Strauss, A.L. "Careers, personality, and adult socialization." *American Journal of Sociology*, 1956, *62*, 253-263.

Blumberg, A. *Criminal justice*. Chicago: Quadrangle Books, 1967.

Carlin, J. *Lawyers on their own*. New Brunswick, N.J.: Rutgers University Press, 1962.

Carr-Saunders, A.M., & Wilson, P.A. *The professions*. Oxford: Clarendon Press, 1933.

Casper, D. "Did you have a lawyer when you went to court? No, I had a public defender." *Law and Social Action*, 1971, *1*, 4-9.

Gintis, H. "The new working class and revolutionary youth." *Socialist Revolution*, 1970, *3*, 13-43.

Gorz, A. *Strategy for labor*. Boston: Beacon Press, 1964.

Gorz, A. "Technical intelligence and the capitalist division of labor." *Telos*, 1972, *12*, 27-41.

Gouldner, A.W. "Cosmopolitans and locals." *Administrative Science Quarterly*, 1957, *2*, 446-467.

Hayes, E.C. *Power structure and urban policy: Who rules in Oakland?* New York: McGraw-Hill, 1972.

Hughes, E.C. *Men and their work*. New York: Free Press, 1959.

Il Manifesto. "Technicians and the capitalist division of labor." *Socialist Revolution*, 1972, *9*, 65-84.

Ivens, C.P. *Office of the public defender in California with special reference to Alameda, Los Angeles, and San Francisco Counties*. Unpublished Master's thesis, School of Criminology, University of California, Berkeley, 1939.

James, H. *Crisis in the courts*. New York: David McKay, 1972.

Janowitz, M. *The professional soldier*. New York: Free Press, 1964.

Kolko, G. *The triumph of conservatism: A reinterpretation of American history, 1900-1916*. Chicago: Quadrangle Books, 1967.

Kolko, G. *The roots of American foreign policy*. Boston: Beacon Press, 1969.

Ladinsky, J. "Careers of lawyers, law practice and legal institutions." *American Sociological Review*, 1963, *28*, 47-54.

Lemert, E.M. *Human deviance, social problems and social control*. New York: Prentice-Hall, 1967.

Levenson, B. "Bureaucratic Succession." In A. Etzioni (Ed.), *Complex organizations*. New York: Holt Rinehart and Winston, 1961.

Lunch, W.M. "Oakland revisited: Stability and change in an American city." Unpublished manuscript. Oakland Project, University of California, Berkeley, 1970.

Mallet, S. *La nouvelle classe ouvrière*. Paris: Éditions du Seuil, 1963.

Marcuse, H. "The movement in a new era of repression: An assessment." *Berkeley Journal of Sociology*, 1971-72, *16*.

Miliband, R. *The state in capitalist society*. New York: Basic Books, 1969.

Mills, C.W. *White collar*. New York: Oxford University Galaxy, 1956.

Niederhoffer, A. *Behind the shield*. New York: Doubleday, 1967.

Platt, A. "Notes on the careers of public defenders in Cook County." Unpublished manuscript, School of Criminology, University of California, Berkeley, 1968.

Platt, A., Schechter, H., and Tiffany, P. "In defense of youth: A case study of the public defender in juvenile court." *Indiana Law Journal*, 1968, *43*.

President's Commission on Law Enforcement and Administration of Justice. *The courts*. Washington, D.C.: U.S. Government Printing Office, 1967.

Shover, N. "Experts and diagnosis in correctional agencies." Unpublished paper delivered at Annual Meetings of the Society for the Study of Social Problems, New Orleans, 1972.

Silverstein, L. *Defense of the poor*. Chicago: American Bar Foundation, 1965.

Skolnick, J. "Social Control in the Adversary System." *Journal of Conflict Resolution*, 1967, *11*, 52-70.

Slocum, W.L. *Occupational careers*. Chicago: Aldine, 1966.

Smigel, E.O. *The Wall Street lawyer*. New York: Free Press, 1964.

Sudnow, D. "Normal crimes: Sociological features of the penal code in a public defender's office." *Social Problems*, 1965, *12*, 255-276.

Tanguay, S. *Role of the prosecutor's office in legal careers*. Unpublished Master's thesis, School of Criminology, University of California, Berkeley, 1967.

Warkov, S. and Zelan, J. *Lawyers in the making*. Chicago: Aldine, 1965.

Weinstein, J. *The corporate ideal in the liberal state, 1900-1918*. Boston: Beacon Press, 1969.

Weinstein, J. "The left, old and new." *Socialist Revolution*, 1972, *10*.

Wood, A. *Criminal lawyer*. New Haven, Conn.: College and University Press, 1967.

5

Channeling Lawyers: A Postscript

Anthony Platt

In Chapter 4 we described the process by which humanitarian lawyers become pragmatic and cynical in the course of their integration into the criminal justice system and also indicated how the public defender's office operates to channel lawyers into the lower strata of the legal profession. This study only *begins* to address some of the fundamental questions about the class position of state workers, the conditions of work in state agencies, and the relationship between the state and private sector. There has been very little investigation of state workers in the criminal justice system. Most research has focused instead on the apparent conflict between bureaucratic and due process imperatives (see, for example, Blumberg, 1967; Packer, 1968; Skolnick, 1967) and on the technological inefficiency of the criminal justice system (President's Commission on Law Enforcement and Administration of Justice, 1967). Without a theoretical understanding of the role of the state and a concrete investigation of working conditions in the criminal justice system, the preoccupation with due process and efficiency tends to abstract the issue of "crime control" from the political economy of advanced capitalism and to encourage reformist strategies of social engineering. In order to avoid this pitfall, we suggest that the following issues need to be addressed and investigated:

Proletarianization of State Workers

Marxist analysis has generally stressed that the state in its modern form serves to guarantee the conditions and social relations of capitalism by absorbing surplus capacity, guaranteeing the necessary preconditions for realizing profits and reproducing the workforce, generating new areas for profitable investment, and preserving capitalist hegemony through repression and ideological domination. According to power elite (Domhoff, 1967; Mills, 1956) and instrumentalist theories (Miliband, 1969), the state and its related political institutions are directly and indirectly governed by representatives of a ruling economic elite. According to structural theories (Poulantzas, 1975), on the other hand, the state is not directly governed by the ruling class, though it acts on their behalf, but operates according to a logic determined by the development of capitalism as a whole. While both theoretical perspectives are in agreement as to the functions of the state in capitalist society, there is considerable disagreement and confusion as to the nature of contradictions within the state apparatus and its internal dynamics.

The specific functions of the criminal justice system as a part of the state apparatus have not been subjected to a rigorous Marxist analysis. The prevailing (and simplistic) view characterizes the criminal justice system as an agency of ruling class policies without a concrete appreciation of how and why the police, courts, and prisons serve capitalist interests. This view, while partly correct, fails to take into account antagonisms *between* the criminal justice system and the ruling class and the growing malaise and militancy of state workers.

The conditions of workers in the state apparatus have undergone considerable change under advanced monopoly capitalism. With the development of state workers' unions, the increasing specialization and technical division of "white-collar" labor, and the brutal impact of inflation on salaried employees, we are witnessing the proletarianization of the managerial and professional sectors of the workforce which, in an earlier stage of capitalism, was more unambiguously identified with bourgeois interests. We need to investigate the historical development of this process, its impact on the criminal justice system, and its implications for organizing specific sectors such as the police, guards, and public defenders.

Rationalization of the Criminal Justice System

In recent years, there has been a proliferation of commission and think-tank studies advocating the need for increased technical and managerial efficiency in the criminal justice system. This has taken the form of support for time-and-motion techniques, creation of standards and goals, development of job specification and a more elaborate division of labor, computerization and other technological devices, and adaptation of corporate business managerialism to the needs of criminal justice bureaucracies. If implemented, these "reforms" will accelerate the depoliticization of criminal justice work through the introduction of technocratic, administrative criteria of efficiency and bureaucratic accountability. Consequently, criminal justice system workers will be forced to surrender what remains of the *craft* aspects of their work and will more and more approximate their counterparts in corporate bureaucracies, assembly lines, and typing pools.

We need to investigate the origins of this rationalization process, its impact on the conditions of work in the criminal justice system, and its implications for organizing workers who are trying to resist the mechanization and trivialization of their "professional" skills.

Stratification within the Criminal Justice System

Critical studies of the criminal justice system generally emphasize the *integrative* aspects of bureaucratic imperatives and examine how the internal dynamics of the police and courts encourage cooperation between the various actors (for example, public defenders and prosecutors), thus undermining the formal requirements of an *adversary* system. While this level of analysis has helped to demystify the actual workings of the law, it has also tended to ignore or obscure contradictions that operate within the criminal justice system. There is considerable variation in salary, training, working conditions, and class outlook among the different strata of the criminal justice system labor force. These differences are demonstrated not only between strata (for example, judges and guards) but also within occupations (for example, the struggle between rank-and-file police and their administrative bosses). Moreover, significant economic and political distinctions are further revealed in the careers of persons who leave the criminal justice system (for example, public defenders and prosecutors), whereby those who have proved themselves loyal subordinates to the capitalist class (such as judges and prosecutors) are rewarded with new positions of privilege, while others (such as guards and public defenders) are easily manipulated, discarded, or replaced.

In recent years there has been a special effort to recruit blacks, chicanos, and women into the criminal justice system. In the late 1960s, the emphasis was on blacks (especially through the so-called "war on poverty," OEO programs). More recently, with the encouragement of the Ford Foundation, women have been recruited into police and prison work. Little is known about the quantitative and qualitative impact of this policy, though the evidence with respect to blacks suggests that it has failed in several respects. However, an authoritative assessment is not possible until we know a great deal more about the effect of these recruitment policies, the levels of authority to which women and people of color were recruited, and their salaries and working conditions. It is also necessary, especially with respect to women, to investigate the role and functions of clerical workers in the criminal justice system.

We need empirical studies of the composition of the criminal justice system labor force, its internal dynamics and contradictions, and its implications for developing class struggles among its most oppressed and alienated sectors.

Organizing Criminal Justice System Workers

In recent years, there has been a growing militancy among different sectors of the state labor force. Public employee unions (such as the American Federation of State, County, and Municipal Employees, American Federation of Teachers, Postal Workers Union, and so forth) have grown enormously and between the mid-1950s and 1970 unionized state workers rose from 5 percent to about 11 percent of total union membership. This process has also had a considerable impact on the criminal justice system. Prison guards are being organized by the Teamsters, public defenders are joining public employee unions, and the police are once again (their previous efforts were aborted by their defeat in Boston in 1919) militantly challenging the constitutionality of no-strike laws.

The organization of criminal justice system workers poses some special problems. First, there is a tendency (especially among the police) to organize along right-wing, racist lines. Second, the socialization of criminal justice system workers encourages them to think of themselves as "middle-class" professionals reinforcing antiworking class attitudes and ideologies. This confusion and mystification of their objective class position creates considerable insecurity and instability, and thus makes them vulnerable to vacillation. Finally, criminal justice system organizations have generally pursued an *economistic* course and limited their demands to "bread-and-butter" issues. Unlike workers in the monopoly sector of industry who can link their demands for wage increases with an attack on corporate profits, public employee organizations can only achieve higher wages through increased taxation and thereby put themselves in direct competition with the working class as a whole (especially by contributing to inflation).

We need to investigate the historical development of public employee unions, the spacial problems involved in organizing criminal justice system workers, and the possibilities for organizing political alliances between public employees and their clients, so as to go beyond an economistic approach (see, for example, the formation of black police organizations such as Officers for Justice in San Francisco and the Afro-American Patrolmen's League in Chicago).

References

Blumberg, A. *Criminal justice.* Chicago: Quadrangle Books, 1967.

Domhoff, G.W. *Who rules America?* Englewood Cliffs, N.J.: Prentice-Hall, 1967.

Miliband, R. *The state of capitalist society.* New York: Basic Books, 1969.

Mills, C.W. *The power elite.* New York: Oxford University Press, 1956.

Packer, H.B. *The limits of criminal sanction.* Palo Alto: Stanford University Press, 1968.

Poulantzas, N. *Political power and social classes.* T. O'Hagan, trans. Atlantic Highland, N.J.: Humanities Press, 1975.

President's Commission on Law Enforcement and the Administration of Justice. *The challenge of crime in a free society.* Washington, D.C.: U.S. Government Printing Office, 1967.

Skolnick, J. Social control in the adversary system. *Journal of Conflict Resolution*, 1967, *11*, 52-70.

Effectiveness in Legal Negotiation

Gerald R. Williams
J. Lynn England
Larry C. Farmer
Murray Blumenthal

Introduction

Negotiation is the primary means of resolving legal disputes in the United States. In 1973, for example, only 8.4 percent of the cases commenced in the federal district courts actually reached trial; the remaining 91.6 percent were resolved without the necessity of adjudication (Bureau of the Census, 1974). Studies confirm that in state and local court systems, from 70 percent to 90 percent of the cases filed are settled by informal agreement between the parties rather than by formal court action (Franklin, Chanin & Mark, 1961; Newman, 1966). The disputes on which these statistics are based nearly always involve parties represented by attorneys and are settled through negotiation between the attorneys on behalf of the actual disputants. Even though the prospect or threat of litigation provides the leverage by which many disputes are settled, legal negotiation has a far greater impact than litigation in numbers of disputes resolved, numbers of persons affected, and amounts of money and property involved.

Despite the social and economic importance of legal negotiation, it has not yet been the subject of major theoretical or empirical inquiry. Studies of the legal system have concentrated primarily on the adjudication process, in which the substantive and procedural rules are explicit, the proceedings and records largely open to the public, and the results more readily quantified and evaluated. One reason for this neglect may be that, until recently, the ideological bases and popular conceptions of law in the United States have emphasized litigation as the correct and just means of dispute resolution, while failing to consider either the frequency or legitimacy of negotiated settlement of disputes. An additional factor may be that, in contrast to the large number of rules governing adjudication, there are very few formal rules relating to legal negotiation: communications between the attorneys are conducted in private, and correspondence, documentation, and even the final outcome are not generally made matters of public record. For these reasons, legal negotiation does not appear to be socially recognized or valued, and it remains inaccessible to study by the usual techniques of library research and legal analysis. On the other hand, its importance in the overall functioning of the legal system and its relative accessibility (compared, for example, to international negotiations) make it an inviting subject of social scientific inquiry.

A major difficulty for social scientists seeking to study negotiating in the legal profession is the difficulty of learning the professional norms and standards that provide the context for the bargaining process. Yet a working understanding of this context is necessary for any social scientist who hopes to conduct meaningful research in a profession as fraternal and esoteric as the legal profession. Thus, a primary thrust of this chapter is to review the current status of social scientific inquiry into the bargaining process, particularly bargaining in the legal context, and then to portray for the interested researcher the normative context in which legal negotiating is currently being conducted.

This article is an attempt to enlarge the theoretical and empirical bases for an understanding of legal bargaining, with an emphasis on the concept of effectiveness in bargaining. The chapter is organized into three sections. First, the literature on bargaining behavior, professional negotiators, and the legal profession generally is discussed as it applies to legal bargaining. Second, a system of hypotheses concerning effectiveness in legal bargaining are developed from the literature. Finally, a set of considerations relevant to the formulation of a theory of effectiveness in legal bargaining is presented.

Discussion of the Literature

There is a substantial body of theoretical and experimental literature relating to negotiation outside of the legal context, and there is a small but growing body of literature describing some aspects of legal negotiation. This literature is rich in hypotheses that have some applications to legal negotiations and bargaining effectiveness. The literature on negotiation has developed primarily in two directions. One direction is typified by theoretical and descriptive studies of bargaining behavior in general. The major concerns in these studies are with the structure of the negotiating process, the variables affecting it, and the attributes of the agreement. Work that may be categorized in this direction includes that based on aspects of game theory (Nash, 1950), that which seeks to supplement or replace game theory with alternative theories (Bartos, 1974), and that which draws upon general theories of human interaction and behavior (Walton & McKersie, 1965).

The second direction consists of studies that attempt to examine bargaining within specific substantive fields and professions, such as international affairs and labor relations (Ikle, 1964; Simpkins, 1971). The major concerns in these studies are with the informal rules that govern negotiations in a specialized area, the strategies specialists adopt in their bargaining, and the characteristics of highly successful negotiators.

General Negotiation and Bargaining Literature

An exploratory description of the principle features of negotiation has been given by Gulliver (1973). According to this description, there must be an arena in which the negotiations take place, a desire by the parties to make a settlement, agreement as to the nature of the dispute, identification of the rules and norms that are relevant to the dispute, a process of offer exchange, an agreement about settlement, and explicit recognition and execution of the agreement. Gulliver's discussion indicates that variables at each step in the process may work together in different combinations to influence the course and outcome of the negotiation.

Many of the general theories of bargaining behavior can be viewed as elaborations of the relationships among the variables in Gulliver's conceptualization. For example, the classic work of Siegel and Fouraker (1960) employs some aspects of economics to develop a theory of bargaining behavior which concentrates on the desire of the parties to settle, on the process of offer exchange, and the agreement. They have developed and tested a theory of the process of negotiations based on the assumption that negotiators have a minimal expectation or level of aspiration. Negotiations arise when attainment of the levels of aspiration of some parties precludes the attainment of the levels of all parties. The bargaining pattern is then expected to develop as follows:

The negotiators begin by expecting and demanding high payoffs, usually their highest.

They experience failure, represented by their opponent's high demands, which makes it apparent that concessions must be made to reach agreement.

The successive bids serve to give the negotiators experience, enabling them to establish realistic levels of aspiration, and on occasion, to concede without making offers below their levels of aspiration. Also, their aspiration levels are modified as negotiations proceed, although there is a minimal expectancy below which the subject will not go under any circumstances.

The search for efficient means of concession-making leads bargainers to solutions in the Pareto optimal set [Siegel & Fouraker, 1960].

The above approach suggests that tough negotiators will be more effective than those who give in readily. In order to test this view, Siegel and Fouraker conducted an experiment to derive information about both the process of arriving at agreement and the outcome in a simulated duopoly. The results basically confirmed their view.

The work by Siegel and Fouraker has generated research into the influence of information and strategy on the parties. For example, Harnett, Cummings, and Hamner (1973) examined the effects of other's toughness on a negotiator who encounters the Siegel and Fouraker bargaining situation. They found that toughness increases profits and does not increase the time it takes to reach agreement. Kahn and Kohls (1972) found that a lack of task-relevant information increases toughness, though the toughness in this case did not increase profits.

Another approach to bargaining which produces similar strategic conclusions is that of Schelling (1963). Schelling's interest centers on what he calls distributive bargaining, bargaining in which a demand for more by one party offers less to the other. The mechanism that drives these negotiations is the set of expectations the parties hold: "... each party is guided mainly by his expectations of what the other will accept. But with each guided by expectations and knowing the other is too, expectations become compounded" (Schelling, 1963, p. 21). The chain of expectations and counter plots can be built up *ad infinitum*, producing inaction. As a result, some criterion must be found to determine the most appropriate time for a concession. It is, says Schelling, when one negotiator is convinced that the other will not make a concession. In his view, the negotiator is most likely to receive a concession from his opponent by convincing the opponent that he (the negotiator) cannot make a concession. Schelling suggests that this is accomplished by making commitments and communicating them to others. Thus, for Schelling, effective bargaining is a result of a successful solution to the problem of communication and control of expectations. The effective negotiator is one who is capable of making an unbreakable commitment, communicating the commitment to the other party, and forcing the other party to select a course of action constrained by the commitment. John F. Kennedy's blockade of Cuba during the missile crisis of 1962 illustrates application of the Schelling strategy. Kennedy committed the blockading force to destroying any vessel attempting to approach Cuba. Once the commitment was made public and credible, it forced the Russians to negotiate within a framework of restricted alternatives or face the mutually undesirable consequences.

Charles Osgood (1962) has developed an alternative both to Siegel and Fouraker and to Schelling. He suggests that the toughness argued for in the Siegel and Fouraker theory and the unilateral commitment suggested by Schelling have seriously detrimental consequences because of the tension and mistrust they generate. The favorable profit which results from toughness is accompanied by greater risks of a breakdown in bargaining. Additionally, when the bargaining is taking place in settings requiring sequential bargaining as in international affairs, labor relations, or legal bargaining, the tension and mistrust eliminate the advantages of toughness. As a result, a negotiator needs to develop a cooperative, trusting atmosphere through concession-making. He recommends that, as a consequence, a negotiator needs to adopt a strategy of Graduate Reciprocation in Tension (GRIT).

It should be noted that the disagreement between Osgood and the other three raises a question as to circumstances in which effective negotiators adopt a strategy of tough bargaining or a GRIT strategy. Research by Bartos (1967) and Harnett, Cummings, and Hamner (1973) indicates that there are settings which confirm Osgood's prediction that GRIT is more effective in the sense that there are fewer unresolved sessions and higher profits, but there are also settings in which his prediction is incorrect.

In addition to the work by Osgood, Schelling, and Siegel and Fouraker, two important theories have been developed that explicitly adopt general theories of human behavior rather than developing theories specifically for bargaining settings. The first, Walton and McKersie (1965), makes a distinction between distributive bargaining and integrative bargaining. Distributive bargaining is basically the same as for Schelling. Integrative bargaining is the system of activities that is instrumental to the attainment of objectives not in fundamental conflict with those of the other party.

The Walton-McKersie model of distributive bargaining assumes that there are two basic processes taking place: a problem-solving process and a bargaining process. The problem-solving process usually precedes the other and is an attempt by the negotiators to obtain information about the other's utilities and expectations, while withholding as much information as possible from the other. The bargaining process is a series of attempts to use the information obtained to change the other's utilities, to change his expected probability of obtaining a highly favorable outcome, and to maintain a high payoff for oneself.

The model of integrative bargaining asserts that there are three basic steps in the process of identifying a mutually beneficial outcome. The first step is the identification of the problem. It consists of the maximum exchange of information by the participants in order to identify the items at issue. Effectiveness depends on the ability of a negotiator to present the issues in a strategically favorable light and to selectively control information flow. The second step consists of the discovery and exploration of alternatives and their consequences. The effective negotiator attempts to be creative in perceiving and exploring the fullest range of alternatives. Invention and creativity are particularly valuable assets for a negotiator. The third and final step entails a settlement through the discovery of the best solution. The successful conclusion of this step requires that the parties clearly evaluate the value, to each individual, of the various alternatives and combine them in the most profitable manner.

Walton and McKersie point out that many bargaining situations require both integrative and distributive bargaining. In both cases, general social-psychological theories, such as balance theory and reinforcement theory, are used to understand the process and predict the outcome.

In a somewhat different conceptualization of bargaining, Douglas (1962) has described it as consisting of three processes or stages. In stage one, the negotiators seek to establish the range or scope of the bargaining. Issues are defined and extreme demands are established. Each party seeks to give the illusion of being fixed to an inalterable position. In stage two, parties begin reconnoitering alternative solutions that fall between the extreme demands of each. To do this, they shift from talking about their own position and begin gathering information about the other's *real* position, at the same time giving clues about areas in which concession might take place and seeking to determine how the other will respond to particular offers. Finally, in stage three a crisis is reached in which the parties must discern the final or last offer of the other and decide whether to accept it. At this stage either agreement is reached or there is a breakdown in the bargaining.

The descriptions of the bargaining process given above do not take into account variations between individuals that may influence the effectiveness of a resolution. There have been several attempts to identify background and personality variables that influence bargaining and bargaining effectiveness. Ikle (1964) notes that reputation, personal ambition, and experience as a negotiator are important variables. Bartos (1967) suggests that sex, age, nationality, race, and some personality traits are related to one's bargaining "toughness" and may be characterized by distinct bargaining patterns. In addition, researchers have stressed the significance of the organizational context of bargaining, thereby suggesting that the position of the negotiator in the organizational hierarchy, the viability of the organization, and the degree of interdependence between the organizations all influence the bargaining (Douglas, 1962; Walton & McKersie, 1965).

Another set of variables affecting the success of negotiators are strategy or tactic variables. Such tactics as making threats or promises, showing commitment to a position (Deutsch & Krauss, 1962; Schelling, 1963), using deception, bargaining from strength (Diesing, 1961), and showing trust (Osgood, 1962) have been found in one way or another to improve success in negotiations. The timing of moves is also considered crucial. Several researchers have indicated that certain tactics are more successful when used in the closing sessions of bargaining (Harnett et al., 1973). It appears that negotiators who make high initial demands usually make more profit than those making low ones (Harnett et al., 1973).

While these variables suggest a rich variety of factors to be examined in an empirical study of legal negotiators, it would be misleading to suggest that all of the research on negotiator effectiveness produces consistent results. Both Bartos and Harnett et al. have noted conditions under which toughness is profitable and others under which it is not. Similar limitations can be noted for almost all of the variables discussed above. Likewise, most of the experimental research has involved nonprofessional negotiators—typically college students—and has been characterized by a lack of professional identities and lack of continuing relationships or interdependencies between the negotiators. Such tactics as making threats may be more successful in these circumstances than where professional identities and continuing relationships are present. These limitations suggest the utility of testing the above theories through an empirical examination of negotiation in a specific professional context such as the legal profession.

Literature on Professional Negotiations

Moving beyond the general theories, there is additional literature that is relevant to a study of legal negotiators and their effectiveness. Ikle (1964) and Bartos

(1967) have identified the existence of informal codes of bargaining behavior among professional negotiators. Bartos, in a critical review of the game research on negotiations, argued that professionals develop their own "code of behavior" in the negotiating situation and that these codes "render [the negotiator's] behavior predictable." Bartos suggests that such professional codes have an important influence on bargaining since they specify the types of behavior that are permissible if the negotiator is to be accepted as a professional. Ikle has investigated negotiations in international affairs and has identified rules of conduct that are included in the professional code. The rules include understandings that the status of participants should not be disputed, concessions should be reciprocated, and flagrant lies, emotionalism, rudeness, and bargaining in bad faith should be avoided. Informal rules such as these may also be usefully conceptualized in terms of the norms and expectations in role theory discussed in the following section.

Professionals have also been singled out as a special class in some of the negotiation effectiveness literature. This literature reveals three primary determinants of effectiveness: reputation, skill in adopting a role, and strategies. Ikle (1964) indicates that one's reputation influences his success in negotiations. Reputations for bluffing, not being firm, and avoiding tests of strength are all detrimental to effectiveness as a negotiator in international affairs. The skill a professional negotiator has in identifying the content of the code applicable to his role and the expectations of the other parties involved influences his effectiveness as a negotiator (Homans, 1961). Homans has found that, when a negotiator is unaware of these matters, the chances of hostility and intransigence are greatly enhanced.

The idea that members of the legal profession have norms or standards of negotiating conduct which are unique to the profession is supported by Donnell (1970). In his role study of corporate counsel, he describes a number of attributes of professionals and professional organizations that may serve to generate and maintain such norms: professionals deal with and become expert in the application of specialized knowledge; their knowledge is gained through a lengthy educational process that includes instruction on formal codes of ethical conduct; they are organized into voluntary (and sometimes compulsory) professional associations which promote and enforce adherence to high standards of professional conduct; and they achieve status among their fellow professionals through adherence to standards of good practice.

The range of professional interests that may be promoted by professional codes have been described by MacIver (1955) to include such extrinsic interests as economic status, social status, reputation, and authority and to include technical interests, such as setting levels and types of training required for entry into the profession and promoting efficiency and quality in the delivery of services to clients.

These studies, combined with the Ikle and Bartos arguments, clearly suggest that the study of legal negotiation should attempt to identify the professional code of attorney-negotiators and should also include consideration of the formal rules of ethical conduct applying to the legal profession as well as articulation on the manner in which they affect legal negotiations.

The formal ethical code of the legal profession is embodied in a number of different sources. The most important statements are the American Bar Association's *Canons of Professional Ethics* and their successor, the *Code of Professional Responsibility*. The *Canons* or *Code* have been adopted, with some modifications, in forty-nine states and in the District of Columbia (Rubin, 1975, p. 579). There are two excellent works describing and interpreting the *Canons* and *Code* (Drinker, 1961; Wise, 1970), but the socialization process by which persons entering the profession learn and adopt these values and standards have not received adequate treatment (Little, 1968; Lortie, 1959). Commentators within the profession appear to feel that lawyers are generally highly committed to the ethical standards of the legal profession (Blaustein & Porter, 1954, pp. 246-247; Wise, 1970, p. vi). However, Carlin (1966) has studied the ethical norms and behavior of attorneys in New York City and found that the New York Bar may be subdivided into categories of high, middle, and low conformers to ethical norms with approximately one-quarter of the attorneys being rated as high conformers, one-half being rated as middle, and the remaining quarter being rated as low conformers—that is, as violators (pp. 54-55). His study also indicated that the level of ethical behavior in attorneys varied with such factors as size of law firm, type of clientele, level of court or agency, work setting, and inner disposition (pp. 166-170), with attorneys on the higher end of these scales observing the higher ethical standards. Such observations have led some observers to conclude that professional ethics are an attempt by elite lawyers to control those who operate on the lower levels of the profession (Schuchman, 1968).

The formal ethical code is enforced by a variety of mechanisms, both through the courts (McCracken, 1955), which ultimately hold the power to regulate the profession, and through state and local bar associations (Hyde, 1955), although the scope and effectiveness of this enforcement is questioned by Carlin (1966, pp. 150-164). The meaning and application of the standards have been elaborated in great detail through opinions of bar association ethics committees, which are made available to the profession (American Bar Foundation, 1967; Maru & Clough, 1970).

The mechanisms by which the courts implement professional standards are described by Thurman, Phillips, and Cheatham (1970), and are shown to include the power courts have to control admissions to the bar (admissions requirements and disbarment proceedings), to control the general structure of bar associations, to define those areas which shall be the exclusive domain of the bar (restrictions against unauthorized practice of law), to promulgate and enforce formal canons of professional conduct, to invoke the contempt power, and to control their own rules of procedure and practice.

The standards of the profession also appear to be maintained as a matter of tradition by informal sanctions within the profession. As long ago as 1854, Sharswood stated in his essay on professional ethics, that:

A very great part of a man's comfort, as well as of his success at the Bar, depends upon his relations with his professional brethren. With them he is in daily necessary intercourse, and he must have their respect and confidence, if he wishes to sail along in smooth waters. He cannot be too particular in keeping faithfully and liberally every promise or engagement he may make with them. One whose perfect truthfulness is even suspected by his brethren at the Bar has always an uneasy time of it. He will be constantly mortified by observing precautions taken with him which are not used with others [p. 73].

Thus, while a lawyer has the ethical duty to "represent a client zealously within the bounds of the law" (Canon 7, ABA *Code of Professional Responsibility*), there appears to be an elaborate structure of formal and informal standards within the profession to which attorneys are expected to conform. As summarized by Drinker (1961);

[Lawyers] have involuntarily assumed, by mutual understanding and recognized custom of the bar over a long period, certain obligations to one another. The recognition and observance of these obligations is primarily what characterized the practice of law as a profession as distinguished from a business. They constitute the most significant part of the lawyer's distinctive code of etiquette and of ethics. These obligations [include the duty] . . . to be candid, fair, and courteous in their dealings with other lawyers . . . [p. 190].

The obligation to avoid haranguing and offensive tactics, to be courteous to opposing counsel, and generally to follow local customs of courtesy and practice are formally stated in Ethical Considerations 7-37 through 7-39 of the ABA *Code of Professional Responsibility.*

In spite of the elaborate specifications of the professional code, the interpretation of its prescriptions in the bargaining context and the effect of the code on negotiations have not been systematically studied, although some exploratory treatments have been made (King & Sears, 1952; Rubin, 1975).

The preceding description of the norms and rules existing within the legal profession suggests the value of construing the activities of a professional negotiator in terms of role theory. First, the role is constructed of a set of expectations, rights, and obligations, such as the code mentioned by Bartos or the rules enumerated by Ikle. Second, the role has attributed to it a position in a social structure with tasks to perform and goals to meet: for example, Lamm (1973) discusses the negotiator's role in terms of the location of the negotiator in the hierarchical structure. Finally, and perhaps most important of all, the role of professional negotiator is conceptualized as part of a role set in which the dynamics of role taking and role making suggested by Mead (1956), Turner

(1962) and Kelly (1965) are relevant. The set of relevant roles consists of the other party, the negotiator for the other party, the party represented by the negotiator, and the negotiator himself. Role theory would suggest that the code plus the expectations held by each of the occupants of the role set about the other occupants will greatly affect, if not determine, the actual interaction and outcome in the bargaining.

Application of role theory to bargaining behavior can be illustrated through the work of Brown (1968). It begins with a negotiator who is seeking to communicate a positive image of himself to the occupants of two roles: the other party to the actual issue at hand and the significant others interested in the outcomes he obtains. In legal bargaining two types of significant others are highly salient for an attorney: his clients, who are his source of financial reward and public approval, and his peers, who provide him with professional evaluation and status within the bar. One consequence of this view is suggested by Goffman (1956, 1959, 1963). He contends that saving face is a prevalent value in our culture. Attempting to project a positive image, people often do things that may be costly to them. Applying this phenomenon to bargaining, Brown (1968) points out that face saving occurs in bargaining and involves attempts by one negotiator to block actions by the others which would cause him to appear foolish, weak, and incapable to significant others.

Legal Negotiations

Although most of the research on professional negotiators has been conducted with international affairs, labor relations, or business-economic problems as the situation focus, there has been some research in the legal context bearing on negotiations. Some of the work on labor negotiations is focused on the role of legal counsel in the negotiation process (Peck, 1972), and a number of studies have been made of plea bargaining in the criminal justice system. The major studies of plea bargaining are by Newman (1956, 1966), Sudnow (1965) and Skolnick (1966).

Newman examined plea bargaining in Kansas, Michigan, and Wisconsin. Most of his work is descriptive, presenting a series of case studies. In his work Newman finds that the form of the bargaining is somewhat dependent on a state's legal structure. For example, there is less plea bargaining in Wisconsin than in Kansas or Michigan because of the degree of sentencing discretion of the judge.

Several aspects of the plea bargaining process are noted by Newman. For example, he identifies a number of issues over which bargaining may take place. They include the charge, the sentence, the recommendation of parole, and the evidence to be admitted. Newman also gives some indications of the bargaining strategies employed. The lawyers often rely upon precedent in their bargaining.

The defense may point to the fact that there is a loss of prosecution time and a risk of loss of the case if the case goes to trial. The prosecution will initially charge the defendant with the maximum defensible crimes based on the facts of the case. Skolnick (1966) is principally interested in the law enforcement system, but his research confirms Newman's position.

Sudnow (1965) describes plea bargaining between the public defender and the district attorney's offices. He stresses two features of legal bargaining. First, informal relations between the representatives of the two offices serve to facilitate reaching a bargain. Second, the bargaining process is highly routinized. The public defender accepts the facts of the case as presented by the prosecution and knows basically how to approach both his client and the prosecution. The prosecution charges the greater offense with the idea that it can later be reduced in exchange for a guilty plea.

Blumberg (1967) examines the criminal law system from the point of view of its effect on the performance of the defense lawyers who represent most nonindigent criminal defendants. He argues that the criminal court and its related personnel, including both prosecutors and regular defense lawyers, are joined by a community of interests that induce the defense lawyer to place a higher value on cooperation with court and prosecution personnel than on defending the interests of an individual client.

An important study of legal bargaining outside the area of plea bargaining deals with insurance claims adjustments (Ross, 1970). Ross interviewed attorneys and insurance claims adjusters and observed a number of bargaining sessions. He applies the theoretical approaches of Schelling, Walton and McKersie, and Stephens, providing insights into the applicability of general theories of negotiations to legal bargaining, at least to the extent that bargaining takes place between attorneys and insurance claims adjusters.

A separate genre of literature on legal negotiation has been produced through the writings of a number of experienced legal practitioners (Baer & Broder, 1973; Hermann, 1965; Hornwood, 1972; Simmons, 1974). These authors draw upon their own experience with legal negotiations and systematically describe the procedures and techniques they have found to be effective. While these works do not represent a social scientific approach to legal negotiation, they probably represent some of the best information accessible to practicing lawyers about the skills of the effective legal negotiator.

These studies present a fairly uniform view of the expectations among attorneys (and insurance claims adjusters) with respect to a number of ethical standards. For example, honesty (Baer & Brader, 1973, pp. 97-98; Hermann, 1965, p. 139), fairness (Hermann, 1965, p. 142), sincerity (Hermann, 1965, pp. 143-144), and cooperation (Nierenberg, 1973, pp. 22-24) are seen as important not only as matters of principle but as expectations which, if violated, will reduce the negotiator's likelihood of obtaining an advantageous settlement. Ross (1970), in his more systematic study of negotiations in insurance claims adjustments, observed these expectations to be embodied in a general obligation that a negotiator bargain in good faith. According to Ross (1970):

To lack good faith is to subvert negotiation, and to perpetrate a fraud. The good faith negotiator must want to reach an agreement, and must be willing to follow the rules in obtaining the agreement. The bad faith negotiator uses the exchange of proposals to gain time, to obtain information to destroy his opponent's case in litigation, or for other reasons apart from the ostensible one of reaching an agreed settlement [pp. 149-151].

While the bulk of the legal literature supports the view that negotiation is a cooperative venture there are some contexts within which a more aggressive strategy is proposed. In their book on public interest advocacy, Meltsner and Schrag (1974, pp. 231-240) describe a series of tactics, a few of which clearly disregard the norms described above. Meltsner and Schrag signal their own reservations about the *propriety* of some of the tactics, but include them because they are considered to be *effective* tactics in certain kinds of situations, whether the negotiator uses them himself or finds them being used against him. The more aggressive tactics include using two negotiators to play feigned conflicting roles (the Mutt-and-Jeff technique); appearing irrational as a means of gaining advantage; and having your client reject an agreed-upon settlement and raise his demands. Meltsner and Schrag also note that where opposing attorneys have continuing relationships together, the negotiations are more likely to proceed in an open, straightforward manner, presumably to avoid future informal sanctions that are said to be imposed upon persons who violate accepted negotiating norms.

It may be observed here that in legal negotiations seeking to resolve a preexisting dispute, an attorney in nearly all cases faces the prospect of taking the case to trial if no satisfactory resolution is reached by negotiation. This alternative of trial, where the attorneys must act in accordance with elaborate and explicit rules and under the supervision of a judge, provides an important recourse for the attorney who is offended or made suspicious by the conduct of the opposing counsel. This prospect of trial undoubtedly provides strong impetus toward a general adherence to the normative expectations of candor, fairness, and cooperation.

Description of the System of Relevant Hypotheses

As the review of literature suggests, social scientists have an interest in bargaining that relates both to the development and validation of a general theory of bargaining and to understanding the bargaining process in specific social contexts. One such context is the legal system. The legal system is significant, in part, because it is characterized by a high volume of disputes, it involves professionals who participate as agents for the disputing parties, and it is relatively accessible to research. The legal system also has a broader significance: persons involved in legal disputes are intimately affected in their personal lives not only by the outcome of the disputes but by the process through which their interests are defined, promoted, and defended. Since the great majority of legal disputes are resolved through negotiation, a clearer understanding of the processes and dynamics of negotiation will assist in assessing the impact they have on the parties involved.

In response to these concerns, the Legal Negotiation Project was developed with the following general objectives: (1) to develop hypotheses about legal bargaining and effectiveness based on legal literature, role theory, and general theories of bargaining; (2) to develop and apply techniques including use of mailed questionnaires, interviews, and case commentaries for obtaining a wide variety of data about legal bargaining from the primary participants, attorneys, and (3) to use the data obtained to test the adequacy of a set of hypotheses about legal bargaining, to develop or elaborate upon theories and models of bargaining, and to make preliminary evaluations of the possible effects of the negotiation process upon the private individuals involved. The remainder of this chapter is a report of the preliminary phase of the Project.

The general hypotheses developed from the literature may be divided into two sets: one set relates to role perceptions of lawyers as negotiators; the other set relates to process and background variables to bargaining effectiveness. The hypotheses will be stated, followed by an explanation of their derivation.

Hypotheses in the first set are related to role concepts as follows:

1. Legal negotiators hold a common set of norms and expectations including the following:
    (a) Both sides will make serious attempts to reach agreement through bargaining (good faith);
    (b) When a client's position is presented, it will be represented accurately;
    (c) The lawyers involved will avoid emotionalism;
    (d) Trust, candor, confidentiality, and flexibility will be maintained;
    (e) Both parties will be prepared on the facts and on the pertinent law.
2. Norms and expectations will differ in emphasis across areas of legal negotiations (e.g., personal injury, divorce, and plea bargaining). In addition, norms and expectations exist that are unique to each subject area.
3. Norms and expectations relating to negotiation can be distinguished from norms and expectations relating to litigation.
4. Lawyers designated by their peers as among the most effective negotiators will be found to differ from lawyers designated as among the least effective by their understanding of and adherence to these norms.

The hypothesis that legal negotiators hold a common set of norms and expectations is based on the extensive claims concerning the existence of an institutionalized code of negotiating behavior which is assumed to have developed within the legal profession (Bartos, 1967; Donnell, 1970; Komarovsky, 1973). In addition to the studies cited, a pilot survey conducted by one of the authors involving interviews of forty attorneys regarding legal negotiations supports this hypothesis. Part of the research on this hypothesis includes an attempt to determine the degree to which there is consensus among legal negotiators about a code of behavior.

The second role-related hypothesis, that the norms and expectations relating to negotiation will differ in emphasis and in kind across areas of specialization within the profession, is based on the assumption that the goals and activities involved in various subject areas of legal bargaining are sufficiently distinct from each other to generate discernible differences in norms and expectations. The third hypothesis, that norms and expectations relating to negotiation can be distinguished from those relating to litigation, assumes that the differences in the negotiation and litigation processes give rise to differences in norms and expectations. This hypothesis serves the additional function of illustrating the potential contrasts between negotiation and other lawyer functions, litigation in particular. The fourth role-related hypothesis, that a lawyer's reputation among his peers for negotiating effectiveness will vary with his own understanding of and adherence to the bargaining code, is designed to test the variables to effectiveness suggested by Ikle (1964) and Homans (1961).

The second set of hypotheses concerning the effectiveness of legal negotiators is taken from the literature on ethics and professional responsibility in the legal profession, professional bargaining, and theories of bargaining. The hypotheses are based on a conceptualization of effectiveness which assumes that an attorney is faced with the problem of resolving a legal dispute in such a way that he satisfies his client, furthers his own reputation, uses legal argument and other professional skills well, promotes the orderly functioning of legal processes, and maintains or enhances interpersonal ties with other actors in the legal system. The important hypotheses derived from this conceptualization are:

1. An effective negotiator will be distinguished from average or ineffective negotiators by:
   (a) developing a better understanding of his client's needs;
   (b) obtaining a more profitable settlement for the client.
2. An effective negotiator will be distinguished from average and ineffective negotiators by his capacity to:
   (a) increase his own economic return;
   (b) enhance his reputation among his peers.
3. An effective legal negotiator will be distinguished from average or ineffective negotiators by:
   (a) his skill in knowing and applying the law;

(b) the extent of his preparation;

(c) his skills and reputation as a trial attorney;

(d) his ability to invent or create new alternatives;

(e) his skill in using basic strategies such as commitment; toughness, reciprocation, initial offers, and information control;

(f) his skillful use of the strength of his position.

4. An effective legal negotiator will be distinguished from average or ineffective negotiators by his skills in interpersonal relationships, including his abilities to:

(a) avoid deception, insults, flagrant lies, emotionalism, rudeness, bargaining in bad faith, and impolite acts;

(b) avoid interrupting or obstructing the routinized aspects of interpersonal relations;

(c) not threatening the other party with loss of face.

The hypotheses derived from the literature and preliminary information about negotiations in the specifically legal context also suggest the following global hypothesis:

Lawyers designated by their peers as among the most effective negotiators will be characterized by positive social traits and attitudes and by the use of more open, cooperative, and friendly negotiation strategies.

This broad hypothesis presents a number of difficulties, including the possibility of apparent verification as a result of the operation of the halo effect. On the other hand, a number of observations argue for its inclusion. First, the literature provides a clear theoretical base for it. Second, a pilot study by one of the present authors provides evidence that attorneys expect each other to be reasonable, open, and cooperative through the course of negotiations and that inexperienced attorneys frequently err by being overly antagonistic and pugnacious in their approach. The interviews did not rule out the possibility that there are occasions or circumstances in which a more antagonistic, aggressive, or hostile approach would be advisable, but they suggested that, on the whole, these were not the most effective strategies.

All of the hypotheses listed above derive their plausibility from one of three sources: the theoretical positions developed for negotiations in general, the literature concerning legal bargaining, or empirical (usually small groups) research. Each source has some severe limitations that must be taken into account when applying them to legal bargaining research and practice. The general theoretical positions and the empirical research typically fail to make adequate allowances for the play of the role expectations, normative constraints, and interpersonal processes that arise as a consequence of the bargaining taking place within the legal system. The legal bargaining literature, on the other hand, is generally either highly a-theoretical or restricted to a single specialty such as plea bargaining. In order to overcome these limitations, it will be necessary to develop a theory of effectiveness in legal bargaining which integrates the hypotheses described above, the functioning of the professional code, the consequences of the organizational structure, and the impact of the situational variables. Two developments must occur to make the theory adequate.

First, the concept of bargaining effectiveness must be made directly applicable to legal bargaining. In research outside the legal context, the problem of the *meaning* or content of bargaining effectiveness has been either highly simple or not explicitly addressed. In most experimental settings, a negotiator's effectiveness is measured by whether agreement is reached, and if so, by the amount of his payoff (generally measured in dollars) relative to that of the other party. For example, when Bartos (1974) studied toughness and bargaining effectiveness in small group negotiations, he assessed effectiveness in terms of the probability of agreement and the amount of payoff received.

In bargaining between attorneys, however, the motives and aspirations of the actors are likely to be so complex as to make assessment of effectiveness based simply on probability of agreement and amount of payoff inadvisable. For example, the literature on the legal profession suggests that the effectiveness of negotiating attorneys needs to include a number of concerns in addition to simple outcome. Lawyers are members of a profession, bound to some extent by its formal and informal norms, its organizational structure, and its system of sanctions and rewards. Their effectiveness must take into account these professional influences, the motives and expectations of their clients, and their ability to maintain ongoing interpersonal relations with fellow lawyers and with other important actors in the legal system. Given the importance of these dimensions, it appears that an effort should be made in future empirical and theoretical work on legal bargaining to integrate them with the hypotheses that have been developed.

Second, even though the hypotheses are supported in the literature, it does not follow that there is a simple causal relationship between the antecedent condition and effectiveness in legal bargaining. In other words; the behavior of some effective negotiators may, in certain situations, depart significantly from that suggested by the hypotheses. Thus, the hypotheses as they are given, in isolation from specific bargaining situations with the combinations of variables that individual situations present, are inadequate as descriptions of effective bargaining behavior. This inadequacy stems, first, from a failure to explain the interaction between normative expectations, the organization of the legal system, and the interpersonal dynamics between attorneys, clients, and other actors in the legal system; and second, from a failure to integrate these interactions with the complex situational variables represented by specific bargaining occasions. As these limitations are addressed and resolved, it will be possible to move to the elaboration of a systematic theory of legal bargaining effectiveness.

References

American Bar Foundation. *American bar association opinions on professional ethics*. Chicago: American Bar Foundation, 1967.

Baer, H., & Broder, A.J. *How to prepare and negotiate cases for settlement* (Rev. ed.). New York: Law-Arts Publishers 1973.

Bartos, O. Concession-making in experimental negotiations. In J. Berger, M. Zelditch, & B. Anderson (Eds.), *Sociological theories in progress*. Boston: Houghton Mifflin, 1965.

Bartos, O. *Simple models of group behavior*. New York: Columbia Press, 1967.

Bartos, O. How predictable are negotiations? *Journal of Conflict Resolution*, 1967, *2*, 481-496.

Bartos, O. *Process and outcome of negotiations*. New York: Columbia University Press, 1974.

Blaustein, A., & Porter, C. *The American lawyer: A summary of the survey of the legal profession*. Chicago: University of Chicago Press, 1954.

Blumberg, A.S. The practice of law as confidence game: organizational cooptation of a profession. *Law and Society Review*, 1967, *1*, 15-39.

Brown, B.R. The effects of need to maintain face. *Journal of Experimental Social Psychology*, 1968, *4*, 107-122.

Bureau of the Census. U.S. Department of Commerce. *Statistical abstract of the United States*. Washington, D.C.: Government Printing Office, 1974.

Carlin, J.E. *Lawyers' ethics: A survey of the New York City Bar*. New York: Russell Sage Foundation, 1966.

Deutsch, M., & Krauss, R. Studies in interpersonal bargaining. *Journal of Conflict Resolution*, 1962, *6*, 52-76.

Diesing, P. Bargaining strategy and union management relationships. *Journal of Conflict Resolution*, 1961, *5*, 367-378.

Donnell, J. *The corporate counsel: A role study*. Bloomington, Ind.: Bureau of Business Research, 1970.

Douglas, A. *Industrial peacemaking*. New York: Columbia University Press, 1962.

Drinker, H.S. *Legal ethics*. New York: Columbia University Press, 1961.

Franklin, M., Chanin, R., & Mark, S. Accidents, money, and the law: A study of the economics of personal injury litigation. *Columbia Law Review*, 1961, *61*, 10-11.

Goffman, E. "Embarrassment and social organization." *American Journal of Sociology*, 1956, *62*, 264-271.

Goffman, E. *Presentation of self in everyday life*. Garden City, N.Y.: Doubleday, 1959.

Goffman, E. *Stigma*. Englewood Cliffs, N.J.: Prentice-Hall, 1963.

Gulliver, P.H. Negotiations as a mode of dispute settlement: Towards a general model, *Law and Society Review*, 1973, *7*, 667-691.

Harnett, D., Cummings, L., & Hamner, W. Personality, bargaining style and payoff on bilateral monopoly bargaining among European managers. *Sociometry*, 1973, *36*, 325-345.

Harnett, D., Cummings, L., & Hughes, D. The influence of risk-taking propensity on bargaining behavior. *Behavioral Science*, 1968, *13*, 91-101.

Hermann, P.J. *Better settlements through leverage.* New York: Aqueduct Books, 1965.

Homans, G. *Social behavior: Its elementary forms.* New York: Harcourt, Brace, & World, 1961.

Hornwood, S.W. *Systematic settlements.* Rochester: Lawyers' Co-operation Publishing Co., 1972.

Hyde, L.M. The duty and obligations of the bar for the maintenance of professional standards. *Southern California Law Review*, 1955, *29*, 81-92.

Ikle, F. *How nations negotiate.* New York: Harper & Row, 1964.

Kahn, A., & Kohls, J. Determinants of toughness in dyadic bargaining. *Sociometry*, 1972, *35*, 305-315.

Kelly, H.H. Experimental studies of threats in interpersonal negotiations. *Journal of Conflict Resolution,* 1965, *9*, 79-105.

King, E., & Sears, D. The ethical aspects of compromise, settlement and arbitration. *Rocky Mountain Law Review*, 1952, *25*, 454-462.

Komarovsky, M. Some problems in role analysis. *American Sociological Review*, 1973, *38*, 649-662.

Lamm, H. Intragroup effects on Intergroup negotiation. *European Journal of Social Psychology*, 1973, *3*, 179-192.

Little, J. Pawns and processes: A quantitative study of unknowns in legal education. *Journal of Legal Education*, 1968, *21*, 145, n. 4.

Lortie, D.C. Laymen to lawmen: Law school, careers and professional socialization. *Harvard Educational Review*, 1959, *29*, 352-369.

MacIver, R.M. The social significance of professional ethics. *Annals, American Academy of Political and Social Science*, 1955, *297*, 118.

Maru, O., & Clough, R.L. *Digest of bar association ethics opinions.* Chicago: American Bar Foundation, 1970.

McCracken, R. The maintenance of professional standards: Duty and obligation of the courts. *Southern California Law Review*, 1955, *29*, 65-80.

Mead, G.H. *The social psychology of George Herbert Mead.* Chicago: University of Chicago Press, 1956.

Meltsner, M., & Schrag, P.G. *Public interest advocacy: Materials for clinical legal education.* Boston: Little, Brown & Co., 1974.

Nash, J. The bargaining problem. *Econometrica*, 1950, *18*, 155-162.

Newman, D. Pleading guilty for consideration: A study of bargaining justice. *Journal of Criminal Law, Criminology, and Police Science*, 1956, *46*, 780-790.

Newman, D.J. *Conviction: The determination of guilt or innocence without trial.* Boston: Little, Brown, 1966.

Nierenberg, G.I. *Fundamentals of negotiating.* New York: Hawthorn Books, 1973.

Osgood, C. *An alternative to war or surrender.* Urbana: University of Illinois Press, 1962.

Peck, C.J. *Cases and materials on negotiation (Unit Five of labor relations and social problems).* Washington, D.C.: The Bureau of National Affairs, 1972.

Ross, H.L. *Settled out of court.* Chicago: Aldine, 1970.

Rubin, A.B. A causerie on lawyers' ethics in negotiation. *Louisiana Law Review*, 1975, *35*, 577-593.

Schelling, T. *The strategy of conflict.* New York: The Oxford Press, 1963.

Schuchman, P. Ethics and legal ethics: The propriety of the canons as a group moral code. *George Washington Law Review*, 1968, *37*, 244-269.

Sharswood, G. *Professional ethics.* Philadelphia: T.&J.W. Johnson & Co., 1854.

Siegel, S., & Fouraker, L. *Bargaining and group decision making.* New York: McGraw-Hill, 1960.

Simmons, R. *Winning before trial: How to prepare cases for the best settlement or trial result* (Vol. 1). Englewood Cliffs, N.J.: Executive Reports Corp., 1974.

Simpkins, W.E. *Mediation and the dynamics of collective bargaining.* Washington, D.C.: Bureau of National Affairs, 1971.

Skolnick, J. *Justice without trial: Law enforcement in democratic society.* New York: John Wiley & Sons, 1966.

Sudnow, D. Normal crimes: Sociological features of the penal code in a public defender office. *Social Problems*, 1965, *12*, 255-276.

Thurman, S., Phillips, E., & Cheatham, E. *Cases and materials on the legal profession.* Mineola, N.Y.: The Foundation Press, 1970, 142-89.

Turner, R. Role taking: Process versus conformity. In A. Rose (Ed.), *Human behavior and social processes.* Boston: Houghton Mifflin, 1962.

Walton, R., & McKersie, R. *A behavioral theory of labor negotiations.* New York: McGraw-Hill, 1965.

Wise, R.L. *Legal ethics* (2nd ed.). New York: Matthew Bender, 1970.

Part IV:
Psychological Factors in
Courtroom Procedures

7

Evidence, Procedure, and Psychological Research

Anthony N. Doob

In this chapter I will briefly discuss some of the problems that arise when a psychologist attempts to do research on questions of evidence and procedure in legal settings. For the most part, because of my background, I will be talking about factors involved in the trial of criminal matters; however, in many instances the problems that arise—indeed, even the exact questions that one might look at—are the same in civil trials.

One very obvious fact about the rules of evidence in a trial is, of course, that they are by their very nature exclusionary. As psychologists we are typically taught that in trying to arrive at a conclusion we should look at all possible aspects of a problem—that is, to take into account all "relevant" data—and then come to a conclusion that we accept only as long as the weight of existing data would appear to support it. Aside from the difference in what is declared relevant in psychology and law, the all-inclusive investigation of psychology is impossible in a trial of a criminal or civil matter. It is not possible in this kind of real life setting, where time and resources are limited, to be allowed the luxury of an exhaustive and never ending inquiry. The trial has to resolve the problem once and for all, and this must be done in a reasonable amount of time. Hence, we have rules of evidence that among other things limit the amount of "data" that the trier of fact (the judge sitting alone or the jury when there is one) can hear.

An example of this conflict between what a psychologist might want to know in order to answer a question and what is admissible in a court of law arises when a defendant's "character" might be related to the crime with which he is charged. Let us assume that in a trial of an assault charge, a man wants to present evidence of his own good character. His reasoning would be that if he could convince the judge or jury that he is not an aggressive sort of person, then the judge or jury would be less likely to convict him. The prosecution, on the other hand, would presumably like to show that he is an aggressive kind of person, and, therefore, would be likely to engage in aggressive behavior. Psychologists would probably want to know about specific incidents where the accused man either did not get into fights with other people. This kind of specific evidence, especially when drawn from situations very similar to the one for which the accused was on trial, would probably be seen by most psychologists as being helpful in deciding whether or not the accused man started the fight for which he was being tried.

However, just a little bit of thought makes it clear that it would be too much of a luxury for a court of law to allow this kind of testimony. Moreover, arguments could easily be made that such testimony would tend to lead the trier of fact away from the incident in question and to other things for which the accused was not being tried. The court could not afford to allow such testimony simply because the trial might never end. The accused man might present evidence suggesting that on a particular occasion even when provoked, he did not start a fight. The prosecution might call witnesses of the incident who would argue the opposite. If this were done, the trial would deteriorate into a trial within a trial and the jury would never hear about the case in question.

The courts tend to resolve the dilemma of what character evidence to let into the trial in a very simple way: for the most part, character evidence involving specific incidents is excluded; only very general statements about the accused's reputation in the community are allowed in as evidence. In this way, very general remarks are allowed (essentially the witness's estimate of the person's reputation in the community) and the trial can then go on and deal with the issue at hand. Clearly, however, from the psychologist's point of view, this general evidence is almost useless. To let in more evidence, however, would be impractical.

Another related reason, more understandable to most psychologists, for the limiting of information that the trier of fact can hear, is that the information might be prejudicial, or that the prejudicial effect of certain evidence would outweigh the value of it as evidence dealing with the fact in issue. Much of the work done by psychologists on evidentiary questions (for example, Efran, 1974; Landy & Aronson, 1969) is of this sort. This research would tend to argue that certain kinds of data about an accused person (or about the case in general) affects the outcome of the trial in predictable ways even though this evidence is not directly related to the fact in issue. Often the implication of this work is that attempts should be made to limit the effects of this kind of "extra-legal" evidence. Thus in these cases the psychologists often argue *for* exclusionary rules.

Obviously the psychologist who decides to do work on evidence does not enter the area with no knowledge. Much research from a variety of different areas of psychology such as person perception, information processing, and memory have clear bearing on the trial. The problem, as always, when one tries to apply general psychological knowledge to a specific social question, is the extent to which one wants to accept the findings from laboratory-based research using nonlegal type materials in predicting effects within the legal system.

From a somewhat different perspective, however, it clearly makes sense to do conceptual replications of some of our standard findings. The reason for this is that when the study is replicated using legal kinds of materials we can be more confident of its validity than we would be without this replication. Moreover, to the extent that it is a close analogy to the question of interest, our confidence will increase.

A final justification for this kind of work that should not be forgotten is that people who may use the results of empirical research on questions of evidence (for example, lawyers, judges, policy makers, and so forth) are more likely to take notice of a study that has as its focus the question that they are interested in than they would an equally good study (from the psychologist's point of view) using other materials or settings.

In picking questions for research, it seems to me that there are at least two separate approaches. The psychologist can do what he/she normally does: pick a question that is of interest to him/her and do research on it. This may or may not be a question of current interest to the legal community and may or may not have general applicability. The only problem with this approach is that if the psychologist is doing the research because he/she thinks it has important social consequences, he/she may be acting in ignorance of other important considerations. In other words, the psychologist might come up with interesting findings but these findings might never be applied to the legal system because of some overriding consideration that the researcher never considered. As I mentioned earlier, one of the reasons for excluding evidence of prior specific incidents of a defendant's behavior to show that he is a good person is that for simple practical reasons our courts are not capable of allowing in such evidence. If one were to do research that showed, for example, that one could predict (to a certain level of confidence) which of two men started a fight by looking into prior fights that they were involved in, this might be interesting from a psychological point of view, but it is unlikely that it would ever have much effect on the trial of assault charges.

The other approach that can be used is to look at the present laws to find out the intent of the law and then to design studies to try to discover whether the law is doing what it is supposed to do. The law of evidence, and the courts that interpret it, make a lot of assumptions about the way in which a judge or jury will use evidence. The psychologist can try to find out whether these assumptions are reasonable. An advantage of this approach is, of course, that the results of the research clearly have some applicability.

The research that I will be discussing on evidentiary questions is of this latter sort: it deals with questions that are closely related to policy questions. Thus they tend to have little applicability to resolving related psychological questions.

The first example of research, that of the effect of evidence of prior criminal convictions of an accused on the outcome of a trial, is clearly related to policy. Had the question and the research that I will describe been approached in a slightly different way, it might have had applicability to the question of the way in which information about a person is integrated. Obviously, I don't wish to imply that the approach that I have followed is better than the more "theoretically" oriented one. It is simply that the applied questions happened to interest me more than the theoretical ones.

Systematic quantitative research on rules of evidence has used the traditional methods of psychological research. On the one hand, various people have done simulations involving experimental manipulations of the questions that one is interested in; on the other hand, people have collected correlational data from real trials (either by watching them or by examining records of them). A third, though less satisfactory method of collecting data on evidentiary questions is, of course, to ask jurors about their deliberations with the aim of trying to find out what factors affected their decisions. I will not be talking about this method for two reasons. In the first place, I am not convinced that people can tell an interviewer what factors were important in their decision-making process. In some of the simulations that we have done, some of our subjects denied that the experimental manipulation had made any effect; yet their data proved otherwise. Secondly, here in Canada, jurors are forbidden (under Section 576.2 of the Criminal Code) from disclosing anything at all about their deliberations.

Clearly the former two methods are not mutually exclusive. Indeed, it is probably the case that one of the best ways of finding out what is really happening is to use both methods. Then, if they come up with the same conclusion, one can be that much more sure that the conclusion is a valid one.

The first example of research that I will be talking about relates to a section of the Canada Evidence Act. Section 12(1) of this act states that "A witness may be questioned as to whether he has been convicted of any offense, and upon being so questioned, if he either denies the fact or refuses to answer, the opposite party may prove such conviction." Although it need not have been interpreted by the courts in this way, as Friedland (1969) has pointed out, it has subsequently had the effect of providing the prosecution "with a statutory right to cross examine an accused on his previous record" (p. 661). In theory, the evidence of the previous criminal convictions of the witness is to aid the trier of fact in deciding on whether or not to believe the witness. Thus if the accused does not testify, the court should not hear of the previous convictions. When an accused man does testify and the jury hears the evidence of the previous criminal convictions, the judge must instruct the jury that they are not to use the evidence of the previous criminal convictions in determining directly whether or not the accused is guilty; rather they are to use this evidence only in determining how much they are to believe the accused.

This "limited use" instruction is based on two questionable assumptions. First of all, it is assumed that a man with a criminal record is more likely, when testifying, to tell lies than is a man without this kind of past. When one considers the situational pressures both for and against telling the truth in a criminal trial—that is, the fact that being caught lying is a serious offense in itself and, on the other hand the fact that lying can often help strengthen one's case—it seems unlikely that even a strong believer in global personality traits would argue that the trait of "honesty" would be very predictive in this situation. As Mischel (1968) points out; ". . . the data on moral behaviour provide no support for the widespread psychodynamic belief in . . . a unitary entity of conscience or honesty" (p. 26).

The second assumption, of course, is that members of a jury can both understand and follow the limiting instructions. Thus it is assumed that they will be able to hear bad things about the accused man and not let that information influence anything except the testimony that he gives. Although there might be some argument about the mechanism by which this evidence affects the outcome of the trial, few psychologists would argue against the proposition that it is harmful to the accused.

There were, however, people involved in criminal justice in Canada who were willing to argue that jurors were able to follow such instructions, and, because it seemed likely that within the next few years Parliament will be forced to review this section of our law, Hershi Kirshenbaum and I decided to look at this question more systematically (See Doob & Kirshenbaum, 1972, for a full report of this research). There were, of course, some data already published. Kalven and Zeisel (1966) reported that defendants who had criminal records (or who did not testify in their own trials) were more likely to be found guilty than were defendants who took the witness stand in their own behalf and who did not have criminal records. However, all of the standard criticisms of correlational findings can be made of those results. For example, it could be argued that the prosecution had stronger cases against those accused men who had criminal records, or that they presented themselves in a less favorable way in some other way, or that they had less competent counsel. Obviously, the list of alternative explanations could go on forever. Moreover, we felt that it was important to have data that used instructions that were reasonably close to those used in Canadian courts. Hence we ran an experiment.

The method that we used was similar to that used by many people who have done what is now called "jury simulation" research. We wrote a hypothetical case of breaking and entering to commit theft. We gave our subjects enough details so that depending on what they believed, they could reasonably decide that the defendant was either guilty or innocent. We had the accused give no real evidence himself. Thus there was no way for the information about criminal record to affect the outcome by way of affecting the credibility of the accused man. Then, for one group of subjects we simply asked them how likely they thought it was that the defendant was guilty of breaking and entering; another group heard the same case but was told that the defendant had a criminal record, while another group heard the case, the evidence concerning the criminal record of the accused, and was given in addition, the instructions that the jury hears in Canada concerning the limited use to which this evidence is to be put.

In summary, then, there were, for our purposes, three groups: First, subjects who were asked to judge how likely they thought it was that a man described in a short written description of a case of breaking and entering to commit theft was guilty. These subjects were given no information about previous criminal convictions of the accused and, presumably assumed that he had no record; second, subjects who heard the same case as the first group, but who also heard that the defendant had a long criminal record for similar kinds of offenses; third, subjects who received the same information as the second group, except who were also instructed that they were not to use the information about previous criminal convictions to determine whether or not they thought that the accused was guilty.

The results were simple and predicted: the presence of evidence of the criminal record of the accused person made the accused more likely to be seen as guilty, and the judge's instructions about the limited use to which this information can be put made no difference. In other words, the people in the second and third groups did not differ from one another, but were both more likely to think that the accused was guilty than were the subjects in the first group. In this experiment, it could be argued that we "loaded" the manipulation in two critical ways: we had a reasonably strong manipulation of prior criminal record (a total of seven previous convictions for related offenses). This was done purposefully to maximize the difference between the record and no record groups so that the judge's instructions could have some effect (in moving the subjects back toward the no record groups). The second way in which we biased our experiment was by having the very last thing that the subjects heard be the limiting instructions from the judge (in that group). We thought that this placing of the instructions (which is not unlike what happens in court) combined with the normal experimental "demands" to do the "right thing" (in this case, presumably, to follow instructions) would give the judge's limiting instructions a better than fair chance of having the effect that, in law, they are supposed to have. However, as I have already said, the only effect that we found was a simple effect of criminal record. The limiting instructions had no effect.

It is probably worth pointing out that we asked our subjects to respond to the question "How likely do you think it is that he is guilty?" We did not ask them anything about what sentence they would recommend if they thought that he was guilty. When trying to find out what variables affect decisions concerning guilt or innocence, the court has one set of data before it; when deciding on the proper sentence for a defendant who has been found guilty, the court typically has a lot of additional information, and by law is encouraged to take a variety of "personal" factors into account. Indeed, the American Law Institute's Model Penal Code states specifically that the presentence report, which the judge should have in most cases, should include such information as "an analysis of the circumstances attending the commission of the crime, the defendant's history of delinquency or criminality, physical and mental condition, family situation and background, economic status, education, occupation and personal habits and any other matters that the probation officer deems relevant to the Court . . . " (American Law Institute, 1962, Section 7.07[3], p. 118). Clearly the American Law Institute sees an important distinction between factors relevant to findings of guilt or innocence and the disposition of convicted persons. Unfortunately, this distinction has been ignored by some psychologists doing work that they perceive to be relevant to understanding the legal process (see, for example, Landy & Aronson, 1969).

It is perhaps ironic that we have such strict rules of evidence in the trials of criminal defendants and then have almost no rules whatsoever about what the judge can hear when deciding on the appropriate sentence for the accused who has been found guilty. With a high proportion of those charged with a criminal offense either pleading or being found guilty, sentencing becomes an extremely important stage of the process. Moreover, given the fact that it has been well documented that judges vary considerably in the principles that they follow in sentencing a guilty defendant (see, for example, Hogarth, 1971; Orland & Tyler, 1974), we would expect that different judges would be affected by very different kinds of information about the crime or the accused.

It would seem worthwhile, therefore, to consider carefully the kinds of information that we want to affect sentencing decisions and follow similar kinds of rules of admissibility at this stage of the trial as are followed in the determination of guilt or innocence. If this kind of principle were followed, judges would not necessarily have available to them certain kinds of information (for example church attendance and marital status) that might otherwise affect them. Empirical research, then, could be done to see whether the evidence available to the judge was having the kind of effects that it was supposed to have.

There are a number of potentially important problems with the simulation I have described that are similar to problems with many simulations. In the first place, this simulation was done with single subjects making private decisions. When one considers, however, that the initial opinions of the individual group members are undoubtedly good predictors of the eventual decision and that information about criminal record may make the jury unanimous (or close to unanimous) on the first vote, then the effects of any variable on individual attitudes are still important.

The second criticism that can be made of this experiment and many others that use the jury simulation technique is that we used only one "case" in the experiment. Although this is a common problem in many areas of psychology—that is, there isn't sampling on the independent variable—we have no way of knowing other than by replicating using different materials whether it is an important problem in this setting.

The third criticism that can be levelled at this experiment is that we did not use a sample of subjects drawn (at random) from the same population that normally sits as jurors. Although we did not sample only university and high school students, we have no way of knowing whether our heterogeneous sample of people chosen haphazardly from a variety of public places is comparable to actual jurors. Finally, of course, because our subjects were asked to "act as if they were real jurors," we have no idea whether they might have behaved in very different ways had they thought that there were some real consequences to their decisions.

In the second experiment that we conducted in Toronto on this topic (Hans & Doob, 1976), we tried to deal with the first two of these questions. By using a completely different hypothetical case we increased the generality of our findings, and by having groups of four people deliberate, we attempted to find out something about the nature of the group deliberations. Because we were not specifically interested in the effects of the judge's instructions, and, therefore, did not need to create a large effect of previous criminal convictions, we used a much weaker manipulation of past record—one previous conviction. One set of subjects simply read the case and made their decisions, while another set read the same case but heard about the previous conviction. This latter group also did hear the standard judge's instructions about the limited use to which this information is to be put.

Interestingly enough, although this manipulation of prior criminal record was not strong enough to have an effect on the verdicts of individual subjects making private decisions, it did have a dramatic effect on the verdicts of our four-person juries: 40 percent of the juries that heard of an accused man's criminal record arrived at guilty verdicts whereas none of the juries that heard nothing about the criminal record arrived at this verdict. Clearly previous criminal activity had a dramatic effect on the groups even though it was not strong enough to affect the individual verdicts.

I suspect that the failure to find this effect for individuals reflects only that it was not a very salient fact in the case. The weakness of the manipulation was probably more important for individuals than groups in that the individuals made their decisions immediately after reading the case, and, it would seem, without spending too much time "weighing" the evidence before them. The groups, of course, had to come to a unanimous group decision which meant that they had more time to consider the details of the case.

More interesting than the verdicts themselves was the way in which this information appeared to affect the discussion. In the first place, the initial statements that were made when the "jury" began to deliberate were much more likely in the record condition to be unfavorable to the accused. As the discussion progressed, it was clear that the information about the previous criminal conviction was affecting the discussion in other subtle ways. Thus the record groups were more likely to discuss matters that hurt the defendant's case; they were more likely to think that the various pieces of evidence that the prosecution mentioned were strong; and so forth. All in all, the nature of the deliberations was quite different as a result of this one piece of evidence.

Obviously, we felt that this second experiment increased both our confidence in the original findings and our knowledge about the mechanism by which the particular piece of evidence was having the effect that it was. Moreover, it made us more convinced than before that the jury was not using the evidence in a manner prescribed by law.

These results are quite similar to those reported by Cornish and Sealy (1973). In the conditions that are closest to those reported here, Cornish and Sealy found that simulated jurors were more likely to convict a man of theft when he had a criminal record than when he did not. This effect, however, was not statistically significant when the previous convictions were for a completely different kind of offense (indecent assault on girls). Unfortunately, other conditions that they ran are really not comparable to the conditions run in the experiments described here.

Having concluded that evidence of prior criminal convictions can hurt the accused and that our limiting instructions offer him no real protection, the obvious question that arises is what policy the government should follow in revising the law. It is clear that the law is in need of revision: it is not doing what it is supposed to do. It seems to me, then, that the policymaker could go in one of two directions. Criminal record of an accused could be kept out of the trial completely unless there is an overriding reason in particular circumstances to let it in. Alternatively, it is possible that it does have some predictive value—that is, a person who was once convicted is more likely than someone with a "clean" record to commit crimes. If this is shown to be the case then one could logically argue that the jury should hear about previous criminal convictions in *all* cases, not just the ones where the defendant testifies. The obvious problem with this second alternative is that it tends to support the notion that a man should be convicted, in part, on the evidence of the kind of person he is, rather than what he has done in the case for which he is being tried.

The choice between these two alternatives is not one that can easily be based on empirical evidence. It is a philosophical or ethical decision and the psychologist has no particular expertise to bring to bear on the decision. Obviously, I favor the more or less complete exclusion of evidence of previous criminal activity. It would be deceptive of me, however, to suggest that this position follows directly from the results of the experiments that I just described.

The final example of the kind of research that I will discuss comes from some research that Pamela Koza and I have done on the Bail Reform Act in Canada. (For a more detailed description of this research see Koza and Doob, 1975a, 1975b.) Without going into the details of the act, this revision in our Criminal Code was devised in order to recognize the rather elementary fact that an accused man, before trial, has not yet been found guilty of an offense. Hence the government should be very hesitant in its use of the power to hold him in custody prior to trial. With a few rather unimportant exceptions, the act does away with the concept of a cash bail set by the Crown. Generally speaking, the philosophy of the act is that the onus is on the Crown to show cause as to why an accused man should be held in custody prior to trial. Furthermore, it sets up two (and only two) reasons for holding someone prior to trial: that there is reason to believe either that he will not show up for trial or that he is a clear and present danger to society. If one of these is proved, then the accused can be kept in custody without bail until his trial.

At each stage of the process, the officer in charge must justify holding an accused. Thus, rather than the normal "arrest" procedures, a police constable is instructed that he is to issue an "appearance notice" (similar to a traffic ticket) unless he feels that he can justify holding an accused for one of the reasons stated above. The desk sergeant at the police station similarly is supposed to release an accused man unless he can demonstrate that one of these conditions is met.

If an accused man is held, he must be taken before a judge and the Crown must "show cause" as to why he should be held in custody. It is at this point that the proceedings are public and relatively easy to monitor, and it was at this point that we began trying to find out what kinds of factors determined whether or not a person would be released. One of the peculiarities of the implementation of these bail hearings in Toronto is that there is generally only one courtroom where hearings are heard each morning. Thus when things are very busy, it is virtually impossible for the court to hear all of its cases before adjournment early in the afternoon. As a result, on busy days, a reasonably high proportion of accused men who were in court would be remanded in custody for a day or two (or occasionally more) for their hearing. One could argue that this is just an unlucky thing to happen to an accused man and that the only real consequence is that he will be in custody for a few days prior to a decision as to whether he should be held in custody until the time of his trial. However, the real problem is that in the long run it may prejudice future decisions concerning this accused man. It is interesting to look at the problem facing a judge who is dealing with a man who is already in custody. The judge must decide whether the Crown has demonstrated the need to keep someone in custody. It would be hard for him to ignore the fact that someone had decided to keep him in custody up to this point. A reasonable inference for a judge might be that he is dealing with a man who must have something wrong with him (for example, he is dangerous or unreliable) and, therefore, he should be kept in custody. Indeed, in support of this notion, we found that those accused men who were eventually detained were far more likely than those who were released to have previously been remanded in custody pending the final "show cause" hearing. It would appear that the process by which an accused becomes labelled as an offender begins early in the criminal justice system.

This finding, of course, is very similar to the effects that I have already discussed with respect to the effects of previous criminal convictions. In the earlier case, previous involvement with the criminal justice system would appear to affect the outcome of a later trial. The present data would suggest that early decisions concerning the disposition of a particular case affect decisions made later on in the same case.

The method used in this study was simple and correlational. We simply watched what was going on and made systematic records of the proceedings. As in any correlational finding, however, it is difficult to be confident that the causal factors can be identified. Interestingly enough, it was findings such as these correlational ones that were important in the promotion of changes in the bail laws that have already taken place. In 1965, Friedland published a book in Canada entitled *Detention before Trial* which, among other things, presented data that demonstrated that in Toronto a man was more likely to be found guilty if he was in custody at the time of trial than if he was out on bail.

Friedland conducted his study in the magistrates courts in Toronto before the changes in our bail system. At the time of the study, cash bail (deposited with the court) was a common condition of release. In one part of an extensive study, Friedland compared two groups of accused men: First, those for whom bail had been set at $500, who had managed to meet the bail, and who, therefore, were not in custody while they waited for their trials nor were they in custody at the time of their trials; second, those who had bail set at the same amount ($500), but were not able to meet it. Obviously, the second group of men waited for and attended their trials in custody. The latter group were more likely to be found guilty whether the offense charged was relatively minor (an offense punishable by summary conviction) or more serious (an indictable offense).

Obviously in this kind of study a number of different factors can account for this effect, even if one assumes that the relationship is a causal one. For example, it is likely that the man in custody cannot prepare his case as well as the man out on bail. He might, for instance, have a harder time finding appropriate witnesses. His lawyer might be less competent. Alternatively, as I have already suggested, it is possible that the judge, who, for the most part can tell whether a man is in custody at the time of trial, might infer that he must be guilty or else he wouldn't be in custody.

To the extent that this kind of inference process existed before the liberalization of our bail laws, it should be even stronger now. With an even higher proportion of accused men being released prior to trial than before, it might even be more likely that a judge would assume that there must be something wrong with an accused who was in custody at the time of his trial. Among other things, now it means that a judge earlier on in the process had decided either that he was dangerous or that he was unreliable.

Koza and I, therefore, tracked a sample of accused who were detained prior to trial through the court system and compared the outcomes of their trials to a sample of people who were on release prior to trial. In our samples, the proportion of people who were found not guilty was so small that comparing the number of guilty findings in the two groups did not make much sense. We looked instead at whether the defendant at the end of the proceedings was in jeopardy of a jail sentence—that is, had been actually sentenced to jail or sentenced to jail only if he did not pay a fine. Once again, the results were clear: being in custody made the disposition more severe.

In order to pin this down a little further, we also ran a jury simulation study where subjects were given a hypothetical case and heard that the accused was either in custody or out on bail prior to trial. Not surprisingly, the subjects inferred that the defendant was more likely to be guilty where he was in custody at the time of the trial. Thus on this particular finding, we have one simulation and two correlational findings that all seem to point to the same conclusion: an accused man is more likely to be seen as guilty if he is incarcerated prior to trial.

Generally speaking, it would seem that there are at least three ways in which evidence that is not directly related to the fact in issue can affect the outcome of the trial. In the first place the trier of fact could make some kind of specific inference about the defendant that might affect the defendant's case. Thus, in the case of prior criminal convictions, they might follow the instructions and use the evidence only in considering credibility. Secondly, the defendant with a "bad" character might be seen as a bad person, and since bad people do bad things, he must be guilty. The last possibility is that the standard of proof necessary for a finding of guilt (or a decision to incarcerate as opposed to using a less severe disposition) might shift according to the nature of the defendant. Thus a member of a jury might feel that he has to be "very sure" that the defendant without a criminal record in fact did the crime in question before he would recommend a guilty verdict. If the defendant had a criminal record, however, the juror might feel that this standard could be relaxed somewhat so that he might feel that he had only to be "reasonably sure" that the defendant did it. It would not seem surprising to find this kind of criterion shift occurring in criminal trials when one considers the disutility of the two kinds of errors that a jury can make (convicting innocent men and setting guilty men free). The disutility of convicting an innocent man who has no previous criminal convictions is probably higher in most people's eyes than the disutility of convicting an innocent man with a long criminal record; similarly the disutility of letting a guilty man out free is higher if he has a criminal record.

The mechanisms that I have described above are clearly very different. We are presently looking at various ways of finding out how different kinds of evidence affect the outcome of trials in different ways.

References

American Law Institute. *Model penal code.* Philadelphia: American Law Institute, 1962.

Cornish, W.R., & Sealy, A.P. Juries and the rules of evidence. *Criminal Law Review*, 1973, 208-223.

Doob, A.N., & Kirshenbaum, H.M. Some empirical evidence on the effect of S.12 of the Canada Evidence Act on an Accused. *Criminal Law Quarterly*, 1972, *15*, 88-96.

Friedland, M.L. *Detention before trial: A study of criminal cases tried in the Toronto Magistrate's Courts.* Toronto: University of Toronto Press, 1965.

Friedland, M.L. Commentary. *Canadian Bar Review*, 1969, *47*, 656-662.

Hans, V.P., & Doob, A.N. S.12 of the Canada Evidence Act and the deliberations of simulated juries. *Criminal Law Quarterly*, in press, 1976.

Hogarth, J. *Sentencing as a human process.* Toronto: University of Toronto Press, 1971.

Kalven, H., & Zeisel, H. *The American jury.* Chicago: University of Chicago Press, 1966.

Koza, P., & Doob, A.N. Some empirical evidence on judicial interim release proceedings. *Criminal Law Quarterly*, 1975, *17*, 258-272. (a)

Koza, P., & Doob, A.N. The relationship of pretrial custody to the outcome of a trial. *Criminal Law Quarterly*, 1975, *17*, 391-400. (b)

Landy, D., & Aronson, E. The influence of the character of the criminal and his victim on the decisions of simulated jurors. *Journal of Experimental Social Psychology*, 1969, *5*, 141-152.

Mischel, W. Personality and assessment. New York: Wiley, 1968.

Orland, L., & Tyler, H.R., Jr. *Justice in sentencing.* New York: Foundation Press, 1974.

Not Necessarily Twelve and Not Necessarily Unanimous: Evaluating the Impact of *Williams v. Florida* and *Johnson v. Louisiana*

Bernard Grofman

Introduction

With recent backlogs of court calendars sometimes stretching into years (see Bloomstein, 1968, pp. 119-122; Zeisel, Kalven, & Buchhotz, 1959, especially chapter 6), there has been widespread interest in dispensing with jury trials whenever possible (Zimroth, 1972, p. 14). There has also been interest in modifying the jury size to less than the traditional twelve persons (see Bloomstein, 1968, pp. 32-33; Institute of Judicial Administration, 1971; Ulmer, 1963, p. 178) and/or in lowering the requirement for a verdict from unanimity to some lesser percentage of agreement among the jurors[1] (for further details, see Bloomstein, 1968, pp. 31-33; Institute of Judicial Administration, 1970; Ulmer, 1963, p. 178) in order to speed the processes of jury deliberation and to reduce the costs in time and money of empanelling a jury.[2] Reversing earlier precedents, the constitutionality of felony convictions reached by juries of less than twelve or by less than unanimity, has now been upheld by the U.S. Supreme Court. In *Williams v. Florida* (1970)[3] the U.S. Supreme Court upheld the constitutionality of felony convictions by state juries of less than twelve. In reviewing *Johnson v. Louisiana* (1972)[4] and *Apodaca v. Oregon* (1972)[5] the Supreme Court held that 10-to-2 and 11-to-1 decisions (in Oregon) and a 9-to-3 decision (in Louisiana) did not violate the Sixth Amendment right to a jury trial. In *Colgrove v. Battin* (1973)[6] the Court upheld six-member civil juries. The full impact of these cases is not yet clear, however.

As Fred Graham wrote in *The New York Times*, "If 9 to 3 convictions are constitutional, how about 8 to 4 or 7 to 5? If undersized juries need not be unanimous, how about 3 to 2 or 2 to 1? And when the Court finally does draw the line where in the Constitution will it find the rationale?" (Graham, 1972b, p. 6).

The research reported in this chapter was partly supported by Grant SOC7514091, Law and Social Science Program, National Science Foundation, for the study of "Modelling Jury Decision Processes."

[1] Nonunanimous verdicts were introduced in Britain in 1967.

[2] Data on comparative costs of six- and twelve-member juries may be found in Institute of Judicial Administration, 1972; and Pabst, 1973, pp. 6-11. Cf. Grofman & Feld (1976).

[3] *Williams v. Florida*, 398 U.S. 78 (1970).

[4] *Johnson v. Louisiana*, 406 U.S. 356, 162Q, 1628 (1972).

[5] *Apodaca v. Oregon*, 406 U.S. 404 (1972).

[6] *Colgrove v. Battin*, 413 U.S. 149 (1973).

The Court's findings in these cases are not such as to provide clear answers to Graham's questions. The court majority held, in effect, that there was nothing sacred about either the number twelve or the unanimity requirements and that both were historical "accidents." What minimum size and what minimum decision rules the Court will ultimately decide the Sixth Amendment *does* require is, as far as I can tell, impossible to determine from the Court's reasoning in these cases, although in *Williams*, Justice White (see Footnote 3, p. 91, note 28), speaking for the majority, indicated that there would eventually be a line drawn somewhere, and that a jury size of six was clearly above that line.

These Supreme Court rulings precipitated considerable outcry from constitutional scholars and civil libertarians, including an editorial in *The New York Times* condemning the Supreme Court's "Retreat on Rights." The rulings have generated pressure on state legislatures to move to smaller juries and to less than unanimous jury verdicts in both criminal and civil cases (Retreat on Rights, 1972, p. 44; see also Graham, 1972a, pp. 1, 28; Manning, 1972, p. 4). For more favorable views of the Court's upholding of nonunanimous juries, see "Backward, Run Backward" (1972, p. 629) and Bloom (1973, pp. 126-129). A summary of the current state of changes in court practices is given by Delsner (1975, p. 1).

Lawyers' reactions to the Supreme Court decisions on size and unanimity requirements appearing in law journals have also been quite sharp (see Saari, 1973; Walbert, 1971; Zeisel, 1971). *Trial's* November/December issue, 1974, contains seven articles dealing with the desirability of reducing jury size and unanimity requirements which range from enthusiastic endorsement of six-member juries (Thompson, 1974) to considerable concern that the recent court rulings will be highly injurious to defendant's rights (Zeisel, 1974). An important recent article on this subject is that of Richard Lempert (1975).

A natural question at this juncture is what difference can the Court's rulings be expected to make. As Ulmer (1963) has put the question:

Since traditional wisdom and practice holds that justice is best dispensed through collegial decision-making, we may ask what theoretical basis can be deduced for such a claim. . . . Does it really matter whether juries decide by unanimous vote, a bare majority, or some vote in between? Does it make a difference whether the size of a decision-making group is 12, 212, or 10,000? [p. 178].

Intuitively it seems reasonable that the fewer the number of jurors required to convict, the more likely is conviction; thus diminishing jury size and/or permitting less than unanimous verdicts should clearly up the conviction rate, but the question remains, however, "by how much?" Still a further question is "How will increases in the conviction rate affect the probability that defendants who are innocent will be wrongly convicted?" No satisfactory answers to either of these questions is presently available. The Court offers no justification, except intuition, for its claim that:

[A] 100 man jury would undoubtedly be more favorable for defendants than a twelve man jury. But when the comparison is between twelve and six, the odds of continually "handing" the jury seem slight, and the numerical difference in the number needed to convict seems unlikely to inure perceptibly to the advantage of either side [see Footnote 3, p. 78, note 47].

The Court in this case (*Williams v. Florida*) is also guilty of misrepresenting the limited empirical evidence available to them. The Court asserts that "studies of operative factors contributing to small group deliberation and decision-making suggest that jurors in the minority on the first ballot are likely to be influenced by the proportional size of the minorities against them" (Footnote 3, note 48). Although the Court here cites Kalven and Zeisel (1966) as their authority, a co-author of the volume has pointed out that the pages cited say the exact opposite of what the Court claimed and, further, the other alleged empirical evidence referred to by the Court (Asch, 1956) also fail to sustain the Court's assertion about size making no "discernible difference" (Zeisel, 1972, pp. 367-369).

We shall attempt to provide some preliminary answers to these and other questions by making some simplifying assumptions about the nature of the jury decision process. We shall use our tools of analysis, probability theory and combinatorial mathematics, building on the work which was done by early scholars, such as LaPlace (1814), Condorcet (1786), and Poisson (1937),[7] and more recent work by Rae (1969), Taylor (1969), and Curtis (1972). We shall also deal with some of the evidence on how juries actually do reach decisions.

We shall restrict ourselves to cases that actually go to trial—that is, not plea-bargained, settled out of court, or otherwise dispensed with—and we shall restrict ourselves to trials which bring in a verdict of innocent or one of guilty on some single count.

Our comments on the implications of varying jury size and/or jury decision rules on verdict outcomes will, obviously, be *directly* relevant only to that small percentage of cases which go to trial. Nonetheless, varying jury size and/or jury decision-rule may have important *indirect* consequences; for example, on the willingness of defendants to engage in plea-bargaining based on their perceptions of the likelihood of a jury of a given size and decision rule bringing in a verdict of guilty in their case. We shall not try to deal with such indirect consequences in this paper.

The assumption of a single-count dichotomous choice avoids the necessity of dealing with bargaining among jurors across counts as to the nature of the verdict. Such bargaining took place, for example, in the Chicago 7 conspiracy trial. Even if there is more than one count in the indictment, our models may still be appropriate as long as each count may be treated separately. (For a

[7] Relevant sections of LaPlace are reviewed in Ulmer (1963); relevant sections of Condorcet are reviewed in Black (1958, pp. 163-165) and more briefly in Ulmer (1963, pp. 179-180) and Barry (1965, p. 293). The most important points of Poisson's argument are discussed and expanded upon in Gelfand & Solomon (1973, pp. 271-278).

simple model of jury behavior when choosing among verdicts of differing degrees of severity, see Grofman, 1974.)

We shall also assume that it makes sense to talk about the defendant's guilt or innocence of the count charged. Clearly, juries make judgments that are more complex than simply "Has the defendant committed the prescribed act?" For example, jurors may make judgments as to whether the defendant's probable punishment "fits" his crime or as to whether the law under which he is accused is indeed a "just" law by community standards. Such judgments on the part of jurors clearly help determine the defendant's probability of conviction. (For more on this point, see Kalven & Zeisel, 1966.) Moreover, even if the physical "facts" of a case are clear, jurors' judgments may still be difficult—that is, involving judgments as to the defendant's "true" motives or the absence of premeditation. Nonetheless, in American jurisprudence the jury's task is to be the decider of the "facts" whether these be physical or psychological and to abide by the judge's instructions as to the law. Our concern shall be with this "idealized" jury process, one in which defendants are either guilty or innocent of the count(s) charged, and one in which determining that guilt or innocence is the jury's sole concern. Such a view of the jury, while descriptively unrealistic is, we believe, of clear normative importance.[8]

Predeliberation Preponderance and Verdict Outcome

If we are to understand the nature of the jury decision process we must look at the relationship between the predeliberation concordance among jurors and the final verdict.

Available empirical data strongly supports the view that when, prior to the jury deliberations, a majority of the jury is in accord as to the verdict, there is a high likelihood that the deliberations will give rise to a unanimous verdict with outcome congruent with the views of the initial majority. Presumably, the majority persuade (or otherwise browbeat) the minority.

In one study of twelve-member juries, 93 percent of the verdicts accorded with the views of the initial majority, 4 percent of the juries remained hung, and in only 3 percent of the cases did the minority persuade the majority (Broeder, 1959). However, the number of jurors on the majority side is not irrelevant. As Rosenblatt and Rosenblatt note:

In a sample of over 200 criminal cases in Chicago and Brooklyn courts studied by the Chicago Jury Project (Kalven and Zeisel, 1966), all of the hung juries observed possessed a minority on the first ballot of at least three. In most of

---

[8] I am indebted to an anonymous referee for emphasizing the need to justify the assumption that one can, even in principle, talk meaningfully of the true "guilt" or "innocence" of a defendant.

them the initial majority was four or five. Likewise an initial minority almost never prevailed in persuading the initial majority unless it, too, numbered at least three. Thus, although the final ballot often showed one lone juror holding out for acquittal, it is only after several others had previously shared that opinion. Thus, the "hanging juror" rarely exists except as one who tenaciously refuses to desert an unpopular view after others have fallen away.[9]

We have reproduced the Kalven and Zeisel data at Table 8-1. As Kalven and Zeisel put it, "it requires a massive minority of 4 to 5 jurors (out of 12) at the first vote to develop the likelihood of a hung jury" (1966, p. 462). Their findings suggest that in juries of size twelve, a predeliberation majority of 11-1 (1-11) will go to unanimity with virtual certainty, and a predeliberation majority of 10-2 (2-10) will go to unanimity with very high certainty while lesser majorities will go to unanimity with lower (but still high) probabilities.

These assertions are buttressed by data from other studies. Padawer-Singer and Barton (1975)[10] found that for twelve-member juries no reversal of the initial majority occurred unless the initial minority was at least four. For six-member juries they found no reversal of the initial majority occurred unless the initial majority was at least two in number. They also found that reversals of the initial majority were twice as likely among twelve-member juries as in six-member juries, and suggested that "different processes may take place in 6- v. 12-member juries and that verdicts are reached on different bases" (Padawer-

Table 8-1
First Ballot Votes and Frequency of Hung Jury in Kalven and Zeisel Data

Guilty Votes on First Ballot	Percent Hung Juries	Predictions of Davis Model 3 in Percents
11	0 $N = 23$	0
10 or 9	0 $N = 56$	10
8 or 7	19 $N = 26$	18
6	0 $N = 10$	25
5 or 4	19 $N = 16$	18
3 or 2	7 $N = 22$	10
1	0 $N = 3$	0

Note: Data drawn in part from Kalven & Zeisel (1966, Table 127, p. 462).

[9] A.M. Rosenblatt and J.C. Rosenblatt, "Six Member Juries in Criminal Cases: Legal and Psychological Considerations," 47 *St. John's Law Review* A15, 631 (1973). © 1973 by St. John's Law Review. Used by permission. All rights reserved.

[10] The Kalven and Zeisel (1966) data are not fully comparable with those of Padawer-Singer and Barton (1975), since the former are reporting first ballot and the latter predeliberation consensus.

Singer & Barton, 1975, Section XI, p. 7). As we shall see below, this conclusion does not really follow from their data (see Table 8-1).

In another study of jury decision-making, R.J. Simon has collected data from mock juries drawn from local jury pools in three different jurisdictions: Minneapolis, St. Louis, and Chicago. Juries were exposed to edited tape recordings of transcripts of trials involving housebreaking (thirty juries) or incest (sixty-eight juries) (Simon, 1967).[11] The relative frequency of decisions observed for each alternative for individual jurors and for twelve-member juries is shown in Table 8-2.

In the housebreaking case the ratio of acquittals to convictions is very similar for individuals and for juries; in the incest case juries are considerably more conviction-prone than are individuals. It is difficult to account for these cases within the confines of a single model. One simple hypothesis (set of hypotheses) is that juries operate by a $K/12$ths rule—that is, if K or more ($K \geq 7$) votes are achieved in the predeliberation period for conviction (acquittal) then the jury will convict (acquit) otherwise the jury will hang. If we take the mean percentage phase of the trial and assume that it is binomially distributed across juries, we may calculate the expected value of P_C (percent convictions) P_H (percent hung juries) and P_A (percent acquittals) for the twelve-member juries under various $K/12$ths decision-rules such as 7/12ths, 11/12ths, and 12/12ths. The results shown in Table 8-2 suggest that these rules overpredict the ratio of the more common to the less common verdict and except for the 7/12ths rule egregiously overpredict the percentage of hung juries. Furthermore, the relatively low rate of predeliberation juror concordance observed by Simon buttresses the view that the observed high rate of jury verdict

Table 8-2
Decisions by Mock Juries and Individuals in Housebreaking and Incest Cases and Predictions from Various Decision Rule Models

	Housebreaking Case				Incest Case			
	N	P_C	P_A	P_H	N	P_C	P_A	P_H
Individual Decisions	360	34%	66%		816	67%	33%	
Jury Decisions	30	27%	56%	17%	68	71%	13%	16%
7/12ths rule	30	7%	80%	13%	68	81%	5%	14%
8/12ths rule	30	3%	61%	36%	68	64%	4%	32%
11/12ths rule	30	0%	5%	95%	68	4%	0%	95%
12/12ths rule	30	0%	1%	99%	68	1%	0%	99%
Davis Model	30	22%	62%	16%	68	66%	18%	16%

Note: Data drawn in part from Davis (1973, Table 4).

[11] I'm indebted to Professor Neil Vidmar for calling this excellent piece to my attention.

unanimity is not attributable to predeliberation jury unanimity as to correct verdict; rather, some form of group conformity process is operative. But, given the poor showing of $K/12$ths rules on the Simon data, the exact form this conformity process takes remains an open question.

Before, however, we too cavalierly write off the usefulness of rules such as the $K/12$ths rules, it is necessary to look at two more recent articles involving experimental work on mock juries, both coauthored by James Davis. In the first of these, Davis, Kerr, Atkin, Holt, & Meek (1975)[12] studied the decision making of mock juries of six and twelve members assigned either a unanimity or a two-thirds majority decision-rule. They found that neither the size nor assigned rule variables exerted a significant overall effect upon the distribution of jury verdicts. They also found that the rule that best predicted overall jury verdicts as a function of predeliberation consensus was a simple two-thirds rule, which was the best predictor under all four experimental conditions.

In the second study, which was confined to six-member juries, Davis, Kerr, Stasser, Meek, & Holt (1975)[13] found a modified two-thirds rule to be best predictor of the relationship between predeliberation consensus and final verdict—a rule in which the jury always voted in accord with the predeliberation majority but did not always hang if no predeliberation majority existed. In this modified form of the two-thirds rule, if the jury were evenly split in its predeliberation views, a verdict of not guilty was predicted 75 percent of the time and a hung jury was predicted for the remaining 25 percent of the time.

In both studies the fit of the two-thirds rule (or its variant) was reasonably good. In the first study in both the six-person unanimous and nonunanimous cases, the predicted overall results were .02 guilty/.88 not guilty/.10 hung versus actual results of .00 guilty/.89 not guilty/.10 hung. In the twelve-person cases, the predicted overall results were .00/.90/.10 versus .00/.72/.28 actual results in the unanimous, and .00/.94/.06 actual results in the nonunanimous case. In the second study Davis et al., report exact relationships between verdict outcomes and the initial jury preference breakdown; we have reproduced those results as Table 8-3. The predicted overall verdict distribution was .40/.52/.08. The actual distribution was .40/.54/.06. Clearly, the modified two-thirds rule predicted very well in the aggregate, even though its detailed predictions (see Table 8-3) are not that good.

Davis has compared predictions of models of the $K/12$th type with a number of other models. See Table 8-4. For example, in his first article (Davis, 1973) he proposed five models for the twelve-member jury case.[14] The

---

[12] I am deeply indebted to Professor Davis for providing me with an advance copy of this article.

[13] I'm indebted to Professor Davis for making available to me a prepublication copy of this article.

[14] All five models predict conviction (acquittal) in the 12-0 and 11-1 (0-12 and 1-11) cases. In Model 1 distributions 10-2, 9-3, . . . , 2-10 yield hung verdicts with probability one. In Model 2 distributions 10-2, 9-3, . . . , 2-10 yield guilty, not guilty, or hung verdicts with

Table 8-3
Distribution of Verdicts Given Predeliberation Preferences in Six-Member Mock Juries

Juror Predeliberation Preferences		Jury Verdicts Obtained			Jury Verdicts Predicted by S-Curve Model[a]		
Guilty	Not Guilty	Guilty	Not Guilty	Hung	Guilty	Not Guilty	Hung
6	0	–	–	–	1.00	.00	.00
5	1	14(.93)	1(.07)	0(.00)	1.00	.00	.00
4	2	16(.84)	3(.16)	0(.00)	.87	.11	.02
3	3	5(.16)	21(.68)	5(.16)	.42	.42	.16
2	4	1(.06)	17(.94)	0(.00)	.11	.87	.02
1	5	0(.00)	6(1.00)	0(.00)	.00	1.00	.00
0	6	0(.00)	1(1.00)	0(.00)	.00	1.00	.00

[a]Parameters are set at $\alpha = .16, B = 3$.
Note: Adapted from Davis, Kerr, Stasser, Meek, & Robert Holt (1975, Table 4, p. 37).

predictions of these models are shown in Table 8-4. Model 1 is a 11/12ths rule. Model 5 is a modified form of the 7/12ths rule. The model which Davis finds to far and away best fit the Simon data is Model 3, one which is not of the K/12ths form.

The fit of Model 3 to the Simon data is shown in row 7 of Table 8-2.[15] As can be seen from Table 8-3, the fit of this model is reasonably good. Since this model has a rather peculiar asymmetry in the 6-6 case, it might appear that a model identical to that of Model 3 except for giving rise to equal proportions of hung juries, acquittals, and convictions in the 6-6 case might improve the fit. However, a glance at Table 8-3 shows this hope to be in vain, since such a change would decrease the number of convictions, and also increase the number of acquittals, thus worsening the fit more than would be compensated for by the increase in the predicted number of hung juries. While a best fitting model can, in principle, be calculated by looking at each of the thirteen possible predeliberation distributions in the two trials dealt with by Simon and assigning the vector to each that minimizes the sum of squares deviation from actual outcomes, the

equal probability (i.e., 1/3). In Model 3 distributions 10-2, . . . , 6-6 yield guilty with probability $1/N$ and not guilty or hung with probability $1/2 (i)/(1-N)$ where i is the number of guilty votes in the predeliberation stage; distributions 5-7, . . . 2-10 yield not guilty with probability $(12-i)/N$ and guilty or hung with equal probability $1/2$ $1-(12-i)/N$. In Model 4 distributions 10-2, . . . , 7-5 yield guilty with probability i/n and not guilty or hung with equal probability, $1/2$ $1-(i/N)$, distributions 6-6, . . . 2-10 yield hung with probability one. In Model 5 distributions 10-2, . . . , 7-5 yield hung with probability one; distributions 6-6, . . . 2-10 yield not guilty with probability one. (See Table 8-4.)

[15] For χ^2 values and data on the fit of the other four models, see Davis (1973, p. 106).

Table 8-4

Verdict Predictions of Five Davis Models of Jury Conformity Processes[a] as a Function of Predeliberation Juror Verdict Preferences

Convict-Acquit	Model 1	Model 2	Model 3	Model 4	Model 5
12-0	(100,0,0)	(100,0,0)	(100,0,0)	(100,0,0)	(100,0,0)
11-1	(100,0,0)	(100,0,0)	(100,0,0)	(100,0,0)	(100,0,0)
10-2	(0,0,100)	(33,33,33)	(83,8,8)	(83,8,8)	(100,0,0)
9-3	(0,0,100)	(33,33,33)	(75,13,13)	(75,13,13)	(100,0,0)
8-4	(0,0,100)	(33,33,33)	(67,17,17)	(67,17,17)	(100,0,0)
7-5	(0,0,100)	(33,33,33)	(58,21,21)	(58,21,21)	(100,0,0)
6-6	(0,0,100)	(33,33,33)	(50,25,25)	(0,0,100)	(0,100,0)
5-7	(0,0,100)	(33,33,33)	(21,58,21)	(0,0,100)	(0,100,0)
4-8	(0,0,100)	(33,33,33)	(17,67,17)	(0,0,100)	(0,100,0)
3-9	(0,0,100)	(33,33,33)	(13,75,13)	(0,0,100)	(0,100,0)
2-10	(0,0,100)	(33,33,33)	(8,83,8)	(0,0,100)	(0,100,0)
1-11	(0,100,0)	(0,100,0)	(0,100,0)	(0,100,0)	(0,100,0)
0-12	(0,100,0)	(0,100,0)	(0,100,0)	(0,100,0)	(0,100,0)

[a]Vectors indicate the predicted percentages of convictions, acquittals, and hung juries, in that order.

raw data for this calculation are not provided by Simon; however, such an idiosyncratic model would in any case be of little value.

Although the Kalven and Zeisel data are not comparable with the Simon data, since they are reporting first ballot rather than predeliberation consensus (and thus we would expect that their data would show a greater consensus than those of Simon), we have, for comparison purposes, applied Davis' Model 3 to the Kalven and Zeisel data. The results are shown in Column 3 of Table 8-1. For simplicity we have weighted cases equally to provide averaged predictions for the Davis model. The fit of the Davis model, while far from perfect, is not unreasonable, with the troublesome exception of the case of an initial 6-6 vote.

As we also observe in the case of the experimental data displayed in Table 8-3, juries that begin evenly split seem rarely to hang—a finding further confirmed in the Padawer-Singer and Barton (1975) study. Why this is so is unclear. Perhaps there is a bias toward acquittal such that an evenly split jury is more likely to tilt to acquittal than either to hang or to convict. (See Table 8-3.) In any case, this result is too well documented to be merely an artifact of sample size.

Davis (1973) concludes that while Model 3 is "more suggestive than definitive . . . nevertheless, the accuracy of Model 3 (for the Simon data) implies that a jury member alone in his decision does not sway the outcome but rather yields to the majority. If the majority favoring guilty is six to ten in size, the probability of a guilty verdict is the proportion of jury members advocating that decision; otherwise the verdict is as likely to be not guilty as hung. If the majority favoring not guilty ranges from seven to ten, the process is identical but now favors the not guilty verdict in proportion to the number of these advocates" (p. 106). However, we are not as convinced as Davis that the process is as straightforward as either Model 3 or a rule of the $K/12$ths form would suggest. It may be that the relationship between percentage favoring conviction and the probability of a unanimous verdict for conviction is curvilinear rather than the combined step function and linear relationship that Davis postulates, or the step function postulated by models of the $K/12$ths form. One possibility would be a power function model similar to that proposed by Gray, Richardson, & Mayhew (1968).[16] In this model the probability of unanimous conviction in the predeliberation stage—that is, for i initial votes for conviction and N jurors:

$$P_C = \frac{\dfrac{(i)^B}{(N)}}{\dfrac{(i)^B}{(N)} + \dfrac{(N-i)^B}{(N)}}.$$ (1)

We assume that no jurors are neutral or undecided. Here, we interpret P_C as the probability that a jury with this predeliberation consensus will bring in a verdict of guilty. This model does not, however, permit for hung juries. A simple modification enables us to accommodate nondecisive verdicts. We let

$$\frac{P_C}{P_A} = \frac{\dfrac{(i)^B}{(N)}}{\dfrac{(N-i)^B}{(N)}} = \frac{(i)^B}{(N-i)}.$$ (2)

Then, for i initial votes for conviction, we let

$$P_H = \begin{cases} \alpha \dfrac{P_C}{P_A} & \text{if } i \leqslant N - i \\[2em] \alpha \dfrac{P_A}{P_C} & \text{if } i > N - i \end{cases}$$ (3)

---

[16] I am indebted to an anonymous referee of another article of mine for calling this model to my attention, albeit in a rather different context.

Here, P_H is interpreted as the probability that a jury with this predeliberation consensus will hang. Parameters α and B may be fitted to jury data. The relationship between initial consensus and probability of conviction specified by equations (2) and (3) will be an S-shaped curve. Thus, high consensus will result in a virtual certainty of conviction (or acquittal); low consensus will result in a high (or at least higher) probability of a hung jury.

Since $P_A + P_C + P_H = 1$ for any given values of i, solving (2) and (3) for the case where $i \leqslant N - i$ yields

$$P_A = \frac{1 - \alpha \dfrac{(i)^B}{(N-i)}}{1 + \dfrac{(i)^B}{(N-i)}} \tag{4}$$

$$P_C = \frac{\dfrac{(i)^B}{(N-i)} \left[1 - \alpha \dfrac{(i)}{(N-i)}\right]^B}{1 + \dfrac{(i)^B}{(N-i)}} \tag{5}$$

$$P_H = \frac{(i)^B}{(N-i)} \tag{6}$$

Similar expressions are obtained for the case where $i > N - i$.

If we let $B = 3$, $\alpha = .16$, we obtain for the six-member jury the values specified in the right hand columns of Table 8-3. As we see, those values provide reasonably good fit to the Davis et al. data except, of course, for the troublesome case of the initial 3-3 split. This bias for acquittal manifested in the data in Table 8-3 can be compensated for in our model by introducing a bias coefficient, c, such that

$$\frac{P_C}{P_A} = \frac{(i)^B}{(N-i)} = c. \tag{7}$$

We shall not, however, here introduce such a further refinement since we would then have almost as many parameters as data points. The model we have presented is, we should note, very similar to the logit model used by Edward Tufte (1973) to plot the relationship between seats and votes in national legislatures and is a generalized form of the famous "cube law" of electoral politics.[17]

---

[17] For a review of the origins of the cube-law conjecture and recent work on the seats-vote relationship see Grofman, 1975.

Basic Findings

When individual jurors have some probability of changing their verdict in the direction of the majority consensus it is not necessary for the jury to begin with a phenomenally high predeliberation consensus to arrive at a unanimous verdict almost all the time. For example, in a jury of size twelve, to obtain a percentage of hung juries of 5 percent, we need postulate only a .90 initial concordance to obtain such a low percentage of hung juries if the jury decision process is that of Davis' Model 3; a .75 initial concordance if the jury decision process is that of the 7/12ths rule; a .83 initial concordance (p) if the jury decision process is that of the 8/12ths rule, and so forth.

Of course, jury size interacts with initial preponderance to determine the probability of a hung jury. We show in Table 8-5 the expected percentage of hung juries as a function of jury size (six versus twelve) jury decision rule (various K/Nths rules) and the initial preponderance among members of the jury pool. We see that, if the effective decision-rule is 5/6ths or unanimity juries of size twelve are *always* more likely to hang than juries of size six. If, however, the effective decision-rule in the jury is two-thirds (the rule for which we have found the greatest empirical support), then whether a jury of six or a jury of size twelve will be the more likely to hang depends upon the preponderance of the majority sentiment among members of the jury pool. If the jury pool is evenly split or if the majority view is held by less than 80 percent of the jury pool (under our two-thirds rule assumption) six-member juries will be *less* likely to hang than twelve-member juries. If, however, a single view is held by 80 percent or more of the members of the juror pool, then six-member juries will be *more* likely to hang than twelve-member juries. This finding is, we believe, quite counterintuitive. Moreover, it suggests that any attempt to determine whether twelve-member juries are more "hanging-prone" than six-member juries is doomed to failure unless it takes into account the extent of predeliberation concurrence among the juror pool and the nature of the jury conformity processes in different sized juries. Whether the conformity process is "different" in smaller sized juries is a question very much at issue. Our reading of the available evidence argues for the proportionality rule—that is, two jurors out of six are equivalent to four out of twelve. This proportionality hypothesis is rejected by some scholars (Lempert, 1975, pp. 678-679). We do not, however, regard the limited evidence as in any way conclusive on this question. (See also Grofman & Hamilton, 1975.)

In the murder case used by Padawer-Singer and Barton (1975), jurors in the predeliberation phase were almost evenly divided as to the defendant's guilt or innocence. In their six-member unanimous juries 28.5 percent were hung and in their twelve-member unanimous juries 35.7 percent hung. Thus, as we would expect, even a case that produced almost total disagreement among the members of the juror pool as to the correct verdict still did not lead to a very high

Table 8-5
Percent Hung Juries as a Function of Jury Size, Jury Decision-Rule, and Preponderant View among Members of the Jury Pool

Jury Size/Rule	2/3rds rule						5/6ths rule						Unanimity rule					
	.5	.6	.7	.8	.9	.95	.5	.6	.7	.8	.9	.95	.5	.6	.7	.8	.9	.95
Preponderance																		
6	.31	.28	.19	.08	.01	.00	.78	.73	.57	.34	.11	.03	.97	.95	.88	.74	.47	.26
12	.61	.50	.27	.07	.00	.00	.96	.91	.75	.44	.12	.02	.99+	.99+	.99	.93	.72	.46
Ratio of Hung 12 to Hung 6	1.9	1.8	1.4	.9	.3	.1	1.2	1.2	1.3	1.3	1.1	.6	1.0	1.1	1.1	1.3	1.5	1.8

percentage of hung juries once deliberations began, because the binomial distribution insures that a sizeable percentage of the juries drawn from a nearly evenly split juror pool will, nonetheless, be highly skewed in one direction or the other in their predeliberation preferences.

The effect of the group conformity process that appears to operate in juries is to exaggerate the initial majority sentiment in the direction of a unanimous verdict consonant with the views of that initial majority. This effect is somewhat more marked, in general, in smaller sized juries if what we look at is the percentage of trials that reach a verdict consonant with the views of the predeliberation majority. However, if we look at the ratio of verdicts consonant with the initial preponderance among members of the jury pool to those consonant with the views of the initial minority—that is, if we exclude hung juries—then it is the larger sized juries that more greatly exaggerate the impact of the views of the initial predeliberation jury pool majority. The relationship between jury verdicts and jury size (six versus twelve) jury decision-rule (various K/Nths rules) and the preponderance among the members of the jury pool is shown in Table 8-6. For example, if we exclude hung juries, a jury pool that begins with a 70 percent agreement as to verdict will give rise to verdicts an expected 91 percent of which will be in accord with that view when a six-member jury is drawn, and will give rise to verdicts an expected 99 percent of which are in accord with that view when a twelve-member jury is drawn!

When juries are allowed to reach nonunanimous verdicts, the probability that the jurors will have already achieved sufficient consensus for a verdict before they begin deliberations is extremely high in smaller sized juries. The percentage of juries with predeliberation accord as to the verdict is shown in Table 8-7 as a function of jury size (six versus twelve), jury decision-rule, (various K/Nths rules) and the preponderance among the members of the jury pool. For example, we may see from Table 8-7 that in a jury of size six, even if the juror pool is 50 percent acquittal and 50 percent conviction in the predeliberation phase, there is a 22 percent probability $(14)/(64)$ that the jury will have a predeliberation majority of five or six, and a 60 percent $(44)/(64)$ probability that the jury will have a predeliberation majority of at least 4-2. On the other hand, if the jurors are evenly divided as to conviction or acquittal, the likelihood of drawing a twelve-member jury with at least nine members in agreement is only 4 percent and the probability of obtaining at least eight members in agreement is only 39 percent $(1588)/(4096)$. However, for high levels of initial preponderance among the members of the jury pool, the differences between six-member and twelve-member juries virtually vanish. Indeed for very high levels of preponderance coupled with low unanimity requirements (for example, $p \geqslant .9$, unanimity requirements of 5/6ths or less), large sized juries are marginally more likely to walk into the jury room in agreement than are smaller sized juries.

It is useful at this point to remind the reader who is looking for differences

Table 8-6
Jury Verdicts as a Function of Jury Size, Jury Decision-Rule, and Preponderant View among Members of the Jury Pool

Jury Size/Rule	2/3rds rule						5/6ths rule						Unanimity rule					
Preponderance	.5	.6	.7	.8	.9	.95	.5	.6	.7	.8	.9	.95	.5	.6	.7	.8	.9	.95
Minority Verdict	.34	.18	.07	.02	.00	.00	.11	.04	.01	.00	.00	.00	.02	.00	.00	.00	.00	.00
Preponderant Verdict	.34	.54	.74	.90	.98	.99+	.11	.23	.42	.66	.89	.97	.02	.05	.12	.26	.53	.73
Ratio of Preponderant Verdicts to Total Verdicts (Excluding Hung Juries)	.50	.75	.91	.98	.99+	.99+	.50	.85	.98	.99	.99+	.99+	.50	.92	.99	.99+	.99+	.99+
Minority Verdict	.19	.06	.01	.00	.00	.00	.02	.00	.00	.00	.00	.00	.00	.00	.00	.00	.00	.00
Preponderant Verdict	.19	.44	.72	.93	.99+	.99+	.02	.08	.25	.56	.89	.98	.00	.00	.01	.07	.28	.54
Ratio of Preponderant Verdicts to Total Verdicts (Excluding Hung Juries)	.50	.88	.99	.99+	.99+	.99+	.50	.97	.99+	.99+	.99+	.99+	.50	.96	.99+	.99+	.99+	.99+

Table 8-7
Percent Juries with Predeliberation Accord as to Verdict as a Function of Jury Size, Jury Decision-Rule, and Preponderant View among Members of the Jury Pool

Jury Size/Rule	2/3rds rule						5/6ths rule						Unanimity rule					
Preponderance	.5	.6	.7	.8	.9	.95	.5	.6	.7	.8	.9	.95	.5	.6	.7	.8	.9	.95
6	.69	.72	.81	.92	.99	.99+	.22	.27	.43	.66	.89	.97	.03	.05	.12	.26	.53	.74
12	.39	.50	.73	.93	.99+	.99+	.04	.09	.25	.56	.88	.98	.00	.00	.01	.07	.28	.54

between six- and twelve-member juries that the nature of those differences will depend upon the extent of predeliberation accord as to verdict among the pool from which jurors are drawn. As we see from Table 8-7, for hard cases—that is, ones with low initial agreement as to verdict—six-member nonunanimous juries (5-1 and 4-2) will behave markedly differently than their twelve-member "equivalents" (10-2 and 8-4) in that the smaller sized juries will exhibit a much higher incidence of decisions that required little or no deliberation time because the jurors walked into the jury room in sufficient agreement to reach a verdict immediately. On the other hand, for easy cases—that is, ones with high initial agreement as to verdict—differences as to deliberation time between six-member nonunanimous and twelve-member nonunanimous juries will be obscured; both sized juries will have a very high proportion of cases in which verdicts are immediately reached. Thus, it may be *very* difficult to establish size differences experimentally without a *very* large sample size and cases which will generate significant size effects.[18]

One related point: if a jury is evenly split we would expect about twice as many "opinion reversals" (i.e., verdicts consonant with the predeliberation minority) in twelve-member juries than in six-member juries, exactly what Padawer-Singer and Barton (1975) find in their study, which is one in which jurors in the predeliberation phase were almost evenly divided as to the defendant's guilt or innocence. On the other hand, if the case is an easy one—that is, one with high predeliberation among the juror pool agreement—then differences in reversal rate between six-member and twelve-member juries should be minimal. If we postulate an S-curve relationship, then the bulk of the reversals will occur in the 4-2 and 2-4 cases in six-member juries and in the 8-4, 7-5, 4-8, and 5-7 cases in twelve-member juries. If the jury pool is evenly divided the latter cases occur about twice as frequently as the former.

Because of the group conformity process that has been observed to operate in jury decision-making it is very likely that shifts from unanimous to nonunanimous verdicts will have minimal impact on verdict outcomes as long as jury size is held constant. It appears to be the case that juries that began as near unanimous end up unanimous with virtual certainty. Thus, we would expect a change from a unanimity to a nonunanimity rule to have zero impact, except perhaps as to deliberation time.[19]

---

[18] Cf. Lempert (1975, pp. 648-653), in which he attempts to estimate the fraction of cases in which jury size can be expected to have a reasonable probability of affecting the verdict. In this chapter we shall not attempt to deal with the issue of minority representation as a function of jury size. See Zeisel (1971) and Lempert (1975, pp. 665-679). We recognize this as an important omission, although we do not concur with Lempert's (1975, p. 699) impression that "the final judgment on six versus twelve will turn on the values that individuals subjectively place on the presence of minority views in the jury room." (Cf. Grofman, 1976, on the weights to be attached to freeing the innocent v. convicting the guilty.)

[19] The Davis, Kerr, Atkin, Holt, & Meek (1975) study, which has some data contradicting this assertion, is marred by deliberation rules that cut off deliberation at a fixed time, which in some cases is before the conformity process can take full effect. This artificially increases the percentage of hung juries among juries requiring unanimity.

Conclusions

We regard the models and results generated in this chapter as only a preliminary to more sophisticated modelling of jury decision processes as sequential decision-making by actors of differentiated status among multiple alternatives. Nonetheless, we feel that the models we have presented can be used as a baseline against which to compare the implications of alternative and more complex models. Limited as our results may be, at least we are explicit about our assumptions and where they lead us, rather than taking glib refuge in intuition, common sense, or misinterpreted social science à la the Supreme Court majority in its recent rulings on the constitutionality of juries which are less than twelve and less than unanimous.

In this chapter we have shown that there *can* be significant verdict and other differences between six-member and twelve-member juries (although not necessarily between unanimous and nonunanimous juries of the same size); but that detecting such "discernible" differences empirically is likely to be quite difficult. We have also shown that modelling size/decision-rule impact necessitates making strong assumptions as to the nature of the underlying group conformity process. Under the assumptions specified in the paper, the impact of jury size will vary tremendously depending upon the extent of predeliberation accord as to verdict.

References

Asch, S.E. Studies of independence and conformity: A minority of one against a unanimous majority. *Psychological Monographs*, 1956, *70*, 1-70.

Backward, run backward. *National Review*, June 9, 1972.

Barry, B. *Political argument*. London: Routledge & Kegan Paul, 1965.

Black, D. *The theory of committees and elections*. London: Cambridge University Press, 1958.

Bloom, M. Here comes the six-man jury. *Reader's Digest*, September 1973, pp. 126-129.

Bloomstein, M.J. *Verdict: The jury system*. New York: Dodd, Mead, 1968.

Broeder, D.W. The University of Chicago Jury Project. *University of Nebraska Law Review*, 1959, *38*, 744-760.

Condorcet, N.C. *Essai sur l'application de l'analyse à la probabilité des decision rendues à la pluralité des voix*. Paris, 1786.

Curtis, R. Decision rules and collective values in constitutional choice. In R. Niemi & H. Weisberg (Eds.), *Probability models of collective decision-making*. Chicago: Merrill, 1972.

Davis, J. Group decision and social interaction: A theory of social decision schemes. *Psychological Review*, 1973, *80*, 97-125.

Davis, J., Kerr, N.L., Atkin, R.S., Holt, R., & Meek, D. The decision processes of 6- and 12-person mock juries assigned unanimous and two-thirds majority rules. *Journal of Personality and Social Psychology*, 1975, *32*, 1-14.

Davis, J., Kerr, N.L., Stasser, G., Meek, D., & Holt, R. Victim consequences, sentence severity and decision processes in mock juries. University of Illinois, Department of Psychology, 1975 (mimeograph).

Delsner, L. Smaller juries increase divided verdicts allowed. *The New York Times*, July 20, 1975, p. 1.

Gelfand, A.A., & Solomon, H. A study of Poisson's models for jury verdicts in criminal and civil trials. *Journal of American Association*, 1973, *68*, 271-278.

Graham, F.P. Justices back state court convictions without unanimous verdicts by juries. *The New York Times*, May 23, 1972, pp. 1, 28. (a)

Graham, F.P. Jury trial: Now the verdict need not be unanimous. *The New York Times*, May 28, 1972, p. 6. (b)

Gray, H., Richardson, J.T., & Mayhew, B.H. Influence attempts and effective power: A re-examination of an unsubstantiated hypothesis. *Sociometry*, 1968, *31*, 245-258.

Grofman, B. The effects of multiple decision alternatives on juror verdicts: The case of single-peaked preferences. State University of New York at Stony Brook, Department of Political Science, 1974 (mimeograph).

Grofman, B. Formal models of electoral systems: A survey of recent research. In R. Wildenmann et al. (Eds.), *German political yearbook*. Munich: Verlag, 1975.

Grofman, B., & Feld, S. A note on clique avoidance in repeated jury selection from among a fixed pool of jurors: Comparisons of manpower savings in six and twelve member juries. *Public Choice*, in press, 1976.

Grofman, B., & Hamilton, V.L. Group decision-making in three member and five member mock juries under unanimous and nonunanimous verdict requirements. Unpublished manuscript, State University of New York at Stony Brook, October 1975.

Institute of Judicial Administration. Juries of less than twelve and verdicts of less than unanimous. New York University, 1970 (mimeograph).

Institute of Judicial Administration. States in which criminal cases may be tried by fewer than twelve jurors. New York University, 1971 (mimeograph).

Institute of Judicial Administration. A comparison of six and twelve member civil juries in New Jersey superior and county courts. New York University, 1972 (mimeograph).

Kalven, H., & Zeisel, H. *The American jury*. Boston: Little, Brown, 1966.

LaPlace, P.S. *Essai philosophique sur les probabilités*. Paris, 1814. (a)

LaPlace, P.S. *Theorie analytique des probabilités*. Paris, 1814. (b)

Lempert, R.O. Uncovering nondiscernible differences: Empirical research and the jury-size cases. *Michigan Law Review*, 1975, *73*, 644-708.

Manning, D.E. The split jury. *Newsweek*, June 19, 1972.

Pabst, W.R. What do six-member juries really save? *Judicature*, 1973, *57*, 6-11.

Padawer-Singer, A.M., & Barton, A.H. Interim report: Experimental study of decision-making in the 12- versus 6-man jury under unanimous versus non-unanimous decisions. Columbia University, Bureau of Applied Social Research, May 1975 (mimeograph).

Poisson, S.P. *Recherches sur la probabilité des jugement en matière criminalle et en matière civile: Précedées des régles generales du calcul des probabilités.* Paris: Bachelieu, 1937.

Rae, D. Decision rules and individual values in collective choice. *American Political Science Review*, 1969, *63*, 40-56.

Retreat on rights. *The New York Times*, May 25, 1972, p. 44.

Rosenblatt, A.M., & Rosenblatt, J.C. Six member juries in criminal cases: Legal and psychological considerations. *St. John's Law Review*, 1973, *47*, 615-633.

Saari, D.J. The criminal jury faces future shock. *Judicature*, 1973, *57*, 12-16.

Simon, R.J. *The jury and the defense of insanity.* Boston: Little, Brown, 1967.

Taylor, M. Proof of a theorem on majority rule. *Behavioral Science*, 1969, *14*, 228-231.

Thompson, E. Six will do! *Trial*, 1974, *10*, 12, 14.

Tufte, E.R. The relationship between seats and votes in two-party systems. *American Political Science Review*, 1973, *67*, 540-547.

Ulmer, S.S. Quantitative analysis of judicial processes: Some practical and theoretical applications. In H.W. Baade (Ed.), *Jurimetrics.* New York: Basic Books, 1963.

Walbert, D.F. The effect of jury size in the probability of conviction: An evaluation of *Williams v. Florida. Case Western Reserve Law Review*, 1971, *22*, 529-554.

Zeisel, H. . . . And then there were none: The diminution of the federal jury. *University of Chicago Law Review*, 1971, *38*, 710-724.

Zeisel, H. The waning of the American jury. *American Bar Association Journal*, 1972, *58*, 367-370.

Zeisel, H. Twelve is just. *Trial*, 1974, *10*, 13, 15.

Zeisel, H., Kalven, H., & Buchhotz, B. *Delay in the court.* Boston: Little, Brown, 1959.

Zimroth, R.L. The crime of plea bargaining. *The New York Times Magazine*, May 28, 1972.

Rules Governing Jury Deliberations: A Consideration of Recent Changes

Charlan Nemeth

Introduction

The institution of trial by jury has a long and cherished history. Transported to the United States with English common law, it came to take on a particular significance as it became a constitutional right. As such, it was acclaimed a fundamental guarantee of individual liberty.

Such an equation of jury trials with democracy and liberty has a deep tradition, perhaps most eloquently stated by Blackstone in 1768. The echoes of such sentiments can be found in Lord Devlin's lectures in the 1950s:

The first object of any tyrant in Whitehall would be to make Parliament utterly subservient to his will; and the next to overthrow or diminish trial by jury, for no tyrant could afford to leave a subject's freedom in the hands of twelve of his countrymen. So that trial by jury is more than an instrument of justice and more than one wheel of the constitution: it is the lamp that shows that freedom lives [Devlin, 1956, p. 164].

This deep regard for the jury system rests on at least two assumptions, namely, impartiality and representativeness. On the one hand the jury system tends to allay fears of political entanglements. On the other hand proponents of the system emphasize that the decision of twelve is better than the decision of one, even if professional experience is lacking. And some even acclaim the importance of the lack of professional experience. The lay jury has a fresh perception of each trial and the introduction of common sense and common experience is considered to be a valuable asset.

Other enthusiasts of the trial by jury have emphasized its role for the community at large rather than for the decision-making process itself. These proponents do not argue that the lay jury is in fact a better and more impartial decision-maker. Rather, they argue that the community must be represented in order to maintain an optimism in the courts as an impartial forum for disputes. The jury system "has a built-in mechanism for sustaining the public trust which supports it" (Cornish, 1968, p. 18). Tribe (1971) has emphasized the symbolic function of a trial by jury: the jury is "significant not only as a means of achieving various ends external to themselves, but also as ends in their own right, or at least as symbolic expressions of certain ends and values . . . a reminder to the community of the principles it holds important" (p. 1391-1392). Thus, the jury system has educative, motivational, and symbolic functions, as well as fact-finding and decision-making functions.

Not all theorists of the criminal justice system share the optimism as presented above. Some question the competence of a group of twelve lay persons, given the intricacies of the law. Others emphasize the great expense in both time and money. Today, when the Courts have a great backlog of cases, these considerations have become increasingly compelling for the critics of the jury system.

While proponents and critics still continue to debate the issue, the Supreme Court has made some recent decisions that have potentially great consequences for the jury system. The cases involved attempts by some of the states to streamline the criminal justice system by changing both the size of the jury and the decision-making rule under which they may operate.

While the jury so revered by Blackstone was a twelve-person jury required to deliberate to unanimity, numerous states now allow for juries of less than twelve persons, as well as for verdicts reached by less than unanimous agreement in civil trials. In criminal trials, nearly a dozen states allow for juries of less than twelve members and five states allow for less-than-unanimous verdicts. Of these latter five states three allow such verdicts only for crimes that would be classified as a misdemeanor or which are tried in inferior courts. Of the two remaining states, Louisiana requires a 9:3 vote for a verdict in cases involving crimes where the punishment is necessarily at hard labor whereas Oregon requires ten of the twelve persons to be in agreement for a verdict except for the crime of first degree murder. These changes in size and decision rule were, in general, made with the aim of "facilitating, expediting and reducing expense in the administration of justice" (*State v. Lewis*, 129 LA 800, 804).

Such changes, however, were challenged in several cases before the Supreme Court. In *Williams v. Florida*, (399 US 78, 1972), the size question was addressed and the Supreme Court affirmed the constitutionality of less-than-twelve-member juries. In *Apodaca et al. v. Oregon* (32 L.Ed. 2d 184, 1972) and in *Johnson v. Louisiana* (32 L.Ed. 2d 152, 1972), the unanimity question was addressed. In *Apodaca*, the appellants maintained that their constitutional rights had been violated since they were convicted by 11:1, 10:2, and 11:1 verdicts, respectively. Johnson argued in a similar vein since he was convicted by a 9:3 vote. The Supreme Court, however, upheld the constitutionality of less-than-unanimous verdicts and ruled that such procedures did not violate either the due process or the equal protection clauses of the Fourteenth Amendment.

Since these decisions, there have been a number of experimental and survey studies attempting to address the implications of allowing juries of less than twelve persons (see, for example, Bermant & Koppock, 1973; Kessler, 1973) and allowing less-than-unanimous verdicts. In the ensuing discussion, we will be mainly concentrating on the unanimity question.

There is general agreement that unanimity leads to more "hung" juries than do less-than-unanimity requirements. Kalven's and Zeisel's (1966) work, for example, shows that jurisdictions requiring unanimity have 5.6 percent hung juries, while jurisdictions requiring less than unanimity have 3.1 percent hung juries. This finding has been corroborated by experimental studies (for example, Davis, Kerr, Atkin, Holt, & Meek, 1975). The studies, however, tend not to find any significant differences in verdict (in cases where a verdict is reached) as a consequence of allowing less-than-unanimous verdicts. "Significant" is used here in the statistical sense; the finding of "no significant differences" means that the differences found could be due to chance over 5 percent of the time.

In its ruling, however, the Supreme Court had larger concerns than simply whether or not unanimity versus non-unanimity would affect specific verdicts. They were concerned with the far greater issue of due process. Thus, the issue was not just the *outcome* of the deliberation but the *process* of deliberation. The justices debated whether or not majority rule would weaken the just and fair consideration of all viewpoints and whether or not the majority would prematurely impose its will on the minority. And they were concerned with whether or not community confidence would be weakened as a result of such a change.

In ruling that nonunanimity did not violate the constitutional rights of the defendant, the majority justices (five in number) argued that not only would the verdict not be significantly changed but also that the process of the deliberation would not be significantly altered. They believed that the majority would not impose its will on the minority as long as the minority had reasoned arguments. In delivering the opinion of the Court, Justice White concluded:

We have no grounds for believing that majority jurors, aware of their responsibility and power over the liberty of the defendant, would simply refuse to listen to arguments presented to them in favor of acquittal, terminate discussion, and render a verdict. On the contrary it is far more likely that a juror presenting reasoned argument in favor of acquittal would either have his arguments answered or would carry enough other jurors with him to prevent conviction. A majority will cease discussion and outvote a minority only after reasoned discussion has ceased to have persuasive effect or to serve any other purpose—when a minority, that is, continues to insist upon acquittal without having persuasive reasons in support of its position [*Johnson v. Louisiana*, 92 S. Ct. at 1624].

The minority justices, four in number, tended to be less convinced of the "conscientiousness" of majority jurors. Justice Douglas, with Justices Marshall and Brennan concurring, offered an alternative view:

Non-unanimous juries need not debate and deliberate as fully as most unanimous juries. As soon as the requisite majority is attained, further consideration is not required either by Oregon or by Louisiana even though the dissident jurors might, if given the chance, be able to convince the majority.... It is said that there is no evidence that majority jurors will refuse to listen to dissenters whose votes are unneeded for conviction. Yet human experience teaches that polite academic conversation is no substitute for the earnest and robust argument necessary to reach unanimity [*Johnson v. Louisiana*, at 1647, 1648].

Thus, the dissenting Justices were fearful that the majority might impose its will on the minority, that the deliberation would stop when the requisite votes are reached and that the nature of the deliberation itself would be less "robust." The dissenting justices maintained that juries can, as can most people, act unreasonably and even improperly at times. Safeguards, then, have to be maintained to promote full and just consideration of all positions.

The issue of community confidence was also raised in the context of the *Johnson v. Louisiana* and the *Apodaca et al. v. Oregon* decisions. Justice Stewart, with Justices Brennan and Marshall concurring, raised this issue in the context of a jury split along group lines:

Community confidence in the administration of criminal justice cannot but be corroded under a system in which a defendant who is conspicuously identified with a particular group can be acquitted or convicted by a jury split along group lines. The requirements of unanimity and impartial selection thus complement each other in ensuring the fair performance of the vital functions of a criminal court jury [*Johnson v. Louisiana*, at 1627].

The justices appear to agree that full and just consideration of all positions is a necessary and vital function of a jury trial. In fact, as stated previously, this has often been an argument for retaining a panel of twelve over a single individual such as a judge. The justices differ, however, in their assessment of how less-than-unanimity requirements would alter this consideration.

Since most studies on this issue have concentrated on verdict distribution rather than on the *process* of deliberation, we have little information on majority-minority interactions or on subjective impressions of the jurors as a result of allowing nonunanimous verdicts. Some studies have assumed that majority-minority interactions would not be affected since there is considerable evidence indicating that juries tend to reach a verdict that was initially held by the majority of its members. Kalven and Zeisel (1966), for example, show that when the guilty position was held by a majority (seven to eleven of the twelve members), 86 percent of their 105 cases went guilty, 9 percent hung and 5 percent went not guilty. When the not guilty position was held by a majority, 91 percent of their 41 cases went not guilty, 7 percent hung and 2 percent went not guilty. Thus, some have concluded that verdicts would not be appreciably altered by allowing some form of a majority rule, since the majority would prevail anyway. Experimental studies (e.g., Davis et al., 1975) tend to corroborate such assumptions by their findings that a mathematical model predicting outcomes based on a two-thirds majority, otherwise hung, tends to most closely correspond to data found with simulated jury deliberations.

These same studies do show that groups under unanimity requirements deliberate longer than do groups under a two-thirds majority requirement and the former also consider their decision rule to be a little more "ideal" than the latter (Davis et al., 1975). However, questions still remain. Is the minority opinion prematurely outvoted when unanimity is not required? Is a minority favoring one position more likely to have its position "fully and justly considered" than a minority favoring a different position? Is the deliberation under less-than-unanimity requirements as robust? Are the subjective impressions of the jurors as favorable—as confident that justice has been administered? What is the nature of the changes, if any, in the interactions between majority and minority as a function of unanimity versus less-than-unanimity requirements?

Our Research

In some of our recent research (see Nemeth, in press-a, in press-b), we addressed these questions experimentally in order to control the distribution of initial votes and to manipulate the decision rule with "all other things being equal." It was necessary to control the vote distribution since there is considerable evidence from the social-psychological literature indicating that the size of the majority and minority affects the social influence processes that occur (see Moscovici & Nemeth, 1974). For example, there is considerable evidence that a minority consisting of one individual is much more likely to conform to an erroneous majority opinion than one who has an ally. In these studies, we used six-person groups with an initial vote split of 4:2. By controlling the vote distribution in such a way that the minority votes were not needed for the two-thirds majority requirement, we could assess the effect of differing decision rule requirements both on the tendency to outvote a minority that is not needed and on the nature of the majority/minority interactions under these different decision rules.

Study 1

The first of these studies used a sample of thirty-seven different groups. The same case was used for all groups, and the evidence was presented in a written form. Very briefly, the case involved the death of a woman whose husband was charged with first-degree murder. The prosecution based its case primarily on two pieces of evidence. The fingerprints of both the husband and the wife were found on the murder weapon, a fireplace poker. These were the only fingerprints found on the weapon. A neighbor testified that the wife was receiving a male visitor on the night in question and that shortly after the visitor's arrival, the husband was seen peering in the windows. An argument ensued, the male visitor left, further arguments were heard, and the husband was seen leaving the house. There was some question as to whether or not the light was sufficient for a positive identification but the neighbor indicated that she was positive that she saw the husband. The defense contended that the husband was away on a business trip. His employer and a motel clerk verified this. However, the business trip was to a city 150 miles away from his home, and his presence at the motel on the night in question could be corroborated only until 7:10 pm whereas the murder occurred somewhere around 11:45 pm.

We first pretested this case on 753 undergraduates at the University of Virginia. Of these subjects, 474 indicated a clear position on the case in the sense that they said that they would vote *and* that they believed that the defendant was either guilty or not guilty. The remaining 279 split their vote and belief. For example, many indicated that they would vote not guilty even though they believed the defendant to be guilty, the reasons being reasonable doubt, insufficient evidence, and so forth. Of the 474 who indicated a clear position, 73 percent took the position of guilty and 27 percent took the position of not guilty. These individuals were allowed to volunteer for the experiment in such a way that we knew in advance that the six people assigned to a particular time would split 4:2 in their initial vote.

Of the thirty-seven groups deliberating this case, nineteen were composed of four individuals taking the position of "guilty" and two taking the position of not guilty; eighteen were composed of four favoring not guilty and two favoring guilty. Half of the groups in each category were required to deliberate to unanimity; the other half were required to deliberate to a two-thirds majority.

In addition to collecting data on verdict, we also collected data on the nature of the interactions. Two types of coding systems were utilized. The first, known as "valence," simply kept a running account of each statement made and whether it favored a verdict of guilty or not guilty. This type of coding system tends to predict the outcome of a discussion of alternatives; when the cumulative sum of comments for one position exceeds the cumulative sum for the alternative by seven or greater, the outcome can be nearly perfectly predicted (Hoffman, n.d.). In this study, such a coding system predicted the verdict in all but one of the groups. The amount of time before such a prediction could be made was considered to be an indicator of "functional deliberation time."

A second coding system is that developed by Bales in 1965, known as the Bales Interaction Analysis. Each comment was coded in terms of who uttered the comment, to whom it was addressed, and which of twelve categories it represented. There were approximately 4.7 comments coded per minute of deliberation. The categories, together with examples of comments that would be coded under each, are as follows:

1. Seems friendly ("I'm sorry"; "that's a good point");

2. Dramatization (joking; undue exaggeration);
3. Agrees ("yes, that's right");
4. Gives suggestion ("let's vote again"; "let's look at the testimony of the neighbor again");
5. Gives opinion ("I think he's guilty");
6. Gives information ("there were only two sets of fingerprints found");
7. Asks for information ("what time did Mr. Smith leave?").
8. Asks for opinion ("what do you think now?");
9. Asks for suggestion ("how shall we get started?");
10. Disagrees ("you are wrong");
11. Shows tension (laughing, stuttering);
12. Seems unfriendly (interruptions; "that's a stupid thing to say").

In addition to these coding systems, we also calculated the amount of time spent in deliberation and we obtained subjective impressions of each participant about the others in his group and about the deliberation process.

Our findings corroborate the previous findings in that there were no significant differences in verdict distribution as a function of unanimity versus two-thirds majority rule, except for the fact that the unanimity groups tended to become hung more often. However, we also found that the minority was more likely to prevail when it took the position of not guilty as opposed to guilty. These data are presented in Table 9-1.

For many of the findings in this study, the decision rule—that is, unanimity versus two-thirds majority—was most important when the majority favored guilty and the minority favored not guilty. It was in this situation that the minority occasionally prevailed, and where there appeared to be the most conflict. When the majority favored not guilty, the verdict almost always was not guilty; requirements of unanimity or two-thirds majority tended not to make a great deal of difference.

This pattern was found for total amount of time spent in deliberation. An analysis of variance on deliberation time showed that groups under a unanimity requirement deliberated longer than did groups under a two-thirds majority rule requirement, but this tendency was particularly true for the 4G/2NG composition, as shown in Table 9-2: ($F_{1,33} = 8.41, p < .05$).

Table 9-1
Verdict Outcome

	Majority			Unanimity		
	Guilty	Not Guilty	Hung	Guilty	Not Guilty	Hung
4G; 2NG	4	5	0	3	2	5
4NG; 2G	1	8	0	0	8	1

Table 9-2
Deliberation Time

	Majority	Unanimity
4G; 2NG	37.89_a	68.30_b
4NG; 2G	41.56_a	29.78_a

Note: Subscripts in common indicate that the differences are not significant at the .05 level.
G = Guilty
NG = Not Guilty

Functional deliberation time showed a similar pattern. This is the amount of time (as determined by the "valence" coding method) needed before the verdict could be predicted. The 4G/2NG groups had a longer functional deliberation time than did the 4NG/2G composition. In other words when the minority took the position of not guilty, it took longer before the outcome of the deliberation could be predicted. This is the situation in which we found that the minority could on occasion prevail; at least, it was not a foregone conclusion that the majority would win. Further there is a trend (though not statistically significant) for unanimity groups to have a longer functional deliberation time than those with a two-thirds majority rule, as shown in Table 9-3.

In keeping with the above, we also found that the total number of Bales comments was greater under unanimity than under majority instructions. Breakdowns by category show a significant main effect ($p < .05$) for majority versus unanimity on categories one (showing friendliness), five (giving opinions), six (giving information), ten (disagreement), and twelve (showing unfriendliness). Specifically, groups required to deliberate to unanimity showed more friendliness and unfriendliness, gave more opinions and information, and showed more disagreement than did groups required to deliberate to two-thirds majority. The decision rule did not affect dramatization, agreement, giving suggestions,

Table 9-3
Functional Deliberation Time

	Majority	Unanimity
4G; 2NG	16.89_a	29.55_a
4NG; 2G	8.00_b	9.78_b

Note: Subscripts in common indicate that the differences are not significant at the .05 level.
G = Guilty
NG = Not Guilty

asking for suggestions, asking for opinions, asking for information or tension release.

All of these findings, with the exception of disagreement, interacted with the initial vote distribution of the group. In situations where the majority favored guilty and the minority favored not guilty—the requirement of unanimity had the most dramatic effect on the types of comments made. It is here that unanimity particularly leads to more friendliness and unfriendliness, as well as to the giving of more opinions and information.

The differences between the unanimity and majority-rule groups are made even more apparent when we consider agreement by individual jurors. Analyzing the videotapes of the deliberations, we coded the last voice vote—that is, prior to the announcement of the verdict. The groups required to deliberate to unanimity followed their instructions: all thirteen groups that did not "hang" reached full voice consensus—that is, the vote was 6 to 0 for the verdict. In contrast, the groups required to deliberate to two-thirds majority did not deliberate until consensus was reached. Only five out of eighteen deliberations reached a 6 to 0 voice vote. Nine ended with one person vocally dissenting, and four groups ended with two persons vocally dissenting. These differences are statistically significant ($p < .05$).

As a slight digression, it should be pointed out that five out of the eighteen deliberations under the two-thirds majority requirement reached a verdict that was initially held by a minority. Full voice consensus was never reached in these groups. Three were characterized by a 4:2 vote and two were characterized by a 5:1 vote. In these situations, the minority prevailed by swaying just enough votes to constitute a majority. They then imposed their will. When unanimity was required, however, the situation was different. When the minority prevailed, they did so by reaching full consensus on their position.

Voice vote does not, of course, necessarily mean true agreement in the sense that beliefs have been changed. To determine any differences between voice vote and actual belief, these individuals were asked their private belief as to guilty or not guilty after the deliberation was completed. Private votes were more in accordance with the group verdict in unanimity groups than in nonunanimity groups. ($X^2_{3df} = 7.5, p < .06$). Further, individuals from unanimity groups reported that they subjectively agreed more with the verdict than did individuals under majority rule ($F_{1,196} = 4.74, p < .05$). And, finally, individuals under unanimity requirements reported that they were more uncomfortable during the deliberation; however, they were more likely to agree that justice had been administered ($p < .10$). These data are shown in Table 9-4.

Let us summarize at this point in order to interpret the findings. We held constant the case, the numbers of people constituting a majority and minority, and the setting. What we varied was the position of the majority (and minority), as well as the decision rule under which they were instructed to operate. In this case, it was either unanimity or two-thirds majority rule. In every group, the

Table 9-4
Jurors' Impressions

	Majority	Unanimity	F test
Reported Agreement with Verdict	3.23	2.55	4.74
Justice was administered	3.51	3.22	2.13
Comfort during deliberation	2.83	3.39	4.00

Note: The lower the number, the more agreement with the label (verdict, justice and comfort).

two-thirds majority was available on the first ballot. The questions were whether manipulation of the variables would cause the minority to be prematurely outvoted, how the interactions between the majority and minority would be affected, and what the subjective feelings of the individual jurors would be.

In general, one might consider the deliberation under unanimity to be more "robust," in Mr. Justice Douglas' terms. The deliberation time was, in general, longer; the functional deliberation time (the time needed before a prediction of outcome could be made) was longer; the total number of comments made was greater; and there was a greater frequency of comments in the specific categories of showing friendliness and unfriendliness, agreeing and disagreeing, and giving opinions, suggestions and information. These differences were particularly apparent when the minority position was not guilty.

While the actual verdicts were not found to be significantly different between unanimity and majority groups, the former deliberated until they reached full consensus, while the latter tended to stop short of reaching voice agreement. Furthermore, individuals indicated more agreement with the verdict and were more likely to feel that justice had been administered when they deliberated to unanimity than when they were under a two-thirds majority requirement.

As with any experimental study, one must raise questions concerning the generalizability of these findings. Only one case was used, and it was presented in a written form. One might question whether or not these findings would generalize to other types of cases, particularly when those cases are presented in a courtroom setting. In an attempt to test the generality of these findings, we conducted a second study in conjunction with the trial court practice course at the University of Virginia Law School.

Study 2

In the trial court practice course, scripts for a variety of cases are used. The "trials" are conducted in an actual courtroom; a real judge presides; live witnesses appear and are examined and cross-examined. The judge gives the jury the instructions that he would choose if the case were real rather than simulated. Third-year law students, as attorneys for the plaintiff and the defense, give opening and closing statements, raise objections, and so on.

For the series of seven trials conducted in the spring of 1974, we brought a "jury" of twelve volunteers to each trial. Thus, there were eighty-four subjects. For any given trial, the twelve individuals sat in the jury box and were treated as actual jurors. After watching the trial (which usually lasted two hours), they were brought to a room for deliberation. The twelve individuals were randomly assigned to one of two groups. The one group of six persons was required to deliberate to unanimity; the other was required to reach at least a two-thirds majority. In other words, all twelve persons saw the same trial; the two groups of six differed only in the decision rule they were assigned.

It should be pointed out that this study does not control initial vote distribution as did the previous study. The groups were created randomly. However, each group had its own control in the sense that the two groups were matched.

Seven different trials were studied in this fashion; four were civil and three were criminal trials. The civil trials involved personal injury, slander, suicide (payment of insurance) and contract default. Two of the three criminal trials involved first-degree murder; the third involved arson.

When we compared the verdicts reached by the two groups for each trial—that is, unanimity versus majority groups—there were no significant differences (see Table 9-5). Whether the group was required to deliberate to unanimity or to a two-thirds majority made little difference. Of the fourteen

Table 9-5
The Relationship of Final Verdict to Initial Vote Distribution

	Majority		Unanimity	
	Initial Vote	*Final Verdict*	*Initial Vote*	*Final Verdict*
1. Murder	2G;4NG	NG	3G;3NG	G (Vol. Mansl.)
2. Arson	6NG	NG	6NG	NG
3. Murder	1G;5NG	NG	6NG	NG
4. Slander	4Pl;2Def	Pl	4Pl;2Def	Pl
5. Injury	2Pl;4Def	Def	3Pl;3Def	Pl
6. Suicide	3Pl;3Def	Pl	4Pl;2Def	Pl
7. Contract	3Pl;3Def	Def	2Pl;4Def	Def

Note: G = Guilty
 NG = Not Guilty
 Pl = Plaintiff
 Def = Defense

deliberations (two groups, each deliberating one of seven cases), there were three juries that started with a 3 to 3 split. The remaining eleven deliberations had an initial majority. Of these eleven deliberations, every verdict was the position initially held by the majority.

Total deliberation time was not significantly different between majority and unanimity groups. However, the trend was for the unanimity groups to have a longer deliberation time. Functional deliberation time, on the other hand, was significantly affected by the decision rule, with groups required to reach unanimity having longer functional deliberation times.

When the Bales Interaction Analysis was computed for these deliberation tapes, none of the twelve categories was found to be affected by the decision rule. At least, the differences were not statistically significant. This is in part due to the small number of cases used and the high variability between cases.

As was found in the previous study, voice vote was affected by the decision rule. Groups required to deliberate to unanimity did just that; every verdict was reached by a 6:0 voice vote. Groups under a two-thirds majority rule, however, did not deliberate to full consensus. The great majority of these groups stopped when a 4:2 vote was reached—that is, the two-thirds majority. Private opinion was also changed to a greater extent when unanimity was required. The mean number of private opinion changes in the direction of the group verdict (relative to the number of possible changes) was .500 for the two-thirds majority groups and 2.00 for the unanimity groups, as indicated in Table 9-6.

As one might expect, the decision rule also affected the subjective reports of agreement with the verdict. Individuals who deliberated under unanimity requirements reported more agreement with the verdict than did individuals who deliberated under two-thirds majority rule. Again, the unanimity groups reported being less comfortable during the deliberation than did the two-thirds majority groups ($F_{1,36} = 4.1$, $p < .05$). And the unanimity groups were more likely to agree that justice had been administered ($F_{1,36} = 3.4, p < .10$).

Table 9-6
Number of Persons Who Changed Their Private Opinions in the Direction of the Verdict

	Majority	Unanimity
1. Murder	0 (of 2 possible)	3 (of 3 possible)
2. Arson	0 (of none possible)	0 (of none possible)
3. Murder	1 (of 1 possible)	0 (of none possible)
4. Slander	0 (of 2 possible)	2 (of 2 possible)
5. Pers. Injury	0 (of 2 possible)	2 (of 3 possible)
6. Suicide	1 (of 3 possible)	1 (of 2 possible)
7. Contract default	1 (of 3 possible)	2 (of 2 possible)

Thus, some of the patterns that were found in the first study, where we controlled vote distribution, were replicated when we used different cases and simulated a trial setting. The verdicts themselves were not found to be significantly affected by the decision rule. However, the process by which agreement was reached showed significant differences. Groups under unanimity requirements reached verbal consensus whereas groups required to deliberate to two-thirds majority did not continue the discussion until all persons agreed. The consequence of this was that the individuals under majority rule tended to agree less with the verdict, had less opinion change as a result of the deliberation, and were less convinced that justice had been administered. The simulated trial study differed from the first study in that the strong differences in the interaction patterns did not emerge. There were no significant differences in the types of comments uttered as a function of decision rule. This, however, may have been due to the small sample size involved.

Discussion

When considering the foregoing studies in the context of the concerns raised by the Supreme Court Justices in *Apodaca et al. v. Oregon* and *Johnson v. Louisiana*, we find ourselves concluding (like many of the previous studies) that verdict distribution may not be significantly altered by allowing less-than-unanimous verdicts. However, the process by which verdicts are achieved appears to be considerably altered. There appears to be an imposition of majority opinion when the minority votes are not needed for a verdict. Few groups under majority requirements deliberated until consensus was reached. Furthermore, there is some indication that the deliberation is not as "robust." To the extent that a predictive coding system like "valance" can indicate the time when the conflict has essentially ended—that is, when the outcome can be predicted very accurately—we find that groups under unanimity requirements tend to maintain the conflict longer. This is corroborated by the individual jurors' own impressions that they were less comfortable during the deliberation when unanimity was required.

Then, of course, one must raise the rather unusual, though sometimes apparent, phenomenon of minority influence. While the minority never prevailed in the simulated study, we did find its occurrence in the first experimental study. And the evidence of Kalven and Zeisel suggests that it may occur somewhere between 3 percent and 5 percent of the time. In accord with the Kalven and Zeisel data, we found that a minority favoring not guilty was more likely to prevail than a minority favoring guilty. And it was under these circumstances that the decision rule made the most difference, affecting both the number and the types of comments made. Unanimity groups made more comments in general, and more task-oriented comments in particular—for example, giving opinions and information. The decision rule also affected the total amount of time spent in deliberation, the subjective impressions of agreement with the verdict, and the belief that justice had been administered.

It should also be pointed out that when the minority prevailed, the *process* of influence was affected by the decision rule. When a two-thirds majority was required, the minority prevailed by swaying just enough votes to constitute a majority. They then imposed their will. By contrast, the minorities who prevailed under unanimity requirements convinced all the members of the original majority to the minority position. They created more private opinion change and more subjective agrement with the verdict, as well as greater agreement that justice had been administered.

While the more goal-oriented readers might consider these to be rather minor consequences, particularly in the light of the fact that the actual outcome of the deliberations appears not to be significantly changed, one must again consider that trial by jury is more than a way of arriving at a decision. In Tribe's (1971) terms, it has "important symbolic and ritualistic functions." It must *appear* to be just, as well as *be* just.

In considering the carriage of justice, it is of some concern that groups not required to deliberate to unanimity tend to stop short of full consensus. It is of some concern that the required majority imposes its will, particularly when one considers that essentially the same outcome is reached by full consensus when unanimity is required. Surely, the amount of time spent in deliberation does not provide great savings for the administration of justice. Proponents of less than unanimous juries generally refer to the savings involved in reducing the number of "hung" juries. Let us even consider the advisability of this savings. The studies discussed here, like others, show that groups required to deliberate to unanimity do "hang" more often. However, this means that a minority remains unconvinced of the majority opinion and, perhaps even more importantly, refuses to give in. Unless one assumes that any adamant minority opinion must be wrong or must be held by "deviants," the question must be raised as to whether or not such groups *should* "hang."

The situation where a minority refuses to conform is particularly compelling in the light of the social-psychological literature on this process. As literally hundreds of studies show, minorities often conform to majority opinion. Particularly when the minority is a single individual, the conformity process is striking. As shown by Asch's (1956) now classic studies, individuals can be shaken in their judgments even when they are making "objective" judgments— for example, the length of lines. When individuals are shown a standard line and asked to judge which of three comparison lines is equal to the standard, they can accurately judge the correct comparison line if they are making the judgments alone. When placed with three persons who unanimously agree that a line obviously unequal to the standard is the correct one, fully a third of the responses by the naive subject is in agreement with the erroneous majority and in disagreement with his own senses.

When an individual is alone in disagreement with a unanimous majority, they not only tend to question their own judgment, but they are also concerned about incurring the disapproval of the majority, that is, of being considered "deviant." In the light of such powerful processes, one must at least wonder about the individual who refuses to conform. Is he simply stubborn and misguided, or is it possible that he interprets the evidence in such a way that, while different from the majority, is still valid and held with great conviction? As a general principle, should this case be retried or should the majority prevail?

In considering the *appearance* of justice, our data suggest that individuals are more likely to agree with the verdict and are more likely to believe that justice has been administered when unanimity is required, as opposed to some form of majority rule. While these individuals' judgments do not tell us about the opinions of the community at large, they at least raise a question about the confidence of the community in verdicts rendered by a less-than-unanimous jury. The problem becomes particularly salient when the minority opinion is represented by individuals who themselves constitute a social minority. For example, will a verdict rendered by ten whites outvoting two blacks be accepted and considered just? Will ten women outvoting two men (or the reverse) give us pause?

Even recognizing that 90 percent to 95 percent of the cases in many jurisdictions never go to trial but, rather, are decided by some form of a pretrial bargaining process, the trial by jury is symbolically important to many persons in the community. Whether their impression is illusory or not, many view the trial by jury as a process by which twelve persons, unbiased and representative of the community, hear evidence for both sides and then deliberate this evidence until they reach agreement. Will the fact that a majority can outvote a minority in this process weaken the confidence of the community in the criminal justice system? Will it weaken even further the very tenuous confidence of groups within our nation that feel underprivileged and underrepresented in that system? And can we afford to make changes that alter this delicate optimism in the criminal justice system, particularly when such beliefs promote the obeying of its laws and the bringing of one's conflicts to it for resolution?

References

Asch, S.E. Studies of independence and conformity: A minority of one against an unanimous majority. *Psychological Monographs*, 1956, *70* (9, Whole No. 416).

Bermant, G., & Coppock, R. Determinants of trial outcome in industrial accident cases: An analysis of 128 cases in the State of Washington. *Washington Law Review*, 1973, *48*, 593-596.

Cornish, L. *The jury*. London: Penguin Press, 1968.

Davis, J.H., Kerr, N.L., Atkin, R.S., Holt, R., & Meek, D. The decision processes of 6- and 12-person juries assigned unanimous and two-thirds majority rules. *Journal of Personality and Social Psychology*, 1975, *32*, 1-14.

Devlin, P.A. *Trial by jury*. London: Stevens, 1956.

Hoffman, L.R. Personal communication, n.d.

Kalven, H.J., & Zeisel, H. *The American jury*. Boston: Little, Brown, 1966.

Kessler, J.B. An empirical study of six- and twelve-member jury deliberation process. *University of Michigan Journal of Law Reform*, 1973, *6*, 712-734.

Moscovici, S., & Nemeth, C. Social influences II: Minority influence. In C. Nemeth (Ed.), *Social psychology: Classic and contemporary integrations*. Chicago: Rand McNally, 1974.

Nemeth, C. From the 50s to the 70s: Women in jury deliberations. *Sociometry*, in press, 1975. (a)

Nemeth, C. Interactions between jurors as a function of majority v. unanimity decision rules. Manuscript submitted for publication, 1975. (b)

Tribe, L.H. Trial by mathematics: Precision and ritual in the legal process. *Harvard Law Review*, 1971, *84*, 1329-1393.

10 The Effects of Videotaped Trial Materials on Juror Response

Gerald R. Miller

Introduction

This chapter reports the results of a series of studies designed to assess the effects of videotaped trial materials on juror decision making and juror information processing. Arguments for the increased use of videotaped materials in courtroom trials have been advanced by numerous legal professionals (see, for example, Barbuto, 1972; Kennelly, 1972; McCrystal, 1972; Morrill, 1970; Murray, 1972; Stiver, 1974; and Trialevision, 1973). The judicial advantages suggested by proponents of greater use of videotape include: (1) increased efficiency in the conduct of trials, thereby relieving the crowded dockets so common in today's legal system and reducing the time required for cases to be heard; (2) added flexibility in taking depositions, thus providing greater convenience for the professional witness and for witnesses geographically removed from the trial; and (3) a more effective means of dealing with objectionable and inadmissible testimony, thus permitting the deletion of inadmissible testimony before jurors hear it and allowing judges more time and thought when deliberating on questions of admissibility.

In attempting to assess the validity of these claims, two general questions seem particularly relevant. First, does the use of videotape actually provide just, effective solutions to purported shortcomings of our present judicial system? For instance, does the deletion of inadmissible testimony result in a difference in the decision making of jurors? Second, and perhaps more important, even if the use of videotape alleviates some of the shortcomings mentioned above, does it produce other undesirable effects that cancel, or even transcend, its advantages? For example, suppose the use of videotape does speed the conduct of trials but results in reduction or juror retention of trial-related information and produces lower levels of juror interest and motivation. To the extent that the values of the legal system place a premium on the role of relevant information in the decision-making process—deciding the merits of a case "on the facts"—and on interested, motivated participation by jurors, more extensive use of videotape

The research reported in this chapter was supported by Grant #38398 of the Research Applied to National Needs Program, National Science Foundation, Gerald R. Miller and Fredrick S. Siebert, Principal Investigators. Many others have contributed greatly to the success of this research program. In particular, Joyce Bauchner, David Bender, Frank Boster, B. Thomas Florence, Norman Fontes, David Hanson, John Hocking, Edmund Kaminski, Denis Lefebvre, Alex Nesterenko, Henry Nicholson, and Scott Poole have worked on one or more of the studies. Thus, the "we" used throughout this chapter is collaborative, not editorial.

would necessitate a tradeoff of one set of desirable circumstances for another. Although the research reported here does not attempt to gauge the relative importance of such tradeoffs, it does indicate the extent to which certain ones may be necessary.

Two general comments about the studies that follow merit emphasis. We have taken the applied dimension of the research task seriously, while at the same time attempting to draw inferences and reach conclusions as rigorously as possible and to formulate statements that permit some confidence regarding generalizability. Thus, while most of the studies are admittedly and unapologetically not theory-building research (at least as that phrase is typically used in the philosophy of social science and social science literature), we have borrowed from various theoretical perspectives in developing research questions. In a similar vein, we have sought to strike an optimal balance between rigorous control, on the one hand, and ecological validity (Brunswik, 1947), on the other. This means that the environmental settings and the juror subjects for most studies fall somewhere between an actual trial (the ultimate in realism) and constructed laboratory scenarios or vignettes (the best situation for rigorous control).

The research reported here focuses on the effects of the videotape medium on individual juror response prior to group deliberation. Obviously, as both common sense and prior research (for example, Anapol, 1973; Strodtbeck & Mann, 1956; and Strodtbeck, James, & Hawkins, 1957) indicate, many things can occur in the jury room to modify these initial perceptions and judgments. Although we admit the importance of such group-process variables, we also believe that the dynamic of jury room interaction is partially determined by the information and impressions that jurors bring to the deliberative task. Since we wished to examine as unambiguously as possible the impact of the videotape medium per se on individual jurors, we chose not to confound our measures with the many variables associated with group deliberation. Later studies are planned to incorporate this phase of the decision-making process.

In addition, when dealing with verdicts and awards, there is an obvious practical problem of subject recruitment when the sampling unit is increased from one individual to twelve individuals. Since we wanted to use actual jurors in some of the studies, we were restricted by the number available and by the time constraints imposed by regular court activities. In our future research, we plan to obtain postdeliberation measures, as well as jury verdicts, from members of six-person juries.

Three sets of studies follow. The first investigations report a direct comparison of a live and a videotaped trial and a comparison of two alternative taping systems. The second set of studies presents some preliminary findings bearing on the inadmissible testimony issue. The final set involves comparisons of information retention by jurors viewing live, monochromatic-videotaped, and color-videotaped testimony. Because of spatial limitations, the studies are described briefly, with references to published reports containing more extensive descriptions. Finally, some implications of the research for establishing policy concerning the use of videotaped trial materials are presented.

A Comparison of Live and Videotaped Trials and of Two Alternative Taping Systems

The first two studies investigated the following two general questions:

Does the medium of trial presentation (live v. videotape) significantly influence juror responses?

Are there differences in the responses of jurors exposed to a split-screen videotaped trial and jurors exposed to a full-screen videotaped trial?

Since the same stimulus trial was used for both studies, as well as for the later research dealing with inadmissible testimony, the steps taken in its selection and preparation merit some detail. Two criteria guided our selection of the kind of stimulus to be used: realism and experimental control. Taping an actual trial seemed to allow for maximum realism but minimum control, while use of constructed vignettes—short segments of testimony—seemed to permit optimal control but low realism.

After consultation with legal experts and behavioral scientists, both extremes were rejected. Instead, we decided to select and reenact an actual trial. This decision allowed for considerable realism and at the same time permitted us to edit content and structure, to control certain potentially relevant variables, and to insert the varying amounts of inadmissible testimony necessary for investigating that issue.

Since videotape has been used more widely in the civil than in the criminal arena, we elected to use a civil case. Furthermore, since we sought a typical area of litigation—that is, a type of case frequently heard—so that results would have maximum generalizability, we decided to use an automobile injury case for the stimulus trial.

Several criteria guided our selection of a specific case: (1) the length of time required to try the case should not exceed four hours; (2) the merits of the opposing parties' cases should be roughly comparable; and (3) the abilities of the contesting attorneys should be roughly comparable. After examining over fifty trial transcripts, we chose a case tried in 1968 in Iron Mountain, Michigan. The key issue involved possible contributory negligence on the part of the plaintiff.[1]

For the most part, the structure and content of the transcript remained unchanged. Editorial changes were, however, made in three areas:

[1] For a more comprehensive description of case selection and a rationale for the criteria used, see Miller and Siebert (1974) or Miller, Bender, Florence, and Nicholson (1974).

1. The names of all participants in the trial were changed and anglicized; thus, the "official" case title became *James and Marjorie Nugent v. Frank Clark.* Besides protecting the identities of actual litigants, this change eliminated any juror bias that might result from the use of ethnic names.
2. Certain details of the trial were altered to conform with the 1973 reenactment date and to facilitate procurement of visual exhibits. For instance, the plaintiff's car in the actual case was a 1962 Mercury; in the reenactment, the year and model were changed to a 1968 Chevrolet.

Finally, after consulting with legal experts, the dialogue was edited to eliminate objectionable material not contested in the original trial and to ensure an identical number of objections by both attorneys. The edited transcript contained six objections by each attorney, four of which were overruled and two of which were sustained.

Since a realistic recreation was essential, a professional director was hired to cast and direct the trial. Save for the judge and bailiff, all trial participants were professional actors. Casting was based not only on the ability to handle lines but also on age and physical appropriateness for the part.

Each actor received a character sketch of the individual to be portrayed. When preparing their roles, actors were directed to avoid the style of television courtroom dramas such as "Perry Mason." In other words, they developed their roles as "ordinary" persons—that is, people who would usually be unsure and uncertain in a trial setting. For purposes of control, all actors were required to learn their lines closely to avoid ad libs and improvisation.

Two systems were used to tape the live reenactment. The primary system was a split-screen arrangement that permitted synchronous recording and playback of three perspectives: a shot of the entire active area of the courtroom on the lower half of the screen, a close-up of the witness in the upper left quarter, and a close-up of the judge and questioning attorney in the upper right quarter. The backup system consisted of a full-screen, single-camera shot of the active area of the courtroom.[2] Both systems employed fixed cameras that precluded panning, zooming, or other editorial decisions.

Study 1: Effects of Live versus Videotape Trial Presentation

Although we had no firm theoretical expectations concerning possible differences in juror responses to live and videotaped trials, several lines of thinking suggested it would be useful to examine this question. At a global level, McLuhan (1964) stresses the hegemony of the medium itself as the primary

---

[2] For diagrams of the split-screen system and equipment specifications, see Miller and Siebert (1974) or Miller, Bender, Florence, and Nicholson (1974).

message in communication transactions. To be sure, most of his insights concern potential differences between alternative media (for example, print versus television), rather than possible variations in media-mediated, as opposed to directly experienced, events. Still, his ideas suggest that the addition of any intervening medium might influence the ways in which information is processed and judgments are formed.

At a less abstract level, the complexity of the juror's stimulus field is drastically reduced by use of videotape. The major problem, however, lies in specifying the extent and direction of differences resulting from a reduction in stimulus complexity. For instance, consider the variable of information retention. Initially, it may seem that restriction of the stimulus field should enhance retention. From a distraction viewpoint, this assumption is warranted. But from a motivational standpoint, the rich milieu of the live trial may better hold a juror's interest. Extensive videotape viewing may become boring and monotonous, causing the juror's attention to lag.

Because of such possible conflicting predictions, Study 1 was question-centered rather than hypothesis-centered. Specifically, these five questions were investigated:

1. Are there differences between verdicts of jurors viewing a live trial and jurors viewing a videotaped trial?
2. Among jurors finding for the plaintiff, are there differences in amount of award between those who viewed the live trial and those who viewed the videotape trial?
3. Are there differences between ratings of attorney credibility of jurors viewing a live trial and those made by jurors viewing a videotaped trial?
4. Are there differences in retention of trial-related information between jurors viewing a live trial and jurors viewing a videotaped trial?
5. Are there differences in motivation and interest between jurors viewing a live trial and jurors viewing a videotaped trial?

Procedures. The subjects viewing the live trial were fifty-two jurors from the Genesee County Circuit Court, Flint, Michigan. The trial was held in a manner conforming as closely as possible to normal trial procedure. The presiding judge explained that the abnormally large jury enabled a group of Michigan State University researchers to conduct a study on jury size. Subjects were told that the litigants had agreed to this procedure and that the jury's verdict would be binding. The judge also explained that the trial was being videotaped for purposes of record. (Researchers accustomed to the psyches of college undergraduates may assume that these deviations from normal procedure engendered suspicion; in fact, for better or worse, the credibility of judges with actual jurors seems extremely high.)

The trial proceeded in fifty-minute segments, through the judge's instructions to the jury. After the trial had ended, the subjects were taken to the jury assembly room where an experimenter administered the "jury size" questionnaire. This instrument contained items to measure the five dependent variables of concern in the study.[3]

After completing the questionnaire, all subjects were thoroughly debriefed by the presiding judge. Personal history forms completed prior to jury service were obtained for analysis of demographic data.

One month later, forty-five Genesee County jurors were shown the videotaped trial. The single variation in research procedure was that the subjects viewed the trial on six television monitors, rather than seeing it live. The judge's preliminary instructions addressed this difference by explaining the split-screen system and assuring the subjects that their verdict would be binding on the litigants.

Results. Table 10-1 contains the negligence verdicts for jurors who viewed the live and videotaped versions of the trial. The data reveal no evidence that the mode of presentation significantly influenced jurors' attributions of negligence. Although jurors found for the plaintiffs somewhat more frequently in the videotaped trial condition, these differences do not approach significance ($X^2 = 2.25; p > .10$).

Jurors were to decide on both an award to Mrs. Nugent for pain and suffering and a derivative award to Mr. Nugent. The mean awards for both Mr. and Mrs. Nugent are also found in Table 10-1. In neither instance did mode of presentation significantly affect the amount of award given by jurors finding for the plaintiff ($t = < 1$ for both Mr. and Mrs. Nugent's awards). While there is a difference of approximately $3,000 in the amount awarded Mrs. Nugent in the live and the videotaped trial conditions, it is more than offset by the substantial variability of awards given by jurors within each of the two conditions.

Juror perceptions of credibility were uniformly high for both attorneys (maximally high credibility = 35 for each of the three credibility dimensions) but did not differ significantly across the two trial conditions (Table 10-2). Likewise, jurors' retention of trial-related information was not significantly

Table 10-1
Negligence Verdicts and Mean Awards for Mr. and Mrs. Nugent by Jurors in the Live and Videotaped Trial Conditions

	For Plaintiffs	For Defense	Mean Award Mr. Nugent	Mean Award Mrs. Nugent
Live Trial	13	31	$2,761	$20,538
Tape Trial	20	21	$2,660	$17,975

[3] For a description of instrument development, see Miller and Siebert (1974).

Table 10-2

Ratings of Credibility for the Contesting Attorneys by Jurors in the Live and Videotaped Trial Conditions

	Plaintiffs' Attorney			Defense Attorney		
	Competence	Trust	Dynamism	Competence	Trust	Dynamism
Live Trial	28.22	26.16	26.96	28.16	26.65	28.41
Tape Trial	27.02	26.18	25.91	28.17	26.67	27.67
t value	1.11	<1	<1	<1	<1	<1

influenced by the medium of presentation. Of a possible score of 40, mean retention for jurors in the live trial condition was 31.1, while the score for jurors in the videotaped trial condition was 29.8 ($t = 1.37$).

Finally, juror interest and motivation did not vary significantly as a result of watching a live or videotaped trial. The mean rating of interest and motivation for jurors in the live trial condition was 4.51, while the mean for jurors in the videotaped trial condition was 4.24 ($t = 1.12$). Since the midpoint of the scale is 3.50, it appears that both groups of jurors were moderately interested in, and motivated by, the task of jury service.

Discussion. When compared with their counterparts who viewed a live trial, jurors who viewed the videotaped trial arrived at similar judgments about negligence and amount of award, had similar perceptions of the contesting attorneys, retained as much of the trial-related information, and reported similar levels of interest and motivation toward the task of serving as jurors. Moreover, numerous jurors expressed enthusiasm for the courtroom potential of videotape and indicated that, in litigation of their own, they would prefer a videotaped to a live trial, a preference consistent with that expressed by the majority of jurors in several of McCrystal's earlier trials (Trialevision, 1973).

The absence of differences in attorney credibility ratings for the two conditions may be reassuring to lawyers who fear that videotape will reduce their courtroom effectiveness. Such an interpretation must be offered cautiously, since the courtroom communication skills of the two role-playing attorneys were probably superior to those of the average trial lawyer. Moreover, both were actors with considerable television experience.

Finally, we must pay homage to the social scientist's aversion to accepting the null hypothesis. Although we agree with Greenwald's (1975) recent argument that much of the conventional wisdom about failing to reject the null is probably misguided, we admit our inability to specify an exact level of significance for our findings of no difference. Still, we constructed our stimuli and instruments carefully and conducted our study in a controlled yet realistic setting. Furthermore, analysis of numerous demographic measures revealed that the two panels of jurors were highly comparable (Miller & Siebert, 1975). Hence, while we plan to attempt replication over a number of trials, we have a good deal of confidence in our results.

Study 2: A Comparison of the Split-Screen and
Full-Screen Systems

Having employed both a split-screen and a full-screen taping system in Study 1, we decided next to compare juror responses to the two systems by using the same five dependent variables examined in the first study. Probably the greatest difference between the two systems lies in the amount of detail that can be captured by the cameras. Although the single camera, full-screen system provides jurors with a realistic shot of the entire active area of the trial, the technical limitations of relatively low-cost equipment prevent close-up views of trial participants, particularly when panning and zomming are prohibited. Thus, while the full-screen shot enables jurors to identify the various participants, it does not permit them to pick up many subtle nuances in facial expression and gesture.

By contrast, the triple camera, split-screen system allows the juror to study the responses of trial participants in greater detail, since one half of the screen shows close-ups of the witness, the questioning attorney, and the judge. The greatest potential disadvantage of the split-screen system is its lack of realism; unlike the full-screen system, which communicates a single shot of a familiar setting, the split-screen system relies upon technology to create a more highly visible, yet somehow more "unnatural" product.

How are these differences likely to affect juror responses? Again, plausible arguments can be made for either, or several, opposing outcomes. On the one hand, the greater detail of the split-screen system might provide more information for jurors, thereby allowing them to make finer discriminations in their perceptions of trial participants or to assimilate more trial-related information. On the other hand the contrived nature of the split-screen system might be distracting, thereby causing jurors to wonder how the effect is achieved. If this happened, assimilation of trial-related information would suffer.

Since we were uncertain which lines of argument might prove most fruitful, we decided, as in Study 1, to pose questions rather than to test hypotheses. More specifically, the questions investigated exactly paralleled those of Study 1:

Are there differences between verdicts of jurors viewing a full-screen trial and jurors viewing a split-screen trial?

Among jurors finding for the plaintiff, are there differences in the amount of award between those who viewed the full-screen trial and those who viewed the split-screen trial?

Are there differences between ratings of attorney credibility made by jurors viewing a full-screen trial and those made by jurors viewing a split-screen trial?

Are there differences in retention of trial-related information between jurors viewing a full-screen trial and jurors viewing a split-screen trial?

Are there differences in motivation and interest between jurors viewing a full-screen trial and jurors viewing a split-screen trial?

Procedures. The subjects were fifty-seven adult members of a Catholic Church group in the greater Lansing (Michigan) area who played the roles of jurors. Aside from the obvious bias in religious affiliation, the demographic characteristics of the subjects were similar to those of a typical jury panel. Constraints concerning the availability of a courtroom and actual impaneled jurors caused us to conduct the study outside the courtroom setting.

Each subject was randomly assigned either to the full-screen or to the split-screen condition. Subjects were told that they would be viewing a reenacted trial concerning an automobile injury case and that they were to assume the role of jurors. The importance of entering into the juror role was stressed, and it appeared that most subjects assumed the role earnestly.

After the instructions had been given, the subjects viewed the appropriate taping of the *Nugent v. Clark* trial. When the trial was completed, all subjects responded to a modification of the questionnaire used in Study 1. Since subjects in Study 1 had difficulty completing the set of semantic differential-type scales used to measure credibility, we used a single, seven-interval scale in Study 2 (1 = minimum credibility; 7 = maximum credibility). This change accounts for the single mean value of credibility in Study 2.

Results. Table 10-3 contains the negligence verdicts for jurors who viewed the split-screen and the full-screen tapings of the trial, as well as the mean awards for both Mr. and Mrs. Nugent. Neither the negligence verdicts ($X^2 = <1; p > .90$) nor the awards to Mr. and Mrs. Nugent ($t = <1$ for both awards) were significantly affected by the type of taped presentation viewed by jurors.

Table 10-3
Negligence Verdicts and Mean Awards for Mr. and Mrs. Nugent by Jurors in the Split-Screen and Full-Screen Conditions

	For Plaintiffs	For Defense	Mean Award Mr. Nugent	Mean Award Mrs. Nugent
Split	11	12	$3,137	$21,200
Full	15	16	$2,919	$19,308

There is some indication that the type of taped presentation influenced jurors' perceptions of attorney credibility, but it is less than overwhelming, since the difference is significant for only the plaintiffs' attorney. The mean credibility ratings for the plaintiffs' attorney were 5.19 in the split-screen condition and 4.81 in the full-screen condition ($t = 2.23; p < .05$). Thus, jurors who saw the split-screen system rated the plaintiffs' attorney significantly more credible than jurors who saw the full-screen system. By contrast, the mean credibility ratings for the defendant's attorney were 5.47 in the split-screen and 5.12 in the full-screen condition. Although the resultant t of 1.75 has a p value of $< .10$, it does not reach the required .05 level.

There is no evidence that the type of taped presentation affected jurors' retention of trial-related information. Of a possible score of 40, mean retention for jurors in the split-screen condition was 30.70, while mean retention for jurors in the full-screen condition was 31.03 ($t = < 1$).

Finally, the data reveal no clear indication that jurors were differentially interested or motivated in the two conditions, though there is a trend toward higher self-report ratings of interest and motivation in the split-screen condition (X, split-screen = 5.3; X, full-screen = 4.94; $t = 1.52; p < 10$). As in Study 1, the ratings of jurors in both conditions are above the 3.50 scale midpoint.

Discussion. Save for differences in ratings of attorney credibility, our results indicate that the two taping systems are about equally effective, at least in terms of the juror responses measured in the study. One possible exception occurs in the case of juror interest and motivation. Although not significant at the required level, the higher self-report ratings of jurors viewing the split-screen taping suggest that it may have been somewhat more interesting than its full-screen counterpart.

We had assumed that the greater detail provided by the split-screen system might result in more favorable perceptions of the attorneys, especially since both were skilled performers. Although admittedly speculative, there is a possible explanation for this effect being more pronounced for plaintiffs' than for the defendant's attorney. As a result of informally observing the two attorneys, we concluded that the strongest rhetorical tool of the defendant's attorney was his vocal dynamism and power, while the primary rhetorical strength of plaintiffs' attorney seemed to lie in his expressive nonverbal behaviors and his skillful use of props, such as his glasses. Obviously, such nonverbal skills could be observed more easily on the split-screen, whereas the vocal abilities of the defendant's attorney could be readily recognized in both conditions.

Hence, we suspect that the credibility of a skilled trial lawyer may be enhanced by the split-screen system, at least when relatively inexpensive equipment is used. Of course, if the single-screen shot could be magnified by means of a projection system, this difference might be eliminated. Moreover, we have no data to suggest whether the converse is also true—that is, a relatively unskilled attorney would profit from the loss of detail that occurs with the full-screen system.

Finally, the fact that ratings of interest and motivation were high for jurors in both conditions suggests that all jurors found the task relatively interesting and motivating, a conclusion that bodes well for the use of either system in actual trial situations.

The Effects of Deleting Inadmissible Testimony from a Videotaped Trial

Proponents of videotape have argued that one of its advantages is that inadmissible testimony may be deleted before jurors are exposed to it. This procedure is said to have at least three advantages: (1) trial time would be reduced; (2) no inadmissible testimony would taint a jury's verdict; and (3) judges could research questions of admissibility thoroughly before ruling on them. (The second purported advantage rests on the assumption that, while jurors are instructed by judges to disregard inadmissible testimony, they may not, or perhaps even *cannot*, do so.)

Some involved reasoning, based on both legal wisdom and behavioral research, is possible regarding this issue. The intended beneficiary of instances of inadmissible testimony may indeed benefit from the introduction of moderate amounts of such material. However, when numerous instances of inadmissible testimony are introduced, their total effect may be quite different. Trial procedure is a highly rule-governed process, and jurors probably expect that attorneys will not violate trial rules. If these rules are extensively violated, then one of two outcomes may occur. Jurors may perceive that the rule-breaking attorney knowingly and intentionally broke the rules, in which case they would perceive him as less trustworthy. Alternatively, the rule-breaking attorney may be perceived as ignorant of the rules of trial procedure, causing jurors to question his legal competence or expertise.

If an attorney's trustworthiness or his competence is adversely affected by rule breaking, the resultant decrement could certainly influence his client's case. This effect could manifest itself in one of two ways: jurors might react unfavorably toward the client represented by the rule-breaking attorney or jurors might feel some measure of sympathy for the client and react more favorably toward his or her case.

Because the preceding analysis involves a number of competing curvilinear relationships, no hypotheses were tested; rather, two exploratory studies were conducted. Both studies were designed to address the following questions:

Are there differences in negligence verdicts among jurors who view differing amounts of inadmissible testimony in a trial?

Among jurors finding for the plaintiff, are there differences in the amount of award among those jurors who view differing amounts of inadmissible testimony?

Are there differences in perceptions of attorney credibility among jurors who view differing amounts of inadmissible testimony?

For both studies dealing with inadmissible testimony, the reenacted trial of *Nugent v. Clark* was employed. After consultation with legal experts, six instances of inadmissible testimony, all designed to be introduced by plaintiffs' attorney, were concocted.[4] During one of the final rehearsals for the live reenactment, a tape containing all six instances of inadmissible testimony was shot. Deletion was then accomplished by systematically editing out varying amounts of inadmissible testimony.

Deletion of Inadmissible Testimony: Initial Investigation

Procedures. The subjects were 120 jurors serving on the Wayne Circuit Court (Detroit, Michigan) jury panel. They were randomly assigned to one of seven conditions (zero deletions of inadmissible testimony to six deletions of inadmissible testimony). After the judge explained the split-screen system to them, each group of jurors viewed the appropriate version of *Nugent v. Clark*. When the trial was finished, the subjects completed a questionnaire containing measures of verdict, amount of award, and attorney credibility.

Results. Table 10-4 contains the negligence verdicts for jurors in the seven conditions, as well as the mean awards to Mrs. Nugent for pain and suffering. (In order to simplify the instructions to the jurors, we eliminated the derivative

Table 10-4
Negligence Verdicts and Mean Awards for Mrs. Nugent by Jurors in the Seven Conditions

Number of Deletions of Testimony	For Plaintiffs	For Defense	Mean Award
0	10	5	$21,000
1	11	9	$14,863
2	13	7	$18,461
3	9	9	$17,055
4	5	4	$21,940
5	15	5	$17,200
6	9	6	$22,500

[4] For a description of the procedures used in developing this testimony and a listing of the six instances, see Miller and Siebert (1974) or Fontes (1975).

award to Mr. Nugent.) The data provide no evidence that either variable was significantly affected by the amount of inadmissible testimony contained in the trial. Although there was a higher proportion of verdicts for the plaintiffs, perceptions of negligence do not vary systematically across conditions ($X^2 = 3.25$; $p > .80$). Similarly, simple analysis of variance of the awards given Mrs. Nugent by jurors in the seven conditions yielded an F of < 1.

In analyzing the credibility ratings, we were particularly interested in those for the plaintiffs' attorney, since he was consistently the rule breaker. Simple analysis of variance of both the trustworthiness and competence ratings of the plaintiffs' attorney produced nonsignificant results (F, trustworthiness = 1.39; F, competence = < 1). Not surprisingly, the credibility ratings for the defendant's attorney did not differ across conditions. Hence, there is no evidence that the amount of inadmissible testimony introduced by the plaintiffs' attorney influenced jurors' perceptions of his credibility.

Discussion. Given that six values of amount of inadmissible testimony were employed, our failure to detect significant differences may seem surprising. Several factors probably contributed to this outcome.

First, unlike some previous studies (Sue, Smith, & Caldwell, 1973), we deliberately avoided highly dramatic, extremely inadmissible items. This decision suggests that the lack of differences may be attributable to one or both of two factors: the *amount* of inadmissible testimony may have been insufficient relative to the four-hour time length or the *content* of the inadmissible testimony may have been neither supportive enough of the plaintiffs' case nor damning enough for the defendant's case to appreciably affect the jurors' responses.

Although our approach may initially strike some as a procedural blunder, our decision was guided by our quest for maximum generalizability. In consultation with legal experts, we selected typical instances of inadmissible testimony to determine the impact of their deletion. Doubtless, we could have identified some item of testimony that would have made a difference, but carried to extremes, this would have been merely an exercise in the obvious.

Sampling problems stemming from the ordinary activities of the court may also have contributed to our nonsignificant findings. Originally, we had been promised 240 jurors to fill the seven conditions. Several unexpected trials on the day of the study reduced this number to about one half. Consequently, the actual sample sizes for each condition were small, introducing a high likelihood of Type 11 error, particularly for the highly variable award measure. In the follow-up study reported next, we attempted to alleviate some of these potential shortcomings.

Deletion of Inadmissible Testimony: A Follow-up

We have already speculated on some possible reasons why the use of varying amounts of inadmissible testimony had no appreciable effect on jurors' responses in the previous study. In addition, however, a problem may have arisen because of our attempt to detect very subtle differences. In our original study of inadmissible testimony, we depended on single-item differences to produce variations in juror response—that is, we relied on the possibility that one additional item, or one less item, would exert a definite impact on juror behavior. Since we had no precise way to gauge the psychological impact of each item, this procedure was risky.

In this follow-up study, we sought to determine if more molar discriminations would significantly influence juror response. We used three of the seven conditions employed in the prior study: (1) the version containing none of the six additional items of inadmissible testimony, (2) the version containing three of these items, and (3) the version containing all six. The questions investigated paralleled those of the previous study:

Are there differences in negligence verdicts among jurors viewing differing amounts of inadmissible testimony in a trial?

Among jurors finding for the plaintiff, are there differences in the amount of award among those jurors who view differing amounts of inadmissible testimony?

Are there differences in perceptions of attorney credibility among jurors who view differing amounts of inadmissible testimony?

Procedures. Because of limitations in the availability of a courtroom and actual impaneled jurors, 144 undergraduate students at Michigan State University were randomly assigned to one of the three conditions. The subjects were told to play the role of a conscientious juror whose verdict would be binding on the litigants.

After the opening instructions, the subjects viewed the appropriate version or *Nugent v. Clark.* They then completed the same questionnaire used in the previous study.

Results. Table 10-5 contains the negligence verdicts for jurors in the three conditions, as well as the mean awards to Mrs. Nugent. In this study, more jurors

Table 10-5
Negligence Verdicts and Mean Awards for Mrs. Nugent by Jurors in the Three Conditions

Number of Deletions of Testimony	For Plaintiffs	For Defense	Mean Award
0	15	26	$15,528
3	20	30	$17,806
6	24	29	$14,964

found for the defendant than for the plaintiff, but the frequency with which this occurred did not vary significantly according to the amount of inadmissible testimony ($X^2 = 1$; $p > .80$). Similarly, while the pattern of mean awards is somewhat consistent with our expectations—that is, when compared with the baseline condition contraining no additional items of inadmissible testimony, Mrs. Nugent's award went up with the addition of three items but declined with the addition of six—the resultant F of 1.16 does not approach significance.

The data also reveal no evidence that the plaintiffs' attorney was seen as differentially credible in the three conditions, which suggests that his introduction of inadmissible testimony did not have a negative impact on his courtroom image. Specifically, the mean ratings of credibility for plaintiffs' attorney were 4.71, in the zero-item condition; 5.01, in the three-item condition; and 4.70 in the six-item condition. Although these means correspond with the pattern observed on amount of award—that is, credibility increased with the introduction of three items but decreased with the introduction of six—the obtained F of 1.70 was not significant.

Discussion. While there are some encouraging patterns in these findings, none of the comparisons are statistically significant. Since the cell sizes are quite large when compared with those of the previous study, we are confident something other than sample size is contributing to the lack of differences. As we have mentioned before, it may be that the stimulus is just not powerful enough—that is, there may not be enough inadmissible material, given the total trial length. Then, too, the large variability within conditions on the amount of awards given to the plaintiff reduces the likelihood of obtaining a significant between-conditions effect. Perhaps if we were to reduce the award requested by the plaintiff (in the trial, the requested award for Marjorie Nugent is $42,500), we could generate a distribution of awards more conducive to a powerful test of the data. We are presently exploring this possibility in further research.

Perhaps the one conclusion to be drawn from these two studies is that relatively commonplace items of inadmissible testimony do not appear to have a marked impact on juror response—apparently jurors can heed the judge's admonition to disregard them. Thus, the advantages to be gained from deletion of inadmissible testimony may be restricted to situations where the material is powerful enough to exert a strong impact on the jurors.

Studies of Juror Retention of Trial-Related Information

The two studies reported in this section dealt with the general question of whether medium of presentation (live, monochromatic videotaped, or color videotaped) affects juror retention of trial-related information. In addition, the possibility that the strength or quality of a witness' testimony might interact with medium of presentation was also investigated.

Retention of Information by Jurors Viewing Live,
Monochromatic, and Color Testimony

This study sought to determine what differences in retention of trial-related information and perceptions of credibility exist among jurors viewing live, monochromatic, and color testimony. Specifically, the study addressed two questions:

Are there differences in the amount or pattern of information retained by jurors viewing live, monochromatic, and color testimony?

Are there differences in perceptions of credibility of attorneys and witnesses among jurors viewing live, monochromatic, and color testimony?

With respect to the first question, even though overall scores on information retention might be similar, the pattern of information retention for jurors viewing live, monochromatic, and color testimony may differ due to differences in the levels and patterns of attention in the three groups. Miller and Campbell (1959) have suggested that interested message recipients will remember more of the last part of a message than of the first part. On the other hand if a presentation is uninteresting, recall of the first part will be better than recall of later segments, presumably because recipients "tune out" later sections. If live testimony results in more personal involvement for jurors than videotape, we would expect jurors viewing live testimony to remember later events to a greater extent. Similarly, if color testimony is more lifelike than monochromatic, retention patterns between the two modes should differ. This possibility is supported by Kumata (1960) and Katzman (1971), who reported dissimilar patterns of information processing for monochromatic and color television. In addition, Schaps and Guest (1968) found that subjects watching color television had better recall of advertisements than those who viewed black-and-white commercials.

The second question has already been examined by previous studies; consequently, the present investigation offered an opportunity for replication. Moreover, if attention factors do in fact differ among live, monochromatic, and color presentations, this difference might also exhibit itself in juror perceptions of key figures in the trial.

Procedures. The subjects who viewed the live trial were thirty-one jurors from the 65th District Court in Flint, Michigan. The subjects were told by the presiding judge that they would be viewing an actual trial where the parties involved had agreed to participate in a jury size study. They were also told the litigants had agreed that the trial could be halted periodically so that questionnaires could be administered.

The subjects viewed a live reenactment, performed by professional actors, of the opening two hours of a trial involving a contested will. The reenactment was videotaped in the courtroom, the subjects having been previously told that videotape was being used for purposes of record.

After the reenactment, the subjects completed a questionnaire designed to measure retention of information from the second hour of the trial and to assess the credibility of the witness and both attorneys. The second hour consisted of the testimony of one witness and was chosen to avoid the confounding effects of delivery style and differing credibility that might result from testing recall of the testimony of more than one witness. Actually, this was the only witness who testified. The first hour was devoted to instructions by the presiding judge and opening statements of the attorneys. While the jurors were completing the questionnaire, they believed that the trial would resume. When they finished the questionnaire, they were debriefed and dismissed.

The videotape of the reenactment was shown in color and monochromatic respectively to two other groups of thirty-one jurors from the 68th District. The judge instructed the subjects that they were viewing a videotaped trial where the litigants had agreed to accept the verdict of the jury viewing the videotape. They were given the same questionnaire administered to subjects in the live condition.

In constructing the retention measure, the testimony was divided into four, thirteen-minute parts. Equal numbers of questions were asked from each part, so that the pattern of retention could be ascertained for equal time periods: (1) by comparing retention from corresponding thirteen-minute sections across live, monochromatic, and color; and (2) by performing analyses of retention for each mode over time.

Results and Discussion. Table 10-6 summarizes the retention scores over the four thirteen-minute time intervals for jurors in the three conditions. Although no differences were found for medium of presentation ($F < 1$), the interaction for medium of presentation over time was significant ($F = 4.03, p < .05$). This effect seems to result from the greater decrement in retention among jurors in the live condition compared with jurors in the videotaped conditions.

In terms of the attention hypothesis discussed above, this finding suggests that videotaped testimony may better hold jurors' interest over time. Moreover, as Table 10-1 indicates, the effect is somewhat more pronounced for jurors in

Table 10-6
Information Retention Scores for Jurors in the Three Conditions

	T_1	T_2	T_3	T_4	$T_1 - T_4$
Live	9.8	8.3	7.7	7.6	8.3
Color	9.0	8.6	8.5	7.8	8.5
Mono	9.4	9.2	7.8	8.0	8.6

the monochromatic condition. This lends credence to the possibility that monochromatic videotape holds juror attention better, perhaps because it requires more effort to view and results in higher perceptual stimulation. We will have more to say about this possibility in the study reported next.

While the information retention patterns differ for the three modes of presentation, the absolute differences in mean retention scores are not large. Consequently, some might contend that the differences, although statistically significant, are not great enough to exert any appreciable impact on the ongoing trial process. Two considerations are relevant in evaluating this argument. First, we tested retention of trial-related information for a single hour of testimony. If the observed differences in retention persist over longer time periods, their cumulative effect on juror knowledge could be considerable for an entire trial. Second, the fact that such small mean differences produced statistically significant results indicates that the effect was remarkably consistent and uniform for most jurors in a given condition. If the within-condition variance in juror retention scores had been at all marked, between-condition differences of the magnitude obtained would not have reached the required level of significance.

Table 10-7 contains the mean credibility ratings by jurors in the three conditions for the witness and both attorneys. Obviously, the mode of presentation did not influence jurors' perceptions of these three principal trial participants. This finding provides additional support for earlier studies that found no differences in credibility ratings across modes of presentation.

Table 10-7
Credibility Ratings for Trial Participants by Jurors in the Three Conditions

		Authoritativeness		*Character*
Witness	Live	81.5	Live	68.4
	Color	85.1	Color	70.0
	Mono	82.0	Mono	64.0
	$F < 1$		$F = 1.69$	
Plaintiffs'	Live	76.6	Live	69.4
Attorney	Color	76.9	Color	70.7
	Mono	78.4	Mono	68.4
	$F < 1$		$F < 1$	
Defendant's	Live	77.7	Live	69.6
Attorney	Color	74.0	Color	70.0
	Mono	79.1	Mono	67.0
	$F < 1$		$F < 1$	

Retention of Information by Jurors Viewing Monochromatic and Color Testimony

Given the higher levels of juror information retention observed for the videotape conditions in the previous study, we conducted a second investigation to examine, with greater specificity, whether there were differences in retention of trial-related information between jurors viewing monochromatic and color testimony. In addition, we also manipulated the delivery characteristics of the witness giving the testimony, primarily to determine if juror response to monochromatic and color testimony might be influenced by the characteristics of a particular witness. We reasoned that a strong witness—that is, one who appears assertive, attentive, and unhesitant—might profit most from the color format, that jurors might retain a great deal of the information presented by such a witness and perceive him as highly credible. By contrast, a weak witness—that is, one who appears uncertain, inattentive, and fumbling—might appear particularly inept in color and might be somewhat more effective on monochromatic tape.

In an earlier study, we also included a condition labeled "modal personality," intended to represent the situation where testimony is read into the record by a third party. Since some procedural problems occurred in that study, the results are not reported here.

Procedures. The subjects were eighty-eight adults from the greater Lansing (Michigan) area who played the role of jurors. They were instructed to view the testimony as though it were part of an actual trial. The subjects were randomly assigned to one of the study's four conditions.

The stimulus used was a videotaped recording of a deposition concerning an industrial accident. A professional actor played the witness role, while two actual attorneys took the attorney role. The participants were seated at a small table and the camera shot was fixed.

The manipulation of witness type was achieved by requiring the same actor to play two different roles. In the strong-witness conditions, he was assertive, attentive, and unhesitant when giving testimony. In the weak-witness conditions, he exhibited verbal and nonverbal cues to suggest that he was uncertain, fumbling, inattentive, and hesitant. It should be noted that the testimony was identical in each condition.

Each subject saw the testimony of one witness type (strong or weak) on either color or monochromatic tape. After viewing the appropriate testimony, all subjects completed a questionnaire designed to measure their retention of trial-related information and their perceptions of the witness' credibility.

Results and Discussion. Table 10-8 contains the mean retention scores for jurors in each of the four conditions. Of particular interest is the fact that retention scores for both witness types were higher in the monochromatic than in the color conditions. Analysis of variance revealed that this difference was statistically significant ($F = 6.55$; $p < .05$), indicating that regardless of the type of witness, jurors viewing the monochromatic deposition retained more information than jurors who viewed the color testimony.

In addition, analysis of the retention data yielded a significant effect for witness type ($F = 6.58$; $p < .05$). Subsequent comparisons revealed that jurors who viewed the strong witness retained significantly more information than their counterparts who viewed the weak witness. The absence of a significant interaction indicates that this difference in retention is comparable for both modes of presentation, although it is somewhat more pronounced in the monochromatic condition.

Table 10-9 contains the mean ratings of perceived witness credibility for jurors in the four conditions. Consistent with the manipulation, the strong witness was perceived as more credible than the weak witness ($F = 9.19$; $p < .05$). More important is the fact that the color mode produced significantly higher ratings of perceived witness credibility, with the difference especially apparent in the strong witness condition. Thus, it appears that use of color videotape enhances the credibility of both witness types but that a strong witness benefits more, proportionately, from its use.

The most interesting and potentially important finding concerned the observed differences in information retention between jurors who viewed the testimony in monochromatic and those who saw it in color: jurors remembered

Table 10-8
Mean Retention Scores for Jurors in the Four Conditions

| | Mode of Presentation | |
Type of Witness	Monochromatic	Color
Strong	39.72	34.59
Weak	36.17	33.31

Table 10-9
Mean Ratings of Witness Credibility by Jurors in the Four Conditions

| | Mode of Presentation | |
Type of Witness	Monochromatic	Color
Strong	5.88	6.43
Weak	4.96	5.12

more of the trial-related information when it was presented on monochromatic tape. There are at least two possible explanations for this result. First, color videotape provides a richer visual stimulus field and, as was suggested earlier, these added stimuli may distract jurors from the testimony. Second, when compared with monochromatic, color videotape is more realistic—that is, it more closely approximates the visual perspective of jurors participating in a live trial. Perhaps this greater realism, which places fewer cognitive demands on jurors, culminates in a state of reduced stimulation that would explain the lower amount of information retention.

Even though information retention was lower in the color condition, ratings of perceived witness credibility were higher. This finding suggests that a significant portion of the information that jurors use in making credibility judgments is nonverbal. If so, much of this information might be lost through the use of monochromatic videotape, either because of its absence from the screen (as in the case of flushed skin) or because jurors do not attend as closely to the less interesting black-and-white visual display. To some extent, then, the findings of this study pose a perplexing and paradoxical problem. Apparently, the monochromatic mode results in better retention of trial-related information, while the color mode produces higher ratings of perceived witness credibility.

Implications for Policy Regarding Use of Videotape

As far as the juror responses dealt with in these studies are concerned, there is no evidence to indicate that the introduction of videotaped trial materials has any markedly negative effect on courtroom communication between trial participants and jurors; consequently, there are no strong grounds for arguing that videotape will exercise a negative impact on juror information processing or decision-making.

In the initial study comparing a live and videotaped trial, we found no significant differences in the responses of jurors exposed to the two presentational modes. In several of the later studies, we actually observed that jurors viewing videotaped trial materials retained more trial-related information than jurors who watched live testimony. Although this finding may initially seem inconsistent with the results of our first study, in which no differences in information retention were found between jurors who viewed a live and those who viewed a videotaped trial, there are at least two possible explanations for the apparent discrepancy, one procedural and one substantive.

Procedurally, the amount of possible control and refinement of the instrument used to measure juror retention of information was somewhat greater in the later studies. This is not to deny the care taken in developing the questionnaire used in the original study comparing live and videotaped trials, but merely to recognize that the shorter time period (one hour as opposed to four hours), plus the experience gained in earlier research, probably resulted in a more powerful retention instrument for the later studies. To the extent that this is true, the likelihood of detecting differences in retention increases.

Substantively, of course, it is possible that the relationship between mode of presentation and amount of information communicated is both complex and nonlinear. In the first study, we were dealing with an "information package" that spanned more than four hours and a number of witnesses; in our more recent undertakings, we were concerned with considerably shorter periods of testimony by a single witness. Perhaps some combination of factors (for example, novelty, interest, and so forth) confers an initial advantage on videotaped testimony; but, after a certain period of time, the influence of these factors dissipates and information retention levels off and equalizes for the two presentational modes. Assessment of this possibility awaits future research that would manipulate time intervals over a larger range of values.

Perhaps the most intriguing, counterintuitive finding concerns retention of trial-related information by jurors viewing monochromatic and color presentations of trial proceedings. Results of two of the studies indicate that jurors retain more trial-related information when the testimony is on monochromatic rather than color tape. It would, of course, be possible to run rampant with post hoc speculations concerning this finding: black-and-white presentations may be something of a novelty in a society where most people watch color television; jurors may have to "work" harder to assimilate information from monochromatic testimony; black-and-white presentations may better fit jurors' expectations of an austere, dignified legal system; and so on. We prefer to save such speculation for future research. One practical observation does, however, seem in order: none of the research reported here suggests that anything is lost in juror information retention by using monochromatic systems rather than their more expensive color counterparts.

Nonetheless, it was noted that the color format does enhance the credibility of witnesses, particularly witnesses with strong presentational skills. This feature of the color medium is potentially a mixed blessing for the legal system. On the positive side, the added peripheral information acquired from color may permit jurors to spot dishonest witnesses more readily. On the negative side, however, our results indicate that color may maximally enhance the impact of a skilled presentation of information. Naturally, a skilled witness is likely to be more effective with any presentational medium, be it live testimony, monochromatically taped testimony, or testimony taped in color. But to the extent that the color mode heightens this effect, it perhaps places a greater premium on variables that should not be central to the decision-making process of jurors. In a nutshell, it may magnify the importance of *image* at the expense of *information*. This is a possibility that should be weighed carefully in arriving at policies concerning the use of videotape in courtroom trials.

Finally, we should emphasize that the research reported above focuses on the possible behavioral impact of videotaped trial materials on jury members. Other writers (for example, Bermant & Jacoubovitch, 1975; Doret, 1974) have not only dealt with this area, but have also raised other important questions concerning the possible influence of videotape on the judicial system. Although our findings have definite implications for those charged with making decisions about the adoption of videotaped trial materials, we realize that a number of system-oriented issues must be resolved before a final verdict can be reached.

References

Anapol, M. Behind locked doors: An investigation of certain trial and jury variables by means of a videotaped trial. Paper presented at the Speech Communication Association Convention, New York, November 1973.

Barbuto, J.V. Potential for TV in courtroom unlimited. *Akron Beacon Journal*, August 2, 1972, p. A12.

Bermant, G., & Jacoubovitch, M.-D. Fish out of water: A brief overview of social and psychological concerns about videotaped trials. *Hastings Law Journal*, 1975, *26*, 999-1011.

Brunswik, E. *Systematic and representative design of psychological experiments with results in physical and social perception.* Berkeley: University of California Press, 1974.

Doret, D.M. Trial by videotape—Can justice be seen to be done? *Temple Law Quarterly*, 1974, *47*, 228-268.

Fontes, N.E. The behavioral impact of inadmissible evidence on jurors: A preliminary investigation. Ph.D. dissertation, Department of Communication, Michigan State University, 1975.

Greenwald, A.G. Consequences of prejudice against the null hypothesis. *Psychological Bulletin*, 1975, *82*, 1-20.

Katzman, N.I. Violence and color television: What children of different ages learn. Unpublished manuscript, Department of Communication, Michigan State University, 1971.

Kennelly, J.J. The practical use of trialvision and depovision. *Trial Lawyer's Guide*, Summer 1972, pp. 183-208.

Kumata, H. Two studies in classroom teaching. In W. Schramm (Ed.), *The Impact of Educational Television.* Urbana: University of Illinois Press, 1960.

McCrystal, J.L. Ohio's first videotape trial. *Ohio Bar*, 1972, *45*, 1-4.

McCrystal, J.L. Video tape trials. *Ohio Bar*, 1971, *44*, 639-642.

McLuhan, M. Understanding media: The extensions of man. New York: McGraw-Hill, 1964.

Miller, G.R., & Siebert, F.S. Effects of videotaped testimony on information processing and decision-making in jury trials. Progress Report 1, NSF-RANN Grant #GI 38398, Department of Communication, Michigan State University, March 1974.

Miller, G.R., & Siebert, F.S. Effects of videotaped testimony on information processing and decision-making in jury trials. Progress Report 2, NSF-RANN Grant #GI 38398, Department of Communication, Michigan State University, February 1975.

Miller, G.R., Bender, D.C., Boster, F.J., Florence, B.T., Fontes, N.F., Hocking, J.E., & Nicholson, H.E. The effects of videotape testimony in jury trials: Studies on juror decision-making, information retention, and emotional arousal. *Brigham Young University Law Review*, 1975, *1975*, 331-373.

Miller, G.R., Bender, D.C., Florence, B.T., & Nicholson, H.E. Real versus reel: What's the verdict? *Journal of Communication*, 1974, *24*, 99-111.

Miller, N., & Campbell, D.T. Recency and privacy in persuasion as a function of the timing of speeches and measurement. *Journal of Abnormal & Social Psychology*, 1959, *59*, 1-9.

Morrill, A.E. Enter—the video tape trial. *John Marshall Journal of Practice and Procedure*, 1970, *3*, 237-259.

Murray, T.J., Jr. Comments on a video tape trial. *Ohio Bar*, 1972, *45*, 25-30.

Schaps, E., & Guest, L. Some pros and cons of color TV. *Journal of Advertising Research*, 1968, *8*, 28-39.

Stiver, C.E. Videotape trials: A practical evaluation and a legal analysis. *Stanford Law Review*, 1974, *26*, 619-645.

Strodtbeck, F.L., & Mann, R.D. Sex role differentiation in jury deliberations. *Sociometry*, 1956, *19*, 3-11.

Strodtbeck, F.L., James, R.M., & Hawkins, C. Social status in jury deliberations. *American Sociological Review*, 1957, *22*, 713-719.

Sue, S., Smith, R.E., & Caldwell, D. Effects of inadmissible evidence on the decisions of simulated jurors: A moral dilemma. *Journal of Applied Social Psychology*, 1973, *3*, 345-353.

Trialevision. *Time*, December 17, 1973, pp. 83-84.

11

Juror Perceptions of Trial Testimony as a Function of the Method of Presentation

Larry C. Farmer   Bert P. Cundick
Gerald R. Williams   Robert J. Howell
Rex E. Lee   C. Keith Rooker

Since its first commercial use in 1956, videotape has found practical applications across an increasingly wide spectrum in the fields of entertainment, industry, and education. Yet there can be little doubt that we are only on the threshold of potential beneficial uses of this medium. During the past five years, for example, there has been increasing discussion in legal, social-psychological, and communications literature recommending a variety of interesting applications of videotape technology to the judicial process (Barber & Bates, 1974; Kornblum, 1972; Taillefer, Short, Greenwood & Brady, 1974; Thornton, 1973). A number of judges, lawyers, and researchers have taken the lead in experimenting with these possible applications and in exploring the legal and procedural ramifications of the use of videotape in the resolution of legal disputes (Bleus & Patterson, 1972; McCrystal & Young, 1972; Stiver, 1974). This research has indicated at least four categories of potential use: facilitating prelitigation negotiation, recording oral depositions, preserving the trial record, and presenting evidence at trial.

Among the potential legal application of videotape the one of greatest interest to the legal profession is the use of videotape to present testimonial evidence at trial. This use was described and advocated as early as 1970 and has been tried experimentally in the courts of several states (Morrill, 1970; National Center for State Courts, 1974). Moreover, the rules of procedure in some states have been revised to allow introduction of certain types of videotape testimony in trials, and the Code of Judicial Conduct now expressly allows a judge to authorize use of electronic recordings in the courtroom in certain circumstances.

The literature concerning the use of videotape for presenting portions or all of the evidence at trial has been generally optimistic and enthusiastic (Kornblum, 1972; McCrystal, 1974; Merlo & Sorenson, 1971). In addition to the efficiencies and conveniences resulting to the individual litigants and their lawyers, media presentation of evidence offers a potential solution to one of the most severe problems facing our judicial system: congestion in the courts.

This article is revised from a more complete account of the experiment originally published in the *Brigham Young University Law Review*, 1975, *1975*, 375-421. The authors wish to thank the Research Division of Brigham Young University and the J. Reuben Clark Law School for providing the funding for this research, Woodruff J. Deem, Professor of Law at Brigham Young University, who served as judge in the experimental trials, and the judges and staff of the Fourth Judicial District Court of Utah, who generously provided staff assistance and access to court facilities. The three judges assigned to the 4th Judicial District Court of Utah not only permitted access to lists of experienced jurors from past jury panels and to the evening use of the courtroom, but also assisted by jointly signing the letter that was sent to jurors requesting their participation.

There are several arguments supporting the idea that videotape trials would save court time. For example, it is argued that by videotaping the evidence and then previewing this record in advance, the lawyers could probably come to agreement on some disputed evidentiary questions. That way the judge would not have to be there at the presentation of the evidence to the jury. Jury time is also saved, principally by the elimination of delays while the court and counsel resolve evidentiary and procedural matters.

In addition, the use of media presentations allows trial testimony to be prerecorded at times convenient to witnesses and attorneys and to be edited of objectionable material before being shown to jurors. It should also broaden the availability of evidence by allowing the testimony of witnesses, who might otherwise be unwilling or unable to take several days to attend and testify at trial, to be prerecorded with very little expenditure of time.

The experimental and scholarly activities to date have laid the foundation for increasing trial applications of videotape recordings, leading one proponent to suggest that "the period of experimentation with videotape is now over" (McCrystal, 1974). This view, however, overlooks a major shortcoming in current experimentation and research: the failure to address the issue of whether the trier of fact may respond differently to a videotape presentation of testimony than to a live presentation of the same testimony. As one observer recently stated, "One overriding question remains, will attending a (televised) movie instead of a trial affect the verdict?" (Johnson, 1974). A comprehensive study by the National Center for State Courts examined this question and concluded that "[t]he impact of the video medium upon a jury's perceptions and decision making process compared with live trials needs to be extensively studied" (National Center for State Courts, 1974). Indeed, general acceptability of the media presentation will undoubtedly depend upon the extent to which trial judges and trial lawyers satisfy themselves (1) that there are no significant differences in juror perceptions between live and media presentations, or (2) that if such differences exist, they will not affect the verdict that the jurors are likely to render, or (3) that if such differences exist, their effects can be predicted in advance so that trial plans can be made in response to them.

A Review of the Research Literature

Until the present time, direct experimental research examining the various alternatives to live trial testimony has been sparse in relation to the importance of the questions involved. In 1973, a pilot study was conducted at Arizona State University Law School comparing the reactions of student "jurors" to the testimony of a single witness presented live, by black-and-white videotape, by audiotape, and by read transcript (Butler, 1973). While this study was subject to significant methodological limitations, it found that the monochromatic videotape presentation produced generally fewer positive ratings of the experimental witness than did the live testimony of the witness.

Additional research has been conducted over the past two years by Miller and Siebert at Michigan State University concerning the effects of videotape on the information processing and decision-making functions of jurors (Miller & Siebert, 1974). This research, a report of which is included in Chapter 10 of this volume, was conducted in two phases. In the first phase, actors using a modified transcript of an actual trial were used to stage a trial in a Michigan courtroom. This staged trial was viewed by a group of jurors and was videotaped for later showings to other groups of jurors. All jurors filled out questionnaires designed to compare their reactions along five dimensions: (1) attribution of negligence, (2) amount of dollar award, (3) perception of attorney credibility, (4) retention of trial-related information, and (5) motivation and interest in the trial proceedings. The researchers concluded that there were no significant differences in juror response across any of the five dimensions tested. However, a reanalysis of these results raises serious concerns about the finding of no difference in juror attributions of negligence. A consistent trend in Miller's data was noted when the verdicts of all of the jury panels which viewed the trial on videotape were examined. The pattern of preferred verdicts resulting from the video trial was consistently different from that of the live trial verdicts.

To demonstrate this change in the pattern of verdict preferences, the data reported in Miller's and Siebert's live-video comparison are presented in the first two rows of Table 11-1 and the results of all other reported video presentations of the trial are given in the additional rows. In thirteen separate videotape presentations of the stimulus trial, there was not one outcome that was like the pattern of verdicts preferred after the live trial. In the live trial, only 30 percent of the jurors found Clark negligent. Proportionately more of the video trial jurors found Clark negligent after every single videotape presentation. This was true regardless of the demographies of the "jurors," the degree of realism surrounding the videotape presentation, the setting in which the trial was shown, and the manipulations of the trial tape. The consistency of the different patterns of verdicts between the live trial and thirteen videotape presentations of the trial strongly indicates a change in the direction of the jurors' preferred verdicts. To test the significance of this pattern, the jurors' verdicts in all the video trials that used real jurors were combined and compared to the live trial verdicts. A significant chi square resulted from this comparison ($X^2(2) = 12.67, p < .001$). Technically, combining of the results of separate studies conducted under varying stimulus conditions can be only suggestive and was only done in this case to point out the possibility of a video effect. Nevertheless, the consistency of the shift in the judgment of Clark's negligence across all of the video presentations of the trial and the improbability of such a consistent shift brings into question the finding of "no difference" between the preferred verdicts of the jurors in the live and videotape trials. In fact, this reexamination of the data suggests just the

Table 11-1
Summary Table of Juror Verdicts for All Presentations of the Clark Negligence Trial

Type of Presentation	No. of Jurors	Subjects	No. of separate presentations included in data	Percentage of Jurors Preferring Each Verdict		
				Clark Not Neg.	Both Neg.	Clark Neg.
Live Trial	44	Jurors	1	43	27	30
Video Trial	40	Jurors	1	35	18	47
Deletion of inadmissible testimony-- video trials	117	Jurors	7	15	23	62
Split-Full screen comparison-- video trials	54	Members of a Catholic adult group	2	28	24	48
Deletion of inadmissible testimony-- video trials	144	Students	3	29	30	41

opposite: that a significantly different pattern for jurors' verdicts occurred in the video trials.

The second round of research conducted by the Michigan State group involved a comparison of (1) the respective amounts of information retained in live, color videotape, and black-and-white videotape presentations, (2) the amount of physiological arousal (as measured by the galvanic skin response test) induced by color and black-and-white videotape and (3) the credibility of the trial participants on color videotape and black-and-white videotape. The findings were (1) that the jurors retained the highest amount of information with black-and-white videotape, followed by color videotape and live presentation respectively, and (2) that the jurors were more physiologically aroused by black-and-white videotape than by color videotape. The findings also indicated that, as compared to black-and-white videotape, color videotape had the effect of enhancing the apparent credibility of witnesses and attorneys.

In a separate study, Bermant, Chappell, Crockett, Jacoubovitch, and McGuire (1975) surveyed the opinions and reactions of jurors serving in California and Ohio civil trials in which all trial testimony was presented by videotape. They found that the reaction of the jurors to the technical aspects of videotape presentation was generally favorable. However, the jurors did have trouble viewing graphic material and thought that more breaks would be necessary when observing videotape testimony. The researchers also found that the impersonal quality of the videotaped presentation bothered a number of jurors.

Although not directly related to the trial setting, educators in psychiatry, clinical psychology, counseling psychology, and teacher training have been conducting experiments to examine the effects of black-and-white videotape feedback as a teaching method. In developing the design for the present research, the authors drew upon this growing body of videotape feedback research for hypotheses concerning the effects of using these media to convey trial testimony.

The Research Design: Rationale and Description

The Need to Assess the Impact of Videotape in the Litigation Process

The research reported here grew out of a concern that the legal literature treating videotape in the courtroom does not directly consider the possibility that videotape presentations of trial testimony may substantially affect the decision-making process of the jury. This is not to say that if there is such an effect it is necessarily bad or improper. Rather, the research reflects a concern that the issue should be raised and confronted in order to determine whether it presents a significant problem.

The Live Trial As a Standard of Comparison

It may be asked why videotape presentations should be compared with live presentations of testimony at all. Historically, the purpose of trial by jury has been to make the most reliable possible determination of factual truth and to arrive at a verdict or award based on that determination. Consequently, the ideal test of the merits of alternative approaches to the presentation of trial testimony would be to compare them with objective and articulated standards of truth and justice. Since such standards are presently unavailable, the traditional substitute is the live jury trial. Secondarily, the extent to which videotape and other media will be utilized in the courtroom will depend largely on their acceptance by trial judges and lawyers whose natural tendency will be to compare any new format for the presentation of trial testimony with the familiar live trial format (Doret, 1974).

Given that the live presentation of testimony is an appropriate standard of comparison, it is not the only one. As previously noted, witnesses cannot always be physically present at trial to give their testimony, and it is therefore accepted procedure in both state and federal courts in appropriate cases to allow the presentation of testimony by read transcript. Since videotape could thus be used either to present the testimony of all witnesses or only the depositions of those witnesses who cannot appear at trial, videotape testimony should be compared not only with live testimony, but also with testimony presented by read transcript. In addition, audiotape is presently being used in Alaska as the official means of preserving trial testimony and as part of the record on appeal (Reynolds, 1970). Moreover, color videotape is now the preferred form of television in American homes and is becoming less expensive to reproduce. It would therefore appear that there are really five means of testimony presentation that should be compared: live, read transcript, black-and-white videotape, color videotape, and audiotape. The research reported here was designed to compare these five alternatives.

Description of the Research Design

Ideally, an actual jury trial should be used as the basis for this type of experimental study. However, because of the need to avoid possible interference with the rights and interests of litigants in an actual trial, it was decided that for the purposes of this research a method closely approximating a live jury trial would be adequate. Two approaches to the creation of such a stimulus trial were considered: (1) the dramatization of an edited trial transcript and (2) the use of a previously settled dispute for presentation in an unrehearsed trial. The dramatized transcript method had the potential advantage of improving experimental control. However, because such a trial would only have been an enactment, it would have been difficult to assess the degree of success in realistically presenting the subtle emotions and complex interactions of a real trial. Consequently, this method was rejected in favor of using a carefully selected, previously settled dispute that was tried as though it had not been settled. By allowing experienced trial counsel to prepare and conduct the trial in the typical fashion, the presentations of the participants were spontaneous and unfolding (rather than memorized and affected). The subtleties of original testimony were present and the whole procedure had the suspense and uncertainty of a real trial. In addition, the original parties to the dispute could be used and thus the participants would have a genuine interest in the proceedings.

The Stimulus Trial. The case selected for the stimulus trial was a land condemnation action. The condemning authority, the City of Provo, Utah, had taken approximately two-thirds of an acre in a prime residential area for street widening purposes. The land in question was near a prominent new building and was well known to most of the participating jurors. As in the typical condemnation jury trial, neither the right to take nor the amount of property necessary to accomplish the public purpose was ever at issue between the parties, and no claim was made for severance damages. Accordingly, the sole issue for the jury was the value of the property taken.

One witness was presented on each side. A co-owner of the property testified that the value of the property taken was $15,960, based on a per acre evaluation of $24,000. A realtor-appraiser who qualified as an expert witness testified on behalf of the city that the rounded amount of just compensation for the property taken was $8,000, based on a per acre value of $12,000. Both witnesses agreed that the highest and best use of the property, both before and after the taking, was future residential development, and both relied for their opinions principally upon what they considered to be comparable land trans-actions. The major difference in approach was that the witness for the city relied upon unimproved acreage transactions, and the land owner upon developed lot sales. Thus the major issue between the two witnesses was whether transactions involving unimproved acreages or developed lots were more comparable to the taking of the subject property. Although this issue was not precisely one of credibility, it did involve a difference of opinion as to the proper approach to the controlling issue of fact.

The Trial Participants. In addition to the landowner and the expert witness previously mentioned, the trial participants included counsel for the respective parties, a judge, a bailiff, and a separate panel of twenty-six to twenty-eight jurors at each trial. Counsel for both the landowner and the city were experienced trial attorneys and had prepared for this case as they would have prepared for any other land condemnation trial. The bailiff normally assigned to the courtroom used in this study served as the court bailiff during each presentation of the stimulus trial, and the two court reporters from the Fourth Judicial District Court participated in the read transcript trial. A law professor with previous judicial experience served as the trial judge.

Jurors were obtained from lists of persons who had previously served as district court jurors in Utah County. A letter requesting their participation in an experimental trial was sent to 244 of the names on the jury panel lists over the signatures of the three members of the district court and the law school dean. The potential jurors were told that they would be compensated at the regular per diem rate of eight dollars. A preference form and a stamped return envelope accompanied the letter, and the potential jurors were asked to indicate all of the days listed on the preference form on which it would be convenient for them to participate. Of the 182 jurors who returned the preference forms, 165 (80 males, 85 females) stated that they would attend at least one of the trials. For this pool of 165 potential jurors, 140 participated in some segment of the experiment, for the average of 28 per trial.

In short, the participants in this trial were people typically associated with jury trials serving in their usual courtroom roles.

The Physical Setting. The setting for the experiment was a courtroom located in the Fourth Judicial District Courthouse in Provo, Utah. The jurors at each trial sat in front of the bar dividing the court and the public sections. However, because the large number of jurors used could not be comfortably seated in the regular jury room, the nearby county commission chambers were substituted.

A Description of the Different Trial Procedures. The trials were held on five separate evenings over a period of a week and a half, and on each evening the entire proceeding occupied slightly more than three hours. On the first night the trial was presented live and simultaneously recorded by high fidelity color videotape equipment. During successive nights, the voir dire examination and selection of jurors were handled live by the same attorneys and the same judge who participated in the live trial. Once these steps were completed, there was a brief recess during which the attorneys and the judge left the courtroom and were replaced by the alternative media. On successive nights these were color videotape, black-and-white videotape, audiotape, and written transcript read by two experienced court reporters. The media presentation included the attorneys' opening statements, the direct- and cross-examinations of the witnesses, and the judge's instructions to the jury. At the conclusion of each presentation, the bailiff ushered the jurors into an adjoining room where they were asked to complete the questionnaire described below.

The various media presentations were all taken from the color video record obtained during the live trial. The black-and-white video presentation was made by turning off the color control switch on the color television monitors. Similarly, both the audiotape and the written transcript were made from the audio portion of the original color recording.

The Questionnaire. The questionnaire was constructed to obtain (1) the jurors' predeliberation dollar award, (2) their ratings of each of the trial participants, and (3) their reactions to the trial procedure. Before the questionnaire was filled out, the jurors were given two pages of instructions containing some sample ratings. Questions that arose during the course of filling out the questionnaires were handled by one of the experimenters.

The first portion of the questionnaire asked each juror to indicate what dollar amount should be awarded the landowner for the condemned property.

The second portion of the questionnaire consisted of a basic unit of twenty-nine bipolar adjective scales selected on the basis of their relevance to the evaluation of witnesses and attorneys by jurors. Each individual bipolar set of adjectives was arranged to yield a 9-point scale in the following manner:

Cooperative: ____:____:____:____:____:____:____:____:____:Uncooperative

$\quad\quad\quad\quad$ 1 $\quad$ 2 $\quad$ 3 $\quad$ 4 $\quad$ 5 $\quad$ 6 $\quad$ 7 $\quad$ 8 $\quad$ 9

Jurors were asked to complete one full set of adjective scales for each of the witnesses and attorneys participation in the trial, for a total of four. The order in which the participants were rated was counterbalanced to insure that the ratings were not systematically influenced by order of occurrence.

The third portion of the questionnaire contained three questions requiring each juror to make a forced choice selection as to which of the two witnesses he would select as a friend, which of the two attorneys he would select as a friend, and which of the two attorneys he would prefer as an attorney for himself.

The final part of the questionnaire listed five nine-point, bipolar adjective scales designed to obtain juror reactions to the trial procedure along the dimensions of interest, understandability, clarity, level of fatigue, and stimulation.

Results

The results of the research design described in the preceding section will be presented in the following order: (1) juror perceptions of the trial participants, (2) amount of the jurors' preferred dollar awards, (3) the relationship between the preferred dollar awards and juror perceptions of the participants, (4) juror preferences for individual participants, and (5) juror reactions to the alternative media presentations.

Juror Bipolar Ratings of the Trial Participants

As noted above, the witnesses and lawyers were rated in each of the five trials using a set of twenty-nine bipolar adjective scales. In order to reduce the complexity of comparing the live and media trial ratings using all twenty-nine items in the scale, all of the ratings given after each of the five trials were included in a factor analysis (the factor analysis program with a Varimax Rotation in Version-5 of the Statistical Package for the Social Sciences was used).

This process yielded five factors, which on the basis of high loading items, were named: (1) competency, (2) honesty, (3) friendliness, (4) appearance, and (5) objectivity (see Table 11-2).

The trial comparisons were made using factor scores derived from the factor loadings of the varimax rotation. The factor scores from the live trial were compared to the factor scores from each of the media trials by a mixed model analysis of variance design. Three treatment conditions were fixed: (a) media, with two levels—live and a media comparison; (b) sex, with two levels—male and

Table 11-2
Adjective Rating Pairs Grouped in Factors

Factor Name	Adjective Pair	Correlational Factor Loading
Competency	precise-vague	.788
	confident-hesitant	.752
	certain-uncertain	.695
	accurate-inaccurate	.693
	knowledgeable-uninformed	.682
	consistent-inconsistent	.613
	clear memory-faulty memory	.612
	convincing-unconvincing	.545
	reasonable-unreasonable	.473
Honesty	trustworthy-untrustworthy	.742
	telling truth-not telling truth	.719
	sincere-insincere	.683
	honest-dishonest	.679
	fair-unfair	.612
	logical-not logical	.601
Friendliness	friendly-unfriendly	.780
	warm-cold	.687
	well-mannered - ill-mannered	.679
	nice-not nice	.622
	pleasant-annoying	.581
	cooperative-uncooperative	.529
Appearance	well dressed-poorly dressed	.884
	clean cut-unwholesome	.835
Objectivity	prejudiced-unprejudiced	.794
	greedy-not greedy	.506
	open-defensive·	.438
Handsomeness	handsome-plain	.634
Calmness	calm-excited	.635

female; and (c) participants, with four levels—landowner, expert witness, counsel for the landowner, and counsel for the city. The fourth condition was random: raters (jurors). The analysis of variance design was an extension of the split-plot design being within the interaction of trials and sex, but crossed with persons. Persons and media were crossed and balanced. The analysis of variance was computed for each live-medium combination for each of the five factors. This resulted in twenty separate factor analyses of the type described above.

The results of these comparisons are easily shown in graphic form. For example, the graphic representation of the jurors' ratings of the competency factor for each of the trial participants in each of the five trials is given in Figure

11-1. In that figure, ratings of the attorney for the city are represented by the white squares. His ratings for each of the trials are given sequentially and connected by a solid line, so that by following his ratings horizontally across the graph one may see how he was rated with respect to competency in each of the five trials.

The portion of this article that follows will illustrate and discuss the jurors' ratings on each of the five factors.

Competency (see Figure 11-1 and Table 11-3). The competency factor is illustrated by the highest loading adjective pairs "precise-vague," "confident-hesitant," "certain-uncertain," and "accurate-inaccurate." The competency factor accounted for the greatest amount of variance (19.4%) in the jurors' ratings. As indicated in Figure 11-1, the attorneys for both parties were rated quite similarly across all trial methods. As between the two witnesses, however, an important difference occurred between the live trial and the read transcript trial. Whereas the jurors rated the landowner as being less competent than the expert witness in both the live trial and the electronic media trials, in the read transcript trial they rated the landowner and the expert witness as being similarly competent. This would suggest that the read transcript presentation interfered with the ability of the jurors to evaluate the competency of the witnesses.

Honesty (see Figure 11-2 and Table 11-4). The honesty factor is described by

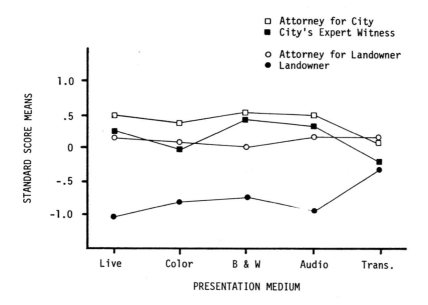

Figure 11-1. Jurors' Competency Ratings of the Trial Participants.

Table 11-3

Summary F-Table: Live and Media Trial Comparisons of the Competency Ratings

Source of Variation	Live/ Color	Live/ B & W	Live/ Audio	Live/ Trans.
A (media)	--	--	--	--
AC (media by participants)	1.03	--	--	7.81**
AC (witnesses)	3.62	--	--	19.11***
AC (attorneys)	--	--	--	1.06
AC (wit. v. atty.)	--	1.83	--	3.25

** $p < .01$

*** $\underline{p} < .001$

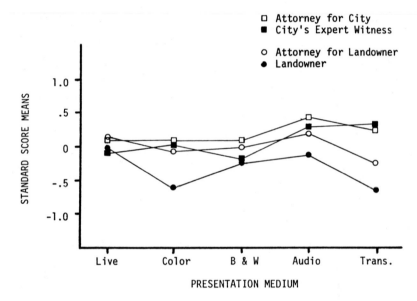

Figure 11-2. Jurors' Honesty Ratings of the Trial Participants.

the highest loading bipolar adjectives, "trustworthy-untrustworthy," "telling truth-not telling truth," "sincere-insincere," and "honest-dishonest." The honesty factor accounted for the second highest proportion of the variance in the jurors' ratings (17.2%). Like the competency factor, the honesty factor was relatively stable across the various trials. The only differences that reached statistical significance were the ratings of the two witnesses (Table 11-3). As

Table 11-4

Summary F-Table: Live and Media Trial Comparisons of the Honesty Ratings

Source of Variation	Live/ Color	Live/ B & W	Live/ Audio	Live/ Trans.
A (media)	1.67	--	1.94	--
AC (media by participants)	1.52	--	--	3.72*
AC (witnesses)	4.19*	--	2.24	9.05**
AC (attorneys)	--	--	--	2.11
AC (wit. v. atty.)	--	--	--	--

   * $p < .05$
 ** $\underline{p} < .01$

compared to the live trial results, the honesty of the landowner was viewed less positively in both the color and read transcript trials, while the testimony of the expert witness was rated about the same in the color trial and more positively in the read transcript trial.

Friendliness (see Figure 11-3 and Table 11-5). The third factor to emerge was that of friendliness. This factor was described by bipolar adjectives such as "friendly-unfriendly," "warm-cold," "nice-not nice," and "well mannered-ill mannered." The friendliness factor accounted for 13.8 percent of the variation of the jurors' ratings. As shown in Figure 11-3, this factor reflected a dimension of juror perceptions that was comparatively very susceptible to media distortions. The comparison between the live and black-and-white trials revealed that the participants as a group were rated significantly less friendly in the black-and-white trial than in the live trial, an effect most visible in the disproportionately low ratings of the landowner. In the color trial, distortions occurred in the ratings of the witnesses as compared to the attorneys. The first significant difference in juror perceptions of the attorneys occurred in the live trial—transcript trial comparison. As shown in Figure 11-3, in the live mode the attorney for the landowner was seen as slightly more friendly than the attorney for the city, whereas in the transcript presentation the attorney for the city was seen as more friendly.

Appearance. (see Figure 11-4 and Table 11-6). The fourth factor, that of appearance, had only two high loading adjective pairs, "well dressed-poorly dressed," and "clean cut-unwholesome." The appearance factor accounted for 7 percent of the variance in the jurors' ratings. It should be noted that the color video trial was the only media trial that did not produce significant differences

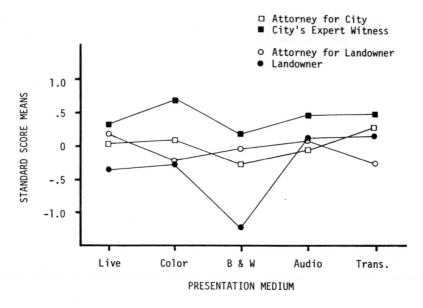

Figure 11-3. Jurors' Friendliness Ratings of the Trial Participants.

Table 11-5
Summary F-Table: Live and Media Trial Comparisons of the Friendliness Ratings

Source of Variation	Live/ Color	Live/ B & W	Live/ Audio	Live/ Trans.
A (media)	--	5.71*	--	--
AC (media by participants)	2.47	2.02	1.57	3.23*
AC (witnesses)	1.04	4.97*	--	1.04
AC (attorneys)	2.41	--	--	4.96*
AC (wit. v. atty.)	3.90*	1.03	3.81	3.68

* $p < .05$

from the live trial on this factor. It is likewise notable that all of the trial participants were rated significantly more negatively in the read transcript trial, and that a similar but less dramatic drop occurred in the audio trial. Obviously the audio and transcript trials provided the least number of clues upon which the jurors could base their appearance ratings. Thus, the jurors' lower ratings were

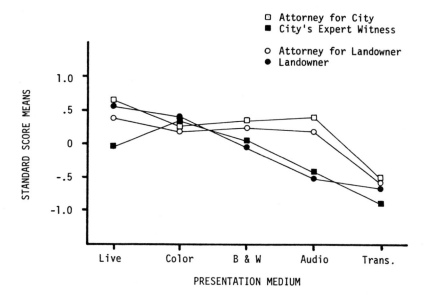

Figure 11-4. Jurors' Appearance Ratings of the Trial Participants.

Table 11-6
Summary F-Table: Live and Media Trial Comparisons of the Appearance Ratings

Source of Variation	Live/ Color	Live/ B & W	Live/ Audio	Live/ Trans.
A (media)	--	1.44	7.68**	31.74***
AC (media by participants)	1.39	1.55	4.16**	--
AC (witnesses)	2.48	4.27*	3.72	1.24
AC (attorneys)	--	--	--	--
AC (wit. v. atty.)	1.45	--	8.77**	--

* $p < .05$
** $p < .01$
*** $p < .001$

probably a reflection of natural uncertainty rather than a less positive evaluation of the participants. There was also a significant crossover in the jurors' evaluations of the witnesses between the live and the black-and-white trials. In both trials, the city's expert witness was rated essentially the same, while the landowner was rated more positively than the expert in the live trial and significantly lower in the black-and-white trials.

Objectivity (see Figure 11-5 and Table 11-7). The fifth factor emerging from the analysis of the bipolar adjective pairs was named objectivity and included such high loading terms as "unprejudiced-prejudiced," "greedy-not greedy," and "open-defensive." The objectivity factor accounted for 6 percent of the variance in the jurors' ratings.

As shown in Figure 11-5, the jurors' ratings of the participants on this factor were very stable between the live and media trials. Of the five factors examined in this study, perceptions of objectivity of the participants were least influenced by the manner of testimony presentation.

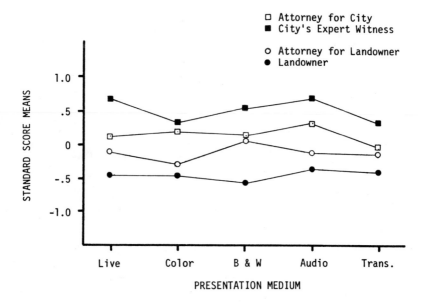

Figure 11-5. Jurors' Objectivity Ratings of the Trial Participants.

Table 11-7
Summary F-Table: Live and Media Trial Comparisons of the Objectivity Ratings

Source of Variation	Live/ Color	Live/ B & W	Live/ Audio	Live/ Trans.
A (media)	--	--	--	--
AC (media by participants)	--	--	--	--
AC (witnesses)	1.35	--	--	1.91
AC (attorneys)	--	--	--	--
AC (wit. v. atty.)	--	--	--	--

The Amount of Compensation Awarded the Landowner. In each trial the jurors were asked to indicate their individual preferences as to the dollar amount that would justly compensate the landowner for the property taken. Tables 11-8 and 11-9 contain summary data on the individually preferred awards as well as four Dunnett's *t* ratios comparing the live trial awards with the four media trial awards (Winer, 1962).

Chi-square analyses were also computed comparing the distribution of awards made after each of the five trials. These analyses were performed because there is evidence that jury awards and verdicts are more related to the number of

Table 11-8
Mean Dollar Awards Preferred by Individual Jurors in Alternate Conditions and *t* Tests Compared with Live Condition

Trial	No. of Jurors	Mean Award	Standard Deviation	Dunnet's t Ratio with Live Condition
Live	28	$ 9,815	$2,073	--
Color	27	$10,330	$2,037	.84[a]
Black and White	26	$10,635	$2,283	1.34[a]
Audio	26	$ 9,205	$2,420	1.00[a]
Read Transcript	27	$10,497	$2,387	1.12[a]

[a]No significant differences were found.

Table 11-9
The Number and Percentage of Jurors Preferring Various Amounts of Compensation to be Awarded to the Landowner

Dollar Award	Live n	Live %	Color n	Color %	Black and White n	Black and White %	Audio n	Audio %	Read Transcript n	Read Transcript %
8000- 8999	13	46	8	30	7	27	19	73	8	30
9000- 9999	2	7	1	4	1	4	0	0	2	7
10000-10999	5	18	7	26	7	27	2	8	7	26
11000-11999	3	11	3	11	1	4	0	0	1	4
12000-12999	3	11	6	22	7	27	3	11	6	22
13000-16000[a]	2	7	2	7	3	11	2	8	3	11
TOTALS	28	100	27	100	26	100	26	100	27	100

[a]Very few jurors preferred amounts above $12,000; thus, these categories were combined.

jurors preferring a certain outcome than to the mean amount of their preferences (Kalven, 1958). Even though there were significant differences in juror
perceptions between the live and media trials, none of the media trial awards
were significantly different from the live trial awards, as indicated in Table 11-8.

The finding of "no difference" in the awards between the live and media
trials, while accurately reflecting the results of this study, can only cautiously be
generalized. Such caution is necessary for at least two reasons. First, the strength
of the city's case relative to the landowner's must be taken into consideration.
The weight of the evidence and the arguments presented in the stimulus trial so
favored the city's position that it would probably have taken dramatic shifts in
juror perceptions to significantly alter the dollar awards. Thus the likelihood of
concluding that no differences existed when they in fact did exist was increased
by the one-sidedness of the trial. To obtain a more precise measure of the
possible differences in juror verdicts resulting from live and media presentations
of the same testimony, it would be necessary for the relative merits of the
parties' cases to be essentially equivalent.

The Relationship of the Dollar Awards to Juror Ratings of Trial Participants

As indicated by the foregoing analyses, there were some significant changes in
juror perceptions between the live and media trials. In light of the general
assumption that significant changes in juror perceptions of the trial participants
will influence both their evaluation of the evidence and the outcome of their
verdict or award, the next step was to explore the potential relationship between
the jurors' ratings of the trial participants and the jurors' preferred dollar awards.
Two types of correlation analyses were made to examine the relationships
between the jurors' ratings of the trial participants and their preferred dollar
awards. First, each of the twenty-nine ratings of each participant were correlated
with the dollar awards made after each trial. Second, a multiple linear regression
analysis was computed using the raw scores of the jurors' ratings of the trial
participants to predict the dollar awards made after each trial.

When the ratings of each participant were correlated with the awards in each
trial, an interesting pattern of significant correlations resulted. As demonstrated
in Table 11-10, the number of significant correlations for the opposing witnesses
reversed between the live and the media trials. In the live trial, seven of the
twenty-nine ratings of the expert witness correlated significantly with the awards
of the jurors, while only three of the landowner's ratings were significantly
correlated with the awards. This finding is not significant by itself, but when the
pattern of correlations with the dollar award in each of the media trials was
examined, a major shift was observed. Although this pattern does not hold
exactly for the attorneys, combining the significant correlations for the corresponding witnesses and attorney to produce the total number of significant

Table 11-10

The Number of Significant Correlations of the Jurors' Ratings with the Dollar Awards

	LIVE	COLOR	B & W	AUDIO	TRANSCRIPT
Landowner	3	9	16	14	10
Expert	7	2	7	2	1
Attorney of the Landowner	1	7	1	0	0
Attorney for the City	8	1	4	1	3
Totals Landowner	4	16	17	14	19
Totals for City	15	3	11	3	4

[a]Correlations that were significant at, or beyond, the .05 level.

correlations for each party resulted in a pattern similar to but more dramatic than that produced by the comparison of the witnesses.

A multiple regression analysis was also computed in which the dollar awards for each trial were predicted from the jurors ratings of the witnesses in the respective trials. Table 11-11 provides percentage data on the amount of the predicted variance in juror awards attributable to the ratings of each of the witnesses and constitutes some of the most interesting data encountered in this study. The percentage of the predicted variance in dollar awards attributable to the ratings of the landowner was much greater in the media trials (64% to 85%) than in the live trials (19%). Correspondingly, the expert witness' ratings accounted for a far greater proportion of the predicted variance in the dollar awards in the live trial (81%) than in the media trials (15% to 36%). These data demonstrate a rather striking shift of award-related ratings between the live trial

Table 11-11

Percentage of the Predicted Variance in the Dollar Award Attributable to the Ratings of the Landowner and Expert

	LIVE	COLOR	B & W	AUDIO	TRANSCRIPT
Landowner	19%	85%	80%	64%	79%
Expert	81%	15%	20%	36%	21%

and the media trials. While this shift did not result in a significant difference in awards in this trial, a similar effect of media presentations might have a significant effect in a trial in which the merits of the respective cases is more evenly balanced.

Juror Preferences for the Trial Participants

At the outset of this study it was hypothesized by one of the authors that the juror awards would vary with the relative personal appeal of the witnesses and attorneys to the jurors. To test this hypothesis, three forced-choice questions were asked of the jurors:

1. If you had to choose between the two witnesses, whom would you prefer to have for a friend?
2. If you had to choose between the two attorneys, whom would you prefer to have for a friend?
3. If you had legal difficulties and had to choose either the counsel for the city or the counsel for the landowner to represent you, whom would you select?

In general, the combination of which witnesses was selected as a "friend" and which attorney as "counsel" resulted in significant differences in the preferred awards (see Table 11-12). For example, the jurors awarded signifi-

Table 11-12
The Relationship Between the Dollar Awards and the Selection of Witnesses and Attorneys as Friends and Counsel

Source	df	MS	F	p
Witnesses as Friends (A)	1	19,835,400	4.61	< .05
Attorneys as Counsel (B)	1	11,356,200	2.64	
Attorneys as Friends (C)	1	15,707,200	3.65	< .10
A X B	1	19,060,700	4.43	< .05
A X C	1	402,421	.09	
B X C	1	733,333	.17	
A X B X C	1	10,186,700	2.37	
Error	126	4,300,520		

cantly more money to the landowner if they selected his counsel as a "friend" in preference to the city's counsel. Conversely, the jurors selecting the expert witness for a "friend" and the counsel for the city as "counsel" gave the lowest award to the landowner. Table 11-13 lists the mean awards associated with the various combinations of juror preferences.

The juror selections were also examined to determine if the number of

Table 11-13

Mean Dollar Awards Associated with Various Combinations of Witness and Attorney Preferences

	Mean Dollar Awards	Number Selecting Combination
Preferred Witness as Friend		
Landowner	11,604	23
Expert	10,409	111
Preferred Attorney as Friend		
Counsel for Landowner	11,538	39
Counsel for City	10,475	95
Preferred Attorney as Counsel		
Counsel for Landowner	11,458	36
Counsel for City	10,555	98
Preferred Witness as Friend Attorney as Counsel		
Landowner + Counsel for Landowner	11,470	12
Landowner + Counsel for City	11,737	11
Expert + Counsel for Landowner	11,436	24
Expert + Counsel for City	9,372	87
Preferred Friendship Combination		
Landowner + Counsel for Landowner	12,220	12
Counsel for City	10,987	11
Expert + Counsel for Landowner	10,856	27
Expert + Counsel for City	9,963	84
Preferred Attorneys as Friend and Counsel		
Counsel for Landowner + Counsel for Landowner	12,104	18
Counsel for Landowner + Counsel for City	10,812	18
Counsel for City + Counsel for Landowner	10,971	21
Counsel for City + Counsel for City	10,138	77

jurors choosing the respective trial participants as "friends" and "counsel" across the various trials changed with the medium of presentation. As indicated in Table 11-11, the number of jurors selecting either the expert witness or the landowner as a friend did not differ between the live trial and the media trials. However, in the black-and-white video trial (see Table 11-14), the number of jurors preferring the attorney for the landowner as a friend was significantly greater than in the live trial, $X^2(1) = 6.4$, $p < .02$. The attorney for the landowner was also preferred as counsel significantly more in both the black-and-white $(X^2(1) = 4.69$, $p < .03)$ and the read transcript $(X^2(1) = 8.21$, $p < .004)$ trials than in the live trial.

It should be noted here that the witnesses generally made very different impressions upon the jurors; one was rated quite positively and the other comparatively negatively. On the other hand the attorneys received quite similar and generally positive ratings in all trials. These results would indicate that media presentation methods will not distort jurors' friendship preferences when one person makes a qualitatively better impression than another in the live situation. However, when the stimulus persons are similarly perceived in the live situation, black-and-white videotape may significantly distort jurors' preferences with regard to friendship, and both black-and-white video and read transcripts may distort jurors' perceptions of competency. Given the significant relationships

Table 11-14
Forced Choice Selections of the Trial Participants as Friends and Counsel in each Trial

| | Number Selected | | | | |
	Live	Color	B & W	Audio	Transcript
Witnesses as a Friend					
Expert	22	24	22	23	21
Landowner	6	3	4	3	6
Attorney as a Friend					
Counsel City	24	22	13	17	23
Counsel Landowner	4	5	13	9	4
Attorney as Counsel					
Counsel City	26	20	17	21	15
Counsel Landowner	2	7	9	5	12

between dollar awards and some of the juror preferences for trial participants, the distortions in juror preferences occurring in the black-and-white trial are a cause for concern.

Juror Reactions to the Trials

The final portion of the questionnaire asked the jurors to rate the trial along five nine-point scales according to how stimulating they felt the trial to be, how interesting they perceived it to be, how easy it was to pay attention, how refreshing it was, and how clear it was. Table 11-15 contains the results of these ratings as compared by Dunnett's *t* test. It should be noted that the transcript trial was rated as less desirable on all five dimensions than the live trial. Moreover, as compared to the live trial, the audio trial was rated as significantly less stimulating and the color trial as significantly less easy to pay attention to. Thus, the black-and-white trial was the only trial in which no significant difference from the live trial occurred.

Table 11-15
Comparisons of Ratings of the Media Trials with the Live Trial

	Mean Ratings				
	Live	Color	B & W	Audio	Transcript
Stimulating–Tedious	3.89	4.19	3.54	4.50[a]	5.74[a]
Interesting–Dull	2.61	3.33	2.35	2.96	4.04[b]
East to pay attention–Difficult to pay attention	2.43	4.00[c]	2.65	3.54	4.95[c]
Refreshing–Fatiguing	5.04	4.70	4.31	5.31	6.07[d]
Clear–Confusing	2.96	4.00	2.46	3.31	5.00[e]

[a]significantly different from Live Condition (p transcript< .001, p audio < .001)
[b]significantly different from Live Condition (p < .05)
[c]significantly different from Live Condition (p color < .05, p transcript < .001)
[d]significantly different from Live Condition (p < .10)
[e]significantly different from Live Condition (p < .01)

Discussion of the Results

There are basically two situations in which videotape may be used to present oral evidence at trial. One is to use videotape only to present witnesses who are unable to attend the trial. The other is to present all trial testimony, regardless of the availability of witnesses. Because read transcripts are already accepted substitutes for the live testimony of unavailable witnesses, the use of videotape in lieu of read transcript testimony involves different questions and different standards of comparison than does the use of videotape to present trial testimony which would ordinarily be given live. These two procedures will therefore be discussed separately below.

Comparative Merits of Deposition Presentation Methods

The primary question involved in the presentation of deposition testimony is whether read transcript of some form of electronic replay is the better substitute for the live appearance of a witness. This study tested the effects on juror perceptions of four alternative methods of deposition presentation: color videotape, black-and-white videotape, audiotape, and read transcript. In general, it was found that all three electronic methods of presentation were superior to the read transcript method in their ability to approximate juror perceptions of and reactions to live testimony, though each of these methods demonstrated unique relative advantages and disadvantages.

Read Transcript. The read transcript procedure was rated by the jurors as less interesting, more difficult to pay attention to, less clear, more fatiguing, and more tedious than the live trial or the other media trials. More, and typically larger, differences in the participants' ratings occurred in the live/read transcript comparisons than in any of the other live/media trial comparisons. In addition the read transcript trial produced the only significant distortions in the participants' competency ratings. As a result the proportion of jurors preferring either one or the other of the attorneys as counsel in the read transcript trial was significantly different than in the live trial. Only the black-and-white trial produced similar distortions in juror preferences. In light of these findings juror perceptions of live trial testimony would be better reproduced by any of the methods discussed below than by read transcript.

Audiotape. Aside from the understandable distortions in the appearance and handsomeness ratings, the use of audiotape to present deposition testimony produced very few differences from the live trial results. The audio trial was rated significantly less stimulating than the live trial, but both the audio and the live trial produced generally more positive evaluations of the trial participants than the other media trials. Given this latter result and the observations of Yenawine and Arbuckle (1971) that audiotape presentations resulted in more emotional involvement than black-and-white videotape presentations, it appears that audiotape produces some unique effects when compared to videotape and read transcript presentation. To illustrate, if one were to close his eyes while listening to a reasonably high quality audiotape reproduction of another person's voice, there would be little difference between that experience and hearing him in person. The read transcript method does not provide anything like this experience and the image projected on the screen by video presentations is so obviously a media presentation that it may dissipate the sense of reality created by the accompanying audio recording. Yet the very fact that audiotape focuses the jurors' attention on one aspect of a person's demeanor—his voice—also creates the possibility that if a person has an unusually pleasant or unpleasant voice, jurors may perceive his audiotaped testimony differently than his live testimony. For example, the landowner in the stimulus trial received his least favorable awards in the audio trial. This may be a result of his comparative disadvantage in audio presentation during the trial. He spoke very slowly, with little tonal variety, and his voice had a raspy quality resulting from a gutteral resonation. The city's expert witness, on the other hand, had a deep, well-resonated voice, and his vocal manner was assured and confident.

Black-and-White Videotape. In addition to being more accurate than either audiotape or read transcript in reproducing the appearance aspects of the live trial, black-and-white videotape was also the only medium tested that did not produce significant differences in any of the five "desirability" ratings such as level of interest and stimulation. These advantages were offset by the significant general distortion of the ratings included in the friendliness factor and in the jurors' preferences (friendship and choice of counsel) for participants similarly rated in the live trial. An intriguing question is whether these distortions were a result of the emotional distancing associated with the use of black-and-white videotape by Yenawine and Arbuckle (1971) and the Bermant group.

Color Videotape. Of the four media tested, color videotape was rated closest to the live trial in its appearance aspects and in its ability to reproduce the "live" jurors' responses to the forced-choice friendship and preferred counsel questions. Like black-and-white videotape, however, the color presentation produced some distortions in the general "friendliness" ratings, and color videotape was the only electronic presentation to produce distortions in the honesty ratings. The color trial was also rated significantly less easy to pay attention to than the live trial.

Conclusion. This research was designed to test whether jurors respond differently to media presentations of testimony than to live presentations of the same testimony. As indicated in the above discussion, significant differences in juror perceptions did occur between the media and live trials. These findings raise the question of whether such differences may in certain trials affect the type or amount of verdict that jurors are likely to render, and the related question of whether the differential effects of the various media can be predicted in advance. Since additional research on a broad scale will be required to answer these questions, the conclusion that any one of the three electronic media would be the method of choice over the other two would be premature. Particular attention should be directed toward an examination of the effects of the limited and focused demeanor cues (vocal characteristics only) and the obvious loss of appearance information when audiotape is used. Also, the consistent distortion of friendliness and warmth cues by black-and-white television deserves special study.

The most conclusive finding in this experiment was that substantially more and greater differences in juror perceptions occurred in the live/read transcript comparisons than in any of the other live/media comparisons—a finding which would suggest that all of the electronic media tested were more accurate than read transcript in reproducing the results of a live trial.

An Evaluation of the Use of Videotape to Present
All Testimony at Trial

In contrast to the use of videotape to present deposition testimony of inaccessible witnesses, the use of videotape to present all testimony at trial involves the presentation of evidence that would usually be presented live. Thus, the primary question involved here is not whether videotape is an acceptable substitute for another medium, such as read transcript, but whether videotape is an acceptable substitute for live testimony. As previously discussed, this study found that while videotaped testimony demonstrated many similarities to live testimony, it also produced several significant differences.

Given the occurrence of significant distortions in juror perceptions of trial testimony in the videotape presentation, the next step is to determine whether these differences indicate that the videotape trial is not an acceptable alternative to the live trial. While current data do not provide definitive answers to this question, some of the findings would indicate that this may be the case.

First, the results of this study indicated that the biasing effects of media presentations do not affect everyone alike. Rather, juror perceptions of trial testimony were found to be related both to the characteristics of the witness and to the medium used. A striking example of this type of media by participant interaction is found in the disproportionate lowering of the landowner's friendliness ratings in the black-and-white video trial relative to the ratings of the other trial participants. In addition, the effects of a media presentation upon juror perceptions of any given individual are difficult, it not impossible, to predict in advance. Thus, given the present state of information, the parties to a trial could not knowledgeably assess whether they would be injured or benefited by selecting a video trial.

Second, the results of the correlational analyses relating the jurors' ratings of individual trial participants to the preferred dollar awards indicated that the impact of the expert witness on the jurors was substantially less important relative to the impact of landowner in all of the media trials. The preferred dollar awards demonstrated relatively strong correlations with the jurors' perceptions of the expert witness in the live trial, but in the media trials the awards were more strongly correlated with the juror's perceptions of the landowner. This question of impact is central to the purpose of a trial, since both parties are attempting to persuade the jurors to accept their point of view. If videotape trials substantially change one participants' impact on the jurors relative to the other trial participants, videotape trials may produce results substantially different from live trials in terms of juror perceptions and decisions. As previously noted, the one-sidedness of the trial selected for this study may have precluded any definitive assessment of this question, but the potential importance of the finding of differences in the relative impact of the media trial participants warrants further and more specific study.

These and other findings of differences between live and media trials should stand as a caution to those proposing the immediate and widespread implementation of videotape trials. Nevertheless, as a final note it must be pointed out that this study did not demonstrate any significant distortions in jurors' preferred verdicts between the live trial and the trials that used media methods to present trial testimony.

Recommendations for Future Research

Assuming, as research has shown, that differences in juror perceptions occur between live and media trials, then the degree and direction of impact these differences may have on jurors' verdicts need to be carefully tested and verified in experimental settings before major policy decisions are made as to the use of videotape in trials.

The most serious potential impact of these differences is that they may influence the outcome of trials. Jurors may plausibly be led by these different perceptions to render a different verdict or to vary the amount of dollar or quality of other awards. This potential biasing effect of videotape presentation of trial testimony suggests the need for research specifically designed to compare deliberated jury verdicts after live and media presentations of the same trial testimony repeated over a number of trials using several witness and attorney types. This research is necessary to determine whether there will be consistent and gross differences between the verdicts or award amounts in live and media trials. If such differences are found to consistently occur in some or all types of trials, that information should be weighed both in the decision of whether to go ahead with media presentations in general and in the decision of whether to accept media presentations in specific instances. In general, research to date has not demonstrated that media presentations can produce dramatic differences in jury verdicts. But, the experimental search to clarify the impact of media usage in the trial setting is of such recent origin that much more work needs to be completed before this result can be broadly generalized.

In designing future studies, researchers should take into account the fact that experimental studies of videotape trials that have been completed to date have compared the results of a live trial with the results of a continuous videotape record of the same trial. The video recording has typically included in a split-screen format both the trial portion of the courtroom and appropriate close-up inserts of trial participants. Consequently, the experimental studies have used videotapes that have included pictures of judges, witnesses, and attorneys. By contrast, actual—as opposed to experimental—videotape trials will present testimony that is recorded at different times, in different places, and, typically, outside of the presence of the judge. Given these differences between the experimental videotape trials and actual videotape trials, the studies completed thus far have produced data concerning the effects of the use of media to present the live trial record, but have not examined all of the differences that might occur in a genuine videotape trial. This methodological consideration is important as current procedures have probably minimized the differences between live and videotape trials. Future studies could more adequately compare live and videotape trials by excluding pictures of the judge and, in general, attempting to produce a record that would appear to be as segmental and discontinuous as that of an actual videotape trial.

References

Barber, J.P., & Bates, P.R. Videotape in criminal proceeding. *Hastings Law Journal*, 1972, *24*, 1-8.

Bermant, G. Critique—Data in search of theory in search of policy: Behavioral responses to videotape in the courtroom. *Brigham Young University Law Review, 1975*, 467-85.

Bermant, G., Chappell, D., Crockett, G.T., Jacoubovitch, M.D., & McGuire, M. Juror responses to prerecorded videotape trial presentations in California and Ohio. *Hastings Law Journal*, 1975, *26*, 975-998.

Bermant, G., & Jacoubovitch, M.D. Fish out of water: A brief overview of social and psychological concerns about videotaped trials. *Hastings Law Journal*, 1975, *26*, 999-1011.

Bermant, G., McGuire, M., McKinley, W., & Salo, C. The logic of simulation in jury research. *Criminal Justice and Behavior*, 1974, *1*, 224-232.

Bleus, W.F., & Patterson, W.A. On trial: Videotape. *Florida Bar Association Journal*, 1972, *46*, 159-161.

Butler, W.F. *The use of video tape in the courtroom to convey demeanor evidence.* Unpublished manuscript, Arizona State University, 1973.

Doret, D.M. Trial by videotape—Can justice be seen to be done? *Temple Law Quarterly*, 1974, *47*, 228-268.

Farmer, L.C. *Juror evaluation as a function of live, color video, black and white video, audio, and read transcript presentations of trial testimony.* Unpublished doctoral dissertation, Brigham Young University, 1975.

Grow, R., & Johnson, R. Opening Pandora's box: Asking judges and attorneys to react to the videotape trial. *Brigham Young University Law Review, 1975,* 487-527.

Johnson, C. Just because you can't televise trials doesn't mean you can't bring a television to court. *Juris Doctor*, 1974, *4*, 25-27.

Kalven, H. The jury, the law and the personal injury damage award. *Ohio State Law Journal*, 1958, *19*, 158-178.

Kornblum, G.O. Videotape in civil cases. *Hastings Law Journal*, 1972, *24*, 9-36.

McCrystal, J.L. The videotape trial comes of age. *Judicature*, 1974, *57*, 446-449.

McCrystal, J.L. Videotape trials: Relief for our congested courts. *Denver Law Review*, 1973, *49*, 463-483.

McCrystal, J.L., & Young, J.L. Pre-recorded videotape trials—An Ohio innovation. *Brooklyn Law Review*, 1973, *39*, 560-566.

Merlo, M.J., & Sorenson, H.C. Video tape: The coming courtroom tool. *Trial*, 1971, *49*, 55-57.

Miller, G., Bender, D., Florence, T., & Nicholson, H. Real versus reel: What's the verdict. *Journal of Communication*, 1974, *24*, 100-111.

Miller, G.R., & Siebert, F.S. Effects of videotaped testimony on information processing and decision-making in jury trials. Progress Report No. 1, March, 1974, Michigan State University, Grant GI-38398, RANN, National Science Foundation.

Miller, G.R., & Siebert, F.S. *Effects of videotaped testimony on information processing and decision-making in jury trials.* Progress Report No. 2, 1975, Michigan State University, Grant GI-38398, RANN, National Science Foundation.

Morrill, A.E. Enter—The video taped trial. *John Marshall Journal of Practice and Procedure*, 1970, *3*, 237-259.

National Center for State Courts. *Video support in the Criminal Courts*, 1974, III, A-2—A-29.

Reynolds, H.J. The case against electronic courtroom reporting. *American Bar Association Journal*, 1970, *56*, 1080.

Stiver, C.E. Video-tape trials: A practical evaluation and a legal analysis. *Stanford Law Review*, 1974, *26*, 619-645.

Taillefer, F.J., Short, E.H., Greenwood, J.M., & Brady, R.G. Video support in the criminal courts. *Journal of Communication*, 1974, *24*, 111-112.

Thornton, J.W. Expanding video tape techniques in pretrial and trial advocacy. *The Forum*, 1973, *9*, 105-121.

Williams, G., Farmer, L., Lee, R., Cundick, B., Howell, R., & Rooker, C. Juror perceptions of trial testimony as a function of the method of presentation: A comparison of live, color video, black and white video, audio, and transcript presentations. *Brigham Young University Law Review, 1975*, 375-421.

Winer, B.J. *Statistical principles in experimental design.* New York: McGraw-Hill, 1962.

12

Individual Differences in Ascriptions of Responsibility, Guilt, and Appropriate Punishment

V. Lee Hamilton

Psychologists and sociologists have begun to apply the tools of social science to predict how jurors will vote in a particular criminal or civil trial, as the chapters by Christie and Berk indicate. This chapter is also relevant to juror decision-making, but has a more theoretical focus. The basic assumptions underlying much research on juror behavior can be stated simply. Whatever makes jurors vote to convict one defendant or acquit another may well be a function of substantial evidence regarding that defendant's guilt or innocence; but what makes jurors take particular views when they disagree on the *same* case is likely to be some function of individual differences between them: differences resulting from sociological characteristics (such as race or social class) or psychological characteristics (such as authoritarianism or dogmatism). The research reported here is based on similar assumptions about juror behavior. Specifically, I have investigated differences in conviction proneness and punishment tendencies that are associated with jurors' authoritarianism.

The psychological concept of authoritarianism (Adorno, Frenkel-Brunswick, Levinson, & Sanford, 1950) has been the variable most frequently used in investigations of juror biases regarding the conviction of criminal defendants. The term *authoritarianism* encompasses an extensive body of literature concerning individuals' affective and cognitive orientations toward authority. The central characteristic of the authoritarian personality is a combination of submission to authority with dominance over subordinates. As Adorno once described it, the authoritarian has a bicyclist's personality: "above they bow, below they kick" (cited in Greenstein, 1969). Other characteristics of the authoritarian relevant to juror behavior include cognitive rigidity, stereotyping of outgroups, ethnocentrism, strict adherence to conventional norms (particularly concerning sex), and punitiveness toward deviants. The original formulation of the authoritarian personality, although theoretically a fusion of Marxian and Freudian ideas, incorporated a Freudian approach to the syndrome's development stressing the child's ambivalent reaction to strict and repressive parents. Much subsequent research has instead moved toward a more cognitive interpretation of authoritarianism (for example, Kelman & Barclay, 1963) or has been relatively atheoretical, simply using measures of authoritarianism originally developed from the Freudian theoretical framework. The use of authoritarianism in jury-related research has tended to be of the latter, cognitive or atheoretical, type.

Paper prepared for Battelle Seattle Research Center conference, Social and Psychological Factors in the Legal Process, June 12-14, 1975.

A series of experiments and surveys have indicated that high authoritarians are more likely to convict a defendant and to punish him severely than are low authoritarians (for example, Boehm, 1968; Epstein, 1965, 1966; Jurow, 1971; Vidmar, 1974). An attitude correlated with authoritarianism—attitude toward capital punishment—has also received research attention recently. High authoritarians have been found generally to favor the death penalty; low authoritarians to oppose it. As one would expect, those who favor the death penalty are more likely to convict defendants, to give harsh punishments, and to espouse retribution rather than deterrence as a justification for punishment (Jurow, 1971; Vidmar, 1974; Vidmar & Crinklaw, 1973; Vidmar & Ellsworth, 1974).

Two theoretical questions have not been adequately addressed in this research, however. First, what are the limits on the conviction-proneness of authoritarians or approvers of capital punishment? Investigations by Mitchell and Byrne (1972, 1973) indicate that authoritarians may be particularly punitive when they perceive a defendant to be dissimilar to themselves. In addition, it seems reasonable to argue that when a defendant is an authority figure himself or obviously submissive to an authority, the typical relationship might be reversed: the authoritarian might actually prove to be acquittal-prone. Second, how general is the typically assumed straightforward relationship between conviction and punishment? Research to date has stressed the continuity between verdict and sentencing and has used measures of guilt and punishment interchangeably (cf. Vidmar, 1972). Yet on commonsense grounds, we know that a number of factors enter into the punishment process that are not considerations in the guilt-determination process (and that may not even be known to a jury). Empirically, however, we know very little about the linkages between assessments of moral blame, legal guilt, and appropriate sanctions in the mind of the individual juror or judge.

The present research was designed to address both of these questions by using an unusual case—one that could elicit both acquittal-proneness in high authoritarians and discrepancies between verdicts and sentences for many of the experimental subjects.

The studies reported here emphasize what might be called "crimes of obedience": cases in which a defendant has acted in response to orders from an authority, but where the actions are considered illegal or immoral by the larger community. Nazi war crimes during World War II are probably the most flagrant historical example of such crimes. Actions by Lt. William Calley and his men at the My Lai massacre in Vietnam provide other examples of such crimes. In civilian life, actions by a number of the lesser figures in the Watergate scandal could well be construed as crimes of obedience.

In addition to capturing our attention because of their historical significance, such crimes provide an excellent testing ground for theoretical issues of individual difference in legal judgments and of the relationships among judgments of responsibility, guilt, and punishment. First—and most important for the study of individual differences—a crime of obedience involves an interpretation of facts more than their establishment. The legal argument concerns *why* the defendant did certain actions rather than *whether* he did them. Second, the defendant in this type of case has been submissive to authority in his actions; hence it can be predicted that high authoritarian jurors should tend to acquit rather than convict him. Third, even when individuals agree that such a defendant should be convicted, we may predict that they may favor a relatively lenient sentence for a number of reasons (see Hamilton, 1974). In summary, a crime of obedience shares with other crimes the elements of possible responsibility, guilt, and punishment. It differs from them in the probable importance of individual differences among jurors, in the potentially unusual relationship between authoritarianism and verdict, and in the potential for differences between probabilities of conviction and the harshness of sentences perceived as appropriate.

Two experimental studies will be discussed here. Both used a military case analogous to the Calley case as the "crime of obedience," since the studies were part of a research program initiated by interest in public reactions to the Calley conviction (see Hamilton, 1974, 1975; Kelman & Lawrence [Hamilton], 1972a, 1972b, 1974; Lawrence & Kelman, 1973). In the first study, attitude toward capital punishment was the major indicator of authoritarianism. A second indicator was an item asking what the participant would do if ordered to commit a similar action; an individual's response that he would obey was taken to be the authoritarian response (Vidmar, 1974). In the second study, a modified repetition of the first, an additional test was made of the relationship between capital punishment attitude and authoritarianism. In both studies, it was predicted that high authoritarians would be more likely to acquit the defendant. The study of the fit between verdict and sentence was exploratory. Thus no predictions were made in the first study beyond the expectation that verdict, responsibility attribution, and sentencing would be highly correlated with one another.

Experiment I

Introduction and Predictions

A jury simulation study based on an actual court martial from the Korean War (*U.S. v. Airman First Class Thomas F. Kinder*, 1954 *Court Martial Reports*) was conducted in 1973. The case resembled Lt. Calley's trial for the My Lai massacre: the defendant argued that he had followed superior orders in killing unarmed prisoners and that he thought his actions to be legal at the time. For reasons of privacy, all names were changed and the branch of the service was changed to the army. The defendant, a young enlisted man with an eleventh-grade education, had obeyed a superior officer's order to shoot an unarmed and wounded Korean prisoner whom he had arrested while on guard duty at his base. The base was 300 miles from the front lines, but there had been rumors of sabotage in the area at the time. The defendant claimed that he thought any order given by his superior was automatically legal, although he also admitted it was ordinarily illegal to kill unarmed prisoners. In the actual case, the defendant was convicted of premeditated murder, but his sentence was ultimately reduced to two years.

The case differed from the Calley trial in not having become famous; in stemming from a different and less controversial war, and in raising no legal question about whether orders to kill were actually given to the subordinate on trial. The case was modified to suit experimental requirements: for example, the number of dead Koreans was raised to six. Also, experimental variations were made in the rank of the superior officer and in the instructions given by the judge to the jurors. Testimony was excerpted from the trial manuscript and a thirty-minute presentation of the case was created, with the testimony on audio tape synchronized to color slides of people in uniforms going through trial procedures in a court room.

A single item about capital punishment opinions was included as an indicator of legal authoritarianism or conservatism. It was predicted that subjects favoring capital punishment would be more likely to acquit the defendant than subjects opposing it. In addition, one dependent measure served as a further indicator of orientation to authority—an item asking what the subject thought he would do in a similar situation (follow orders and shoot, or refuse to shoot). Obviously, subjects who said they would shoot could be expected to acquit the defendant more often than subjects who said they would refuse. In addition, predictions were made about sociological variables on the basis of previous research (Kelman & Lawrence, 1972b). It was predicted that subjects who were more educated and of higher social status would be more likely to convict the defendant and to hold him responsible for the killings. Older subjects were expected to be slightly acquittal-prone; the group most likely to hold the defendant responsible and to convict him was expected to be those aged twenty-five to thirty-four. Self-defined political liberals were also expected to be somewhat more likely to convict than conservatives, although that trend was very weak in the earlier study. No specific predictions were made about the relationships among responsibility assessment, guilt, and punishment, although they were expected to be highly related.

Method

Participants and Sampling. Participants were 302 adults aged eighteen and over, sampled from Cambridge, Massachusetts, and two adjacent cities. Although most participants were obtained by random sampling methods, the sample was predominantly female (60% to 40%) and subjects were typically young, well-educated, and liberal. Participants were paid $5.00 for being in the study.

Design and Procedure. Experimental variations are presented fully in Hamilton (1974). Briefly, one experimental variation concerned the rank of the superior officer who ordered the defendant to kill. For half of the subjects, this superior was a captain; the others heard that he was a sergeant. The defendant was always a corporal. The second manipulation involved the judge's charge to the jury. The judge either instructed that the verdicts available were not guilty or guilty of premeditated murder, or also included a lesser guilty verdict of unpremeditated murder. All subjects in a given session of the experiment heard the same version of the trial. Here, all relationships among the independent variables will be tested based on the full sample ($N = 302$). Relationships between independent and dependent variables will be assessed using the 198 subjects who formed the main experimental design.[1]

Upon arriving for the experiment, all participants were handed a questionnaire. The questionnaire included demographic items (for example, age, sex, race, and education) and questions about legal issues including attitudes toward capital punishment. Participants then watched the trial presentation. In the basic procedure, participants then filled out questionnaires giving their individual opinions about the case; deliberated for an hour in randomly composed six-person juries; and finally filled out questionnaires concerning their individual post-deliberation opinions.

Thus participants gave individual judgments on the dependent variables—assessments of responsibility, guilt, punishment, and other measures—both before and after they deliberated in juries. Here we shall deal with individual opinions only, since our interest is in individuals' different perceptions of the case. We shall also stress the opinions given before deliberation, because they were not affected by the group discussion.

Results

Verdict and Responsibility. As shown in Table 12-1, most predictions about the relationship between sociological variables and dependent variables were confirmed. The significant correlations, while small, are comparable to the correla-

---

[1]Two control groups were also used. One group ($N = 54$) went directly from the presentation of the trial to group deliberation and skipped the preliminary individual questionnaire. Individuals in the second control group were told, before they filled out the initial questionnaire of dependent measures, that they would not be deliberating in groups. The first control group provided a control for the filling out of the pregroup individual questionnaire. The second group provided a control for the effects of anticipated group discussion on individual viewpoints.

Table 12-1
Experiment I: Intercorrelations of Independent and Dependent Variables

	Age	Education	Occupation	McGovern Vote '72	Favor Capital Punishment	Subject Would Shoot
Verdict	-.250[c]	.159[a]	.224[a]	.251[b]	-.167[a]	-.224[b]
Responsibility of Defendant	-.276[c]	.179[a]	.232[a]	.201[a]	-.239[c]	-.272[c]

[a] $p < .05$
[b] $p < .01$
[c] $p < .001$

tions found in a national sample interviewed two years earlier concerning the Calley case (Kelman & Lawrence, 1972b). Participants who were younger, more educated, and from higher status occupations were more likely to convict the defendant. The linear correlation for age was significant despite the fact that the conviction rates were highest in the thirty- to thirty-four-year-old group and second highest among twenty-five- to twenty-nine-year-olds, creating a peak in convictions for the group aged twenty-five to thirty-four, as predicted. Effects of political party membership could not be meaningfully tested in this Cambridge area sample, because of the virtual absence of Republicans. However, there was a substantial correlation between reported presidential vote in 1972 and verdict, with McGovern voters more likely to convict. Again, this was consistent with the prediction that liberals would be more conviction-prone.

Relationships between these independent variables and assigned responsibility were generally stronger than the relationships with verdict, despite a substantial correlation between the two dependent variables ($r = .629, p < .001$). Attributing greater responsibility to the defendant was associated with being younger, more educated, from a higher status occupation, and a McGovern voter. The linear correlation between age and responsibility was maintained even though the peak period for responsibility attribution was the ages from twenty-five to thirty-four, consistent with the pattern found for verdicts.

As Table 12-1 also shows, attitude toward capital punishment was related to both verdict and responsibility attribution. As predicted, participants approving of capital punishment tended to acquit the defendant and to assign him less responsibility for the crime. Not surprisingly, capital punishment attitude was also correlated with a number of variables previously shown to predict either capital punishment attitude or authoritarianism. Subjects who approved of capital punishment were likely to be older ($r = .299, p < .001$), less educated ($r = .262, p < .001$), from lower status occupations ($r = .271, p < .001$), Nixon voters ($r = .522, p < .001$), and Catholic ($r = .300, p < .001$), in comparison with disapprovers of capital punishment.

A second indicator of orientation to authority was the participant's response concerning whether or not he would shoot prisoners under orders. To avoid making subjects sensitive to the issue, this item was asked among the dependent measures—that is, after the viewing of the trial. As predicted, 63 percent of participants who said they would follow orders and shoot acquitted the defendant, while 65 percent of those who said they would refuse the orders convicted him ($X^2 = 11.506$, $d.f. = 1$, $p < .001$). In addition the shooting response was correlated with approval of capital punishment ($r = .252$, $p < .001$), as was also found in an earlier study (Vidmar, 1974). Self-identified "shooters" and "refusers" also differed in how they assigned responsibility to the defendant and to his superior officer for the crime. The responsibility ratings, shown in Table 12-2, indicate that refusers assigned more responsibility overall, particularly to the defendant; shooters assigned the defendant much less

Table 12-2
Experiment I: Correlations of Independent Variables with Sentence Assigned

	Sentence
Age	−.073
Education	−.130
Occupation	−.010
McGovern Vote	.079
Favor Capital Punishment	.073
Subject Would Shoot	−.134

responsibility, but assigned the superior slightly more. Thus people who say that they themselves would shoot sharply differentiate who should be blamed; those who say they would refuse, do not.

Sentence Assigned. The sentence given to the defendant was less predictable from sociological variables, as Table 12-3 indicates, despite significant correlations between sentence and the other two dependent measures ($r > .4$ with both verdict and responsibility). When all sociological variables were considered together, this lower predictability proved to be because variables highly correlated with one another affected sentence in opposite ways: for example, among people with the same education level, higher occupational status predicted assigning higher sentences; among people of the same occupational status, more education predicted assigning lower sentences. Higher income and voting for McGovern also significantly predicted higher sentences when all variables were considered together.[2]

Initially, capital punishment attitude was not significantly correlated with sentence assigned. However, when all correlated sociological variables were controlled, the relationship was significant:[3] participants approving of capital punishment tended to give *higher* sentences, despite their already discussed tendency to acquit the defendant and to assign him low responsibility.

The apparent inconsistency between harsh sentencing and lenient judgments of guilt and responsibility by approvers of capital punishment is explained in

[2]With these sociological variables controlled, approval of capital punishment was still significantly associated with leniency in verdict and responsibility assigned to the defendant.

[3]The simultaneous effects of sociological and personality variables were assessed using the statistical technique of stepwise linear regression. For sentence, a number of variables were significantly contributors to an R^2 of .130. Longer sentences were significantly predicted by higher income, McGovern voting, lower education, higher occupational status, and approving of capital punishment. Presumably, the lack of a significant zero-order correlation between McGovern voting and sentence was a function of the strong association ($r = .522$) between a McGovern vote and *disapproval* of capital punishment. Similarly, although the zero order correlations of both income and occupation with sentence were negligible, both had a direct relationship to sentence with education controlled.

Table 12-3

Experiment I: Responsibility Attribution by "Shooters" and "Refusers" to the Defendant and His Superior

| | | Person Rated | | |
		Subordinate	Superior	Row Marginal
Subject Would	Shoot	26.889	93.00	59.944
	Refuse	55.508	85.239	70.373
	Column Marginal	41.199	89.119	

Note: Average responsibility attributed: 0 = not all responsible; 100 = completely responsible.

Table 12-4, which shows average sentences grouped by capital punishment attitude and verdict. Initially (Table 12-4A), the interaction between capital punishment attitude and verdict is not statistically significant, but the pattern is apparent: participants approving of capital punishment are indeed more likely to acquit than participants disapproving; but when they *do* convict, approvers of capital punishment sentence the defendant substantially more harshly. The gap between approvers and disapprovers becomes greater still in the individual opinions given after group deliberation (Table 12-4B). At that point, approvers who convict the defendant assign a sentence three times longer than the sentence assigned by disapprovers who convict. Thus, contrary to expectation based on the pattern of verdicts, approval of capital punishment was directly rather than inversely related to sentence, but only among those participants who convicted the defendant: those participants who approved of capital punishment were more punitive in sentencing the defendant when they did convict him.

Discussion

Results from the first experiment generally supported the predictions. Sociological variables found to predict opinions about Lt. Calley in our 1971 national sample also predicted judgments of this defendant, although the Cambridge area sample was quite different from a national sample. As predicted, approval of capital punishment and "shooting" on the hypothetical item were correlated with one another, with acquittal of the defendant, and with rating the defendant as less responsible for the crime. Surprisingly, when approvers of capital punishment did convict the defendant (although they were less likely to do so than disapprovers), they punished him more severely.

The unexpected pattern of acquittal-proneness plus punitive sentencing tendencies found in capital punishment approvers may reflect a two-step

Table 12-4

Experiment I: Mean Sentence Assigned, Grouped by Attitude toward Capital Punishment and by Verdict

4A. Subjects' initial individual judgments

		Capital Punishment Attitude			
		Approve	*Don't Know*	*Disapprove*	*Row Marginals*
Verdict	Not Guilty	$\bar{X} = 1.450$ $N = 20$	$\bar{X} = .533$ $N = 15$	$\bar{X} = 3.585$ $N = 41$	1.856
	Guilty	$\bar{X} = 28.955$ $N = 22$	$\bar{X} = 20.467$ $N = 15$	$\bar{X} = 15.293$ $N = 75$	21.572
	Column Marginals	15.202	10.500	9.439	

4B. Subjects' final individual judgments (after group deliberation)

		Capital Punishment Attitude			
		Approve	*Don't Know*	*Disapprove*	*Row Marginals*
Verdict	Not Guilty	$\bar{X} = 2.500$ $N = 22$	$\bar{X} = 0.846$ $N = 13$	$\bar{X} = 2.188$ $N = 32$	1.845
	Guilty	$\bar{X} = 30.900$ $N = 20$	$\bar{X} = 26.067$ $N = 15$	$\bar{X} = 9.294$ $N = 85$	22.087
	Column Marginals	16.700	13.456	5.741	

Note: Sentence ranged from 0 to 100 years.

judgment process. The first step, assessment of responsibility and guilt, is governed by orientation toward authority and other individual differences in how responsibility is assigned to wrongdoers. The second step, assignment of sanctions, may be governed by factors such as whether or not an individual views punishment as fundamentally retributive. These different factors may be traced to a common foundation in the original description of the authoritarian syndrome (Adorno et al., 1950) that included both submission to authority and punitiveness toward deviants, criminals, or outsiders.

The relationships of certain other variables to sentencing were also consistent with a two-step notion. For example, education and occupation were both directly related to verdict: more educated and higher status participants were conviction-prone. Yet, when the two variables were considered together, more educated participants tended to give lower sentences, while those from higher status occupations gave more severe sentences.[4] It may be argued that greater

[4]This was determined in the regression reported in Footnote 3.

education produces both increased emphasis on individual responsibility and increased leniency or humanitarianism in sanctioning; in cases such as the crime of obedience, this leads to convicting a defendant but not punishing him.

These results thus suggest two modifications of previous findings about capital punishment attitude or legal authoritarianism and legal judgments. First, under some conditions, opponents of capital punishment rather than its supporters are more likely to convict a defendant, reversing the usual relationship (for example, Jurow, 1971). Second, conviction and sentencing may be two distinct steps in judgment: the first, linked to perceptions of authority and of individual responsibility; the second, also involving other factors such as authoritarian punitiveness or retributive orientation. Thus verdict and sentence should be investigated separately, rather than used relatively interchangeably (cf. Vidmar, 1972). In this highly educated, liberal sample, the dominant tendency was to combine convicting the defendant with punishing him lightly or not at all. In an earlier study (Vidmar, 1974), it was noted that we have little understanding of *why* people want other people punished—that is, of the utilitarian and retributive motives for punishment. The present findings suggest that it would also be useful to study reasons for convicting defendants and the relationship between convicting and punishing. Legally, conviction and punishment are far from perfectly linked; the psychological linkage now appears as complex and multifaceted as the legal one.

Experiment II

Introduction and Methods

In order to expand on the suggestive findings from Experiment I, and to test their consistency over time and population samples, a partial replication was conducted two years later in a different region of the country. In the second study, the measurement of individual differences between participants preceded the trial presentation by a substantial period of time in order to reduce any effect of the measurements on judgments of the trial. A number of these initial measures were directly concerned with the issue of authoritarianism and the law.

A more detailed, two-question measure of capital punishment attitude was adopted from another study (Jurow, 1971). It was expected that these questions would provide a more accurate and reliable measure of participants' true attitude. In addition, a set of punishment ratings for fourteen potentially capital crimes was also adopted from the Jurow study, to provide an index of how punitively the participants would sentence defendants in other cases prior to their entering this experiment. The Calley case was added to Jurow's set of crimes, both to check how judgments of it related to the other judgments and to test the simple correlation between judging the Calley case and judging the experimental trial. A version of the F-Scale, the original instrument used to measure authoritarianism (Adorno et al., 1950), was included so that the relationship between capital punishment attitude and authoritarianism could be assessed directly. Finally, although the same trial and experimental manipulations were used as in Experiment I, the trial was presented by written transcript rather than audiovisual simulation.

The study was conducted with a university student sample on Long Island, New York. The students participated to fulfill a course requirement or to obtain extra credit.

Approximately three to five weeks prior to participation in the trial simulation, 167 participants filled out questionnaires containing the individual difference measures. A number of sociological variables were included, with a measure of self-rated liberalism/conservatism added. (The latter was a scale marked from "far left" to "far right" on which the participants indicated their political position.) Two questions from Jurow (1971) assessed attitude toward capital punishment—one five-choice general item and one five-choice specific item—asked about participants' own probable behavior as a juror. It was predicted that these items would be related to verdict and sentence as in the previous study: participants favoring capital punishment would be more likely to acquit the defendant, but would punish him more harshly if they convicted him. In addition, a forced-choice F-Scale was used: the short form of the Berkowitz and Wolkon scale (Robinson & Shaver, 1973, p. 332), plus two additional items from their scale. Subjects chose one of two alternatives and then expressed degree of agreement with the chosen alternative, resulting in a seven-point scale with no middle alternative allowed. It was predicted that authoritarianism would be related to approval of capital punishment and that it would show the previously discovered pattern of responses to the case: acquittal plus punitiveness.

The Jurow Penalty Scale, a set of fourteen serious crimes (all murders except the Rosenberg spy case), was also used to assess initial punitiveness. As already noted, the Calley case was added to the list of crimes forming that scale. It was predicted that harsh sentences for all cases *except* the Calley case would be positively related to one another and to approval of capital punishment and authoritarianism. Sentencing on the Calley case would be negatively related to the other measures.

Three to five weeks after obtaining individual difference data, subjects participated in the jury simulation. Relationships among the independent variables will be assessed using the 167 participants who filled out the initial questionnaire. Relationships between independent and dependent variables will be assessed using only the 142 participants who both filled out the initial questionnaire and attended the subsequent jury simulation.

Upon coming to class, participants read the case used in Experiment I. They also expected to deliberate in groups after finishing the initial reading and evaluations. After reading the case, which took twenty to thirty minutes, participants filled out questionnaires giving their initial verdicts, sentence recommendations, and attributions of responsibility to the defendant and to his superior. Other items, such as the hypothetical "would you shoot" item, were eliminated for brevity. Some participants were then told that their participation was completed; others entered into group discussions not relevant to the present study. All data analyses from Experiment II, therefore, are based on participants' initial judgments only.

Results

Individual Differences. Predicted relationships among individual difference items were generally confirmed. The distribution of responses to the capital punishment items and to the Penalty Scale for punitiveness are presented in Tables 12-5 and 12-6. The individual item distributions in these scales may be of some interest in understanding the overall pattern of responses made by subjects. It is evident from Table 12-5 that on the whole these subjects lean toward opposition to capital punishment, particularly on the general attitude item. When asked about their own behavior as a juror, in the specific attitude item, many subjects opt for the intermediate response—that is, they would "consider all of the penalties provided by the law and the facts and circumstances of the particular case." Perceived social desirability may be a problem with this item, since the pro-capital punishment responses could well appear unreasonable and the intermediate response may be seen as the approved stance for a juror to take.

Correlations among independent variables and between independent and dependent variables are presented in Table 12-7. As expected, the two items tapping capital punishment attitude were highly correlated. However, the general capital punishment item was a substantially stronger correlate of punitiveness as measured by the Penalty Scale. This may reflect the contamination of answers to the specific item by social desirability. As expected, approval of capital punishment was significantly related both to being highly authoritarian and to being a self-identified conservative. Authoritarianism and conservatism were also related to higher punitiveness on the Penalty Scale. Surprisingly, however, they were not significantly related to one another, as found in other studies.

Predictions concerning the Calley penalty item were partially confirmed. Contrary to prediction, the item does show a low positive correlation with the average penalty for the other fourteen cases (mean penalty score in Table 12-7); yet penalty assigned to Calley was uncorrelated or even somewhat negatively correlated with many of the individual items. In addition, the Calley item was discarded from the overall Penalty Scale on the basis of a factor analysis of all fifteen penalties: all other items loaded strongly on one factor, but the Calley loading was below the acceptable level for inclusion in the factor. Thus penalties

Table 12-5

Experiment II, Preliminary Questionnaire: Responses to Capital Punishment Attitude Questionnaire

Check the *one* statement which *best* summarizes your *general views* about capital punishment (the death penalty) in criminal cases:

34%	1. I am opposed to capital punishment under any circumstances.
37	2. I am opposed to capital punishment except in a few cases where it may be appropriate.
9	3. I am neither generally opposed nor generally in favor of capital punishment.
14	4. I am in favor of capital punishment except in a few cases where it may not be appropriate.
7	5. I am strongly in favor of capital punishment as an appropriate penalty.
101%	Total %
164	Total N

Assume *you are on a jury* to determine the sentence for a defendant who has already been convicted of a very serious crime. If the law gives you a choice of death or life imprisonment or some other penalty: (check only one)

35%	1. I could not vote for the death penalty regardless of the facts and circumstances of the case.
18	2. There are some kinds of cases in which I know I could not vote for the death penalty even if the law allowed me to, but others in which I would be willing to consider voting for it.
43	3. I would consider all of the penalties provided by the law and the facts and circumstances of the particular case.
3	4. I would usually vote for the death penalty in a case where the law allows me to.
1	5. I would always vote for the death penalty in a case where the law allows me to.
100%	Total %
165	Total N

Note: Figures are rounded percents of total sample who choose each option.

Table 12-6
Experiment II, Preliminary Questionnaire: Rounded Percentages of the Total Sample Assigning Each Punishment to Each Crime on the Jurow Penalty Scale

Defendant	Circumstances	Penalty						
		(Write-in)[a] (Scored as 0)	10 Years, Possible Parole After 3 (Scored as 1)	20 Years, Possible Parole After 7 (Scored as 2)	Life, Possible Parole After 20 (Scored as 3)	Life, No Parole (Scored as 5)	Death (Scored as 5)	Mean Penalty
1. Lee Harvey Oswald	murder of President John F. Kennedy	1%	1%	6%	23%	41%	28%	3.867
2. Jack Ruby	murder of Lee Harvey Oswald	1	3	16	40	26	14	3.307
3. James Earl Ray	murder of Martin Luther King	1	1	5	27	39	27	3.829
4. Dr. Sam Sheppard	hired a gunman to murder his wife, Marilyn, to collect life insurance proceeds	1	2	10	34	37	17	3.534
5. Sirhan Sirhan	murder of Senator Robert F. Kennedy	1	1	7	23	39	29	3.859
6. Nathan Leopold Richard Loeb	wealthy young college students who kidnapped and murdered an 8-year boy, Bobby Franks, for "thrills"	3	2	10	24	32	30	3.685
7. Mark A Fein	wealthy young business executive who borrowed $30,000 from a loan shark (who was also his bookmaker) to bet on horses. When loan shark demanded the money back, Fein and a gangster he hired, killed him	1	3	16	37	33	10	3.285

Table 12-6 (cont.)

Defendant	Circumstances	(Write-in)[a] (Scored as 0)	Penalty					Mean Penalty
			10 Years, Possible Parole After 3 (Scored as 1)	20 Years, Possible Parole After 7 (Scored as 2)	Life, Possible Parole After 20 (Scored as 3)	Life, No Parole (Scored as 5)	Death (Scored as 5)	
8. Salvatore Agron	Agron, aged 18 and a member of a teenage youth gang, kicked and stomped to death a boy of 13, who was sitting on a bench in Central Park and who objected when Agron pushed him off the bench	2	6	15	31	23	23	3.352
9. Dennis Cook	Cook, an unemployed drifter, raped and then murdered a 24-year old woman who was returning home from work on a deserted street, late at night	1	2	8	30	35	24	3.675
10. Paul Warner	Warner, married for 20 years and father of two children, discovered his wife was having an affair with his business associate, Steven Fox. When Warner told Fox he knew of the affair, Fox replied: "It's your tough luck." Enraged, Warner brooded about the situation for two weeks, and then placed dynamite in Fox's car. When Fox started the motor in the morning, the car exploded, killing Fox instantly	1	16	29	34	18	2	2.564

		1	2	3				
11. Adolph Eichmann	Nazi Colonel who arranged for the murder of 6,000,000 Jews in Nazi Germany during World War II	1	2	3	10	37	47	4.215
12. Ralph Bolden	Shot the owner of a liquor store to death after robbing the store of $50	0	1	20	30	31	18	3.436
13. Louis Johnson	When riding in a taxi, Johnson pulled out a knife and demanded money. The cab driver slammed on the brakes and then leaped at Johnson. Both fell on the back seat, fighting. During the fight, Johnson stabbed the cab driver, who later died	0	11	27	29	24	9	2.950
14. Julius and Ethel Rosenberg	Convicted of espionage (giving atomic secrets to Soviet Union)	0	26	22	23	23	6	2.619
15. Lt. William Calley	U.S. Army officer who shot and killed 22 or more South Vietnamese civilians at My Lai, South Vietnam	3	32	16	26	17	6	2.424

Note: Each percent is based on the row total for that crime. Row totals ranged from N = 158 to N = 165.

[a]Some subjects wrote in that defendants should get psychiatric care or a lower sentence.

Table 12-7

Experiment II: Relationships among Independent and Dependent Variables

7A. Correlations Among Independent Variables

	General Capital Punishment	Specific Capital Punishment	Mean Penalty Score[a]	Calley Penalty	Mean F-Scale Score	Liberalism-Conservatism
Gen C.P.	—	.683[d]	.577[d]	-.048	.222[c]	.368[d]
Spec C.P.		—	.333[d]	-.076	.220[c]	.361[d]
Penalty			—	.197[b]	.323[d]	.244[c]
Calley				—	-.078	-.033
F-Scale					—	.076
Lib-Cons						—

7B. Correlations Between Independent and Dependent Variables

	General Capital Punishment	Specific Capital Punishment	Mean Penalty Score[a]	Calley Penalty	Mean F-Scale Score	Liberalism-Conservatism
Verdict	-.161	-.028	-.072	.338[d]	-.101	.062
Responsibility of Defendant	-.141	-.063	-.115	.285[d]	-.042	.045
Sentence	-.047	-.038	.064	.419[d]	.138	-.010

[a]Mean for Jurow's Penalty Scale without adding Calley case.
[b]$p < .05$
[b]$p < .01$
[c]$p < .001$

for all other cases essentially "hung together" as expected; the sentence for Calley, as predicted, stood out distinctly from all others. In addition, the case received the lowest mean punishment rating of all, as the averages in Table 12-6 show.

Most of the other fourteen cases (and the mean for all fourteen) showed highly significant positive correlations with general and specific capital punishment approval, and none showed a negative correlation. (These tendencies corroborate the findings in Jurow, 1971.) This penalty for Calley was slightly negatively related to both, although it did not show the predicted significant negative relationship. It also showed slight negative relationships with average F-Scale score and with conservatism. Thus the penalty assigned to Calley by these subjects is anomalous—perhaps as anomalous as should be expected, given a format that may have encouraged consistency across cases. The direction of the findings, if not their size, supports the predictions concerning punitiveness toward Calley.

Dependent Variables. As in the previous study, the major dependent variables were significantly correlated with one another. Verdict and responsibility assigned to the defendant were highly related ($r = .644$, $p < .001$); verdict and sentence, somewhat less so ($r = .464$, $p < .001$). The sentence-responsibility relationship was also high ($r = .457$, $p < .001$). These correlations are somewhat larger than those reported in the first experiment.

Fewer sociological variables were available for testing in this second study, for the participant group was composed of individuals of roughly the same ages and educational levels; however, one measure of *parental* status was available: family income. Students from higher-income families tended to assign more responsibility to the defendant ($r = .279$, $p < .001$), similarly to participants in the first study who were highly educated or in high status occupations themselves. Females were also more likely to convict the defendant than males ($r = .181$, $p < .05$) and had lower authoritarian scores ($r = -.189$, $p < .05$).

The best predictor of responses to the experimental trial was the Calley penalty item. Not surprisingly, that item was most strongly related to the sentence assigned to the defendant: those who punished Calley severely also punished the experimental defendant severely. Participants who assigned Calley harsh punishments also were significantly more likely to convict this defendant and to assign him more responsibility for the crime. These reactions seem to be a straightforward case of generalizing from Calley to this defendant and from sentence to verdict and responsibility.

The measures related to authoritarianism did not affect the dependent variables as strongly as predicted. Approval of capital punishment (either general or specific) was not significantly correlated with any dependent variable. However, when major sociological and personality variables were considered together, general attitude toward capital punishment significantly predicted both verdict and responsibility attribution: participants who favored capital punishment, as predicted, were more lenient toward the defendant.[5] Scores on the Penalty Scale and self-rated conservatism were not related to the dependent variables. Thus punitiveness in sentencing fourteen other crimes did not predict sentencing the defendant in a crime of obedience. With other variables controlled, F-Scale score was the only variable other than the penalty assigned to Calley that predicted sentence: as predicted, subjects who had higher authoritarianism scores were more likely to assign long sentences.[6]

Further analyses were also performed on sentence duration to see if capital punishment approval might produce harsh sentences only among those who convicted the defendant, as found in Experiment I. The average sentences are presented in Table 12-8. In contrast to Experiment I, it appears that in the second study those subjects who were either strong supporters *or* opponents of capital punishment gave somewhat longer sentences than subjects moderately opposed. Thus the relationship between attitude toward capital punishment and sentencing is more complicated than the direct relationship found in Experiment I.

Despite failing to replicate fully the unexpected pattern of acquittal-proneness plus punitiveness found in Experiment I for approvers of capital punishment, the second study generally supported the predictions derived from the first. In both, approval of capital punishment was associated with a tendency to

Table 12-8

Experiment II: Mean Sentence Assigned, Grouped by Attitude toward Capital Punishment and by Verdict

| | | Capital Punishment Attitude | | | |
		Approve	Disapprove Moderately	Disapprove Strongly	Row Marginals
Verdict	Not guilty	$\bar{X}$ = 2.097 N = 31	$\bar{X}$ = 2.517 N = 29	$\bar{X}$ = 2.320 N = 25	2.311
	Guilty	$\bar{X}$ = 30.417 N = 12	$\bar{X}$ = 16.741 N = 27	$\bar{X}$ = 25.773 N = 22	24.310
22	Column marginals	16.257	9.629	14.046	

Note: Sentences ranged from 0 to 100 years.

[5] Assignment of responsibility to the defendant was significantly predicted by three variables using stepwise regression. Subjects who had sentenced Calley harshly, who had high income parents, and who disapproved of capital punishment assigned more responsibility. These variables accounted for 21.5 percent of the variance in responsibility (R^2 = .215).

[6] Only two variables significantly predicted sentence in a stepwise regression with an R^2 of .209. Those subjects who had assigned harsh sentences to Calley in the Penalty Scale and who had high F (authoritarianism) scores gave longer sentences to this defendant.

acquit; for crimes other than crimes of obedience we expect the opposite relationship. Indeed, in the second study punitiveness in sentencing fourteen other crimes was unrelated to judging the military crime of obedience. Only the penalty assigned to Calley predicted reactions to this case. The second study also corroborated a number of predictions about authoritarianism and punitiveness: that high F scores and approval of capital punishment would be associated with acquittals; that high F scores, capital punishment approval, and punitiveness on the other fourteen Penalty Scale cases would tend to be negatively related to the Calley penalty; and that high F scores would be related to capital punishment approval. Predictions about sentencing—the arguments that those subjects who had high F scores or who favored capital punishment would be likely to assign harsher sentences when they convicted the defendant—were confirmed for F scores, although not for capital punishment attitude.

Discussion and Conclusions

Crimes of obedience are not like other crimes. Thus in these experiments using a military crime of obedience it was possible to differentiate authoritarianism and conviction-proneness and to distinguish among verdicts, assessments of responsibility, and sentences.

In both studies, major sociological variables showed relationships to the dependent variables similar to those found in the earlier survey with a national sample (Kelman & Lawrence, 1972b). As in the national responses to the Calley trial, those subjects who were older, less educated, and lower in social status (or had lower status parents) tended to be more lenient about both verdicts and responsibility attribution. Thus certain relationships found in the earlier sample were confirmed some two to four years later, using a different case, in two different regions, with both adult and student samples. These trends lend confidence in the stability of reactions to such crimes and in their generalizability to the public as a whole.

In Experiment I, it was predicted and found that those who approved of capital punishment would give more lenient verdicts than those who opposed it. There was a complex effect of both capital punishment attitude and education on verdict and sentence: although subjects who favored capital punishment and who were less educated were more likely to acquit, they were also more likely to give long sentences when they convicted the defendant. From these data it appears that responsibility attribution and verdict represent one stage in judgment, governed by orientation toward individual responsibility and toward authority; sentencing is a separate stage, governed by retributive or punitive tendencies as well. Thus we have differentiated here between what might be called labelling and sanctioning steps. The judgments of responsibility and verdict represent *labelling*: the defendant is responsible; he is guilty. The sentencing step indicates what should then happen to a person to whom a label is applied—that is, the *sanction* that should accompany being guilty or responsible for a crime.

Results from the second study, using a different sample and method of presenting the case, generally corroborated the predictions based on the first experiment. There was a substantial relationship between willingness to punish Calley and willingness to blame, convict, and punish the experimental defendant. The judgments of Calley, in turn, were not related to capital punishment attitudes and only weakly related to judgments of fourteen other serious crimes (the Penalty Scale). Authoritarianism, measured by a forced-choice F-Scale, was related to both punitiveness on the Penalty Scale and to favoring capital punishment, but not related to judgments of Calley. In the experiment, more authoritarian subjects tended to acquit the defendant and were significantly more likely to assign harsh sentences; this was generally the predicted pattern. Approvers of capital punishment, as predicted, were also more likely to acquit the defendant and to hold him less responsible than those opposed to capital punishment.

An important feature of the results of the second study was the failure to replicate fully the previous combination of punitive sentencing and acquittal-proneness found for approvers of capital punishment. Instead, there was a tendency for strong supporters and opponents of capital punishment to resemble one another—that is, for both to give longer sentences than subjects moderately opposed to capital punishment. Several explanations may be conjectured for such a pattern. First, the measures of capital punishment attitude in the second study differed from the simple item used in Experiment I. Perhaps they were actually inferior to the measure used initially. It is more likely, however, that the measures used in Experiment II (or at least the general attitude measure) were in fact better indicators of capital punishment attitude, providing a better index of support for or opposition to capital punishment; with these better indicators, then, a non-linear relationship could be observed in the second study that had been hidden in the first. It is common to find in the political realm that strong partisans resemble one another more than either resembles indifferent citizens (in likelihood of voting, for example, or in intensity of feeling and activity—for example, Flanigan, 1972; Lane & Sears, 1964). Individuals who feel strongly one way or the other about capital punishment may be such partisans. Just as both strong Democrats and strong Republicans vote, although for different parties, it is possible that strong advocates and opponents of capital punishment sentence this defendant harshly, but for different reasons or for different mixtures of the same reasons.

The samples as well as the items differed between experiments. Hence it could be argued that the students in Experiment II differed in some important way from the adults in Experiment I. This is not a likely cause of the differences in results, however, because the authoritarianism results in the student sample were consistent with predictions: harsher sentencing despite a tendency to acquit among high authoritarians. One could argue, of course, that attitude toward capital punishment has a different relationship to authoritarianism among the students, but the complexity of the necessary argument makes it important to first eliminate the simpler explanation that rests on the different capital punishment attitude items. This can be done by using all the capital punishments items together in a single study. In any case, the bulk of the results from Experiment II supported and extended those from the first study.

Taken as a whole, what do these findings suggest about attitude toward capital punishment, authoritarianism, and conviction-proneness? In the case used here, in which the defendant followed an authority's order in committing his crime, we saw that approval of capital punishment may mean acquittal-proneness under the right circumstances. The circumstances of a crime of obedience actually provide support for theoretical interpretations of capital punishment attitude that focus on authoritarianism. The significant correlations between capital punishment approval and F-Scale scores and the relationship of the F-Scale scores to other measures in Experiment II also support this theoretical argument. Yet it is important to think critically about just what our theories involve us in here, for the notion of authoritarianism is troublesome for social scientists. Since the idea of the authoritarian personality first caught hold in social science (cf. Adorno et al., 1950), many scientists have objected to the theory, the method, or both (cf. Christie & Jahoda, 1954; Kirscht & Dillehay, 1967; Rokeach, 1960). Why is a person who approves of capital punishment or scores high on tests for authoritarianism usually more likely to convict a defendant or to endorse severe punishment? It may be that the concept of authoritarianism gives us more than we bargained for in answering the question.

We need to explore the relationships among capital punishment attitude, authoritarianism, and punitiveness more thoroughly. At best, most of the associations found among these variables are of modest size; the results from the current studies were no exception to the rule. The associations of these variables with verdicts and sentences, although often significant, have also been modest, as they were in these experiments. It would be useful to work toward a better understanding of just what it is about authoritarianism scores, or agreement with capital punishment attitude items, that produces the usual results in jury studies. It might be suggested that the relationships commonly found among such variables as F-Scale scores, capital punishment attitude, and punitiveness may reflect a more basic orientation—something like "traditionalism" or "legal traditionalism." Such a concept would eliminate some of the less persuasive or less palatable aspects of the old concept of authoritarianism, such as tendencies to see plots in high places or sexual rigidity or repressed hatred of one's parents (cf. Adorno et al., 1950). It seems plausible that certain beliefs—respect for authority, a search for order and stability, a belief in the efficacy of punishment and possibly in retribution as the basic reason for punishment—may hang together without the need for some·of the glue provided by the old authoritarian syndrome. If so, we will do both our theories and our subject groups a service by dropping labels that carry unnecessary and even pejorative meanings.[7]

Finally, we need to ask what we have discovered about the relationships among judgments of responsibility, of guilt, and of punishment. In both of these studies, responsibility and guilt judgments were more closely related to one another than either was to sentencing. In both studies, there was evidence that different factors influence sentencing and the other judgments—and even evidence that some of the same variables influence them in opposite ways. It was suggested here that such "inconsistencies" are more apparent than real: that the pulling apart of these judgments here may reflect a meaningful two-step judgment process. *Labelling* an offense and *sanctioning* it were the steps suggested. A simple pairing of labels with sanctions is not what happens in law; other factors enter into the sanctioning judgment. Similarly, judgments by individuals in the public show a complex process relating labels to sanctions. To investigate how verdict and sentence are differentially influenced may help us to understand how both psycho-logic and legal logic are complexly determined, and how psycho-logic must sometimes be adapted to fit legal categories.

In summary, these studies using a military crime of obedience suggest two issues that should be explored in the study of "normal" crime. First, how do we conceptualize the links among capital punishment attitude, authoritarianism, and conviction-proneness? We have shown that the approver of capital punishment may want to acquit some defendants more often than the opponent of capital punishment; we have also shown that verdicts and sentences are not always related in simple fashion, and variables such as authoritarianism may affect them in opposite ways. We have also argued that further investigation needs to be done into the meaning of authoritarianism in this context. Second, how do we view the relationships among judgments of responsibility, guilt, and punishment? We have argued that the first two judgments represent labelling, determined in part by an individual's orientation toward authority versus individual responsibility; and that the punishment judgment is also governed by other factors such as personal retributiveness. Vidmar has suggested that we need to explore *why* people punish: their beliefs in the deterrent effect of punishment and in its moral "rightness" as retribution (Vidmar, 1974; Vidmar & Crinklaw, 1973). These findings indicate that, if we are to fully understand the desire to punish, we should also explore labelling versus sanctioning rather than simply study reasons for sanctioning. If we can separate in our own thinking the labelling of wrongdoing from the punishment of it, we may gain a better understanding of how the member of the public, or the juror, relates a crime to its punishment.

---

[7]Richard Christie has commented that he now uses a shortened version of the F-Scale containing only such items as those suggested here; he calls this scale a "traditional moralism" scale. He finds that these are the items from the old item set that have retained their meaning and their predictive power.

References

Adorno, T., Frenkel-Brunswick, E., Levinson, D. & Sanford, R. *The authoritarian personality.* New York: Harper, 1950.

Boehm, V. Mr. Prejudice, Miss Sympathy and the authoritarian personality. *Wisconsin Law Review*, 1968, *1968*, 734-750.

Christie, R., & Jahoda, M. (Eds.). *Studies in the scope and method of "The authoritarian personality."* Glencoe, Ill.: Free Press, 1954.

Epstein, R. Authoritarianism, displaced aggression, and social status of the target. *Journal of Personality and Social Psychology*, 1965, *2*, 585-589.

Epstein, R. Aggression toward outgroups as a function of authoritarianism and imitation of aggressive models. *Journal of Personality and Social Psychology*, 1966, *3*, 574-579.

Flanigan, W. *Political behavior of the American electorate.* Boston: Allyn & Bacon, 1972.

Greenstein, F. *Personality and politics.* Chicago: Markham, 1969.

Hamilton, V.L. The crime of obedience: Jury simulation of a military trial. Unpublished doctoral dissertation, Harvard University, 1974.

Hamilton, V.L. Obedience and responsibility: Jury simulation of a military trial. In preparation.

Jurow, G.Y. New data on the effect of a death qualified jury on the guilt determination process. *Harvard Law Review*, 1971, *84*, 567-611.

Kelman, H.C., & Barclay, J. The F scale as a measure of breadth of perspective. *Journal of Abnormal and Social Psychology*, 1963, *67*, 608-615.

Kelman, H.C., & Lawrence [Hamilton], L.H. American response to the trial of Lt. William L. Calley. *Psychology Today*, May 1972, pp. 41-45, 78-81. (a)

Kelman, H.C., & Lawrence, L.H. Assignment of responsibility in the case of Lt. Calley: Preliminary report on a national survey. *Journal of Social Issues*, 1972, *28*, 177-213. (b)

Kelman, H.C., & Hamilton, V.L. Availability for violence: A study of U.S. public reactions to the trial of Lt. Calley. In J.D. Ben-Dak (Ed.), *The future of collective violence.* Lund, Sweden: Studentlitteratur, 1974, pp. 125-142.

Kirscht, J., & Dillehay, R. *Dimensions of authoritarianism.* Lexington: University of Kentucky Press, 1967.

Lane, R. & Sears, D.O. *Public Oopinion.* Englewood Cliffs, N.J.: Prentice-Hall, 1964.

Lawrence, L.H., & Kelman, H.C. Reactions to the Calley trial: Class and political authority. *Worldview*, 1973, *16*, 34-40.

Miller, F.D., & Hamilton, V.L. Decision making processes in simulated juries. Paper prepared for Public Choice Society, Chicago, April 1975.

Mitchell, H.E., & Byrne, D. Minimizing the influence of irrelevant factors in the courtroom: the defendant's character, judge's instructions, and authoritarianism. Paper presented at the Midwestern Psychological Association, Cleveland, Ohio, May 1972.

Mitchell, H.E., & Byrne, D. The defendant's dilemma: effects of juror's attitudes and authoritarianism on judicial decisions. *Journal of Personality and Social Psychology*, 1973, *25*, 123-129.

Robinson, J.P., & Shaver, P.R. (Eds.). *Measures of social psychological attitudes.* Ann Arbor, Mich.: Institute for Social Research, 1973.

Rokeach, M. *The open and closed mind.* New York, Basic Books, 1960.

Vidmar, M. Effects of decision alternatives on the verdicts and social perceptions of simulated jurors. *Journal of Personality and Social Psychology*, 1972, *22*, 211-218.

Vidmar, N. Retributive and utilitarian motives and other correlates of Canadian attitudes toward the death penalty. *The Canadian Psychologist*, 1974, *15*, 337-356.

Vidmar, N., & Crinklaw, L.D. Retribution and utility as motives in sanctioning behavior. Paper presented at the Midwestern Psychological Association, Chicago, May 1973.

Vidmar, N., & Ellsworth, P. Public opinion and the death penalty. *Stanford Law Review*, 1974, *26*, 1245-1270.

13

Probability v. Precedence: The Social Psychology of Jury Selection

Richard Christie

Introduction

A critical problem in the utilization of social science research techniques in jury selection is the working relationship between the social scientists and lawyers involved in a particular case. The cooperation can be smooth and effective or it can be difficult, if not impossible. My experiences have given me cause to reflect on why there should be such variability. To the best of my knowledge, there are as yet no systematic case histories of such cooperation; therefore, the following observations are speculative.

Critical to the whole problem of cooperation is the fact that social scientists and trial lawyers have quite different histories of professional socialization. Graduate training in the social sciences places a heavy emphasis upon research methodology. Questions are viewed as best answered by the application of statistically based techniques. Thus the selection of a fair and unbiased jury is viewed as analogous to a research problem.

Legal training, on the other hand, is characterized by the study of previous cases and the whole intricate system of legal precedent that may apply to a particular case. The practice of criminal law demands the effective implementation of these principles through argument in a specific arena—the courtroom. Here, skills in advocacy, within a highly specific setting, are paramount.

The basic point in making this distinction is that social scientists and lawyers tend, by virtue of differential training and professional experiences, to have different conceptual approaches to the problem of jury selection. This is neither good nor bad; it simply is. To the extent these differences are recognized and reconciled, cooperation becomes smoother.

Methods of Jury Selection

The techniques used by those of us working with lawyers on jury selection are in no way a radical departure from more traditional legal practice; they are more a

In much of the discussion, the word "we" occurs. This is not simply an editorial convention. I am one tip of an iceberg. The material upon which the discussion is based comes from the work of hundreds and hundreds of volunteers in various cases. Much of the thinking reflects the continuing collaboration with Jay Schulman that began with the Harrisburg 7 case, as well as more recent association with other members of the National Jury Project.

265

matter of degree or style than of kind, as illustrated in Table 13-1. More comprehensive descriptions of social science techniques may be found in Kairys, Schulman, & Harring (1975). Since these techniques are in a constant process of revision and refinement, they have not been uniformly employed in all of the trials in which we have been involved. It has also not been possible to use them consistently because of restrictions of time and resources.

The techniques listed in the righthand column of Table 13-1 are by no means used by all lawyers. Kairys et al. (1975) make the flat statement, "Most criminal lawyers are not interested in jury selection." Among those that are, experienced trial lawyers have one enormous advantage over social scientists in the evaluation of jurors. They have participated in scores of jury selections and thus have a much greater experiential knowledge on which to base their evaluations. When they are interested in problems of jury selection, they can develop an uncanny ability to discriminate between potentially good and potentially bad jurors.

Among the presumed majority who are not particularly interested in jury selection, several distinctions may be drawn. Some have a pre-Freudian view of man; they assume that jurors are rational and that, if the case is presented logically, any juror will arrive at the correct conclusion. Therefore, any potential juror is as good as any other, so why bother with intensive screening? Another clear category consists of those who have great faith in their own powers of persuasion and view the voir dire as an opportunity to "educate" the jurors on the crucial points they wish to make during the trial. Although they may not think all jurors are rational, they tend to consider them educable, a proposition that some of us with academic backgrounds might view with a degree of skepticism.

Returning to the five categories of jury selection techniques presented in Table 13-1, let us consider them in order.

Table 13-1

Comparison of Methods of Lawyers and Social Scientists in Jury Selection

Area	Social Scientists	Lawyers
Venire characteristics	Surveys and demographic studies	Experiences with previous jury pools
In-court observations	Systematic ratings	Intuition based upon experience
Venire reputations	Information networks	Informal contact
Jury composition	Application of findings from small-group research	Selection of key jurors
Follow-up	Systematic interviews of jurors and peremptory challenges	Informal feedback

Surveys

The use of surveys as an aid in jury selection began with our participation in the Harrisburg 7 trial[1] (Schulman, Shaver, Colman, Emrich, & Christie, 1973). A random sample of registered voters in the judicial district was drawn prior to the trial and was interviewed. Questions were designed to classify the respondents on a civil-libertarian dimension as well as to provide demographic information. The data were then analyzed to find out which identifying background variables might be related to different positions along the ideological continuum.

A modified version of this questionnaire was used for the Gainesville 8 trial.[2] Here it was possible to do a multiple regression analysis and to determine weights for relevant background characteristics. In practice this meant that as each venireman was questioned, the relevant information was checked off and computed by the formula. In this manner each venireman was given a score on demographic favorability/unfavorability, which could then be converted into a rating of his attitudinal position relevant to the base sample of those previously interviewed. In our experience lawyers have found this type of survey very useful, as it has provided them with an overall picture of the sort of jurors they could expect to find.

Lawyers often accept survey findings, even when such findings do not conform to their initial preconceptions. This is particularly true when there is a convincing explanation. For example, in Harrisburg, the expected finding that younger people would be more liberal did not emerge. However, the area was economically depressed, even prior to the current recession, and there were no major liberal arts colleges in the area. Bright, young high school graduates tended to leave the area for their higher education, and, once they were gone, there was little to bring them back. Those people left were the ones who fit comfortably into the conservative, predominantly fundamentalist Protestant, rural, small-town ambience and thus were not different ideologically from the older people.

Juror Rating Techniques

In Harrisburg the rating method we used involved asking lawyers to rate veniremen on a scale of one to five (one = bad; five = good). There was general agreement among the lawyers that a few of the veniremen would be good jurors. (Usually these individuals stood out so clearly that the prosecution could also identify and subsequently strike them.) There were more veniremen who were predicted to be bad for the defense. There was, however, great disagreement about the remainder, the middle group from which the actual jurors are usually selected after the extremes have been eliminated through challenges for cause

---

[1] *U.S. v. Ahmad* (Cr. No. 14950, Middle District of Pennsylvania, Harrisburg Division).
[2] *U.S. v. Briggs* (ND Fla 1973) 366 F Supp 1356.

and use of the peremptory challenges. In addition to disagreeing on the classification of a large portion of the veniremen, the lawyers also varied in the way they used the rating scale: some rated almost everyone as low or bad, whereas others tended to have a much more benign view and rated everyone as favorable.

In the Camden 28 case,[3] a different strategy was employed. The defendants were asked to rate the veniremen, and fifteen of them did so. The first jury vote in the case was six for conviction and six for acquittal. Comparison of the vote with the pooled ratings made at the time of the voir dire indicated exactly chance predictions; the defendants, in other words, were not skilled at rating jurors.

Because of the difficulties we experienced with both of these methods, in Gainesville we decided to have psychologists make ratings. It was assumed that the variable of authoritarianism was relevant to the kind of biases that the jurors might have (Adorno, Frenkel-Brunsick, Levinson, & Sanford, 1950) and that this variable would be related to the civil-libertarian dimension tapped in the survey. Two raters independently evaluated each venireman on this dimension, using a thirty-point graphic rating scale. Since the voir dire was very brief and was conducted by the judge, the ratings had to be based upon the responses of individual veniremen to the judge as an authority figure more than upon the content of what was said. These ratings were then used as part of the final evaluation. (The evaluation procedure is discussed in more detail in the description of the Gainesville trial; see below.)

The problem of the relative efficacy of social scientist versus lawyer assessment of veniremen is still a puzzling one. It is clear that lawyers vary tremendously in their ability to make the appropriate discriminations; the same is true of social scientists. The crucial questions cannot be answered until we have more systematic evaluations of the same group of veniremen by different kinds of evaluators, together with follow-up evaluations.

Information Networks

Defense lawyers frequently know some of the veniremen, and their friends and associates know others. This is especially true in relatively small jurisdictions. One logical extension of this knowledge has been the use of information networks that are based on studies of community research. Basically, the social structure of the community is not random. There are networks of power relationships and channels of interpersonal relationships. If these are known, it is possible to contact people in key positions concerning their knowledge of the public reputation of persons on the venire panel.

This is a risky procedure on several grounds:

---

[3] *U.S. v. Anderson* (DNJ, No. 602-71, May 19, 1973).

Many of the people in the best position to give information by virtue of their social position are not willing to cooperate with the defense, especially if the defendant is unpopular for political reasons (as has usually been the case in the trials with which we have been involved).

Unless one has good reason to trust such evaluations or evaluators, erroneous information can be easily obtained.

Unless the persons obtaining the information are discreet, the procedure may backfire—that is, if a potential juror learns that the defense is seeking information about him, he may change an initial predisposition in favor of the defendant to a bias for the side of the prosecution. Some people resent having questions asked about them, even when the information is not personal or private but in the public domain.

Yet another problem occurred in Gainesville, where the judge did not release the jury list until the actual start of the trial and the list did not include veniremen's addresses. This had been anticipated, however, and Jay Schulman had volunteers sitting by telephones, with directories available, so that addresses could be determined as soon as a legal assistant ran out of the courtroom with the list. Once the addresses had been obtained, appropriate key informants were contacted. Since the voir dire was very short, this meant that the entire operation was hurried and that incomplete information was obtained.

In other trials, it has been possible to establish more adequate networks. Again, there has been a wide variation in the quality of the information; but in some cases, key information that has been obtained on a few veniremen has prevented serious mistakes in jury selection from occurring.

Application of Findings from Small-Group Research

There are two key methods involved in making the final selection of jurors. First is to combine information from the demographic ratings made on individual veniremen with in-court observations and network information in order to determine which veniremen would be most likely to be unfavorable; these are then eliminated from consideration. The second is to decide how those individuals remaining might fit together as a jury.

In the great majority of cases, most potential jurors are prosecution-oriented. Very few could fairly be called "initially favorable to the defense." If they have signed peace petitions, participated in peace demonstrations or civil rights activities, ever been on a jury that voted for acquittal, or had any public history of protest, the prosecution will invariably strike them. There may be a few closet dissidents who have escaped the FBI's central files, but there are not enough to count on in the average jury array. This means that the central problem in jury selection is the careful evaluation of those who are not so biased that they cannot be fair and impartial jurors.

In actual practice, the majority of ratings of veniremen based on demographic and in-court observations are in substantial agreement. If they are bad on both indices, they are truly bad for the defense; if they are good, they stand out. The cases that create problems are those in which there are discrepancies. If someone has a bad demographic rating but comes across well under questioning, one must ask whether this individual is strongly antidefense but is putting on an act so that he can get on the jury and cast a vote for conviction, or whether he is someone who simply does not fit the ideological niche suggested by his demographic characteristics. Similar problems emerge with the opposite pattern. Suppose someone has the demographic characteristics associated with a favorable set of attitudes but appears prosecution-prone during the voir dire. Is he likely to be a favorable juror for the defense and hedging in his answers only because he is afraid the prosecution will strike him? Material from the information network is frequently useful in making decisions in such cases.

After determining overall ratings of favorableness, the next thing that must be considered is how the jury will interact. A jury is not an aggregate of twelve autonomous individuals. Leaders will emerge; some people may try to become leaders and be rebuffed; some will fit passively into almost any group structure; some will become isolates; and so forth. Anticipation of this process in a particular jury is not merely a matter of mechanically applying rules. In general, an individual's status and power within the jury group will mirror his status and power in the external world. Empirically, then, we would expect a higher status within a jury for men; for those with a higher education or a more prestigious occupation; for whites; and for older individuals. Status may or may not be related to demographic ratings and in-court ratings; this varies with the sociological characteristics of the population in a particular court district. A further assumption is that cliques will form around friendship choices that tend to be related to persons of similar status.

The mechanics of jury selection vary from trial to trial and depend on factors such as the degree of confidence in the evaluations, the range of judged differences among veniremen, the success with which undesirable jurors are struck for cause, the number of peremptory challenges available to both sides, successful guesses as to whom the prosecution will be most likely to strike, and the way in which peremptory challenges are exercised.

Follow-up Interviews of Jurors

One professional hang-up typical of working with a research orientation is wanting to understand the relationship between independent variables (in this case, input into jury selection) and the dependent variables. It is important to find answers to the following questions:

Who influenced whom in the decision made by the jury?

Did individual jurors perform as their demographic profile and/or in-court rating would have predicted?

Did the group process develop along anticipated lines?

A major frustration in research on actual juries is that each case has its unique aspects; unlike scientists performing laboratory experiments, we cannot run *n* replications, look at the overall results, and check out experimental hypotheses. As a compromise, our procedure has been to interview jurors afterwards in an attempt to reconstruct what happened.

We initiated this procedure with our first case, that of the Harrisburg 7. Paul Cowan, who had covered the trial for the *Village Voice*, was persuaded to interview some of the jurors for us; we then analyzed the seven tapes he obtained. This was an eye-opening experience. Cowan had used material obtained from one interview to formulate questions for succeeding interviews, as opposed to the more usual social science technique of having one set of highly standardized questions, to be asked of everyone. Cowan's method enabled him to obtain information about jury schisms that none of the lawyers or the reporters covering the case dreamed existed.

Summary

We can summarize the methods we have used in jury selection as follows:

1. They differ from lawyers' techniques more in degree than in kind; they are not foreign in principal to methods used by experienced trial lawyers.
2. They constitute an approach that views jury selection as a research problem in which we try to make explicit the relevant issues and collect data to check out our assumptions.
3. They require us to use a variety of techniques, in full knowledge that, although each gives us better than chance probability of success, each also has a high probability of error. It is, therefore, dangerous to assume that a single method will be adequate.

An Illustrative Example: The Gainesville 8 Trial

To clarify how these jury selection methods work, we will describe some of our experiences in the Gainesville 8 trial. We have since gone on to more sophisticated data analysis techniques and are now using a variation of the Morgan and Sonquist Automatic Interaction Detection Program, which permits the identification of discrete subgroups of the basic sample. Since the trials in which we have used these latter methods are still in the process of jury selection, however, it is not prudent to discuss the details here.

In the Gainesville trial, the demographic profiles were clearcut; courtroom observations were based on relatively little information but were in high agreement with the demographic predictions; the range of variability among veniremen was very wide; and the restrictions on voir dire meant there were no successful challenges for cause. The defense had 18 peremptory challenges and the prosecution six; but the system of challenges was unusual in that, after the prosecution struck, they could not go back and subsequently eliminate anyone still seated.

The hypothesized sociometric structure of the Gainesville jury is illustrated in Figure 13-1. The prosecution struck the only two Jews (both young); a middle-aged, white, male social worker; two white, female college students; and one young, white hippie (an unemployed cabinetmaker). The defense strategy was strongly influenced by the fact that the prosecution passed over the person identified as Juror No. 1. She had a college degree and taught art classes; her husband had an administrative position at the university; and she came across in court as self-assured and low authoritarian. Network information indicated that

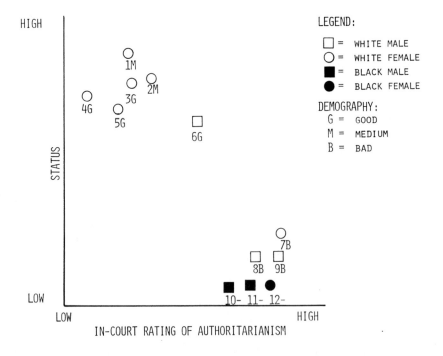

Figure 13-1. Hypothesized Sociometry of the Gainesville 8 Trial Jury.

she was politically conservative but fair. She appeared to be a natural leader. Basing their strategy on this assumption, the defense team then decided to strike high-status males who looked like potential leadership rivals, especially since none of them came across as favorably as she did. This action was in addition to striking older, low-status, white males and females. Two of the five blacks on the panel were also struck, despite the fact that they were relatively young, because they appeared to identify very strongly with white middle-class values.

There appeared to be three natural groupings, if the assumptions we made about status similarity and clique formation were correct. The first was made up of very articulate, middle-class white women: Jurors No. 2, 3, 4, and 5.

Jurors No. 2 and No. 3 were both college graduates and married; No. 4 and No. 5 were both college students. No. 4 had the lowest rating on authoritarianism of any panel member and was married to a graduate student. No. 5 was a mystery in terms of outside information but seemed both intelligent and colorless.

The second clique was made up of three black jurors. There were not enough blacks in the survey to provide a clear demographic portrait. No. 10, however, was a twenty-seven-year-old grocery chain employee who appeared to be relatively independent and a strong person. No. 11 was a twenty-four-year-old Vietnam veteran who had been drafted and who now worked as an attendant in the local Veterans' Administration Hospital. Since a good deal of the testimony involved explosives and weapons, we assumed that he would be somewhat knowledgeable about questionable aspects of the government's case and that, in combination with No. 10, he would not be pro-government. No. 12 was a single woman in her fifties, from a rural area, who supported herself by working in a vegetable-processing plant in season and by housework at other times. It was assumed that she would align herself with the other two blacks.

The third clique represented a risky, calculated gamble. These were both rednecks (one of whom was proud of the fact) who were employed as a power-line crew member and as a plumber's helper, respectively. They were relatively young (thirty-three and twenty-four) but, more importantly, very inarticulate. We assumed, both on the basis of demography and on courtroom ratings, that they would be pro-prosecution but that they would be incapable of persuading anyone else on the jury of the merits of their position. One of the findings of experimental research is that high authoritarians are more susceptible to group pressure than are low authoritarians, and we hoped this would hold true in jury deliberations.

This left two hypothesized isolates. No. 6 was a twenty-seven-year-old male elementary school teacher who had been recently divorced. He belonged to the National Guard, but this was interpreted as a way of keeping out of the draft rather than representing high authoritarianism. He did not appear particularly intellectual (our code name for him was "bubblehead") and, in our judgment, seemed more likely to be influenced by the central group of high-status women.

No. 7 was a fifty-year-old widow, with less than a high school education, who worked as a cottage mother at a school for mentally retarded children. She was given a high authoritarian rating and a poor demographic rating, and she fell into none of the hypothesized clusterings. It was assumed that she would be pro-prosecution but that when the crunch came, she would be most influenced by the high-status women.

In addition to our assumptions about status similarity and clique formation, there was an additional underlying assumption about our prediction that nine jurors would vote for acquittal and three for conviction (at least initially). It was based on our sitting in with the defendants' and lawyers' review of the anticipated government case—one we thought would not convince an unbiased jury. There was only one juror, No. 3, that we suspected might be favorably inclined toward the defense, and this feeling was based on reports that she had been seen at a health food store and might have smoked pot.

Somewhat similar considerations have gone into weighing jury composition in subsequent cases. I am not aware of lawyers independently attempting to take all of these factors into account, although some have reported scrutinizing jurors for potential leaders or for someone who might hold out to hang a jury.

After the completion of the Gainesville trial, interviews were obtained with all twelve jurors as well as with fourteen of the eighteen defense peremptory challenges (four of the six struck by the prosecution, and two of the four alternates). This enabled us to ascertain a number of things.

We had anticipated an initial 9:3 split in the jury. The first straw vote after deliberations began was nine for acquittal and three, not for conviction, but for discussing the matter further. The only problem with our prediction was that two people switched from the sides we had anticipated.

It turned out that Juror No. 7, our older, low-status white woman, was known as the most religious Bible-quoting person in her rural county. During the trial she prayed almost constantly for guidance. No. 12, our older black woman, was also a great one for praying; and these two women sometimes not only prayed together, but alternated visits to one another's churches on Sundays. (The jury was sequestered, and there were not enough marshals to take everyone to his home church on Sunday.) In the course of these prayers, God told her that the devil was in the government's chief witness (an FBI informant), and the defendants were therefore innocent. This defection shook up Juror No. 9, the young plumber's helper. He was from the same rural county as Juror No. 7 and was relying on her to argue for conviction; he was so stunned when she voted for acquittal that he was even less articulate than usual and finally joined in the unanimous verdict for acquittal.

His redneck compatriot also voted for further discussion but yielded to the pressure of Juror No. 1 (who had been elected foreperson). She had sized him up as a potential troublemaker from the beginning and used her not inconsiderable powers of blandishment throughout the trial to keep him in line. His capitulation was a classic example of low-status-high authoritarian bowing, not only to group pressure, but to a high-status person.

The one person who really put our prediction to shame (we do not feel chagrined about failing to predict heavenly intervention for Juror No. 7) was Juror No. 5, the woman student who, at twenty, was our youngest jury member. She had been very hard to read when questioned by the judge. She had sounded intelligent and calm; this, combined with her youth and status of student, led to a prediction of low authoritarian. Beneath the cool exterior, however, there was a lot of heat. In her interview (which lasted about five hours) it turned out that she was not only the daughter of an ultra-conservative real estate appraiser, but was also an Ayn Rand objectivist. Although jurors were not allowed to take notes during testimony, every night Juror No. 5 sat in her room and wrote down all the points the prosecution had made during the day—but none that the defense had made. The cause for the defense was saved, however, by Juror No. 4, the part-time student who had the lowest rating in authoritarianism of any of the jurors. This young woman was incredible. She had an almost photographic memory of everything that occurred during the trial and was able to rebut the one-sided notes of the young objectivist who finally capitulated. It is a moot point whether a more extensive voir dire would have picked up this young woman's rightest political views, although she was very open about them in the interview.

Included among the interview questions were some authoritarianism and civil liberties items, a number of which had been on the questionnaire administered to the original sample. Responses to these were compared with the predictions made by both the demographic index and the courtroom ratings. Aside from the wild misplacement of Juror No. 5, the major surprise was that the three black jurors were not quite as authoritarian as had been predicted. Juror No. 10, who was skeptical about the government and its case, was especially interesting because he came the closest of any juror in sizing up the reactions of the other jurors. No. 12, the black woman from the country, was very interesting in her own right. She was extremely independent, with a strong sense of personal integrity, and was skeptical about the government because she had been given a very difficult time when she registered to vote.

What about clique formation? Did it go as predicted? One answer comes from the room arrangements in the motel where jurors were quartered when sequestered. Their rooms extended along both sides of a corridor, and one room, well down the corridor, was set up as a TV and recreation room. The three high-status white women claimed the rooms on either side of and across from the recreation room, with the other two who were hypothesized as falling in this cluster taking adjacent rooms. The three blacks took rooms along one side close to the entrance of the corridor, and the two rednecks had adjoining rooms across from them. The older white woman took a room on the periphery of those occupied by the high-status white women. "Bubblehead" appropriately took a room between the high-status white women and the two red-necks.

Interestingly enough, the four alternates segregated themselves by their ascribed status and occupied the four least desirable rooms at the entrance to the corridor next to the marshal's room.

Accounts of interaction among the jurors during the month they were sequestered followed fairly closely the rooming arrangements which, in turn, followed the sociometry design indicated in Figure 13-1.

Limitations of Jury Selection Techniques

Some reactions to our work have been highly negative and have implied that somehow we were rigging juries. Such attacks are interesting on two counts; first, because these critics obviously do not know what we are doing; second, because none of them have attempted to find out what the procedures are.

A more troublesome problem has been trying to disabuse lawyers of the notion that somehow we have a magic formula that will enable them to get their clients off the hook. There are no mysteries in the use of computers to analyze survey data nor in the assessment of the body language of potential jurors. Our procedures are perfectly straightforward and rational. This means that there are some cases in which no amount of hard and systematic work can produce a jury that will acquit the defendant. I am not talking about cases in which the evidence is so clearcut that no method of jury selection could outweigh the evidence but about cases in jurisdictions where, given the existing system of jury selection, it is almost impossible to select a jury of "twelve men [persons] good and true."

Basically, the constraints on the value of doing a jury project are twofold. There must be enough ambiguity in the evidence of the case to give a reasonable juror cause for thought; and the initial composition of the jury pool must be heterogeneous enough to permit discrimination among potential jurors. The following two cases illustrate the futility of attempting to use the techniques outlined in this discussion when the latter condition—heterogeneity of the jury pool—does not hold.

Wisconsin v. Mendoza

Mendoza was a seventeen-year-old chicano accused of murdering two policemen shortly after the bars closed in South Milwaukee on a night in the summer of 1974. The officers were young and physically robust. They were off duty, dressed in civilian clothes, and, according to the police autopsy, legally drunk. They had been shot at point-blank range with a handgun (loaded with dumdum bullets) that belonged to one of the officers. There were no eye-witnesses, so the entire episode had its puzzling aspects. Two weeks before the trial was scheduled to start, the judge, without consulting either the prosecuting attorney or the defense attorney, announced that he was moving the trial out of Milwaukee to Monroe County. The announced reason was "too much pre-trial publicity," most of which, interestingly enough, was unfavorable to the police department. The legal propriety of the judge's action was unclear, since the defense lawyer could find no incident of similar behavior in Wisconsin jurisprudence—that is, there was no precedent.

Monroe County is located almost all the way across the state from Milwaukee.. Jim Shellow, the defense attorney, had never set foot in it, so he called us (Christie and Schulman), explained the civil rights aspects of the case, and asked if we would help in the jury selection. I called Schulman, who was tied up in Buffalo on the Attica cases. Neither of us could go to Wisconsin for the survey, but Sid Harring, a young lawyer from Wisconsin with graduate training in sociology, was interested and free to go. We then swung into action.

Shellow sent me a detailed list of the crucial issues in the case, as he saw them, and I drafted them into questionnaire format. I also called a former student who was teaching at the University of Wisconsin at LaCrosse, which is in a county adjoining Monroe, and he recruited eight students to serve as interviewers. Shellow recruited ten students from his class in the law school at Madison. The following chronology may sound implausible, but this is what happened.

I flew into Buffalo on a Wednesday night after class. Harring and I spent the night going over the Attica questionnaire; we used those items that seemed relevant to the Mendoza case and grafted new items onto them. In this way, we produced a draft of the questionnaire. I went on to Oklahoma the next morning, and Harring went over the questionnaire draft with Schulman. In the afternoon Harring flew to Milwaukee, went over the questionnaire with the lawyers, and had the questionnaires printed up. Friday night, the interviewers gathered in Sparta, Wisconsin (the county seat), for a training session. On Saturday and Sunday, 203 face-to-face interviews were obtained. This is easier to describe than it was to do, since the area is predominantly rural and not all the interviewers had cars.

One parenthetical note: this operation was conducted entirely by volunteers. In my experience, the dedicated souls who work with us on these cases obtain interviews of higher quality than those obtained by commercial interviewing firms. This is true even when, as is usually the case, the interviewers have had no previous interviewing experience and have received only a single training session prior to going into the field. One of the young women interviewers, who was eight months' pregnant, set an all-time record for the projects with which I have been associated by obtaining seventeen interviews without a single refusal.

On Monday, Harring flew back to Buffalo with the interview protocols. He had had one of his undergraduate research classes at Buffalo State College set up to do the coding of interviews, this was done on Monday night, and the data were keypunched onto cards the following morning and sent to the computer center at the State University of New York in the afternoon. Preliminary analyses were ready by Wednesday morning—less than a week after the questionnaire was drawn up.

The preliminary analyses indicated that Monroe County very definitely was not the best place to try a chicano for the murder of policemen. The county's population of about 30,000 has remained relatively constant over the past twenty years, although 10,000 emigrated during the 1950s and 5,000 during the 1960s. This reflects the fact that young people leave Monroe County as they attain maturity and depart for school or employment elsewhere. The remaining population is older than national norms, almost 100 percent white, and low in education; in addition, there are very few professionals. On attitudinal items, the population is distinguished by being uniformly high on measures of traditional moralism and is highly prejudiced against blacks and chicanos (although no chicanos reside in the county). The only ray of hope was the fact that there seemed to be a considerable amount of suspicion of police, and especially big-city police. With this in mind, we went over with Shellow a series of projected voir dire questions that would hopefully enable us to identify those jurors who would not accept police testimony uncritically. (It might be noted that the police work in the case had been incredibly sloppy.)

The first problem we encountered had to do with the method used in empaneling jurors. There were three jury clerks, each responsible for a third of the county. In examining them, Shellow discovered that the selection procedure was idiosyncratically informal. One gentleman testified that he knew everyone within a ten-mile radius of his home. (He had lived in the same house for seventy-five years.) When selecting jurors from the voting list, he would eliminate women who did not drive, school teachers (who were not legally exempt), farmers whose hired hands were laid up, etc.

The judge accepted Shellow's challenge as to jury composition. His resolution was to have the jury clerks add two morticians, three pharmacists, and nine school teachers to the panel and redraw names. Shellow's objections to this procedure were overruled, and the box was filled with twelve veniremen. In capital cases in Wisconsin, the jury is automatically sequestered, and each side is allowed six peremptory challenges. Since it was anticipated that the trial would last at least three weeks, there were many excuses for hardship. This did not materially affect the jury, since almost everyone looked equally bad from the defense's point of view.

What was worse, however, was the fact that the judge ran a very tight court. The lawyers had to obtain permission from the judge to stand and were not permitted to communicate with those members of the defense team who were not allowed in the well. Even worse, the judge ruled as irrelevant the questions that had been prepared for the voir dire, so it was impossible to attempt to screen out those with a blind and abiding faith in the virtues of the Milwaukee police force.

To make a long and frustrating story short, we predicted that exactly two of the twenty-four veniremen who had been empaneled would make fair and impartial jurors. They were, of course, the first two struck by the prosecution, since the contrast between them and the other jurors was so obvious. In my estimation, under the conditions that prevailed, there was no possibility of obtaining a fair and impartial jury in this case; therefore, any amount of work on jury selection would not have helped. Mendoza was found guilty. The case is currently being appealed.

The Banks Trial

In a trial about to start in Custer County, South Dakota (as of this writing), in which Dennis Banks is being charged with incitement to arson, among other things, we are not even attempting a jury selection project. In this trial, each side has twenty peremptory challenges. Motions for additional defense peremptory challenges, individual voir dire, and other requests were denied in a pretrial hearing. Evidence from surveys indicates that the people of South Dakota are less sympathetic to Indians involved in that complex of cases known as "Wounded Knee" than is a national sample, that registered voters in the Western District of South Dakota are more antagonistic to Indians than those in other districts of the state, and that those in Custer County (which is in the Western District and abuts the Pine Ridge Reservation) are the most prejudiced of all. None of this information was viewed as being relevant to the motions. I believe that, if everyone of the approximately 2,600 registered voters in Custer County were empaneled, it would be unlikely that thirty-two fair and impartial veniremen could be found; and I so testified. The defense strategy in this case was to get the objections on the records and, if Banks is found guilty as expected, to appeal the case.

Some Reflections on Lawyers

Prior to being enticed into the Harrisburg case by Jay Schulman some four years ago, my experience with lawyers was minimal. This was not necessarily a reflection of excessive rectitude and lack of need for their services but more one of the isolation of academic life from the "nitty gritty" world of criminal law. I confess that I find lawyers a fascinating lot, both individually and in their professional roles. This fascination may not be unrelated to the fact that prior to my involvement with lawyers, I had spent about fifteen years doing research on Machiavellianism, or interpersonal manipulation. More relevant to the present discussion, however, are some observations about the characteristics of lawyers who were able to work on jury projects, contrasted with those who found it difficult to interact with social scientists.

The first and most obvious characteristic of lawyers who have worked well with us was their concern with juries. Criminal lawyers are usually more interested in juies than are lawyers specializing in civil trials. This may reflect the fact that, by and large, criminal cases are more likely to involve civil liberties; most of the lawyers with whom we work are on the liberal rather than conservative end of the ideological continuum.

A second distinguishing characteristic is that young lawyers are much more attuned to our techniques than are older lawyers. David Kairys and I recently spoke at a series of meetings on the jury system sponsored by the National Jury Project and the National Lawyers Guild. The striking fact about the audiences was their youth—my eyeball estimate was that almost 90 percent were in their twenties and early thirties. This is, of course, the college generation that was radicalized during student protest days. Of equal importance, I think, is the fact that many of them had been exposed to sociology and social psychology as undergraduates and that almost all had had at least some undergraduate courses in psychology. I was quite surprised when some of them came up at breaks in the meeting and asked very specific and technical questions about some of my published research; some had even done research projects using scales that I had developed.

Their educational experience contrasts markedly with the undergraduate training received by lawyers thirty to forty years ago, prior to the almost exponential expansion of social psychology and prior to the empirical, rather than speculative, work in sociology. It is very difficult for people who received such training to feel at home with the probabilistic concepts underlying social research. Even some of the older lawyers with whom we collaborated success-fully often gave the impression that they did not fully resonate with our way of conceptualization.

There are other factors that sometimes lead to difficulties in working with older lawyers. Platt's comments (in this volume) about young legal-aid lawyers' burning out fast and losing their idealism jibe with my impressions. However, among those that do survive as successful defense lawyers, there is another socializing process that leaves its mark on professional style: the development of an aggressive personality. Someone has to lose in every case, and defense lawyers lose more often than prosecuting attorneys. Quite simply, this means that good courtroom lawyers have to have very strong egos to be able to engage in continuous and dubious battle. Most of the lawyers with whom I have worked, develop tremendous commitment to the cases in which they are involved (if not always to their clients), and the losing of an important case can be a traumatic event. I find myself glued to radio news broadcasts whenever a jury I have helped select is in deliberation, and my involvement has nothing to do with earning my bread and butter—and not that much to do with my professional reputation. Social scientists who work with lawyers, then, ought to be fore-warned that it is not unrealistic to expect possibly abrasive personal contacts in these working relationships. Many experienced trial lawyers talk about the courtroom as an arena in which they try to dominate the course of action. This aggressiveness can carry over to relationships with members of the defense team.

There are also, however, many benefits for social scientists who work with lawyers. Just as I have had to rethink a lot of sociological assumptions as a result of conducting surveys and interviews with jurors, I have learned a lot of psychology from lawyers. At its best, the process of interaction can be a highly productive enterprise. When collaboration is possible, it can be extremely profitable; lawyers see certain aspects that social scientists do not; and social scientists are sensitized to look for things that most lawyers do not even know exist. The blending of the two viewpoints can thus lead to the selection of fairer and less biased juries and can, therefore, serve the cause of clients better.

References

Adorno, T., Frenkel-Brunswick, E., Levinson, D., & Sanford, R. *The authoritarian personality*. New York: Harper, 1950.

Kairys, D., Schulman, J., & Harring, S. (Eds.). *The jury system: New methods for reducing prejudice.* Prepared by the National Jury Project and the National Lawyers Guild. Philadelphia: Philadelphia Resistance Print Shop, 1975.

Schulman, J., Shaver, P., Colman, R., Emrick, B., & Christie, R. Recipe for a jury. *Psychology Today*, May 1973, pp. 37-44; 77; 79-84.

14 Social Science and Jury Selection: A Case Study of A Civil Suit

Richard A. Berk

Introduction

At about 4:45 A.M. on December 4, 1969, members of the Chicago Police Department raided the Illinois Black Panther Party headquarters. Within approximately ten minutes, over eighty rounds of ammunition had been fired and Party Chairman Fred Hampton lay dead. One other occupant (Mark Clark) was killed, four others in the Panther apartment were seriously wounded, one police officer was injured by flying glass, and another was shot in the leg. The alleged purpose of the raid was to search for weapons.

Of the many shots fired, at most three came from Panther weapons. More likely, the Panthers fired a single shot or no shots at all. Some evidence suggests that Fred Hampton was drugged at the time of his death (see Commission of Inquiry, 1973) or was in any case unconscious when the raid occurred. There is also evidence clearly linking FBI agents to the planning of the operation. Documents released in 1973 as a result of the federal freedom-of-information suit of Carl Stern (NBC reporter) clearly indicate that the National Black Panther Party was a prominent target in a disruptive counterintelligence program called "Cointelpro." Moreover, in recent depositions, William M. O'Neil, Jr., confessed to his role as a paid FBI informer who infiltrated the Chicago Black Panther organization. From information supplied by O'Neil, FBI special agent Roy Martin Mitchell was able to draw a map of the Panther apartment, on which was indicated the room where Hampton slept; this map was used in the December raid. In short, a wide range of evidence implies at least a de facto assassination of Hampton, directed by the Cook County State's Attorney, implemented by the Chicago Police Department, and covertly endorsed by the Federal Bureau of Investigation. (For a good summary of the facts of the case, see Green & Warden, 1975.)

During the two years following the raid, two federal grand juries and a state grand jury were empaneled; one of the federal grand juries handed down obstruction of justice indictments against State's Attorney Edward V. Hanrahan and several Chicago police officers. All were eventually acquitted. Not surprisingly, the failure to obtain even a single conviction left many people unsatisfied.

In late December of 1969, a private Commission of Inquiry chaired by Roy Wilkins and Ramsey Clark had been formed to gather information about the raid and to produce an independent report. Approximately two years later, they arrived at conclusions that in general validated earlier public skepticism about the "official" version of the raid:

Whatever their purposes, those officials responsible for planning the police actions, and some who directly participated, acted with wanton disregard of human life and the legal rights of American citizens.

The search warrant for the premises, assuming it was legally supportable, could have been executed in a lawful manner with no significant risk to life.

The hour of the raid, the failure to give reasonable warning to the occupants, the overarming of the police, the wildly excessive use of gunfire all were more suited to a wartime military commando raid than the service of a search warrant.

There can be no possible legal or factual justification for this police use of firearms. There was no "shootout". The police did virtually all, if not all, of the shooting and most of it blindly. If the one shot that can be attributed to a Panther was fired, and was fired first, it could not justify the more than 80 shots that were fired by the police. If any of these shots were fired in the mistaken belief that they were being fired in response to fire from the Panthers, that such a belief was entertained by police officers would evidence the inadequacy and consequent irresponsibility in planning and control of an operation involving the use of lethal force.

It is not safe to entrust enforcement of laws to authorities who permit the use of a machine gun the way Chicago Police did during the episode.

Many statements made after the episode by participating police officers, such as that of Sergeant Groth that "Our men had no choice but to return their fire," are not credible.

State's Attorney Edward V. Hanrahan's statements that the police acting under his authority "exercised good judgement, considerable restraint, and professional discipline" and that "the immediate violent criminal reaction of the occupants in shooting at announced police officers emphasizes the extreme viciousness of the Black Panther Party" render him unworthy of public trust.

The failure of the Chicago police and other state and local officials to employ basic investigative practices such as fingerprinting, preserving evidence, examining all firearms, sealing the premises, and examining and photographing the bodies before removing them, as well as gross errors on the part of these officials in ballistics, autopsy, and other examinations, are professionally inexcusable and can only undermine confidence in the competence and integrity of the police and legal system.

The "exclusive" account of the police action given by State's Attorney Hanrahan's office to the Chicago *Tribune* and the filmed reenactment of the episode by the police for CBS-TV demeaned public office, misinformed and prejudiced the public, and violated professional ethics.

Systems of justice—federal, state, and local—failed to do their duty to protect the lives and rights of citizens [Commission of Inquiry into the Black Panthers and the Police, 1973, pp. viii-ix].

As it became clear that "justice" would not be forthcoming from the criminal justice process, a civil suit seeking damages was filed for the dead and surviving Black Panthers. Named as defendants were the FBI, the State's Attorney Edward V. Hanrahan, and several police officers. After numerous delays due to pre-trial motions, continuances, and a general lack of cooperation from the FBI, the State's Attorney's Office, and the Chicago Police Department, the trial date was set for early April 1975. The trial date was then moved back to November 1975 (as of this writing).[1] There are still numerous legal issues to be settled before the trial can begin (the State Supreme Court has already been involved twice), and the starting date may well change again.

While the legal issues in this trial are fascinating and the backroom politics worthy of lengthy treatment in themselves, this chapter will focus on the ongoing actions of a volunteer (except for two who were paid small salaries) research group gathering social science type data to assist the plaintiffs in selection of jury members for the trial. Of necessity, the account will be incomplete. Data that will be used to help select the jury are not yet ready for analysis, and it is not even clear precisely who the defendants will be. Tactical maneuvering by the defense may well bring about a separation of trials for federal and local officials.

The Intended Role of Social Science Data

At the time the civil suit was filed, there already existed substantial experience in using social science methods for jury selection. Moreover, in nine criminal trials where the defense had relied on direct social science input, the defense had won seven times. Whether this in any way can be attributed to social science input, a seven-for-nine batting average can not casually be dismissed.[2] Consequently, soon after the plaintiffs decided to sue for damages, an effort was mounted to provide substantial social science assistance. This chapter will specifically consider the use of survey data, primarily to help in the selection of jurors and secondarily to provide credible information for other courtroom activities (for example, arguing for a change in venue if Chicago citizens are shown by the survey to be overwhelmingly hostile to the plaintiffs).

In order to understand the survey design, it is necessary to get some notion of how survey data might be used. In this civil suit, there will probably be six jurors and two alternates (other alternatives are still possible). In the jury

---

[1] As of the summer of 1976, this case was being heard in U.S. District Court of the Northern District of Illinois, Eastern Division (*Iberia, Hampton, adminstratix, etc. et al. v. Edward Hanrahan et al.*, no. 70 c 1384, consolidated).

[2] To date, no rigorous evaluation of the social science input has been undertaken. Even impressionistic evidence is not very helpful, since support for the effectiveness of social science assistance is at best equivocal. In all fairness to social science advocates, the absence of any respectable assessment may be attributed in part to a variety of methodological difficulties inherent in such an evaluation. For example, a persuasive account would have to consider the processes by which the jury reached a decision. This kind of data would probably have to be generated through retrospective juror accounts that would be vulnerable to a variety of distortions. In any case, for a useful summary of these early experiences see Christie (in this volume); Ginger, 1975; and Kairys, Schulman & Harring, 1975.

selection process, the plaintiff's attorneys will be provided with a certain number of opportunities to dismiss potential jurors without cause (that number has still to be determined) and then must demonstrate marked bias for any other dismissals. Information supporting such a charge will likely come from responses to questions posed by the plaintiffs. However, it is not yet clear how those questions will be asked. It may be possible for attorneys to address jurors directly. More likely, questions will be submitted in writing to the judge who will then select some subset that he himself will ask. At some later point in the proceedings, attorneys for the plaintiffs will be permitted to dismiss some jurors and to challenge the fitness of others.

There are a number of competing and complementary processes by which attorneys for the plaintiffs might reach decisions about jurors and many different kinds of substantive input to these processes. Currently, I anticipate the active participation of the plaintiffs, their attorneys, various "professional" advisors, and members of the jury selection project (essentially the people who helped gather and analyze the survey data). The professional advisors will likely include some mix of sociologists, psychologists, and psychiatrists. After a juror (or jurors) has responded to a series of questions, the entire group will discuss what the answers might reflect. Somehow, a collective decision will be reached. The critical point is that input from the survey will comprise only one piece of information, and its impact will have as much to do with the interpersonal skills of its proponents as the intrinsic worth of the material.

Among participants in the jury selection project, motives for social science input are very diverse. First, there is a significant minority who feel that the American system of justice is fundamentally corrupt and that any tactics that will assist their side are justified. Appeals are made to a higher order of justice in which the formalities of courtroom procedure are at best tools to be exploited. Since it is assumed that trials are essentially political, a political view of courtroom conflict is advanced. Whether the view is based on assumptions of class warfare or racial warfare, the ethics of revolutionary insurgency are dominant.

Second, some participants hold an equally hostile but less fundamentally critical view of American courtroom justice. They reason that the basic ideology of the system is sound, but some important subset of public officials have thoroughly corrupted it. Immediate justice for the plaintiffs requires fighting fire with fire and using whatever means possible to achieve a substantial settlement. There is no reluctance to use whatever tactics are necessary, even if "subversion" of the system is implied, because the system has already been subverted.

There is a third group far less alienated from American courtroom justice. They basically accept the system as it is; this acceptance includes a notion that courtroom "advocacy" means doing nearly anything within the law to present the best possible case. They argue (1) that lawyers always try to select the best possible jury for their clients (a practice widely accepted as part of advocacy);

(2) that to do so, the most reliable information should be obtained; and (3) that social science data may impart some of that reliability. They also argue that all parties have the right to social science input. While they understand that access to professional assistance takes money (or a cause that draws volunteers) and that, in general, poorer clients may not have the advantage of such assistance, in this case they do; and that is all that matters.

Just as there are different motives for using social science skills for jury selection, there is a range of feelings about how effective that strategy will be. A small minority believes that the survey data in particular will be extremely helpful. Insights available through no other means will emerge, and emerge in a form easily translated into questions for prospective jurors. For example, the data might reveal that white Chicagoans from neighborhoods with more than 25 percent black residents will be extremely hostile to black militants in general and the Panthers in particular. Then, one could simply ask where a prospective juror lived and, after noting from census data the racial composition of the neighborhood, easily eliminate certain types of people from the jury.

In my view, this level of belief in survey data is extremely naive. To begin with, a decision to exclude a particular juror is binary: either yes or no. Yet, aggregate data analyses will at best reveal where people fall on various continua or the *probability* that they fall in one of two (or several) categories. Therefore, somewhat arbitrary cut-off points must be constructed to transform what are essentially continuous data into the nominal categories (for example, "reject" or "not reject"). There are well known difficulties with these kinds of transformations here (see, for example, Blalock, 1964, Chapter 4), made all the more worrisome by their real consequences. In short, there exist no easily defined criteria to judge how good is good and how bad is bad. Using some location in the distribution of potentially good jurors (for example, the top decile) provides a specific decision rule but, still, an arbitrary decision rule. Perhaps the top decile is not good enough.

More fundamentally, one must develop powerful predictors of desirable jurors. This implies a set of definitions specifying what makes a juror desirable and then the development of some weighting procedures by which a range of characteristics may be aggregated. With regard to the former, desirable juror attributes must be grounded *not* in some unspecified situation (for example, "What do you think of the Black Panther Party?"), but in the actual group context in which jury decisions are made. Hence, there are a variety of predispositions one might want to measure: feelings about the plaintiffs and defendants, attitudes already formed about the case, acquiescence, leadership, maturity, authoritarianism, and so on. Then, once these attributes are selected and defined, some form of weighting is clearly necessary to produce an overall assessment for each juror. This will be a difficult undertaking. For example, is hostility towards the plaintiffs more, or less, important than leadership ability?

Equally critical, a juror's decision is not a response to a projective test.

There is objective content that may be subject to rational and conscious consideration. Hence, attitudes and predispositions may be relevant only at the margins; that is, where the facts are ambiguous. Perhaps much of the case will not fall within this gray area. In addition, while no doubt juror proclivities somewhat color perceptions of the facts, cognitive skills rather than attitudes or personality traits may be the pivotal factors. A more effective questionnaire might seriously address verbal and analytical abilities. However, it might be that if one had a weak case based on the facts, one might purposely choose a jury that was not only biased towards one's side, but not bright enough to perceive the facts.

Once these kinds of questions are settled, the difficult task of developing questionnaire items remains. There is not space here even to begin to address these issues. Suffice it to say that here are many problems that are not easily overcome. (For an excellent review of this literature, see Sudman & Bradburn, 1974.)

The particular kind of trial in which I am involved has special properties that make the application of survey data (or any social science data) even more problematic. For most previous trials where social science data has been used in jury selection, the defense sought assistance. Hence, if one sympathetic and stubborn juror could be found, the worst outcome was a hung jury. For plaintiffs, the roles are reversed. Their success depends on finding an entire jury that will be likely to see the facts their way. Clearly, the margin for error is much smaller and our social science methods will be more severely tested. There are also a variety of sampling problems which I will consider briefly later.

In the face of all the difficulties noted above, a heavy reliance on the survey data seems unrealistic. While real benefits may appear, they will at best be modest. First, the very construction of a survey instrument will perhaps sensitize the plaintiffs' lawyers to additional attributes possessed by unsympathetic jurors. For example, drawing from the growing work on victimization surveys, lawyers might be alerted to look for jurors who had been crime victims. Such jurors might be less sympathetic toward the Panthers and more sympathetic toward the police. Similarly, unanticipated characteristics of good jurors might be suggested. For instance, membership in fully integrated unions could be positively associated with sympathy for the Panthers. The point here is that even *before* the data are gathered, the serious consideration of survey questions may raise issues that would have been ignored.

Second, our interviewing process may have many of the same benefits as the questionnaire construction: issues may be raised that would have escaped notice. For example, interviewers have noted that many respondents seem torn between their biases against the Black Panther Party and their support, in theory, for a "fair trial." Since it will probably be rather difficult to convince jurors that the Black Panther Party is not their enemy,[3] courtroom

---

[3] Whether the Black Panther Party was indeed the enemy of most Americans involves complicated questions which cannot be considered here. While I would argue they were not, I cannot justify my views in a couple of sentences.

argument might be most productively phrased in terms of equal justice for all. Appeals to ideals of American justice may have far more impact than efforts to dispel anti-Panther attitudes.

Third, the results of the data analysis itself may provide some nontrivial assistance. Most dramatically, a few striking counterintuitive findings may appear.[4] Perhaps a bit more realistically, the survey data may highlight a subset of intuitive insights from among the many that exprienced trial attorneys already employ. There exists an extensive lore on jury selection, some with social science trappings, and a few law firms even have specialists whose major contribution is assisting in jury selection. Hence, there is certainly no shortage of beliefs about how to select a jury. The survey data may play an important role in suggesting which of many plausible factors may be especially salient in this case. The data may show, for instance, that women are more likely to be sympathetic to the plaintiffs than men. While this would probably not surprise our attorneys, the salience of gender rather than some other "obvious" variable like age or occupation is an important finding. Given the few questions the judge will likely permit, any procedure that makes the questioning process more efficient is far from trivial.

Unfortunately, given the host of methodological problems, any selection of a subset of factors (variables) will be very imprecise, and only very large differences in importance should be taken seriously. Further, the only useful large differences will be those that can be translated into factors assessable in court. Obviously, it will be impossible to give each juror the California Personality Inventory (CPI). Only if the insights of such an instrument could be efficiently summarized with acceptable courtroom questions would there be any direct impact on jury selection. This assumes, of course, that enough space in the questionnaire could be allocated to instruments like the CPI to make their findings more reliable.

There is an even weaker but nonetheless important role for the survey data. The data may simply reaffirm our lawyers' hunches about important jury selection variables, but in so doing, legitimate whatever processes generated these hunches. In other words, even the ordering among many plausible variables may not be news, but with our lawyers' insights supported, they may feel less anxious about acting on their ideas and be able to more easily move on to other issues. The problem of which questions to ask in court may be for all practical purposes solved. Equally important, our lawyers may gain additional confidence in their intuitive insights and be able to apply themselves more creatively and effectively.

---

[4] Note that the goal is prediction. Causal explanations are of use only to the degree that they allow us to generalize our predictors to situations we have not measured. Understanding per se is probably an unnecessary luxury. For example, suppose that we find people from large families are likely to be unsympathetic to the plaintiffs. If this effect is large and not a result of sampling or measurement error, potential spuriousness does not matter. We could still use family size as a way to eliminate unacceptable jurors. Casual understanding would be important only if it led to better predictors (such as social class), for which family size was only a surrogate.

Design of the Survey

The survey was undertaken with two goals in mind. Most important was the hope of ascertaining for potential jurors those characteristics that would efficiently predict sympathy for the plaintiffs or, at least, an open mind on the issues. Besides such obvious variables as race, age, and sex,[5] a broad net was cast for unanticipated relationships. A secondary goal was characterizing the entire pool of potential jurors for a variety of motions that might be introduced in court. Of particular interest was the possibility of arguing for a change in venue if the vast majority of potential jurors had already made up their minds on the facts of the case.

Unfortunately, the survey's two goals suggested different sampling strategies. To effectively characterize the pool of potential jurors through an analysis of marginals, one would prefer a simple random sample of the population of potential jurors. That would be the best and simplest way to guarantee representativeness a priori. In contrast, an analysis in which associations among juror attributes and attitudes were primary would suggest a more complicated design insuring that certain subtypes of people who might turn up in court were represented in the survey in sufficient numbers to justify statistical procedures on those subtypes (for example, one would need enough widows living alone to accurately describe that group). If one knew the distributions of these subtypes in the overall population, one might attempt a disproportionate, stratified probability sample and oversample where necessary. Alternatively, one could guarantee sufficient cell sizes through quota sampling. However, because quota sampling is a nonprobability procedure, it trades internal validity for external validity—that is, less potential spuriousness for less generalizability. These and other more subtle methodological considerations were further complicated by our lack of resources and the anticipation of operating with inexperienced, volunteer interviewers.

Eventually, the following sampling strategy was devised. In practice, jurors are selected from voter registration lists from the greater Chicago area. Since we could not go door to door, we decided to use telephone interviews, and if there were more than one registered voter per household, we would choose among them randomly. Telephone numbers would be selected by random digit dialing (a common way to generate a random sample of phone numbers),[6] with calls made in the evenings to insure that employed people would be at home.

---

[5] Common lore suggest that blacks, younger adults, and women tend to be more sympathetic to plaintiffs, especially when the defendant is the government or a large corporation.

[6] In essence, random digit dialing is done with phone numbers whose composition is random. The three digit exchanges are assigned four random numbers thus making up complete phone numbers. This produces a list of phone numbers which can then be used by interviewers, which in turn generates a probability sample representative of the universe of phone numbers. While many non-working numbers are included, they obviously cannot produce respondents and therefore do not affect the content of the sample of interviews.

There were several immediate compromises apparent in our sampling strategy. First, while random digit dialing eliminates the problem of unlisted numbers, some registered voters do not have phones. In particular, low-income families and minorities might be proportionately underrepresented. Second, to simplify the selection of respondents within each household, only one person would be asked for an interview. Therefore, registered voters in families with more than one registered voter would be proportionately underrepresented. It is difficult to determine how serious either of these sampling biases are, especially since we were only interested in the population of registered voters. For citizens of the greater Chicago area in general, clear distortions would occur; for our smaller population, it is hard to say.

In essence, our sampling strategy was a simple random sample. To compensate for the possibility of having small numbers of certain types of respondents, we decided to gather a rather large sample of 1,500. We hoped the large sample would provide a sufficient number of diverse registered voters. However, we also knew that telephone interviews on controversial topics often produce low response rates, and several fall-back positions were developed. If the response rate dropped much below 75 percent, the simple random sample would, for all practical purposes, be destroyed. Indeed, the 75 percent figure was perhaps not conservative enough. Were this to occur, a priori representativeness for the greater Chicago area would be lost, and then a shift to quota techniques would involve no additional penalties. In other words, if the random sample were already blown, why not take advantage of the benefits of quota sampling?

We also set up a schedule specifying how many interviews had to be "in the house" on various dates if the total of 1,500 were to be gathered in time for analysis. If we were to fall seriously behind schedule, the pure sampling strategy would be abandoned (allowing for call-backs) in favor of techniques that would produce more completed interviews per phone call. In particular, we would accept the first registered voter who came to the phone rather than try to interview the appropriate random respondent within a household. In short, to the degree that our probability sample was seriously violated or our production of completed interviews fell far behind schedule, any pretense of probability sampling would be dropped in favor of gathering as many interviews in the remaining time as possible. If complemented by quotas for important subtypes of respondents, our fall-back position would produce a sample with the potential for high internal validity, even though statistical external validity would be seriously jeopardized. In addition, the use of significance tests to assess the degree of error due to random sampling would be inappropriate.[7]

After the sampling strategy was devised, a questionnaire was developed by

---

[7] Basically, significance tests specify the range of error attributable to random sampling error. However, these tests require that the data be in the form of random variables. If one does not have a probability sample, one does not have data in the form of random variables, and therefore, significance tests are technically inappropriate and often misleading. (See, for example, Kmenta, 1971, Chapter 6.)

drawing on previous research and our hunches about variables of particular importance for Chicago respondents. For example, the interviewing was scheduled to occur just after mayoral primary elections, and voter preferences were thought to reveal a great deal. Indeed, former State's Attorney Edward V. Hanrahan was one of the candidates!

The questionnaire was extensively pilot-tested, not only for appropriateness for respondents but also for its ease of delivery. Since we would be working with inexperienced volunteers, a simple instrument was critical. In addition, to speed up subsequent coding and keypunching, most questions were written in a closed format—that is, response categorie were provided—and column numbers for the computer cards were put on the questionnaire so keypunchers could work directly from completed protocols. These procedures could well occur under severe time constraints. Eventually, a revised questionnaire was prepared; it required approximately twenty minutes for the interviewer and respondent to complete the questionnaire.

While the questionnaire was being developed, a variety of statistical techniques were anticipated. The availability of SPSS (Statistical Package for the Social Sciences) made routine analyses easily accessible. In addition, I had recently devised an interactive—that is, on-line rather than batch processing—statistical program with some capabilities beyond SPSS to facilitate more complicated approaches. Finally, AID (explained below) was explored and prepared.

Given the rather crude level of results probably obtainable with a twenty-minute telephone survey, I anticipate that simple crosstabulations will be more effective. Complicated statistical techniques used on crude data only serve to obscure errors and give the impression of more rigor than really exists. AID is an elaboration of crosstabulation analysis that selects predictors in order of their "predictive" power. I have serious objections to AID procedures, not the least of which is its pronounced tendency to build on Type I errors. Therefore, if more sophisticated procedures are required, AID results will be compared with other techniques; and, where contradictions occur, AID results will be rejected.

The statistical analyses will be complicated by the need to translate findings into a form amenable for courtroom use. In other words, a series of decision rules that can be understood and applied by participants in the jury selection process, will have to be developed. For example, one might produce a "score card" on which visible biographical data (sex and race) could be recorded, along with answers to various questions. A number that could be summed to an aggregate assessment might be provided for each entry. Then, totals above a certain level might indicate acceptance of a juror: below a certain level, rejection; and totals in between, an ambiguous status.

For a while, I also considered using Bayesian procedures to assess juror qualities. In essence, Bayesian statistics allow one to build into the analysis a prior insights that can then be altered on the basis of sample data. For example, if a lawyer's "eyeball" assessment is that the chances a juror will be sympathetic are 50-50, this expectation can be included as "data." Classical statistical techniques do not have this facility. While the courtroom setting would be ideal for Bayesian approaches, a consideration of the likely properties of the sample data indicated that many necessary assumptions would not be met. Hence, Bayesian estimation had to be disregarded.[8]

Another possibility builds on Decision Theory, which provides guidelines for making decisions under the condition of "uncertainty" (see Raiffa, 1970). Basically, one develops a branching tree, indicating the probabilities of all possible outcomes along with consequences of various decisions. Eventually, one has a kind of "flow chart" with all "payoffs" mapped on it. Unfortunately, once again, our data are not likely to be in a form directly amenable to this kind of analysis. However, the flow-chart mode of presenting alternative decisions can be quite useful without the formal rigor of Decision Theory. For example, the printout of AID automatically appears in a flow-chart format. Suppose the most powerful AID predictor of sympathy for the Panthers is sex; women are more sympathetic. Under a box showing the proportion of sympathetic men and a box showing the proportion of sympathetic women would appear the next most powerful predictor. Suppose the next variable is age: those under thirty are more sympathetic. Now there are four boxes—two for men (under and over thirty) and two for women (under and over thirty)—showing the proportions sympathetic in each group. This procedure can be carried out until the case base becomes too small or until no more useful predictors are found. In application, one would first observe whether the potential juror is a man or woman. If a woman, one would then determine her age and move to the next branch in the tree and so on, until the last question was reached. In short, the printout provides an order for asking questions that will obtain the best predictions with the minimum number of inquiries.

Implementing the Study Design

To date, we have been operating under a variety of constraints often avoided by academic research. To begin, we initially had no office space equipped with telephones. While we have been able to raise enough money to provide a small central office from which the project can be coordinated, people have had to gain access to phones as best they can. For calls within Cook County it has been possible to use private phones of friends and sympathizers. For long distance calls, other arrangements have been made on a case-by-case basis. Typically, volunteers wind up footing the bills for these calls.

Along with a lack of phones, many other material resources are very

---

[8]For an easy introduction to Bayesian methods, see Wonnacott & Wonnacott, 1970, Chapter 10.

scarce. Paper had to be obtained for duplicating and questionnaires; access to duplicating equipment had to be managed; and pens, pencils, and other office supplies had to be "liberated" at any opportunity. However, we have also been fortunate in receiving gifts for many of our needs.[9]

Technical assistance has come from a variety of sources. The sampling procedures have been provided by friends who work for a local survey research outfit. Several graduate students have given freely of their time during the questionnaire construction. I have been involved in various parts of the study, particularly in planning for the statistical analyses. While overall the level of technical expertise has been adequate, coordinating these efforts has been a major problem.

We have not yet begun to keypunch the data, but have been fortunate to find volunteers to do that work and keypunch machines to which we can gain access. Similarly, computer facilities have been found and necessary statistical programs made available.

Coupled with a lack of response, there have been several organizational difficulties. The group coordinating the survey believes strongly in democratic decision making. While this position is morally upright, it has led to interminable meetings and somewhat inefficient operational procedures. Fortunately, we have been blessed with two people of unusual commitment, energy, and skill who have weathered these delays while living up to democratic ideals. Despite many frustrations, the job is getting done.

The recruitment, training, and supervision of interviewers has generated another set of serious problems. People were recruited through friendship networks and contacts in a variety of Chicago left-of-center political organizations. To everyone's credit, political differences have been put aside, but coordinating this diverse group living in many different areas of the city has not been easy. In essence, we have developed procedures to decentralize the interviewing processes so that individuals and small groups are responsible for meeting certain quotas of interviews. As the interviews are completed, they are sent to the central office where they are examined. Some control of interviewing quality is maintained by contacting people whose performance does not measure up.[10]

---

[9] Occasionally, other sorts of arrangements were made to obtain necessary resources. One law firm in the city has offered us a considerable sum of money if we give them our survey results after we have finished the analysis. After much breast beating about compromises, we decided to accept the offer.

[10] While the quality of interviewing has been excellent, productivity has been uneven. Some people have done nearly 100 interviews and others have done less than ten. There has also been variability in the degree to which people have met their organizational responsibilities. Some people made promises and kept them, others have meant well but often failed to deliver. One of the critical things we have learned over time is who can be counted on and who cannot. Indeed, obtaining those insights was one of the early hurdles that had to be overcome. The group had to learn that democratic ideals did not mean that everyone was capable of the same level of commitment and performance. Further, to some important degree, performance had to be linked to responsibility and power. The people who did the work deserved the right to make the decisions.

While the survey has been hindered by resources and organizational difficulties, the results so far look very promising. Nearly 1,000 interviews are "in the house" with sufficient time to code, keypunch, and analyze the data. However, our response rate has been only about 60 percent and as planned, we have implemented our fall-back strategy of quota sampling. In particular, men seem less likely to cooperate, so we have recently been oversampling for men.

One important consequence of the 60 percent response rate is the destruction of the probability sample. This implies that precise estimates of sampling error are impossible. We have also come to realize that the original plan for a very large sample (over which there were some significant differences of opinion) mismatched the relatively imprecise measurement procedures inherent in a twenty-minute telephone interview with unnecessarily powerful sampling techniques. In other words, given the inevitable and nontrivial measurement error produced by the questionnaire, very small standard errors (assuming we had managed an acceptable probability sample) are somewhat beside the point. Further, some preliminary analysis of the data suggests all important types of people will be sufficiently represented for the level of statistical sophistication our data will sustain. Consequently, it is likely that we will stop gathering interviews well short of the original goal of 1,500. Given our limited resources and the judgment that our sample is just about as large as our data will require, we have decided to use our energies on other aspects of the civil suit. If later data analyses belie this decision, we have, in any case, sufficient time to collect more data.

Fortunately, the quality of interviews appears excellent. Respondents seem to have little trouble answering all the questionnaire items, and the response categories seem to capture their sentiments. Where necessary, interviewers have been conscientious and written down additional respondent comments in the margins. In short, the questionnaire works, and most of the credit goes to a group of energetic volunteers who were motivated solely by ideals.

We have also been fortunate in the virtual absence of political harassment from the outside. In the recent Attica trial, for instance, it was discovered that an FBI informer was working in the jury selection project. *The New York Times* reported that the informer tipped off the prosecution about defense strategies. While we probably have an informer or two in our midst, he/she has not caused any visible problems to date. Early in the project's history it was decided that any serious efforts to discover informers would be time consuming and disruptive. Therefore, we have chosen to ignore the problem, at least for the present.

Conclusions

It has still to be demonstrated that social science research can directly and significantly assist in the selection of particular jurors. Previous experiences have not been seriously evaluated; and given the conceptual, methodological, and operational problems described in this chapter, it is doubtful that any careful assessment of our procedures would reveal striking benefits. If the survey in particular has any impact, it likely will be in alerting lawyers to juror attributes that might have been ignored and in legitimizing the intuitive insights of experienced trial attorneys. While these benefits are not trivial, they are very far from the "revolution" in jury selection that some journalists have predicted.

Given the marginal impact of empirical research on jury selection procedures, there seem to be little grounds for worrying about the moral and political implications. Lawyers always try to pick the most sympathetic jury possible. Social science techniques seem at most to be quantitatively different from the usual approaches, and perhaps no more effective.

It seems likely that the contribution of social science research will remain small for many years to come. One must not forget that, ultimately, jury decisions are based on the assessment of empirical facts and that objective reality (or, more accurately, consensual reality) may explain the lion's share of juror decisions. In this context, it is less clear what contribution social science insights can make in jury selection. Prior attitudes and personality characteristics may be important only when many of the case's critical facts are ambiguous. And even here, the insights social science can offer are probably small. We simply do not know enough to be of much help.

This is not to deny that some indirect benefits can occur. The publicity surrounding social science impact on jury selection has brought many important issues to the surface and focused attention on the jury selection process. The question of blatantly biased juries in certain locales seems especially critical, but the more general problem of defining "a jury of one's peers" has also been raised. In addition, lawyers may now take more care in choosing jurors and may feel free to call in consultants who specialize in this phase of jury trials. Indeed, a growing cadre of professionals from different academic disciplines, who are developing national reputations, is being recruited for important and controversial cases. Nevertheless, one must understand that their input is based far more on impressionistic personal experience than on formal social science.

References

Blalock, H.M. *Causal inference from nonexperimental data.* Chapel Hill: University of North Carolina Press, 1964.

Commission of Inquiry into the Black Panthers and the Police. *Search and destroy.* R. Wilkins & R. Clark, Chairmen. New York: Metropolitan Applied Research Center, Inc., 1973.

Ginger, A.F. *Jury selection in criminal trials: New techniques and concepts.* Tiburon, Calif.: Lawpress Corp., 1975.

Green, L., & Warden, R. New furor in the Panther case. *Chicago Daily News*, May 22, 1975, pp. 5-6.

Kairys, D., Schulman, J., & Harring, S. (Eds.). *The jury system: New methods for reducing prejudice.* Prepared by the National Jury Project and the National Lawyers Guild. Philadelphia: Philadelphia Resistance Print Shop, 1975.

Kmenta, J. *Elements of econometrics.* New York: Macmillan, 1971.

Raiffa, H. *Decision analysis.* Reading, Mass.: Addison-Wesley, 1970.

Sudman, S., & Bradburn, N.M. *Response effects in surveys.* Chicago: Aldine, 1974.

Wonnacott, R.J., & Wonnacott, T.H. *Econometrics.* New York: John Wiley, 1970.

Index

Adolescence: ideological maturity in, 76; socialization in, 73-74

Adversarial system, 8

Alameda County (Calif.) Public Defender's Office, 17-18, 81-105; development of, 84-85, 102-103; as legal socialization agency, 103, 104; recruitment for, 84-89

American Bar Association: ethical code of, 120

American Law Institute: Model Penal Code of, 140-141

Anthropology: and legal socialization, 68-69

Apodaca et al. v. Oregon, 21, 149, 170, 172, 181

Attica trial, 295

Audiotape: as trial testimony, 214, 232

Authoritarianism: defined, 239; measurement of, 250; studies on, 239-262

"Authoritarian personality": as juror, 23, 239-262

Autonomy: views on, 74-76

Awards: juror ratings and, 226-229

Bail, 145-146

Bail Reform Act (Canada), 143

Bales Interaction Analysis, 174, 180

Banks, Dennis: jury selection in trial of, 279

Bargaining. *See* Legal negotiation; Negotiation

Bayesian procedures: in jury selection, 292-293, 293n

Behavior modification: use in prison, 12

Benevolence: toward blacks, 48-55; toward mentally disabled, 34-48; toward women, children, 55-56

Berkowitz and Wolkon scale, 250

Black Panther Party civil suit, 23,

283-296; jury selection project in, 285-296

Blacks: benevolence toward, 48-55; mentally disabled and, 49-50; social response to, 48-55; spatial segregation of, 49, 53; special admissions programs for, 51-54; stigma of, 48-55

Blackstone, William: on jury system, 169, 170

Brown v. Board of Education, 52

California Personality Inventory, 289

Calley, William, 240-258 *passim*; and Jurow Penalty Scale, 255, 256, 257

Camden 28 case: jury selection in, 268

Canada: criminal justice in, 139. *See also* Bail Reform Act; Canada Evidence Act; Criminal Code (Canada)

Canada Evidence Act, 138

Capital punishment, 13, 240-262 *passim*

Chicago Jury Project, 152-153

Chicago 7 trial, 151

Children: legal socialization in, 16, 65-67; and social interaction, 69; as stigmatized group, 55, 59. *See also* Juvenile proceedings

"Civil inattention": defined, 39-40

Civil service exam: in public defender system, 85-86

Class differences: in socialization, 71

Cloning, 58

Code of Judicial Conduct: and electronic recordings, 209

Colgrove v. Battin, 21, 149

Compensatory programs: for blacks, 50-55; for mentally disabled, 50; and U.S. Supreme Court, 51

Cook County (Ill.) Public Defender's Office, 17-18, 94

Correctional institutions: American concept of penitentiary, 4; challenges facing, 12

299

About the Editors

Gordon Bermant is Project Director and Research Psychologist at the Federal Judicial Center, Washington, D.C. He was for seven years associated with the Battelle Memorial Institute, as Research Scientist in the Law and Justice Study Center, Center Fellow in the Battelle Seminar and Study Program, and Coordinator of the Battelle Institute program in the Behavioral and Social Sciences. He received the Ph.D. in Psychology from Harvard University. He has been Research Fellow at the University of California, Berkeley, Associate Professor of Psychology at the University of California, Davis, and Affiliate Professor of Psychology at the University of Washington. He is co-author of *Biological Bases of Sexual Behavior*, editor of *Perspectives on Animal Behavior*, and co-editor of *Primate Utilization and Conservation, The Ethics of Social Intervention,* and *Markets and Morals.*

Charlan Nemeth is Associate Professor of Psychology at the University of British Columbia in Vancouver, B.C., Canada. She was earlier on the faculties of the University of Chicago and the University of Virginia and has been a visiting professor of Psychology at the University of Bristol (England) and at the Sorbonne (Paris). Dr. Nemeth received the A.B. from Washington University, the M.A. from the University of Wisconsin and the Ph.D. from Cornell University. Her research interests are in the area of influence processes in small groups and these interests have more recently been tied directly to psychology and the law. She is the editor of *Social Psychology: Classic and Contemporary Integrations* and has authored numerous journal articles. She is a consultant to the Social Sciences Review Branch of the National Institutes of Mental Health.

Neil Vidmar is Associate Professor of Psychology at the University of Western Ontario, London, Canada. He received the A.B. from MacMurray College in 1962 and the Ph.D. from the University of Illinois in 1967. From 1973 to 1974 he held a Russell Sage Foundation Fellowship in Law and Social Science at Yale Law School. Dr. Vidmar's various articles on law and psychology have been published in the *Journal of Personality and Social Psychology,* the *Journal of Applied Social Psychology, Stanford Law Review*, and *Wisconsin Law Review.*